MW00571484

Computer Information Systems

HBJ

Harcourt Brace Jovanovich, Publishers
and its subsidiary, Academic Press

San Diego   New York   Chicago   Austin   Washington, D.C.
London   Sydney   Tokyo   Toronto

Steven C. Lawlor
Foothill College

Computer Information Systems

Cover: © Erich Hartmann/Magnum Photos, Inc.

Acknowledgments for literary selections, illustrations, and photographs appear in a section at the back of the book beginning on page 424, an extension of the copyright page.

Many of the products designated in this book are trademarked and their use has been respected through appropriate capitalization and spelling.

Copyright © 1990 by Harcourt Brace Jovanovich, Inc.

All rights reserved. No part of this publication may be reproduced or transmitted in any form or by any means, electronic or mechanical, including photocopy, recording, or any information storage and retrieval system, without permission in writing from the publisher.

Requests for permission to make copies of any part of the work should be mailed to: Copyrights and Permissions Department, Harcourt Brace Jovanovich, Publishers, Orlando, Florida 32887.

ISBN: 0-15-512653-9

Library of Congress Catalog Card Number: 89-84374

Printed in the United States of America

PREFACE

Information—how it is gathered, developed, presented, and ultimately used—is one of the most important topics in the world today. Students, both in their current academic environment and later in their professional careers, will be continually called upon to generate and use information. Their future employers will require them to produce concise, timely, and effective reports, and to use information efficiently in the decision-making process. With the sheer volume of information available today, business people have come to expect precision, accuracy, and conciseness. Only that information delivered in the most easily understandable and effective form is likely to receive attention.

Computer Information Systems is more than just a textbook—it is an entire package of instructional materials on the subject. The textbook provides the foundation, and a broad selection of supplements offers the additional building blocks that allow teachers to tailor the course to their own special requirements. The result should be a well-structured learning experience for the study of information systems.

ORIGIN AND DEVELOPMENT OF THIS TEXT

This package is the culmination of experience gained from teaching Computer Information Systems at Foothill College in Silicon Valley for the past 10 years. It has been thoroughly class tested in various stages by me and by my colleagues, whose suggestions have been incorporated along with those of the thousands of students that used preliminary versions.

Each stage of the manuscript was extensively reviewed for technical accuracy, stylistic treatment, depth and breadth of content, and, most especially, for effectiveness of presentation. The approach used represents a consensus of those who class tested the book as well as the many professors who reviewed the manuscript, responded to our surveys, and participated in our focus groups.

This extensive reviewing and class testing allowed us to develop a book and an ancillary package that present subject matter deemed most important by instructors actively engaged in teaching this course, and to do it in such a way that the student is provided with an easily digestible presentation of the material.

FEATURES OF THE TEXT

Information processing depends on the smooth operation of a system—a quite complicated system at that. Thousands of pieces of hardware and lines of software, as well as the many people and procedures to guide them, must work together to make the system effective. We must, of course, know about the individual parts of the system, but to completely understand one part requires that we be able to relate it to the entire system.

The all-too-common way to solve the problem has been by what might be called the "dictionary approach." Authors who favor this approach tend to "toss out" a great many terms and definitions and hope that students will be able to "put it all together." This is not what a good textbook does.

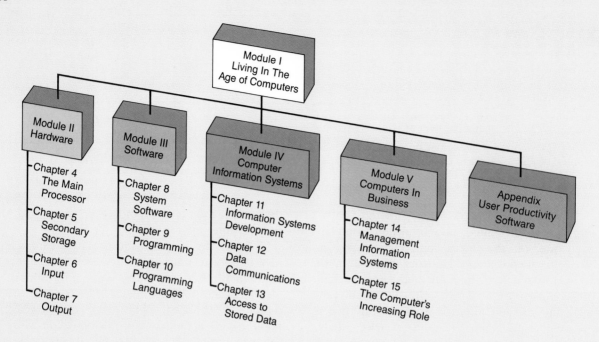

A Systems Approach

We have developed a teaching system whose objective is a real understanding of information systems and not just the short-term ability to memorize terms and definitions. The heart of this system involves a two-tier presentation. In Module I, "Living In the Age of Computers," we present the overall system, in everyday terms. Once a foundation is established, we discuss the individual pieces in greater detail in Modules II-V, believing that they can now be related to the whole.

A Top-Down Modular Design

Since virtually everyone designs information systems and programs using top-down modular design methods, it seemed reasonable to design a teaching system using the same principles. In our system, Module I is the overall controlling module. Modules II through V and the Appendix act as submodules, each taking on a major part of the overall system—hardware in Module II, for example—and treating it in more detail. Modules are then further broken down into chapters, as in Module II which consists of four chapters dealing with the main processor, storage, input devices, and output devices.

Modular Flexibility

In any good modular design, the modules may be treated independently. That is certainly true of this book, and after Module I, modules may be taught in any order. Modular flexibility is further enhanced by the treatment of applications software—word processing, spread sheets, and databases. Because depth of treatment varies greatly from course to course, we have reserved our specific treatment to a self-contained appendix, while incorporating coverage of their vital role and many uses into our systems approach.

End-User Perspective

Computer Information Systems presents computers and information systems from the perspective of the end-user rather than that of the computer technician. Such an approach is especially important for business students who need to appreciate what to expect of a good system and to understand what kinds of information are needed to serve this system.

This emphasis on an end-user perspective is also valuable for beginning students who decide to pursue a career in information systems. Those students will eventually be providing or processing information for end-users and must understand the needs, wants, and frustrations of their audience.

Conceptual Orientation

Computer Information Systems lays broad, careful foundations for conceptual understanding and builds individual concepts on those bases. Terms are defined and used in context within chapters, while short, precise definitions of the same terms are given in a glossary at the back of the book. The conceptual orientation used in this book was far more difficult to achieve than a dictionarylike approach would have been. But it should prove far more rewarding to teacher and student alike.

Readable Writing Style

A book that is difficult to read tends not to be read. *Computer Information Systems* is a careful, accurate presentation of the subject, but it is presented in an easy, informal manner that will not intimidate the novice computer user. Technically sophisticated concepts are presented in everyday language and only after a proper foundation has been laid. Computer jargon is used only where it has become part of the language, and never in defining terms or presenting concepts.

An Integrated Approach to Microcomputers

Virtually all of the students in the courses for which this book is intended will face microcomputers—both as stand-alone systems and as the gateway to larger information systems. *Computer Information Systems* stresses microcomputers but does not present them in isolation. Most of the basic concepts of computer systems and components are similar in all classes of computers—differing in size, speed, and capacity, but not in function. As we develop each concept, we are always careful to relate it to all applicable computers. But since students are, or soon will be, most familiar with microcomputers, we usually use a microcomputer application or example.

Photo Essays

To enhance design and complement coverage, *Computer Information Systems* contains five full-color photo essays. They are placed at appropriate points in the text, but are completely self-contained sections. They can be used for supplementary browsing by the students or as a basis for lectures to enhance the course. The topics are:

- The Making of an Integrated Circuit
- Computer Hardware
- Computer Graphics and Art
- The History of Computers
- Microcomputers

CHAPTER COMPONENTS

Each chapter begins with a short ***Preview*** that introduces students to the subject of the chapter and lists the various concepts to be learned. Concepts are best reinforced by showing them in use, and *Boxes* within the chapter do just that. Typically drawn from current literature, they augment the text by providing real-world situations. *Focus articles* at the end of chapters are intended to draw the chapter material together.

We have designed *Computer Information Systems* to be both readable and visually exciting. There are nearly *200 four-color photographs* in the book, carefully chosen to show examples of the materials themselves or to show them in use. And there are almost *150 pieces of line art,* much of it three dimensional, that provide visual explanations of textual material.

A *Summary* at the end of each chapter reinforces the learning experience and a *Key Word List* provides students with a check of their grasp of chapter terminology. A *Glossary/Index* at the end of the text serves as a reference for the student, providing both a formal definition and the page references where the term is used.

Finally, *Computer Information Systems* has three complete sets of questions at the end of each chapter. *Review Questions* test recall of the terms and concepts in the chapter. *Think About It* offers more complicated questions requiring the student to apply text information to a specific situation. And *Challenges* contain case problems that call for students to do some outside research in order to devise a solution.

FOR THE STUDENT

Computer Information Systems presents a solid, integrated approach to studying computer information systems. We realize, however, that there are many ways to teach the course—some put less emphasis on application software and some put more on learning a programming language. Accordingly, we have included the conceptual coverage of these topics in the textbook and put the practical, more specific coverage in a selection of supplements. By picking and choosing among them, the professor may provide students with the specific tools needed for their own teaching objectives.

Introducing BASIC

Introducing BASIC, by Steven Lawlor, uses industry-accepted top-down, structured, program-design methodology, illustrating and implementing that methodology with IBM PC BASIC. It gives the student programming tools that can be used with any language in the future. This supplement solidly reinforces the chapters on structured design and programming in the textbook. *Computer Information Systems* may be ordered as a package with this supplement.

Pascal

For those wishing to teach Pascal, HBJ offers *Structured Programming Using TURBO PASCAL: A Brief Introduction, Second Edition,* a Turbo Pascal supplement by Margaret Anderson of the University of Georgia. This supplement incorporates solid structured methodology and covers the fundamentals of the language through arrays, structures, and files.

Application Software

To accommodate the various requirements for teaching application software, HBJ has an extensive list of textbooks and supplements, including two computer lab manuals written by Douglas Robertson of the University of Minnesota to support an introductory course. Each has accompanying software and data on disk for student exercises.

- *The Big Three.* Tutorials cover WordPerfect, Lotus 1-2-3 (and the Lotus workalike VP-Planner Plus), and dBASE III PLUS. WordPerfect is the best-selling word processing package on the market today; Lotus has been and continues to be the commercial leader in spreadsheets; and dBase III PLUS remains the database standard, outselling dBase IV and all other database packages. Educational versions of WordPerfect, dBase III PLUS, and VP-Planner Plus are available to adopters.

- *The PC Series.* Tutorials cover PC Type+, PC Calc+, and PC File+, long respected in academic circles for their power, flexibility, and convenience. Business has responded to their ability to share certain kinds of files and to import files created by some commercial packages. Full versions of the software are available to adopters.

Instructional Software

In addition to the software accompanying the application supplements, HBJ will provide two other software packages to adopters.

1. *Graphic Demonstration Software.* This set of programs shows computer concepts in action. The programs are meant to be used as a lecture adjunct. While an instructor talks about a concept, it can be dynamically illustrated on a computer screen.

2. *BASIC Program Demonstrations.* These programs can be used to demonstrate concepts of BASIC programming. They contain significant pauses to allow instructors to lead students through a program while showing its step-by-step actions on a computer screen. Because the demonstrations are self-guiding and self-explanatory, they can also be run by students at a personal computer.

Study Guide

The *Student Study Guide* can be used to reinforce the concepts in the chapters as well as to provide a good yardstick for measuring the student's grasp of those concepts. The professor may assign exercises or students may use the Guide as an optional study aid. For each chapter in the textbook, the *Student Study Guide* contains the following: (1) a chapter synopsis with learning objectives; (2) a section-by-section outline of the chapter, highlighting key concepts; (3) a key-term matching exercise; (4) "Did You Think That . . ." Exercises, dispelling common myths or misconceptions about computers; (5) "Data Check" exercises requiring the student to interpret tabular, graphic, and illustrative material; (6) true–false, multiple-choice, and applied study questions; and (7) answers to all *Study Guide* exercises and questions, including the "Computers in the News" exercises.

FOR THE PROFESSOR

Instructor's Manual

After an overview of the entire ancillary package, the *Instructor's Manual for Computer Information Systems* provides the following material: (1) suggested course outlines, including sample syllabuses; (2) a bibliography of books, guides, and related publications; (3) an annotated list of film and video resources; (4) a chapter synopsis that includes learning objectives; (5) a suggested teaching/lecture outline; (6) a "Topics for Expansion" section containing suggestions and resources for discussion; (7) answers to all end-of-chapter questions and exercises; and (8) transparency masters.

The *Instructor's Manual* also includes a section of *Introducing BASIC* which contains suggested teaching outlines and solutions to all the exercises.

Test Bank

A Test bank for *Computer Information Systems* contains nearly 2,500 questions in a variety of true–false, multiple-choice, and short-answer formats for each chapter. The questions are graded according to difficulty and keyed to the appropriate textbook page. The test bank is available both in hard-copy form and in a computerized version for the IBM, Apple, or Macintosh microcomputer. The SOPH-TEST test-generation program allows the adopter to select, modify, and print both test items and answer keys from the test bank. The IBM and Macintosh versions offer advanced features such as the capability to browse through the test bank.

Transparencies

A packet containing 100 full four-color transparencies is available to adopters. These include reproductions of most of the illustrations in the book. In addition, the *Instructor's Manual* contains transparency masters of the flowcharts found in *Introducing BASIC.*

Videos

HBJ has compiled an extensive video resource list to accompany *Computer Information Systems.* HBJ will provide single tapes on specialized topics or a series of tapes, depending on course requirements, free to adopters. Minimum purchase requirements apply. See your HBJ representative for further details.

ACKNOWLEDGMENTS

There are a great many people to whom I am deeply in debt for their hard work and encouragement in the development of this project from concept to finished book. I would like to begin by expressing my thanks to the thousands of students who patiently studied from the preliminary versions of the text and who offered much constructive criticism. I would also like to thank the people at Harcourt Brace Jovanovich who deserve special mention for their dedication, effort, and helpful suggestions: Richard Bonacci, acquisitions editor; Eleanor Garner, permissions editor; Paul Raymond, associate editor; Lyn Hastert, marketing manager; Julia Ross, manuscript editor; Cheryl Solheid, designer; Sarah Randall, production manager; Cindy Robinson, art editor; and Cynthia Sheridan, production editor.

Finally, I would particularly like to thank the developmental reviewers who evaluated the manuscript at various stages and shared with us their technical and pedagogical expertise: Gary R. Armstrong, Shippensburg University; Frank E. Cable, Pennsylvania State University; William R. Cornette, Southwest Missouri State University; J. Patrick Fenton, West Valley College; Barbara A. Gentry, Parkland College; Fran Goertzel Gustavson, Pace University; James R. Walters, Pikes Peak Community College; Karen L. Watterson, Shoreline Community College; and John David Witherspoon, Monroe Community College.

IN APPRECIATION

Key to the development of the materials for this project are those who class tested, those who reviewed, those who participated in focus groups, and those who assisted us in innumerable beneficial ways. Their listing here hardly expresses the special debt I owe them.

Gary R. Armstrong,
   Shippensburg University

Rick Aukerman,
   Oklahoma State University

Frank E. Cable,
   Pennsylvania State University

William R. Cornette,
   Southwest Missouri State University

J. Patrick Fenton,
   West Valley Community College

Barbara A. Gentry,
   Parkland College

Fran Goertzel Gustavson,
   Pace University

Richard Hatch,
   San Diego State University

Dennis R. Heckman,
   Portland Community College

Russell K. Lake,
   Parkland College

Jan Lindholm,
   University of Central Florida

Stephen Mansfield,
   McHenry County College

Joan K. Pierson,
   James Madison University

Edward H. Rategan,
   College of San Mateo

Thomas C. Richards,
   University of North Texas

Noel C. Smith,
   University of Texas at Arlington

Gerald E. Wagner,
   California State Polytechnic University—Pomona

James R. Walters,
   Pikes Peak Community College

Karen L. Watterson,
   Shoreline Community College

John David Witherspoon,
   Monroe Community College

Robert C. Wurm,
   Nassau Community College

CONTENTS

Brief Table of Contents

Module 1

LIVING IN THE AGE OF COMPUTERS

 3

BUSINESS INFORMATION 54

Module 2

HARDWARE

6

INPUT 131

7

OUTPUT 155

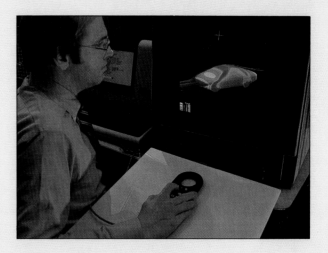

Module 3
SOFTWARE

Module 4

COMPUTER
INFORMATION SYSTEMS

Module 5
COMPUTERS IN BUSINESS

14
MANAGEMENT INFORMATION SYSTEMS 342

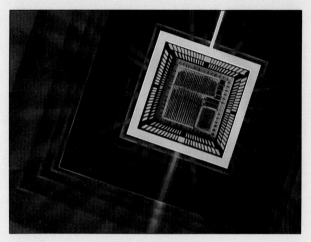

 15

THE COMPUTER'S INCREASING ROLE 366

Appendix

USER PRODUCTIVITY SOFTWARE 400

GLOSSARY/INDEX 428

Computer Information Systems

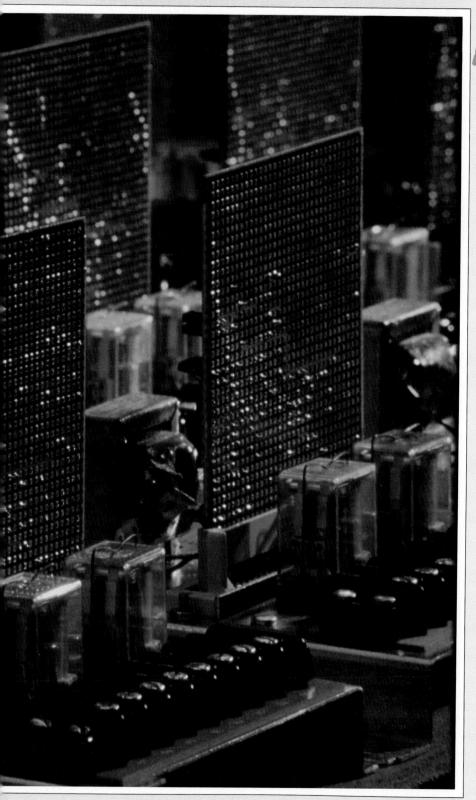

Module 1

LIVING IN THE AGE OF COMPUTERS

Computers support our modern technological world in ways that may not even be apparent—until some vital computer-based system crashes. In Chapter One, we see how, where, and why computers are used today, as well as what advantages computers have over humans—and the advantages humans retain over computers.

Chapter Two introduces the main components of the computer system, while Chapter Three discusses information systems and the computer industry, distinguishing between what is raw data and what is information, and outlines the essential elements of a computer information system.

3

1

THE COMPUTER REVOLUTION

PREVIEW
This chapter will form an introduction to computers and their relationship to us and our society. From this chapter you should gain an understanding of:

■ The computer's presence in our daily lives and the extent to which we depend on them.

■ The rapid rise of computers from nonexistence to prominence.

■ What a computer is and what makes it different from other machines.

■ Why we use computers.

■ The kinds of things we use computers for.

■ How computers have changed our lives.

Computers have invaded all areas of American life. Today, there are more computers and computer-type devices than there are people in the United States, and these machines perform almost a half million calculations per citizen per second. In three years, the number of machines will double and the number of calculations will increase more than threefold. Everywhere we turn we encounter either the machines (in automobiles, home appliances, video games) or the results of their operations (utility bills, grade reports, pay checks).

To some people's way of thinking, computers have provided wonders that would be otherwise unattainable. They help launch spaceships, contribute to miraculous medical advances, and give business the means to account for the millions of transactions taking place every day. To others, they pose a threat to employment and privacy. There are computer-controlled robots replacing people on the factory floor and data on almost everyone in the country is entered into at least a dozen computers' data banks. Regardless of your own opinion, computers are here to stay, so you might as well learn about them.

Because most of us do not see the computers themselves, we fail to recognize their impact on our daily lives. To appreciate the extent to which we are affected by computers, let us, hypothetically of course, give all computers and computer-related devices a one-day vacation. During this day we will follow a typical American, Delbert Freed, and see how he fares.

These clean-looking cabinets hide the miles of wire and billions of components that make up a large computer system.

In contrast to large computers performing many tasks for many people concurrently, smaller personal computers perform one task for one person at a time.

THE SAD TALE OF DELBERT FREED

Delbert woke up with a shaft of sun stabbing at his eyes. Usually, when his alarm went off, that burning spot hit the wall two feet above his head. "I'm late," he thought, as he rolled over to check his clock. What was usually a red LED readout was now just a faint 88:88, the remnants of a dead digital clock. His watch, with the second hand that usually did a constant, jerky dance from second to second, was stuck at 12 midnight.

The World Times
Computers Take Day Off

"Stupid computer vacation," he mumbled as he reached for the phone, "I gotta find out the time." Had Delbert been a little more awake, he might have saved his energy. He knew full well that almost all telephone calls are routed by computer-controlled switching circuits and that the thing would be dead. The radio? Forget it. So he took a cold shower in a dark bathroom. Cold and dark because Delbert's lights and hot water heater needed electricity, and his city's power distribution system was computer controlled.

By the time he'd tied his shoelaces, Delbert was really depressed. Remembering the advice on a wise and philosophical bumper sticker, "When the going gets tough, the tough go shopping," he decided to go out and buy something extravagant. After prying open his garage door with a crowbar (naturally his digital-coded, automatic garage door opener wouldn't work), he hopped in his car.

Delbert's car was not cooperating. Instead of starting, it whined and sputtered. No way for a car with only 3,000 miles to act. When it finally cranked over, it coughed, choked, and filled his garage with black smoke. Had he bothered to read his owner's manual, he would have found that computers controlled the car's fuel mixture, ignition timing, and almost all the smog-control equipment. As he chugged and belched away from his house, an ironic little grin crossed his face. At least he wouldn't have to worry about Officer Reilly's radar trap at the end of the block. Of course, he couldn't get his car over 35 m.p.h. anyway.

Officer Reilly didn't have much time to think about his nonworking radar because he was busy directing traffic at the intersection. The entire city's computer-controlled traffic light system was out. The rest of the force was busy with a rash of burglaries. When most of the industrial- and residential-intrusion alarm systems go on vacation, the local felons get to work. Delbert remembered his wide-open garage door and unprotected house.

But Delbert cheered up as he thought of his impending shopping spree. Today was not only his day off, but payday as well. He would drive to his office, pick up his check, and go out and blow it. As he lurched into the parking lot in front of the personnel office, he saw a hand-lettered red sign proclaiming "NO CHECKS TODAY, COMPUTER DOWN." Of course, he thought, the computer figures and writes all company checks.

Luckily, he still had a wallet full of charge cards and could stop at his bank's 24-hour, automatic teller to get some cash. As you might imagine, trying to use the automatic teller was a mistake. As hard as he shoved, the little slot would not accept his card.

A cloud of fumes followed him downtown, where he saw long-faced, dejected people everywhere. His stockbroker couldn't get the latest, or any, stock information; the tune-up shop was trying to tune cars by ear and intuition instead of electronic diagnosis; and a bunch of angry high-school kids were hanging around outside the video-arcade game palace. The only working machine? An antique pinball game.

Rounding the next corner, Delbert felt relieved at the sight of a bit of normalcy, a riot at the supermarket. The shoppers must be protesting high prices again. A harried-looking Mrs. Fassbinder coming out of the market told him that they were really protesting the long lines at the checkout counters. The cash registers, which automatically pick the product codes off the packages and figure the totals, were sitting idly by while checkers

fumbled with pencils and scraps of paper, trying to add up the bills. Not even their hand-held calculators would function today.

Finally, Delbert reached Smitty's clothing store and spent the next three hours blissfully ignoring the crazy world outside. He purchased a slick-looking, three-piece suit with shirt and tie to match. At least the salesman was a human, not a computer or a robot.

The salesman gave Delbert the bill, $326.82, and Delbert handed over his credit card, saying, "Charge it!"

The salesman, in a very proper British accent with only a hint of south Bronx, said "What am I to do with this? I would have to call for approval and the credit-card company's computer is indisposed today. I'm sorry, sir, but unless you have cash, I cannot sell you the suit."

At this point, Delbert hit bottom. He figured the only thing he could do to save his sanity would be to go home and watch Monday night football. After chugging home and turning on the television set, he found, to his surprise, that the game was on. The electric company had gone back to its old manual systems. The game itself was a little ragged because people were having to do what the computer usually did. For example, leaning against the animated scoreboard were huge cards with hand-painted numbers on them. But at least the players were not computers.

Near the end of the second quarter, during a field-goal attempt, the center hiked the ball over the quarterback's head, 21 players dove for the ball at the same time, it squirted out from underneath the pile, and the kicker picked it up and ran it in for a touchdown. At this point, you might expect the announcer to spout some computer-generated statistic like "That's only the second time in NFL Monday night regular-season football between two teams from east of the Mississippi where a soccer-style kicker with less than four years in the pros has run more than seventeen and a half yards for a touchdown."

Instead, computerless, he said, "Gee, I wonder whether that's ever happened before?"

Delbert turned off the set and went to bed.

THE COMPUTER EXPLOSION

The story of Delbert Freed is fictional only because the idea of a one-day vacation for computers is absurd. But it does illustrate the extent to which we have all come to depend on computers. A world without them is possible, but it would set us all back 40 years.

How did we get to this state? Did computers just sneak up on us? In a way, they did. Like the automobile, before the computer existed, we seemed to live satisfactorily without them. But now that we have them, we refuse to let them go. Like the automobile, computers are not indispensable, they just make life easier for us.

The Advancing Technology

Physically, humans in their current form have been around for the last 50,000 years or so, but man's living patterns have been changing constantly over that period. As man advances, the pace of the advance quickens. For example, the urban revolution, the movement toward the cities, has been going on for about the last 1,000 years; the industrial revolution, the use of machines and the factory, for about the last 100 years; and the computer revolution, the use of computers to provide information and control many processes, only for about the last 30 years.

Advances in computer technology have occurred in four major areas: cost, size, speed, and reliability. The first gadgets we would call electronic computers were made in the 1940s. By today's standards, they were expensive, big, slow, and unreliable. The ENIAC (Electronic Numerical Integrator And Computer), for example, cost about $3,000,000 in today's dollars ($485,000 in 1946), weighed 30 tons and took up 1500 square feet of floor space, could perform about 500 calculations a second, and averaged about 12 minutes of running time between failures. It was an important early step, however.

During the 1950s, reliability and speed increased, cost and size decreased, and the computer started being thought of as a viable business and scientific tool, if you could afford it. In the 1960s those trends continued and big businesses and scientific organizations could not afford to be without computers. In the 1970s, computers became inexpensive enough to be available, and indispensable, to all but the smallest organizations.

Computers have gone through rapid changes in their relatively short time in existence. (a) 1950S–UNIVAC 1 (b) 1960s–IBM 360 (c) 1970s–DEC PDP 10 (d) 1980s–Compaq 386

Now, in the personal-computer era of the 1980s, many people have access to one at school or the office, and might have one at home.

In this time period, our four criteria have advanced a long way. A modern IBM PS/2 personal computer system costs about $4,000, fits on a desk top, performs a million calculations per second, and has a reliability measured in thousands of hours.

The Advancing Industry

Because computers are getting better and cheaper, more individuals and organizations are buying more of them. Consider these computer industry facts:

- The number of computers sold in the world doubles about every two and a half years.
- The amount of data processed doubles about every year and a half, which confirms our suspicion that computers are getting more powerful all the time.
- The price of a computer with comparable capability is halved about every two years. Look at the difference between the 1940s ENIAC and the 1980s PS/2.
- In 1988 the world's information-systems companies had estimated sales of about $243.1 billion.
- All of the above facts were assembled with the aid of computers.

BOX 1-1

Non-Computer Users Need Not Apply

Applying to college is becoming as easy as ABC. The Georgia Institute of Technology's Apply By Computer (ABC) system lets any student with a terminal and a modem dial into the school's computer network and electronically fill out an application for admission. Although only 1 percent of last year's applicants used the system, the school believes the numbers will increase as more high school students gain access to computers, either at home or in school. The whole process takes about ten minutes. A prospective student can also use the system later to find out the status of his or her application.

While computerized admission is admittedly in its infancy, its proponents believe it is the wave of the future. Among them are officials of the University of Richmond in Virginia. Its copyrighted Computerized Application Process (CAP) allows students to fill out their applications on a floppy disk in either an IBM or an Apple personal computer. The program greets the student with the UR insignia, accompanied by the school's fight song. After the last blank has been filled in and the alma mater is played, the student mails the disk back to the school, along with an application fee.

"The CAP system makes the process a lot easier and more enjoyable for the students," says Thomas Pollard, dean of admissions at Richmond. So far, about 600 students have requested the disks to apply for the 1989 school year, and Pollard thinks the number may reach 1,000. Next year, he hopes to have a system in place that will send applications out to students who have a computer and a modem.

Both schools agree that it is just a matter of time before other colleges begin similar programs. "I've been amazed by the positive response from the students, counselors, and other colleges," says Earl Babbitt, information systems coordinator for Georgia Tech.

Application by computer saves the schools time and money by eliminating much of the paperwork that would otherwise be involved. Because the student's electronic application is loaded directly into the school's computer, the system also improves the accuracy of the admissions process.

Applying to college may be getting easier, but getting in is still the hard part.

Source: Kenan Woods, *PC/Computing,* Nov. 1989, p. 64.

These charts show both the fantastic growth of computers and the shift toward smaller ones over the last 30 years.

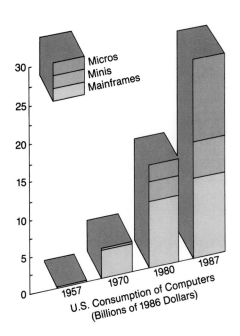

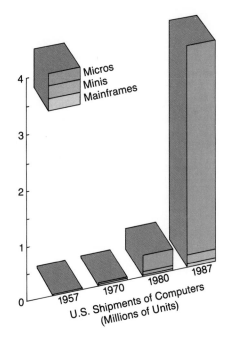

The Global Industry

We used to think of computers as being as American as apple pie. No longer. The rest of the world has caught up. International Business Machines Corporation (IBM) is still the largest computer company in the world, with about a 22 percent share of the total worldwide information-systems sales, but of the top ten information-systems companies, only five are based in the United States. Three are in Japan, one in Germany, and one in Italy.

WHAT IS A COMPUTER?

A **computer** is a machine that can manipulate data by itself. We give it instructions, we give it data, and then we can walk away while it does its work. A computer used for word processing can take text typed at a keyboard (like this book, for example) and store each character in its memory banks. It can reformat the text to fit within the margins of a page, or allow whole paragraphs or pages to be moved from one place to another.

A computer used for financial analysis can take numbers, perform calculations on them, and display the results in columns or perhaps graphic form. A computer in an automobile can sense temperature, exhaust composition, and power demands, and make adjustments in the engine. Each of these tasks involves manipulation of data—accepting data, assembling them, using them in calculations, combining them, moving them, and either displaying or reacting to them.

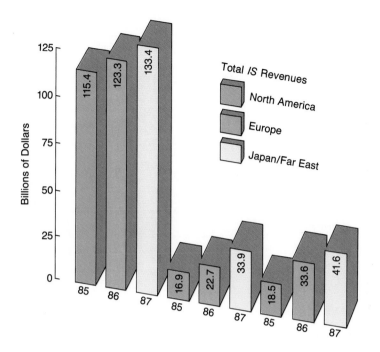

The bars show the locations of the leaders of the international information technology business and the relative size of their IS revenue.

Many machines can manipulate data—typewriters, adding machines, calculators, and slide rules—but they all require humans to give them a constant stream of instructions while they work. Once we give the computer its instructions, it can work on its own.

To see how using a computer might compare with other methods of solving a problem, let us assume you are a department manager with eight employees and a bonus of $1,000 to distribute to them. You know approximately how much each should get, but since the total must add up to exactly $1,000, you will have to juggle the figures a little. So you sit down with a pencil and paper and make a first stab at it. "Let's try giving Jones $250; Smith, $150;" and so forth. Now you add them up with your calculator. "250+150+ . . . ." The total comes out to $1275 so you go back to the figures, make some adjustments, take calculator in hand and go through the process again and again until it satisfies both you and the $1000 total requirement.

Another way of handling this chore is to think up the numbers and make the final decisions, but have your assistant do all the work. You will have to instruct your assistant to type the names and numbers in two vertical columns, add the numbers (someone has already instructed him to use a calculator), and type the total at the bottom. Then you can give him the data and tell him to follow your instructions. When he is finished, you can look at the report and say, "Let's knock $25 off Jones, $15 off Smith, but leave Brown the same" and have your assistant perform the same task as before. After going through this process a few times, you should have your bonus distributed.

A third way is to use a computer the same way as you would have used your assistant. Give the computer the instructions, then the data, and have it follow the instructions. You can look at the typed report, change the data,

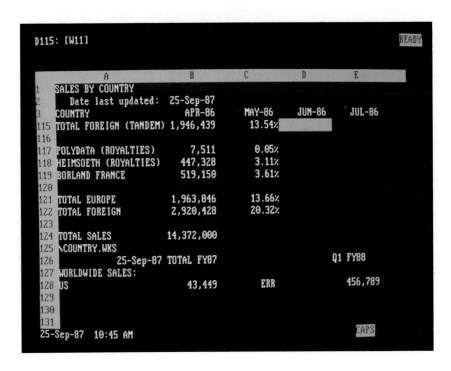

and have the computer follow the instructions again until you are satisfied with the result.

The Stored Program

Both the calculator and the computer can tally a column of numbers, but you must continuously feed the calculator instructions—add, subtract, and so forth—each time you use it. The advantage of the computer is that once you give it a set of instructions, called a **program,** it can remember it. You can have it perform, or **execute,** those instructions (**run** the program) hundreds or thousands of times because, once the program is stored in the computer, it can be called on at a moment's notice. The **stored-program concept** is the capacity for the computer to store, or remember, a set of instructions. With other machines, such as a calculator, to perform the same operations 100 times, you would have to give it the instructions 100 times.

Hardware and Software

A computer system, then, consists of two important ingredients. **Hardware** is the actual equipment. Keyboards, screens, printers, boxes full of wires and circuit boards and such are all hardware. An automobile is a noncomputer example of hardware. **Software** are the sets of instructions, the programs, that tell the hardware what to do. One cannot work without the other. Your car, for example, cannot get you anywhere unless you instruct or drive it.

```
10 REMARK THIS PROGRAM ASKS FOR TEMPERATURE IN DEGREES
20 REMARK FAHRENHEIT AND PRINTS OUT THE SAME TEMPERATURE
30 REMARK CONVERTED TO DEGREES CELSIUS.
40 INPUT "TEMPERATURE IN FAHRENHEIT:";FAHRENHEIT
50 CELSIUS = (5/9)*(FAHRENHEIT-32)
60 PRINT "TEMPERATURE IN CELSIUS IS:";CELSIUS
70 END
```

This is a program which instructs the computer to accept a number from the person running the program (40 INPUT . . .), perform a calculation based on that number (50 CELSIUS . . .), and display the result (60 PRINT . . .).

WHY WE USE COMPUTERS

Will the wild imaginings of science-fiction writers come true and computers take over the world? Why should they? Computers, like hammers, microwave ovens, and automobiles, are simply tools that we use to make our lives easier, more productive, and more pleasant. Society exists for humans and unless computers benefit us, we simply will not use them.

The Advantages of Computers over Humans

To be useful, any tool must have an advantage over the human without the tool. For example, you can pound a nail much faster and more comfortably with a hammer than with your fist. Let us examine the advantages of the computer over the human without the computer.

How fast can you add 16 and 9? A second? Half a second? Not bad, but an average computer could perform that calculation in perhaps one millionth of a second. You say you can type at 80 words per minute with very few errors? Some computer printers can produce about 500,000 words per minute with virtually no errors. Speed and accuracy are obviously advantages of the computer.

A computer is tireless. It will work 24 hours a day without sleep, lunch, or coffee breaks. Computers are dependable. They do break down, but not as often as humans, and they are repaired more quickly. Computers are consistent. Once you give them their instructions, they will do the same thing the same way over and over.

A computer requires very little training. Humans spend years in school and additional time learning on the job. You merely have to plug the computer in and give it a program, and it will function productively.

Because of all these capabilities, computers can perform mathematical and clerical tasks considerably less expensively than humans. If it requires a large volume of repetitive calculations or organizing data into reports and such, you can bet that a computer can do it faster, more accurately, and more cheaply than humans.

The Advantages of Humans over Computers

It looks as though we humans are in danger of becoming obsolete, relegated to a life of lying in the sun while the computers do all the work. Fortunately, or unfortunately, this is not the case. Humans have advantages

---

TABLE 1-1   Computer versus Human Advantages

Human Advantages	Computer Advantages
Thinking	Computational speed
Judgment	Accuracy
Creativity	Dependability
Motivation	Little training required
Flexibility	Lower cost in many cases
Mobility	
Storage Density	

---

which make us not only more efficient than computers in many cases, but indispensable.

Humans can think. Computers can only follow directions. Someone has to think up the directions (write the programs) for computers to follow. Because of our thinking ability we can exercise judgment. If you could program a computer to walk off a cliff, it would do it. A human so instructed would consider the consequences and question the instruction.

People are creative. Computers are only consistent. To be creative, one must think of new ways to approach things. Computers will take the same approach each time, unless we create a new one for them.

People are motivated and take initiative. We derive satisfaction out of a job well done and will strive to do it better. Computers just follow instructions.

Humans are more flexible in communications. Computers require communication in very precise, detailed terms with nothing either left out or ambiguous. We can gloss over mispellings and deal with a variety of languages, dialects, and slang. Can you imagine the very literal, inflexible computer's reaction to the popular colloquialism, "It's raining cats and dogs"? (Incidentally, did you notice that "mispellings" was misspelled? Did it really make any difference in your understanding of the passage? If that were a computer instruction, it would have been rejected.)

People are more mobile than computers. We can move about more freely and can manipulate things with our fingers and hands. Not only that, our senses—sight, hearing, touch, taste, and smell—can guide us in our movements. True, computer-controlled robots are becoming more sophisticated in both mobility and senses, but it will be quite a while before a robot will be the mechanical equal of a human.

The human brain can store more data in less space than computer data-storage devices. No one really knows the true capacity of the brain but it is estimated that it can store data 10 to 20 times more densely than a computer. (Of course, some of us are more dense than others.)

WHERE COMPUTERS ARE USED

Information versus Control

Almost all of the uses of computers can be divided into two broad categories—information and control. Some computers' principal function

Electronic engine control module

is to provide information such as sales figures, holiday mailing lists, or the size of the national debt. These are the machines we will spend most of the rest of this book discussing.

Other computers, however, have as their principal task controlling various pieces of machinery. For example, many late-model cars have a small computer in them that adjusts the fuel mixture and timing continuously as the car is being driven. Commercial airliners are equipped with autopilots, computer devices that can fly the plane. Many of our home and business air-conditioning and heating systems are computer controlled. Robots used in manufacturing are directed by computers.

Business Information

The computer is as much a fixture of modern businesses, governments, and other organizations as the telephone, the typewriter, or the desk. Almost every business either has one or more computers, or uses the computers of some other service company. These computers provide the business with records of transactions, financial reports, analyses of business activity, payroll information, product inventories, and a host of other valuable pieces of information. If you asked a businessperson what the company's most valuable asset is, the answer might well be the collection of data stored on its computers.

The computer has become an integral tool of modern business.

Office Tasks

The automated office is rapidly becoming a reality, due mainly to computers. Instead of typing and retyping letters and reports, office workers are **word processing,** using computers to manipulate text. They use either specialized computers or word-processing software on their office computers that allow them to enter text, store it, change it, move it around, and print it out on demand. If Mr. Smyth's name was spelled "Smith," the entire page need not be retyped, the "i" can be changed to a "y" and the word processor will reprint the page.

Word processors have replaced typewriters in many offices.

Conventional office memos and business letters are becoming extinct. Instead of sending paper from one place to another, people are composing their correspondence on their computers and using **electronic mail,** a process in which the message is sent from one computer to another and is stored in the receiving computer until the addressee decides to read it.

Database management software allows computers to store large amounts of data, and to search for and call them up on a moment's notice. The file clerk now uses a keyboard and a computer instead of a room full of paper.

The **personal computer,** a small computer dedicated to just a single person, is rapidly replacing the calculator on the desktop. Not only can these computers calculate, with the right software they can perform various financial analyses, print charts and graphs, do word processing, send electronic mail, and accomplish practically anything a large computer can.

The Home

A few years ago, with the introduction of the home computer, some industry sages predicted that every home would have one. The lady of the house could keep her recipes and shopping lists on it, her husband could balance the checkbook, and Junior and Sis could do their homework and play video games. Their computer-in-every-home prediction was no more accurate than their stereotypical view of the American family. However, a high percentage of homes have purchased computers and still others use computer-related devices.

A computer is more complicated and difficult to use than a mixer or a calculator, and often it is less trouble to keep recipes on 3 × 5 cards and balance the checkbook by hand. But the home computer can offer a lot of fun and satisfaction. Most can play a variety of games and do word processing, and creating a program yourself that plans well-balanced weekly menus or keeps track of household expenses can be very satisfying.

Even if you do not have a home computer, chances are that many of the appliances in your home have computer circuitry in them—including appliance timers and alarm clocks, energy-saving thermostats, digital garage-door openers, telephones, televisions, lawn sprinkler systems, and security devices. For better or worse (most of us like to think for better), the computer has invaded the home.

In the home, the same computer can play video games, write letters, and manage the budget.

BOX 1-2

Northrop Designs Own Systems To Answer Pressure To Integrate

At Northrop Corp., people no longer say "back to the drawing board" because they stopped designing on drawing boards in 1984.

W. Richard Howard, vice-president of information resource management joined the company five years ago. He is working on a goal set 10 years ago by the company: to design strictly in a three-dimensional computer database.

As a leading design engineering company, Northrop realized it could significantly improve its quality and output by moving to sophisticated 3-D engineering workstations.

Ten years ago, however, there were no 3-D workstations to buy, so Northrop developed a system internally. The first product designed by the new system was the B2 bomber, the first aircraft in history designed totally in 3-D.

Under Howard's guidance, the system went a step further, moving the 3-D capabilities through the manufacturing process and finally into the logistics and support operations. Because of the 3-D

capability, Northrop was able to put all its critical processes—design, production planning, fabrication, quality inspection and assembly—on a common database, thus increasing quality and productivity.

Northrop uses the 3-D system, based on IBM mainframes and different types of computer-aided design workstations, on the new Advanced Tactical Fighter project as well. Howard acknowledges that such a system gives Northrop a decided strategic advantage.

Source: Glenn Rifkin, *Computerworld,* Sept. 12, 1988.

Design and Manufacturing

Computer-aided design (CAD) is shortening the time it takes to design products, and contributes to making the products better by allowing the designs to be more accurate. Computers do not design things—that requires the creativity of people—but they can be of great assistance to the designers. Once a design is created on the computer, it can often be given to other computers that control the machines that manufacture the item. This is part of what is referred to as **computer-aided manufacturing (CAM).**

Health Care

The family doctor with the benevolent smile and smooth bedside manner still exists, but the physician now has a host of computerized machines to help. Most hospitals and many private physicians keep both billing information and medical records on computers. In addition, computers are used extensively with diagnostic and treatment equipment. Seriously ill patients have their blood pressure, pulse, respiration, and chemical balances monitored by computers which alert the staff if the patient's condition worsens. X-rays, CT (computerized axial tomography) scans, and magnetic-resonance imaging use computers to assemble and graphically

Instead of drafting boards, designers and draftspeople use computers.

BOX 1-3

Seeing Inside the Human Body

In 1970 the computer was used to enhance X-rays to produce three-dimensional images of the inside of the body. The process, called computerized axial tomography, or CT scanning, provided doctors with even clearer pictures of the body's internal geography. X-rays, however, can be harmful if overdone, and are much better suited to viewing bone rather than soft tissue.

In 1971, Raymond Damadian, M.D., predicted the development of a magnetic-resonance imaging machine to "see" inside the human body, a dream he admitted might cause him to be perceived as unrealistic, especially since he said it could be done within three years. He gathered his believers around him, formed the FONAR Corporation, and set to work. It actually took six years, but in 1977 the machine was finished and a revolutionary method of detecting and diagnosing disease in humans was born.

Magnetic resonance is the phenomenon that begins as spinning atoms align themselves with an external magnetic field. The energy of a radio wave with the same frequency as the spin of the atom will be absorbed by the atom. When that radio wave is turned off, the energy is released and can be detected by a radio receiving coil. FONAR's MR scanner detects the position and strength of the released energy and puts the data through a Data General ECLIPSE S/140 computer, which assembles the data and creates three-dimensional graphic images.

Because MR scanners make images based on chemistry, not photography, they have a distinct advantage over X-rays and CT scans. Tissue and water give off strong magnetic resonance signals,

From: *"Magnetic Resonance Imaging: A Dream Come True,"* Technique, Vol. 3, No. 2, 1988.

present data for diagnosis. The computer in medicine is almost as common a tool as the stethescope.

Doing Things Humans Can't

Most of the things for which we use computers could be done, and perhaps were previously done, by humans. Computers are efficient at repetitive tasks that require no thinking, and most humans are quite willing to relinquish this drudgery to them.

However, some tasks could not be done without the aid of computers. NASA simulates the airflow around a flying body using equations that are so complicated and require the processing of so much data that even their

* efficient at repetitive tasks.

while the response of bone is weak. This is nearly the opposite of X-rays and CT scans, which reveal bone in sharp detail while showing other parts with less clarity. Therefore, MR scanners enable doctors to analyze soft body parts—such as the heart, kidneys, and brain—as never before.

"MR is a dramatic new technology because it allows you to image in any projection angle, it uses no radiation, and produces images unobscured by bone," says Dr. Charles Manetz, radiologist at Henrico Doctor's Hospital in Richmond, Virginia. According to Manetz, the MR scanner is especially useful in discriminating among different types of soft tissue. "Most of the things we are looking for, notably tumors, must be located within other areas of soft tissue density and differentiated."

MR scanning is used in the diagnosis of multiple sclerosis, heart problems, cancer, and even mental illness

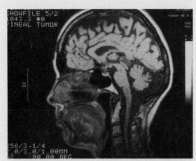
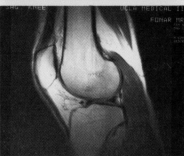
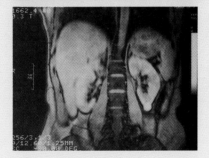

because its ability to reveal chemical information can show subtle chemical changes often associated with such disorders. It is also popular in sports medicine because it can provide detailed images of ligaments, tendons, and muscles surrounding bones and joints.

MR scanning is currently somewhat expensive; the machine costs about $1.5 million and an individual scan between $650 and $1350, but the costs can be reduced by increasing the number of patients that can be scanned. "My real dream" says Damadian, "is to have FONAR scanning clinics all over the country . . . so if you don't feel well, you'd just walk into one of them and be scanned and diagnosed on the spot." Considering the growing medical need for less intrusive ways of seeing inside the body, and the strength of Damadian's convictions, such a goal may not be unreasonable.

computer, capable of over a billion calculations per second, can only produce approximations. It would take a mathematician about 130 years (not including overtime or coffee breaks) to do what their computer does in a second.

A new, experimental jet fighter is not only extremely efficient and maneuverable but also extremely unstable because the designers put the small wings up front and the big wings in back facing forward. The plane, in effect, flies backward. A human pilot could not make corrections fast enough to control the plane, so the pilot directs a computer and the computer flies the plane. Without the computer, the plane would disintegrate within a few seconds. Fortunately, they built in three computers, any one of which could fly the plane.

Humans would have liked to have been there, but they couldn't, so computers controlled this landing vehicle on Mars.

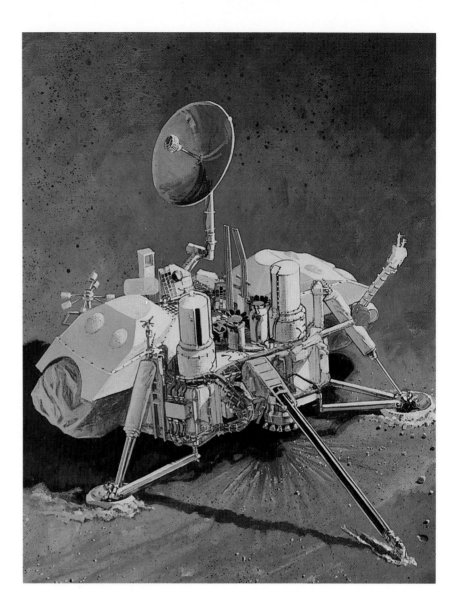

Other computer devices replace humans in dangerous environments, such as space or areas of high radiation. Human life is much more valuable than a collection of wire and silicon chips.

HOW COMPUTERS HAVE CHANGED OUR LIVES

As Delbert Freed found out, computers are playing an increasingly prominent role in our lives. Is this good or bad? Will our use and dependence on computers have a positive or negative effect on the quality of our lives? It is not our intent to debate the point here or try to direct you to any conclusions, but you should be aware of some of the changes in society that have come about as a result of the computer.

Source: *Businessweek,* Feb. 8, 1988.

BOX 1-4

Eureka! Now There's a Laptop for the Blind

These days it seems the only thing a personal computer can't do is see for the blind—unless, that is, it's made by Robitron Pty., Ltd., a computer peripherals maker in Melbourne, Australia. In March the company plans to begin marketing a three-pound laptop computer in the United States designed for the visually impaired. Called Eureka, it offers a synthesized voice that calls out the letter or number that is typed on a special braille keyboard. The $2,300 computer runs software programs designed for IBM's PC and stores up to 300 pages of text. It is intended to help a blind person do simple text editing, perform scientific calculations, or even compose music. A key-activated, built-in modem automatically dials phone numbers.

Pop composer Stevie Wonder was so taken with Eureka that he bought three of them during a concert tour Down Under and gave one to his friend Ray Charles. Now Wonder is thinking about promoting the machine. Another booster, the Baltimore-based National Federation of the Blind, will run an article on Eureka in April in its 26,000-circulation publication.

Efficiency

No one would argue against the notion that computers have made many tasks more efficient. The automated checkout stands in the supermarkets make the lines move faster and the bills more accurate. Accounting by computer requires only a third as many people as hand accounting. An engineering drawing that took a month to complete might take two days with the aid of a computer. We can make changes in this book and have the computer print out a new copy without having to retype the whole thing.

The computer's efficiency stems from its speed and consistency in making calculations and moving data. For tasks that do not require that (such as digging holes in the ground or painting a landscape), our tool, the computer, is inappropriate and simply not used any more than we would use a hammer to cut our lawn.

Information

Watching a sports event on television these days is a great example of the information explosion that we are going through: the percent of baskets Magic Johnson has sunk from thirty feet out in the last two years, the odds

Driving by the Glow of a Screen

Electronic maps put a high-tech fantasy on the dashboard.

More than two decades have passed since moviegoers first watched James Bond tail a Rolls-Royce to Goldfinger's Alpine retreat by tracking a moving blip across a screen on the dashboard of his Aston Martin. Now advances in computer technology have turned this Hollywood fantasy into automotive reality.

In California, some 2,000 motor vehicles—from Michael Jackson's Mercedes-Benz to Palo Alto garbage trucks—have been equipped with a gadget called the Navigator, which helps drivers get to a destination by displaying their vehicle's location on a glowing green map. And beginning next month, visitors to three hotels and six Budget Rent a Car stations in and around San Francisco will have access to counter-top DriverGuide units, which can calculate the shortest route between any two addresses in the Bay area and print out a concise set of directions. Later this year, DriverGuide will also become available in a smaller, dashboard version.

The Navigator, introduced by Etak, a Menlo Park, Calif., company, is an electronic road map that calculates position by means of dead reckoning. Data from a solid-state compass installed in the vehicle's roof and from sensors mounted on

its wheels are processed by a computer in the trunk and displayed on a dashboard screen. The car's position is represented as a fixed triangle; the map, showing a web of streets and avenues, scrolls down as the car moves forward and rotates sideways when it turns.

DriverGuide, produced by Karlin & Collins, a Sunnyvale, Calif., firm, is the electronic equivalent of rolling down a window and asking for directions. The prototype unit looks like an automated-teller machine, but it issues information rather than cash. By punching buttons and choosing from a variety of screen menus, users specify where they want to go. Twenty

seconds later, the machine spits out a printed sheet of driving instructions constructed from a data base that contains the location of every intersection and alleyway in the Bay area, including 3,400 turn restrictions and 4,800 traffic lights. Says Barry Karlin president of K&C: "We save fuel, and we save time."

How the devices will fare in the marketplace remains to be seen. Their current price tags will certainly limit sales: Navigator sells for $1,395, and the DriverGuide is expected to cost about $1,000. Toyota already offers a computerized dashboard map on an expensive model sold only in Japan, but while U.S. automakers are testing the devices, none have plans to offer them as options before the early 1990s.

Etak and K&C remain optimistic and are busy expanding their cartographic data bases. Etak has computerized the maps of 85% of the nation's urban areas, while K&C is programming Los Angeles, Miami and Atlanta. Both companies speak confidently of the day when onboard computers will act as mobile information systems, displaying everything from the latest traffic conditions to the location of the nearest hospital. Predicts Karlin: "Ten years from now, nobody will need to drive with a road map folding and flapping in the steering wheel."

Source: Philip Elmer-DeWitt, *Time*, April 29, 1987.

on George Brett hitting at least a double against a left-handed pitcher, the statistical comparison of Joe Montana's passing game to other NFL quarterbacks in play-off games. All of these "stats" are assembled by computer.

Businesses require fast and accurate information on which to base decisions. This information can be used to make products better, cheaper, and more appropriate for us. "They don't make 'em like they used to" you say? Perhaps, but most of us would prefer one of today's cars over a 1948 Hudson.

Entertainment

Computer games, computer animation in the movies, computer circuits in televisions to make reception better, computer ticket sales for events, the list goes on and on. No computer has ever written a good book, however.

Law Enforcement

Much of detective work is digging out and assembling information. Since this is the computer's strong point, it is only natural that computers are being used more and more in the field of law enforcement. For example, in a recent case a mass murderer was brought to justice on the basis of his fingerprints left at the scene of one of his crimes. The fingerprint match was made by a computer capable of checking 650 fingerprints a second. The police department estimated that if a human expert had to look through all the city's 1.7 million fingerprint cards, it would have taken him 67 years.

Threat to Privacy

Almost in opposition to the law enforcement benefits of the computer is the risk of loss of individual privacy. Various agencies have the ability to assemble so much information on each of us that it is somewhat intimidating. A credit-card company's computer, for instance, can trace one's movements by assembling a trail of credit-card purchases. Some people say, "If you didn't do anything wrong, what do you have to hide?" Others object to living in such a computerized fishbowl.

Enforced Change

Computers have become so pervasive in our society that to someone who has not grown up with the computer, or doesn't adapt readily to the way a computer operates, this can be frightening. Imagine, if you can, having lived in a society whose most advanced transportation was the horse, and then being forced to drive a car on the Los Angeles freeways to work.

Employment Displacement

The computer has changed the way we do business. It has also changed the requirements for the jobs that businesses have to offer. Many occupations have become almost obsolete, while new jobs—requiring different skills and abilities—have been created. An auto worker has just lost his job to a robot. An economist would say that in the long run it makes little difference because other jobs are created in the robot industry. Try telling that to the auto worker who is struggling to feed his family while desperately trying to learn computer programming.

Dehumanization

Delbert couldn't buy a suit because the computer wasn't working. You call information for a phone number and a computer voice (affectionately called "Louise") intones it to you. Your charge card bill is fouled up because of erroneous data in the computer, and no people seem to take enough interest to dig in and change it. You can buy a "psychiatrist" program for your personal computer that will listen to your troubles and sympathize with you. Where have all the people gone? We are still here, but the computer's impersonal, lockstep method of operation has certainly influenced many of the things we do.

Like most advancements, the computer is a mixed blessing. It can do wonderful things for us but there are costs. It is up to each of us individually and all of us collectively to determine where the advancements are worth the costs.

SUMMARY

Computers play an important role in our daily lives. It would change our way of living drastically if they were suddenly taken away. Many things we take for granted—such as credit-card purchases, traffic lights, and paychecks—depend on computers in their operations.

Modern-day computers did not exist 40 years ago. Their rise to their current status of an almost indispensable tool was brought on by rapid advances in technology which increased their speed and reliability, and lowered their size and cost.

A computer is a machine that manipulates data by itself. Its hardware, the equipment, is controlled by software, sets of instructions called programs, to perform a task without human intervention. Once we give a computer a program, the computer can store the program and execute it any number of times.

We use the computer as a tool to get something done more efficiently than we could without it. It has a number of advantages over humans such as computational speed, accuracy, and dependability. Little training is required, and often times tasks can be performed at lower cost. Humans, on the other hand, are indispensable because of their mobility and ability to think, which include judgment, creativity, motivation, flexibility, and "data storage density."

Computers are used for many things, such as business information and office tasks, home tasks and entertainment, designing and manufacturing, and controlling various pieces of machinery. Computers can also be used in applications where it would be impossible to use a human, such as exploration of outer space.

The use of computers has brought about many changes in our society. It can force us to change how we do things, invade our privacy, threaten our jobs, and tend to dehumanize us. But computers also increase our efficiency, provide us with more information than we ever had before, and entertain us.

KEY WORDS

(in order of appearance in text)
Computer
Program
Execute
Run
Stored-program concept

Hardware
Software
Word processing
Electronic mail
Database management

Personal computer
Computer-aided design (CAD)
Computer-aided manufacturing
(CAM)

REVIEW QUESTIONS

1. What four major characteristics of computers have changed much in the last 40 years?

2. How often does the number of computers sold in the world double?

3. How does a computer differ from a calculator?

4. What is a program? What is the stored-program concept?

5. What is the difference between hardware and software?

6. What are the advantages of a computer over a human?

7. What are the advantages of a human over a computer?

8. Do computers make mistakes?

9. If you gave a computer an instruction that was not logical, would it follow it?

10. How does a control application differ from an information application?

11. List some of the ways the computer has helped our society.

12. List some of the ways computers pose a threat to our society.

THINK ABOUT IT

1. If all computers and computer-related devices took a one-day vacation, how would your life be affected? Compare your situation to Delbert Freed's.

2. Could a present-day computer system "take over the world" as some science-fiction writers suggest? If so, how? If not, why not?

3. If you had a complicated formula to solve but were only going to solve it once, would it be more practical to use a computer or a calculator and pencil and paper? Why?

4. We know that we can use a computer to process the words we use to write a report or a book. Could the computer actually write the book without us? How or why not?

5. If you had (or have) a computer in your home, for what kinds of things would you (or do you) use it?

CHALLENGES

1. How would the computer industry have been different if computers increased in speed and reliability, decreased in size, but the costs per piece of data processed remained constant instead of decreasing?

2. A computer program must be stated very precisely and with no ambiguities. Write a "program" or set of instructions, clearly and in detail, for tying a shoelace.

3. With computers taking over so many of our clerical and mechanical tasks, what will happen to the people who used to perform these tasks? Will employment shift from one area to another? Will overall employment go up or down? Is the short-range outlook different from the long-range?

2
THE COMPUTER SYSTEM

PREVIEW
Computers come in all sizes, but their basic components and functional units are fairly similar. Here we will discuss what computers are made of, what the basic building blocks are, and how they work together. After reading this chapter, you should know:

■ What the individual components are, what they look like, and something about how they fit together.

■ The units of the main computer processor, what their functions are, and how they interact.

■ What other kinds of machinery are needed to make an efficient, effective computer system.

■ The role of software in making a computer system work.

■ How we use computers to solve problems.

■ The size and capability categories for computers and what differentiates them.

To many of us, the computer is a wondrous, magic box. In this chapter we are going to take the cover off the box and see what's inside—how it looks, and what makes it tick. Although computers come in many different boxes, we can look inside any of them and find many of the same things. The computers vary in size and capability, but the components and the functional units all follow the same principles.

COMPUTER CONSTRUCTION

Computers are made of plastic, metal, bits of wire, nuts and bolts, and so forth. Some components, such as the mechanism used to print out computer reports, are mechanical, but most are electronic, containing no moving parts at all. The computer performs calculations and other internal operations by means of sets of electronic circuits. Each of these circuits contains a number of electronic components, principally **transistors** (some of which are coupled with capacitors or resistors), which we will consider the electronic building block of the computer. Even a simple home computer may contain over a million of them.

The Integrated Circuit

Wiring together a million components, each with two or more leads, would certainly drive the cost of a home computer well above the under-a-thousand-dollar price tag to which we have become accustomed. Fortunately, electronic-component suppliers have developed manufacturing technologies that allow the computer builders to buy most of the components in prewired sets. An **integrated circuit** (IC) is a set of components connected together on a single piece of silicon. Some of the newer ICs may contain over a million components on a single silicon chip.

The ICs themselves may be only about a tenth to a half-inch on a side, much too small to connect wires to, so they are attached and wired to **packages,** plug-in modules that protect the IC chip and are large enough to handle. These packages may be anywhere from a half- to two-inches long and have between 10 and 128 pins, or plug connections, sticking out of them. Some of the more sophisticated packages used on the larger computer systems even have built-in cooling systems to keep the IC from overheating.

The Printed Circuit Board

Even a simple computer is made of many ICs, and just wiring these together would become prohibitively expensive. So, engineers have designed the **printed circuit board (PC board),** a piece of flat plastic on which a pattern of electrical conductivity, serving the purpose of wires, is etched or "printed."

There are holes in the boards where connections are to be made. Components, such as ICs, IC sockets and others, are mounted and soldered through the holes to the metal on the board. Typically, one or more sides of the board have areas where small, flat fingers of metal reach to the very

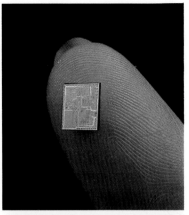

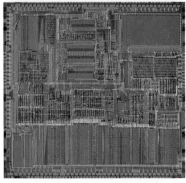

Integrated circuits such as this one (top) may contain thousands or even millions of individual electronic components. (Bottom) This 32-bit Intel386™ microprocessor has 275,000 transistors and can run multiple applications from operating systems simultaneously.

ICs and other components are assembled onto PC boards which, in turn, are connected to other PC boards.

BOX 2-1

The Next Major Battleground

A new breed of chips challenges 25 years of computer design

Silicon Valley has not seen such a bumper crop since it stopped growing peaches and prunes and began producing computer chips. Hardly a week has gone by this spring without a ballyhooed announcement of a new semiconductor or a line of high-speed computers. At the center of the excitement is a new breed of microprocessors that promises to give computer manufacturers their biggest performance boost in a decade. Lightning fast, the chips make it possible to put the power of ten to 20 refrigerator-size minicomputers into a single desktop-size machine.

Of all the announcements, none has generated as much anticipation as the one to be made this week by Motorola, the largest U.S. supplier of semiconductors (1987 sales: $6.7 billion). The electronics giant has etched 1.7 million transistors into a three-chip microprocessor called the 88000 that it hopes will become a standard component of the next generation of high-performance computers. Motorola may be right. Even before the new product was formally unveiled, more than 30 prospective customers, including Data General, Convergent and Tektronix, had formed a users group to set guidelines for designing hardware and software to take advantage of the new chips. Says Motorola Vice President Murray Goldman: "This is the next major battleground in the computer world."

How do the new chips achieve their performance breakthroughs? In a word: RISC, for reduced instruction set computer. RISC is not a new technology, but a fresh approach to computing that challenges 25 years of semiconductor design. It focuses on a computer's most basic commands: the instructions that are embedded, or hard-wired, into the silicon circuitry of the machine's central processing unit. The first computers made do with a handful of primitive commands, such as LOAD, ADD and STORE, which programmers combined to perform complex tasks. Lacking a command to multiply 6 times 5, for example, they had to instruct their computers to add five 6s together.

Over the years, the basic instruction sets grew in length, as miniaturization allowed computer designers to etch more circuits into silicon chips. The most advanced microprocessors began to resemble state-of-the-art calculators that could compute everything from square roots to compound interest at the touch of a button. By the time Digital Equipment introduced its best-selling VAX 11/780 computer in 1977, the machine's instruction set had swelled to 304 commands.

Source: Philip Elmer-DeWitt, *Time,* April 25, 1988, p. 79.

edge. These are called **edge connectors** and allow sets of wires to be plugged into the board, or allow the whole board to be plugged into another board.

An Assembled Computer

For small machines, the complete, assembled computer may be entirely contained on one circuit board. Larger computers have a number of curcuit boards plugged into "slots" or sockets on a master curcuit board called a **motherboard** or **backplane.** The motherboard provides power and the proper circuits to connect the various boards plugged into it.

But the increased complexity had its cost. Studies showed that 20% of the instructions were doing 80% of the work. The rest were like expensive extras on a limousine: rarely used luxuries that took up space and slowed performance. The advocates of RISK, declaring that it was time to go back to basics, stripped away the nonessentials and optimized the performance of the 50 or so most frequently used commands. Says Ben Anixter, vice president at Advanced Micro Devices, a Sunnyvale, Calif., firm that is introducing its first RISC chip in two weeks: "It is like going from the complicated old piston airplane engine to the turbojet."

At first, the industry was reluctant to switch to RISC. But the new crop of chips has made believers out of almost everybody. Sun, a company best known for its engineering computers, got into the chip business last summer when it began licensing a RISC processor to AT&T, Unisys and Xerox. MIPS, which introduced its second generation of the chips last month, supplies microprocessors to Tandem, Prime, and Silicon Graphics, Hewlett-Packard has built an entire line of computers around RISC technology.

Most important, IBM is making a major commitment to RISC. IBM Vice President Andrew Heller suggests that RISC technology could produce startling advances in electronic speech recognition, machine vision and artificial intelligence—all of which require superfast microprocessors. Says Heller: "Computers that can listen and talk back, and recognize objects on sight, are not so farfetched. RISC will help make all that a reality, and it's going to happen this century."

A technician working on a disassembled computer.

Still-larger computers have circuit boards connected to many mother-boards or other pieces of apparatus and mounted in one or more metal skeletons called mainframes. Whatever the size or configuration, the computer will have a number of plugs to connect it to other pieces of equipment such as keyboards and printers and the like.

Many computers come with extra, unfilled sockets called **expansion slots** on their motherboard. These allow you to plug in new circuit boards, providing the computer with extra capabilities. For personal computers, for example, you can buy boards that will enhance the computer's graphics capability, provide for more input and/or output devices, or allow communications over telephone lines.

HARDWARE

All the things described above and everything you see when you look at a computer system is hardware—display screens, keyboards, printers, lights, wires, and circuits. Let us examine the main functional components of computer hardware so that we understand something of what happens when it executes our instructions. Computers vary in size, capacity, effectiveness, and cost, but they all have these same basic functional components.

The Central Processing Unit

The heart of any computer system is the **central-processing unit** or **CPU.** It is made entirely of electronic components, principally ICs, and has no mechanical parts. Belying its importance to the computer, the CPU is one of its smallest parts. For example, in a personal computer it is a single chip of silicon about one-fourth inch on a side. Small though it may be, it carries on three of the most important functions in the system.

(1) Its first job is to **control** the rest of the computer system. To have the computer do a job for us, we give it a program of instructions and direct it to execute, or perform them. In its control function, the CPU acts as our foreman inside the system. It takes each of our instructions in turn and follows it, telling the other parts of the system what to do to accomplish the instruction. The system may consist of many different pieces of hardware, but they are all controlled by the CPU. For example, if we instruct the computer to display a character on a screen, the CPU will retrieve the character from its storage place and send it down the proper wires to the display screen.

(2) **Arithmetic operations**—addition, subtraction, multiplication, and division—are performed in the CPU. If we are figuring paychecks and our instructions call for multiplying the number of hours worked by the pay rate, the CPU will move the proper figures into its arithmetic unit and perform the operation.

(3) The third main function of the CPU is **logical operations.** These are comparisons—seeing if this is bigger than that, or these are equal, or those are not equal. The need for arithmetic operations is obvious—what good would a computer be that could not calculate? Logical operations are just as important, however. For example, our company probably includes overtime in its paychecks. To determine whether or not to pay overtime, we must direct the computer to compare the number of hours worked with 40. If the number of hours is greater than 40, then the overtime premium will be paid.

The capacity for logical operations is another factor that makes a computer different from a calculator. The latter adds and subtracts, but it does not compare.

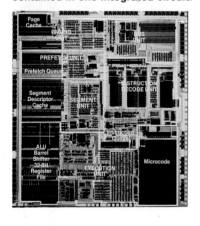

In microcomputers the entire central-processing unit is contained in one integrated circuit.

Main Memory

Marvelous though it is, a CPU alone is not an effective computer system. It can control, add, subtract, and compare, but it cannot remember what it is

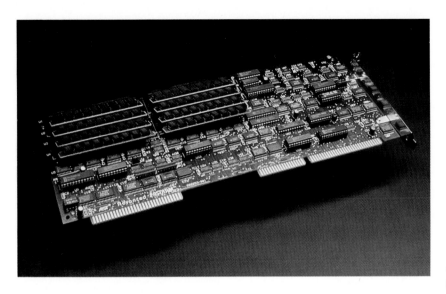

This main memory board can hold 8,192,000 characters of data.

supposed to add or the results of the calculation, nor can it remember the instructions it was supposed to follow to perform its task. Our computer system must include **storage** devices to remember both data and programs.

Main memory is the computer's primary storage device. Modern main memories are made up of transistors, often coupled with capacitors, on one or more integrated circuits. These components are arranged in sets, each of which can hold a small chunk of data—a character, for example, so it takes thousands to millions of these sets to build a useful memory. Main memory is fast; the CPU can get data from it in a fraction of a millionth of a second. But it is also somewhat expensive and therefore limited in capacity, so it is used only as temporary, working storage. Into it we put the program we are currently working with and the data that the program is using. Once that program has finished, we clear it out of main memory and bring in the next one.

Advantages & Disadvantages of main memory.

Secondary Storage

Secondary storage can hold data and programs permanently. It is inexpensive compared to main memory, but hundreds of times slower. The data are stored on some **medium,** some material which can hold the data. The medium for the data in this book is paper. Typical computer secondary-storage media are hard or floppy **disks,** or **magnetic tape.** These are not really such exotic materials. Some home computers, for example, use standard audio cassette tape and a portable cassette recorder for secondary storage.

While main memory is limited, secondary storage, even in a home computer can be virtually unlimited. Most computer systems have at least some secondary-storage devices that use **removable media,** disks or tapes that can be removed from the machine and replaced with other disks or tapes. This means that the secondary storage is limited only by the amount of shelf space available to hold the media. An IBM PC may be able to hold 1,440,000 characters on a single floppy disk but, since these disks can be taken out and others put in, billions of characters on thousands of disks can be stored on the shelves.

Input and Output Devices

For a computer to be useful, we must be able to communicate with it, feeding data and instructions into it (input) and pulling the results of its labors out (output).

The most common input device is a **keyboard.** What we type on the keyboard is transmitted to the CPU, which, as part of its control function, decides what to do with it. In Chapter 6 we will discuss the keyboard and its interaction with the rest of the computer in more detail, and we will look at a number of other input devices, such as bar code readers and voice input.

The most common output device is the **video-display unit (VDU),** usually using a **cathode-ray tube (CRT)** as a screen. The CRT looks like a television screen and, in fact, may well be—showing computer data rather than soap operas, however. Displays are said to produce **soft copy,** temporary output which is replaced as soon as new output is generated.

The second most popular device is the **printer,** which produces **hard copy,** permanent output on paper.

The CPU, as part of its control function, directs information to the output devices.

Quite often we combine an input device, usually a keyboard, with an output device, typically a VDU, in one unit to form a single, input/output **(I/O)** device, called a **terminal.** We will discuss printers, VDUs, and many other output devices in greater detail in Chapter 7.

(Left) The most common type of input and output devices are keyboards and video displays. (Right) Printed reports are a common form of computer output.

**Terminals combine a keyboard
with a video display.**

To be effective, any computer system must have at least one device from each of the above categories. For the home, for example, you could buy a small computer from Commodore or Radio Shack which includes the CPU, main memory, and the keyboard in one case for less than $150. To it you would add secondary storage, consisting of at least a cassette tape machine costing as little as $40, and some type of VDU, probably an ordinary color television set. Most people also feel that a printer is a necessity, and you could pick up one especially made for this computer for about $30. This comes to a total outlay of about $220 plus a color television which you probably have lying around anyway.

For your advanced research lab, you could dig a little deeper into your pocket and spend about $20,000,000 for a Cray 2 computer system which includes many CPUs, millions of characters of main memory, billions of characters of secondary storage, and hundreds of input and output devices, all of which can be working at the same time.

The difference in the two systems is not the categories of components—they are the same in small systems and large—but the speed and capacity of the components.

Source: Charles P. Lecht, *Computerworld*, Feb. 22, 1988, p. 21.

BOX 2-2

Friends and Foes Join to Build PCs

Lift the veil and find a map of the world, from Singapore to El Salvador

While replacing a board in one of my personal computers, my attention was drawn to a chip that bore the words "El Salvador" and the logo of Texas Instruments, revealing the country and company of origin. This bit of information led me to wonder how many other countries and companies had contributed to this PC's manufacture.

Without checking every component, but having removed just a few boards, I managed to come up with at least 11 countries and 16 companies. The countries included Japan, Singapore, Malaysia, Taiwan, South Korea, Indonesia, Australia, the Philippines, El Salvador and the U.S.

The company symbols were not easy to decipher, but I recognized those of Motorola, Intel, IBM, Fairchild, Hewlett-Packard, Nippon Electric, TI, National Semiconductor, Advanced Micro Devices, Beckman Instruments, Yokugawa Electric, Hitachi, Siemens, Fujitsu, Electronic Associates, and AST Technologies.

Some of the companies were operating in several of the countries, the notable example being TI, whose logo I found on components from at least five countries.

Included in the overall country list are nations harboring clone manufacturers as well as legendary computer industry foes such as IBM, Fujitsu, Hitachi, NEC and Intel—competing and cooperating at the same time. Omoshiroi (Japanese for "interesting"), I thought.

Exploring the component origins of the first machine led me to lift the bonnets off several other systems, each produced by a different manufacturer, either Japanese or American. They all sported a similar country and company mix.

SOFTWARE

We have now assembled the equipment for a complete system, but it won't do anything without instructions—software.

Application Programs

An **application program** is one that performs a specific task for individual users of the system. Some examples are programs to write paychecks, process text (word processing), do financial analyses, or play games. If you

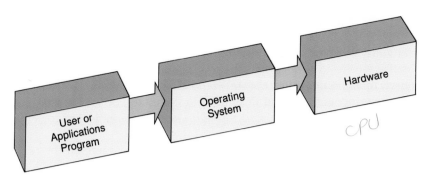

The Operating System
The operating system is a program that goes between the user or application programs and the system hardware. It translates the user's instructions into ones that the machine will understand.

use the supplement, Introducing BASIC, you will be writing such application programs.

System Programs

Since computer hardware is so complex, the instructions that direct it must be quite detailed and complicated. You, whether directly or through an application program, would prefer to give the computer simpler, more general instructions. **System programs** help you by translating your general instructions into the detailed, specific ones required to direct the CPU. One of those system programs, the **operating system,** is placed between you and the actual hardware. Many of your instructions or those in your application programs are intercepted by the operating system and replaced by instructions in the detail required to direct the hardware. The operating system, then, is your helper inside the computer.

For example, printing an entire sentence on the display screen typically requires only one instruction from us. However, to actually execute this instruction, the CPU must find where that sentence exists in main memory, take each character in the sentence from main memory and send it down the proper wires at the right speed to the display, check at each character to see if the end of the sentence is reached, and so forth. All this involves the execution of perhaps five or more instructions per character. The operating system translates your one general instruction into the many specific instructions the CPU requires to perform the task.

Another function of the operating system is to match standard software to the requirements of a particular hardware configuration. Each type or brand of computer may be slightly different—the display screen is connected to different wires, the printers run at different speeds, and so forth. By making the operating system slightly different to accommodate these peculiarities, the same instructions from the user will have the same effect on different computers.

HOW COMPUTERS THINK

They don't!

Computers don't think as you and I think of thinking. Computers follow sets of instructions that we give them. In following the instructions, the computer will be consistent, detailed, and exact. It will never be imaginative or ambitious, or, on the other hand, lazy. Human thinking is just too, well, human. Our thinking depends upon a certain amount of uncertainty, flexibility, and even mood.

If we were to drive from Chugwater, Wyoming, to King of Prussia, Pennsylvania, the most direct route would be the road going just north of Mishawaka, Indiana. Can you imagine your computer, or your car for that matter, deciding to take the road through Greenup, Illinois, just to see a new section of the countryside?

Either machine would consistently take the same route all the time unless it were instructed to do otherwise; in which case, neither machine would ever discover the little town of High Hill, Missouri—much to its loss. Creative human thinking involves varying from the norm and trying new things for no other reason than "It looks like it might be good."

Problem Solving

Computers are not creative, but they can solve problems for us. Because they solve problems following our instructions, and because we humans have had tens of thousands of years of experience in problem solving, we usually instruct our computers to solve problems in typically human problem-solving patterns.

For example, if we had to develop a comparison of sales in the various product lines for our chain of department stores, we would gather all the sales data, organize them into product lines and total them, and then list them in some readable fashion. If we used a computer to do the same task, we would have it follow the same pattern—feed it the data, have it organize and total it, and instruct it to print out a report that is easily readable by humans.

When software developers design new programs, the first thing they consider is how they would solve the problem without the aid of the computer. Then, they apply that process to the computer. Only rarely is it more efficient to vary from the human process.

Artificial Intelligence

A move is afoot to make computers think like humans. This development of **artificial intelligence** involves analyzing and systematizing human thinking processes, and programming computers to follow the same ones. Until recently, such a dream (or nightmare) has not been practical because we know very little about the human thinking process, and those processes are so complicated that trying to imitate them requires tremendous computer resources that were just not available.

Even when this branch of computer design becomes commonplace, it will still be difficult, if not impossible, to program in the sometimes wild and crazy aberrations that make up human creativity

COMPUTERS IN ALL SIZES

Computer systems range from pocket size to room size. We usually classify them as microcomputers, minicomputers, mainframes, or supercomputers, but the lines separating these classifications are not clear-cut, and hence the definitions are somewhat fuzzy. However, the characteristics discussed here are typical of computers in each range.

Microcomputers

As the name implies, **microcomputers** are the smallest computers. This does not mean that they are not effective. Some of today's micros can do more at a higher speed and a fraction of the cost than the large computers of a few years ago. Because of this, sales of microcomputers such as Apple, Compaq, and the IBM personal computer are growing at a much greater rate than sales in the other three classes.

Microcomputers usually have a one-chip CPU. The entire central processing unit, including control and arithmetic/logic functions, fits on a quarter-inch square of silicon. The computer system itself must be larger than that because it must include circuits for memory and other functions: a keyboard for input, and a display or printer for output. Some entire microcomputers can fit in a pocket. Most, however, sit on a desk top.

Micros range in price from about $200 to $25,000, depending on the sophistication of the particular machine and the kinds of extra equipment you add to it.

Micros have small CPUs and main memories. Their CPUs can handle only one to four characters at a time and their main memories can hold from about 64,000 to 640,000 characters (although some allow main memories of well over 10,000,000 characters). Those two facts combine to make them considerably slower than the other classes of computers. A micro might perform an addition operation in ten millionths of a second.

We find microcomputers in a lot of different applications. Many special-purpose machines—such as cash registers, telephone switch-

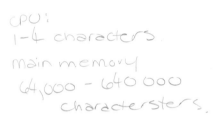

CPU:
1-4 characters.
main memory
64,000 - 640 000
charactersters.

A microcomputer is shown here.

Here we see a minicomputer.

boards, and automatic bank tellers—have micros built in. Video arcade games and home television games are microcomputer systems.

Home and personal computers are microcomputers. Businesses are using personal computers increasingly as main computers for small firms, to prepare data for larger computers, or as analytical tools for individual employees. In fact, personal computers are rapidly replacing the calculator on the desk top. Authors, like us, use personal computers on which to write our books.

Minicomputers

The name is somewhat misleading. **Minicomputers** are only "mini" when compared to modern mainframes. True, their main processors would typically fit inside a suitcase, but compared to any computer of ten years ago, they are functional giants.

Most newer machines have main memories of 1,000,000 to 32,000,000 characters and will process instructions at speeds from 0.5 to 15 MIPS (Million Instructions Per Second). Minicomputer system prices range from about $20,000 to $150,000. A small- to medium-sized business might use one as its primary computer, while a larger company might link a number of them together into a network of computers.

Mainframes

When the computer industry was new, all computers were big, bulky machines with many layers of components, all housed in one or more large metal frames called main frames. Computers have gotten physically smaller, but we still call the large ones **mainframes.** Main processors can be the size of a desk or larger, may have more than one CPU, and a typical mainframe system with accessory equipment usually fills a large room. That

This type of computer is called a mainframe.

room must have strict environmental controls, carefully regulating heat, humidity, and dust. Few minis and no micros have such requirements. Main memories in these machines usually store from 2 to 64 million characters, although some have the capability for over a billion.

Mainframe CPUs are extremely fast—from about 5 to 80 MIPS. They range in price from $150,000 to millions of dollars.

Medium to large companies use mainframes as primary computers, and larger companies add them to a group of computers connected together in a network.

Supercomputers

Supercomputers are the behemoths of the computer industry. They are high-capacity, high-speed "number-crunching" machines. They are not typically used for normal business information-processing applications but for special scientific or engineering tasks where huge numbers of repetitive calculations must be made within a reasonable amount of time. Supercomputers are used for jobs such as predicting where oil might be from masses of seismic data, assembling intelligence information from data gathered by listening posts and satellites, or simulating the airflow over the surface of an aircraft in flight. If the "Star Wars" defense systems becomes a reality, it will require even more advanced supercomputers than the ones available today.

The Cray-2 is one of the largest supercomputers. It has a main memory of 2 billion characters, can perform 1.2 billion arithmetic operations per second (that is about 50,000 times faster than a personal computer), comes in a C-shaped cabinet less than four feet high and five feet across, and can be yours for about $18 million. The most expensive was Illiac IV, a $40,000,000 machine built for the United States Army by the Burroughs Corporation. It was installed at NASA's Ames Research Center in California.

A supercomputer is the largest type made.

BOX 2-3

Just Dig While You Work

Where does the world's foremost designer of high-speed computers get his inspiration? Apparently deep in a dirt tunnel beneath his Wisconsin home, according to John Rollwagen, the chairman of Cray Research. As Rollwagen tells it, Seymour Cray, the company's elusive founder, has been dividing his time between building the next generation of supercomputers and digging an underground tunnel that starts below his Chippewa Falls house and heads toward the nearby woods. "He's been working at it for some time now," says Rollwagen, who reports that the tunnel is 8 ft. high, 4 ft. wide and lined with 4-by-4 cedar boards. When a tree fell through the top of the tunnel several years ago, Cray used the opening to install a periscope-equipped lookout.

For Cray, the excavation project is more than a simple diversion. "I work when I'm at home," he recently told a visiting scientist. "I work for three hours, and then I get stumped, and I'm not making progress. So I quit, and I go and work in the tunnel. It takes me an hour or so to dig four inches and put in the 4-by-4s. Now, as you can see, I'm up in the Wisconsin woods, and there are elves in the woods. So when they see me leave, they come into my office and solve all the problems I'm having. Then I go back up and work some more."

Rollwagen knows that Cray is only half kidding and that some of the designer's greatest inspirations come when he is digging. Says the chairman: "The real work happens when Seymour is in the tunnel."

Source: *Time*, Mar. 28, 1988, p. 57.

The Shift to Microcomputers

The million-dollar mainframe computer was always the mainstay of a business's information system. It was big, powerful, could handle masses of data, and serviced a number of users concurrently. It still is the heart of most large companies' information efforts, but its role is changing and microcomputers are taking over many of its functions.

As more users are becoming directly involved with the computer, they are finding that the microcomputer gives them an increased amount of flexibility and power. Processing can be done on the desktop rather than in some anonymous back room and, more importantly, the user can control that processing. If needed software doesn't exist, the user can write it using a relatively simple programming language such as BASIC, or any number of software packages that facilitate organization and manipulation of data.

In a corporate environment it is common to have a two-year backlog of programming projects for the mainframe, and completion times measured in months. Many users have taken refuge in the personal computer. They appreciate the convenience of being able to start on a project

Source: Robert L. Perry, *Business Solutions,* Sept. 1987, p. A15.

Business Focus BOX 2-4

PCs Help Welch Put Competitors In a Jam

"In a market as tough as ours, a quicker introduction is very important and often means the difference between success and failure," says Domenic Montemurro, manager of cost accounting, at Welch Foods Inc., Westfield, N.Y. Montemurro's 11-person cost accounting department, which plays a vital role in new product development, has found an advantage that helps the cooperative get to market first with "hot" new products. That advantage, of course, is the personal computer.

Montemurro says, "We are constantly analyzing a steady stream of requests to estimate the costs and profitability of new products and extensions to product lines. Doing these cost analyses with a calculator is very, very cumbersome. Setting the estimates up on the PC saves a tremendous amount of time."

Montemurro cites the hugely successful Welch's Squeezable Jellies and Jams product line as a prime example of his PC's essential role. "Prior to the introduction, we had to do dozens of costs analyses with the PCs. I'm sure the PC was instrumental in getting the line to market much sooner, probably weeks sooner, than it would have been if we had done them manually.

And we did more extensive analysis, produced reports in a more timely manner, and delivered them faster than we otherwise could have."

He notes with pride, "We were first to market with a squeezable line, although we had heard several competitors were researching a similar product."

Montemurro's boss, Controller Bill Grieshober, points out that cost accounting was the first department at Welch Foods to both recognize the value of and take advantage of the PC more than three years ago.

Despite the staff's accomplishments with PC technology, Montemurro's department has only one PC for its exclusive use. "There is a room right next door with two more PCs that we have access to," he says, admitting that his staff monopolizes the room. "When we are very busy, we may have five people from the department scattered around the building using PCs."

Welch Foods certainly gets its money's worth from these PCs. Montemurro says that, on average, his staff uses PCs for 40 to 60 hours a week. Besides new product analyses, the biggest job the department faces is the annual budget

reviews for the manufacturing plants. "We are responsible for reviewing more than 2,000 accounts in each plant. Prior to PCs, many of these accounts were not looked at in depth," Montemurro says. "Now year-to-year comparisons and trend analyses are very easy. We can more readily identify misspending and budgeting mistakes. We probably save the company hundreds of thousands of dollars a year with our ability to analyze these complex budgets more thoroughly."

Grieshober adds that Montemurro's staff coordinates its budget analyses with his office's plant and company budget process. "We do all of our plant budgets on PCs. Each plant accountant has a PC, and we swap disks with each one during our month- to six-week-long budget process."

Despite their value, PCs at Welch Foods do not change the basic nature of the accountant's job. Rather, Montemurro says, PCs allow him to do more and better quality work.

There is no doubt that the use of PCs in accounting helps Welch Foods put the squeeze on its competition.

TABLE 2-1   **Computer Size Comparison**

	Size of Main Processor	Main Memory (1,000s chrs)	Cost of System ($1,000s)	Speed (MIPS)
Micro				
Min	Book	64	0.2	.1
Max	Shoe box	10,000	25	3
Mini				
Min	Shoe box	1,000	20	0.5
Max	Suitcase	32,000	150	15
Mainframe				
Min	Small desk	2,000	150	10
Max	Closet	64,000	10,000	100
Super				
Min	Small desk	10,000	1,000	50
Max	Closet	100,000	20,000	10,000

This chart shows typical characteristics of each class of computer, but the lines separating the classes are by no means rigid.

immediately and finish it in days or even hours. The result is that many tasks that formerly would have been done on the mainframe are now being accomplished on micros. Processing is becoming "decentralized" and spread among many smaller computers.

The increased use of micros has been made possible by advances in both hardware and software. It is now possible to do relatively large projects on microcomputers because the speed and capacity of these little giants rival that of the mainframes of a few years ago. IBM, which controls over three-quarters of the mainframe market, admits that its top-of-the-line PS/2 microcomputer, costing under $10,000, has the same raw processing speed of its 1975 370/168 mainframe costing about $3.5 million.

In the software arena, microcomputer productivity software packages (discussed more fully in the Appendix) make it relatively easy for the more casual user to get sophisticated results from the micro.

Is the mainframe dead? Not by a long shot. Much of the processing has gone to the micros, but mainframes have been advancing, too, and can handle massive amounts of data that will continue to exceed the micro's practical capacity for the foreseeable future. In addition, mainframes are being used to handle the communications tasks between all the micros in the company. The mainframe's role, then, is shifting away from being the computer that everyone uses toward being the storehouse for the organization's common data base, and allowing the micros to share those data and communicate with each other.

SUMMARY

Computers are made of a variety of components, but the majority of them are integrated circuits, each of which contains thousands of transistors and other electronic components. These ICs are mounted on printed circuit boards, which in turn are plugged into other PC boards called backplanes. The computer consists of one or more of these assembled and wired together and contained in one or more cabinets or frames.

The heart of any computer system is the central processing unit (CPU). It is small, but without it the system would not operate. Its three functions are control (following instructions and directing the rest of the system), arithmetic operations (calculations), and logical operations (comparisons).

The CPU stores no data, so it needs a main memory to work with. Main memory consists of thousands or millions of data-storage spaces which can be accessed very rapidly by the CPU. In main memory we store programs that are currently running and data for those programs.

We use secondary storage, disks or tapes, for permanent storage. It is cheaper and the storage media are usually removable, which makes secondary storage virtually unlimited. However, access to it is much slower than to main memory.

To feed data to the system and receive the information from the system we need input and output devices. The most popular input device is the keyboard. The most popular output devices are the visual display unit and the printer.

To be useful, the hardware must be directed by software. We separate software into two different categories: application programs that are written for specific tasks, and system programs that assist both application programs and computer users in performing their instructions.

Although the dividing lines are not always clear, computers are separated into classes according to their size and capabilities. Microcomputers are the smallest, minicomputers somewhat larger, mainframes are the big workhorses, and there are a few supercomputers, mainly dedicated to scientific tasks requiring the processing of mountains of data.

There is a shift in emphasis from centralized processing and mainframe computers to decentralized processing and microcomputers. This has been facilitated by the increased processing power of the micros and the availability of micro software that allows data handling by less-sophisticated users.

KEY WORDS

(in order of appearance in text)

Transistor	Storage	Hard copy
Integrated circuit (IC)	Main memory	I/O
Package	Secondary storage	Terminal
Printed circuit board (PC board)	Medium	Application program
Edge connector	Disk	System program
Motherboard	Magnetic tape	Operating system
Backplane	Removable media	Artificial intelligence
Expansion slot	Keyboard	Microcomputer
Central-processing unit (CPU)	Video-display unit (VDU)	Minicomputer
Control	Cathode-ray tube (CRT)	Mainframe
Arithmetic operation	Soft copy	Supercomputer
Logical operation	Printer	

REVIEW QUESTIONS

1. What is the principal device or "building block" of a modern computer?

2. What is an integrated circuit?

3. What is the purpose of a motherboard or backplane?

4. Name the three basic functions of a CPU.

5. How is an arithmetic operation different from a logical operation?

6. What do we keep in main memory? In secondary storage?

7. What are the most popular input and output devices?

8. Which devices produce hard copy and which produce soft copy?

9. Describe the difference between application and system programs.

10. Why do computers have operating systems?

11. Do computers think? Can they create?

12. What branch of computer science concerns itself with making computers imitate human thinking processes?

13. What characteristics differentiate mainframes, minicomputers, and microcomputers?

THINK ABOUT IT

1. Outline a sequence of instructions that would accept ten test grades between 0 and 100 from a keyboard, average them, and assign and display letter grades as follows: 90–100, A; 80–89.9, B; 70–79.9, C; 60–69.9, D; below 60, F. Be very detailed in your instructions. Label appropriate operations as input or output, logical or arithmetic.

2. Of these components—CPU, main memory, secondary storage, input devices, and output devices—which could the computer function without? Why?

3. If we were to design a computer to think and create like human beings, how would we have to modify its methods of operations?

4. We know that with the rapid rate of advancement of computers, today's equipment will be obsolete tomorrow. Other than simply wearing out, under what conditions should old equipment be replaced? When something better comes along? When you are embarrassed to admit you have old equipment? Why?

CHALLENGES

1. A number of companies make machines called "programmable calculators." Do they have main memories? Secondary storage? Do they perform logical operations? Would you classify them as computers or calculators?

2. Investigate a local company and see what classes of computers (micros, minis, or mainframes) it uses.

3. Look at some computer manufacturer's sales brochures or visit a computer store and, for a particular computer, see how many instructions per second it will perform, how much main memory it has, how much secondary storage it has, and the minimal cost for a system with one input, one output, and one secondary storage device.

The Making of an Integrated Circuit

1. This is the raw material (trichlorosilane) from which silicon wafers are made.

2. Here we see the interior of a furnace for growing silicon crystals.

3. The refining process results in a silicon ingot.

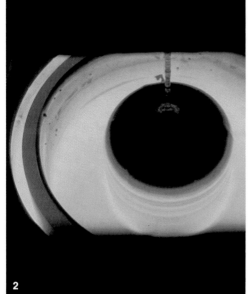

4. These are known as epitaxial (having orientation controlled by the crystal substrate) silicon wafers.

5. The ingot is sawed into wafers, which are then polished.

6. An epitaxial furnace such as this deposits epilayers on the wafers.

7. Some of the processes involve putting materials on top of the wafer, while others involve putting impurities into the silicon (to give it different electrical properties).

8. These men are discussing the photo mask for a silicon chip. A blow up of the mask is behind them.

9. The mask's pattern is projected onto the silicon wafer through a layer of photosensitive material. The pattern is printed on the wafer, and the wafer is then developed.

10. Here the photosensitive material is removed, and all but the required circuit pattern is etched away.

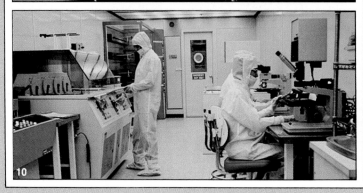

9

11. This super blow up of a wafer shows the result of the etching process.

12. At various steps the wafer is visually inspected and electronically tested.

13. Individual chips in wafers are separated by a diamond saw and defective ones removed.

14. This is the silicon wafer after being separated into transistors.

15. The chip is attached to a "package," with individual wires between the chip and the package.

16. After packaging, each individual integrated circuit undergoes a final set of electrical tests.

17. The result of these processes are integrated circuits, ready to use in a supercomputer or a microwave oven.

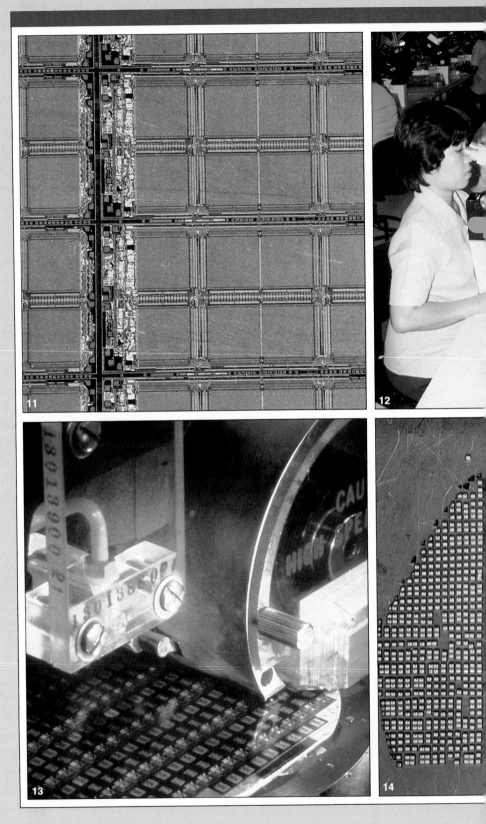

15

16

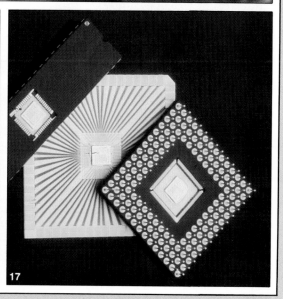

17

3

BUSINESS INFORMATION

PREVIEW
This chapter gives a general overview of modern methods of providing information to organizations. The emphasis is on using the computer as a tool in the process. After reading it you should understand:

■ Something about the information industry—its size, growth, and who the major suppliers and users are.

■ Why we demand so much information today.

■ The meanings of the terms "data" and "information" and how one is transformed into the other.

■ What elements are combined to form a computer information system.

■ How we organize data for our information systems.

■ Where we use computers in information systems.

THE INFORMATION INDUSTRY

The world's demand for information is growing rapidly and shows no sign of abating. For example:

- In 1987, the world's top 100 information-systems companies had sales of over $208.9 billion. IBM alone had information-systems sales of $50.5 billion.
- The computing capability the computer industry sold between 1987 and 1989 equaled all the capability sold from the beginning of the computer era until then.
- In 1970 there were about 200,000 data processing computers in the world. In 1988, including personal computers, there were about 50,000,000.

Who uses this information? We all do, from Harry down at the corner service station wanting to know how much his next shipment of tires is going to cost, to the presidents of corporations worried about the future state of the economy. The largest single information user is the United States government which, in its various branches, has more than 30,000 computers and stores more than a trillion trillion characters of data. If all this information were printed out, it would cover the entire earth almost twice over.

Our government may be the largest *single* user, but collectively American business uses more information than any other group—more than governments, scientific research institutions, or educational institutions, and about as much as all businesses in the rest of the world combined. Businesses record financial transactions, customer data, orders, shipments, inventories, production schedules, and costs with computers; and they continually use this information to make business decisions.

Why So Much Information?

Businesses are in business to earn a profit—the excess of revenues (the amount a business brings in through sales and fees) over expenses. Information is expensive and expenses reduce profits, yet American business spent $500 billion just for data-processing staff salaries over the past ten years. So why has business spent all this money?

Information costs money

To be profitable, a company must make accurate and timely business decisions. The more a decision maker knows about a situation, the more accurate the decision. The faster the decision maker can get information, the more timely the decision. Increase the accuracy and timeliness of a decision and its potential profit increases. For example, because Activision quickly and accurately determined the success of Atari home video game systems, they were able to profitably produce and market their own Atari-compatible cartridges, creating new sales of several million dollars.

Information, then, is an important factor in business profits. If a business gathers more information and does it faster, its profit potential increases. That extra profit, however, may be reduced or even eliminated by the extra cost of the information. To achieve maximum profit, a business must strike a balance between enough information to make a reasonably good decision and the cost of that information. In other words, the cost of the information should not exceed the added profit generated by the decision.

Imagine that you work as the marketing manager for Amalgamated Foods and are thinking of introducing a new breakfast cereal, Crunchy Critters, in the Midwest. You have tasted the cereal and you like it. You decide, though, that you should probably know more before you spend over a million dollars in advertising, production, and distribution just to introduce it. What information would help you make an intelligent decision? The following categories are listed here roughly in decreasing order of importance:

- Population of the targeted sales area
- Percentage of the population below 13 years of age
- Number of families in the area
- Average family income
- Family cereal buying habits
- Taste preferences of children in the area
- Sample taste tests of product in the area
- Willingness of families to change products
- Whether each individual child in the area likes the product
- The amount of buying influence each child exerts over his/her parents

If you could obtain all that information, you might reasonably predict the cereal's profitability, but it would probably cost you more than you would make selling the product. How much information would provide a

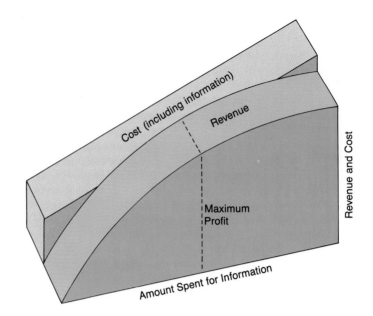

How Much Information?

Increased expenditures on information, when used correctly, can lead to increased revenues. As more information is gathered, however, it tends to overlap other information or not be as pertinent to the situation. Revenues will still increase, but not at a decreasing rate. The trick is to spend just enough on information to realize maximum profit, the greatest difference between revenues and expenses.

reasonable assurance of success but not blow all your profits? Some of the information is cheap. You can obtain such information as population, age of population, and number of families in the area from government census reports tallied by computers. Other information would be prohibitively expensive. To find out whether a given child could convince his or her mother to buy a $1.49 box of cereal would probably cost $150 per child for research, testing, and computer time. The ideal amount of information lies somewhere in the middle.

Judging from the amount of money business has spent on information recently, Americans seem to think they need more and more information on which to base a good decision. What did companies do 30 years ago, before the information explosion? Wasn't information just as important then? Of course it was, but before the development and widespread use of modern computers, information cost a lot more to process. Therefore, the ideal point before information costs ate up the profits came quickly, forcing businesses to base decisions on a relatively small amount of information.

Now, because businesses can obtain information more cheaply, they seek more of it and are growing more sophisticated in using it. If ABC Company makes better decisions and provides better service than XYZ Company, then XYZ Company had better improve or ABC will put XYZ out of business. Increased competitive pressures require increased use of information.

Why Information Is Cheaper Now

While we have been saying that information is less expensive now than ever, we have also said that American business spends billions per year on computers and information-gathering activities. It seems contradictory, but

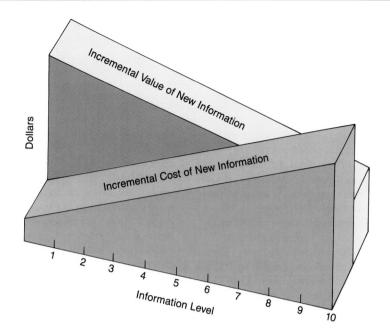

In a typical information-gathering situation, the least expensive relevant information is sought first. It is usually most valuable because little else is known. As you move up levels to more expensive information, it is not usually as valuable because, among other things, it overlaps earlier information.

it really isn't. True, we are spending more for information but we are getting much more information for the money. For example, 30 years ago it would take three hours and about fifty dollars to make up a profit-and-loss statement that can now be done in three minutes at a cost of about three dollars.

Computers account for most of the information cost reduction. They are fast—a human can do a simple addition in about half a second, a computer in about a millionth of a second. They are accurate—even most so-called computer errors are really human errors. And they are becoming cheaper and more powerful all the time. It has been said that if the automobile industry exhibited the same changes in price and capability as the computer industry, a Rolls-Royce would get about 20,000 miles per gallon and cost about $4.98.

The Computer as a Tool

The computer did not invent information. If anything, the need for more information spurred development of the computer. Years before computers existed, people, with the aid of calculators, pencils, or beads and stones, processed data and provided information.

For example, every ten years we in the United States perform a census, a count of the people and certain of their characteristics. Today, it would be unthinkable to attempt such an undertaking without the aid of computers, but our first census was taken in 1790, obviously before the advent of computers. In fact, over 4,000 years ago, the Babylonians took a complete survey of their agricultural and land holdings. They certainly did not use computers.

BOX 3-1

Information at Brinkman's

Brinkman's is a medium-sized sporting goods store located in a major suburban area. In the 14 years it has been in business, it has grown from a small hunting and fishing shop to a department store carrying a complete line of sports equipment and apparel. The increased size of the operation started management thinking of computerizing their information processing. Before spending a fortune on computer equipment, however, they decided to make a systematic study of their needs. Their first step was to determine what information they were currently using.

As with most businesses, one of the most significant categories of information is accounting. This includes figures for the following:

- *Sales.* Sales of the various products in the different departments.
- *Cost of goods sold.* How much the items that Brinkman's sold cost them.
- *Expenses.* Payroll, rent, advertising, taxes, insurance, supplies, and all the other costs of doing business.
- *Inventories.* How much stock they have on hand.
- *Accounts receivable.* How much others owe to them.
- *Accounts payable.* How much they owe to others.
- *Various assets.* Cash, store fixtures, office machines, the building, and so forth.

The "bottom line," net profit or loss (sales less cost of goods sold, less expenses), concerns management most.

Besides the basic accounting figures, Brinkman's needs other important information. For example, Brinkman's runs an aggressive marketing and advertising program that includes frequent special sales. To make the sales successful, management must know which items will attract customers to the store and how low to price those items, so they keep careful records of past sales—which items were on sale, how many of each item actually sold, how many nonsale items moved during the sale, the number of people who passed through the store, and the type of advertising that brought them to the store.

Brinkman's also maintains a customer mailing list containing not only names and addresses but also information on the customers' favorite sports, their last purchase, and whether they are small, average, or large spenders. From this information Brinkman's targets its mailings to those groups of customers most likely to respond to a particular offering.

To build goodwill among its customers, Brinkman's sponsors a number of activities, including a ski school, tennis lessons and tournaments, and sailboard lessons and regattas. Each event is advertised separately

and special fliers are mailed to specific categories on Brinkman's mailing lists. Brinkman's gauges the effectiveness of these events by carefully tracking costs, revenues, and new sales generated.

To maintain the proper amount of stock on the shelves, Brinkman's has complicated inventory and order-processing information needs. Management must know how much of each item they have on hand, when to order more, the status of their orders, and whether to order an unusually large quantity in anticipation of impending price increases by suppliers.

Having employees requires even more information. For each employee, Brinkman's must know name, address, social security number, all kinds of tax information for state and federal governments, insurance data, work schedules, vacation information, and which of Brinkman's outside activities he or she might participate in. The employees themselves must know the items in stock, their prices, whether they are on sale, where they are located, and something about each item so that they can talk intelligently to customers.

This analysis covers only the major information needs of Brinkman's. There are thousands of others, from numbers of bad credit cards to the number of items of sportswear a customer has taken to the dressing room, that are not covered here but are very important to Brinkman's operation. Information represents an important asset to Brinkman's or any business.

The evolution of information technology.

Computers now generate most accounting information, but long before they existed, we performed accounting by hand. Most of the written records of early civilizations almost 5,000 years ago were accounting data—tax records, harvest yields, and inventories of the king's treasures.

Although most present computer applications could be performed manually, using a machine involves much less time, money, and human drudgery. The accounting system is much the same as before, but the accountant uses the computer as a tool to make the job more efficient, much like a carpenter drives nails with an automatic hammer rather than a rock. This frees the accountant for thinking and creating rather than moving numbers around.

INFORMATION SYSTEMS

In this book, our principal concern is not computers, and certainly not the entire field of computers. We are primarily concerned with providing information. However, since the computer is the major tool used to help us in providing information, it will necessarily become a major part of our discussions.

Data Versus Information

(Opposite page) The United States census, taken every ten years, is a massive information undertaking.

Data (the plural for datum, a word almost no one uses) are raw facts. When data are combined, organized, summarized, and presented appropriately,

How to fill out your Census Form

See the filled-out example in the yellow instruction guide. This guide will help with any problems you may have.

If you need more help, call the Census Office. The telephone number of the local office is shown at the bottom of the address box on the front cover.

Use a black pencil to answer the questions. Black pencil is better to use than ballpoint or other pens.

Fill circles "O" completely, like this: ●

When you write in an answer, print or write clearly.

Make sure that answers are provided for everyone here.

See page 4 of the guide if a roomer or someone else in the household does not want to give you all the information for the form.

Answer the questions on pages 1, 2, and 3.

Check your answers. Then write your name, the date, and telephone number on page 4.

Mail back this form on Tuesday, April 1, or as soon afterward as you can. Use the enclosed envelope; no stamp is needed.

Please start by answering Question 1 below.

Question 1

List in Question 1

• Family members living here, including babies still in the hospital.

• Relatives living here.

• Lodgers or boarders living here.

• Other persons living here.

• College students who stay here while attending college, even if their parents live elsewhere.

• Persons who usually live here but are temporarily away (including children in boarding school below the college level).

• Persons with a home elsewhere but who stay here most of the week while working.

Do Not List in Question 1

• Any person away from here in the Armed Forces.

• Any college student who stays somewhere else while attending college.

• Any person who usually stays somewhere else most of the week while working there.

• Any person away from here in an institution such as a home for the aged or mental hospital.

• Any person staying or visiting here who has a usual home elsewhere.

1. What is the name of each person who was living here on Tuesday, April 1, 1980, or who was staying or visiting here and had no other home?

_____

_____

_____

_____

_____

_____

_____

_____

_____

_____

_____

_____

_____

Note

If everyone here is staying only temporarily and has a usual home elsewhere, please mark this box ☐.

Then please:
• answer the questions on pages 2 and 3, and
• enter the address of your usual home on page 4.

Please continue ↗

BOX 3-2

At Westinghouse, 'E-Mail' Makes the World Go 'Round

It was a typical summer weekend for Westinghouse Electric Corp. President Paul E. Lego. In between golf games and jogging near his home in Upper St. Clair, 15 miles southwest of Pittsburgh, Lego got in five hours at his IBM PC/AT computer. He sent out a flurry of electronic-mail memos to managers located as far off as Japan and Australia. He read electronic progress reports from company representatives negotiating a new contract with Westinghouse's unions. He immediately responded via "E-mail" with bargaining suggestions and fired off another memo to a lieutenant, asking him to send data to Lego's office computer by Monday morning.

At 6 a.m. on Monday, during his 30-minute drive downtown, Lego, 58, called on his cellular phone to map out the day's strategy with Chief Executive John C. Marous, who was motoring in from Fox Chapel, a town 10 miles northeast of the city. Arriving at his office on the 23rd floor, Lego checked his computer for messages and found the information he had requested the day before. Another workweek had begun.

Welcome to the brave new world of Westinghouse, where personal computers and telecommunications have dramatically changed the lifestyles of Lego and thousands of employees. Electronic mail and voice-message systems have ended the annoyance of telephone tag. Teleconferencing has drastically reduced travel to meetings. The bottom line, Lego says, is that these tools have contributed up to one-third of the company's stunning 6% annual increases in white-collar productivity since the early '80s. That's important since Westinghouse's salaried ranks have soared to 73% of its work force today, from 46% two decades ago. In terms of white-collar productivity, "Westinghouse is probably the best in the world," says Iwao Koshimae, deputy director of the Kansai Productivity Center, a nonprofit think tank in Osaka. Japanese companies are studying Westinghouse's methods for use at home.

The centerpiece of Westinghouse's office system is E-mail, which was begun in 1980. Some 6,000 PCs connect 10,700 of the company's managers and employees as well as 1,000 customers. The system links operations around the U.S. with offices in 37 foreign countries. Lego may spend 15 hours of his 80-hour workweek using E-mail from his home and office. "It makes it possible both at home and at work for me to have continuous access to important information," he says.

It also makes life easier. A decade ago, if Lego wanted to contact a manager in Tokyo, he'd dictate a letter to his secretary, who would take it to the telex center, where it would be retyped. It often took eight hours for the message to arrive in Tokyo. Or he might call at 5 p.m., forcing a Tokyo manager out of bed at 6 a.m. Tokyo time. Now, Lego can send a message before heading home and have an answer in his computer the next morning. Because E-mail costs 90% less than overseas calls and letters and 75% less than telex, the savings add up quickly.

Lately, Lego even has become a portable executive. At a recent meeting in Hawaii with licensing partners Mitsubishi Electric Corp. and Mitsubishi Heavy Industries Ltd., Lego and Marous brought laptop computers. "Both of us stayed in constant contact with Pittsburgh and the rest of the world," says Lego.

The new technology isn't entirely wonder and light. Executive Vice-President William A. Coates concedes that the reams of electronic memos can mean too many weekend hours spent in front of the PC. Still, there's no going back. "People are amazed at how quickly we can move information around," says Coates. "It gives us a competitive edge."

Source: Gregory L. Miles, *Businessweek*, Oct. 10, 1988, p. 110.

they become information. **Information** is useful facts on which one can immediately base a decision. **Data processing,** or **information processing,** is collecting data, transforming it into information, and disseminating that information.

To illustrate the difference between data and information, consider the case of Value Stores, Inc., a grocery chain. In each of its 300 stores, a computer connected to the cash registers at the checkout stands keeps track of each sale. The sale of a single can of peas is data, a fact. This fact by itself does not give the store manager enough information on which to base a decision. However, if the manager knows the total sales of peas for a week, he or she will find the information very useful. This week's sales can be compared with last week's, with last year's at this time, or with previously projected sales. This information can be used to answer such questions as: Should Value increase its inventory of peas? Drop their price? Advertise them more? Will the store run out of stock?

The store manager, by combining the sales of peas with those of corn, carrots, and so forth, can see how the whole canned goods section is faring. By combining all the store's sales and comparing them to expenses, he or she can tell whether or not the store is profitable.

Whether facts are data or information depends also on who possesses them. Knowing canned peas sales in the store helps the single store manager do the job, but to the Value Stores regional manager, who oversees 40 stores, canned peas sales in a single store for a week does not mean much. In order to make decisions, the regional manager would want to combine canned peas sales with all canned goods sales for all the other stores over a week or even a month. Weekly canned peas sales for a particular store, then, would represent information to the store manager but data to the regional manager.

The Data Processing Cycle

In turning data into information, almost all data processing efforts go through the same overall steps, commonly called the **data-processing cycle.** Data are gathered together and **input** (entered into) the system, where they are **processed** (combined, summarized, and so forth), and information is **output** (delivered by the system). If you write a report for a

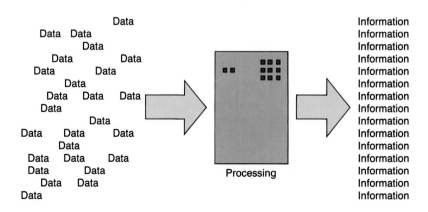

Data processing.

class (or a business), you follow the same cycle. You gather data (input), organize it in your mind and on paper (process), and write the final information report (output).

Value Stores inputs each sale (including canned peas) through the cash registers, processes those data at periodic intervals (collects all the sales of canned peas), and outputs information (total canned peas sales for the week). The cycle is continuously repeated as Value Stores carries on its business and evaluates its performance.

ESSENTIAL ELEMENTS

Data processing does not necessarily require the use of computing machinery. However, since we are mainly interested in computer data processing, let us look at four necessary elements required to turn data into information by using computers.

1. Hardware.
2. Software.
3. People.
4. Procedures.

The details of these various elements will be covered in later chapters, but let us examine them briefly now.

The Machine Elements

To have an effective computer information system, we must have a computer system, so the first two elements are **hardware,** the equipment, and **software,** the instructions that guide the equipment.

The Human Elements

No matter how modern and sophisticated the machines, they are useless without people. **People** run them and people derive the benefits from them. The objective of data processing is to provide information for various people in the organization. We call these people **users.** Users seldom work within the data processing department itself but are marketing managers, salespeople, accountants, production supervisors, or anyone else within the organization who needs information to do a job productively. The

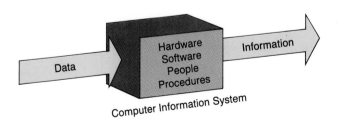

The elements of a computer information system.

```
4.5 Running Day's Sales Report.
    4.5.1    Load 15", 6-part, green-bar paper (#3171)
             on printer #2.
    4.5.2    Load DAYSSALES tape from data entry.
    4.5.3    Load CUSTOMERFILE from CUSTOMER tape (#127).
    4.5.4    Load PARTSFILE from inventory tape (#044).
    4.5.5    Load DAILYSALES program from accounting tape #4
             (#024).
    4.5.6    Run DAILYSALES program.
    4.5.7    Store updated PARTSFILE on inventory tape (#044).
    4.5.8    Distribute copies of report to distribution list
             #6 plus Mr. Greenfeld.
```

computer-information system exists for all of them. If it does not satisfy their needs, it is useless.

Systems analysts are the bridge between the users and the data-processing department. They react to changing user needs by designing and implementing computer information systems for them. They examine the user's information needs; specify the hardware, software, personnel, and procedures required to satisfy those needs; and get the system into operation. Systems analysts do not design hardware, instead they use existing hardware and integrate it into the systems they design.

Though analysts indicate what programs the system needs and what the programs should do, **programmers** actually write them. In some organizations, especially small ones, these jobs might be combined and performed by **programmer-analysts.**

Computer **operators** turn the computer on, load programs into it, supply paper for its printers, and do the many other tasks required to run it. **Data-entry operators** put raw data into the system, most often using some kind of keyboard.

Like any other department in the company, the data processing efforts are directed by **managers.**

People, like machines, need to know what to do, so we give them guidelines or **procedures** like those in the above figure. Unlike machines, however, people are much more flexible in their decision-making processes. Therefore, the procedures do not have to be quite as detailed or precise as a computer program, but they must exist.

Any data-processing effort requires these four elements: hardware, software, people, and procedures.

Procedures

This is part of a computer operator's procedures manual. This particular section outlines the steps the operator must go through to have the computer generate a certain report.

DATA FORMATS

The data in an information system exists for our, human, use. Therefore, it should be organized the way we logically think about it. We shall see that this is not always the easiest way to physically store the data on the computer. This allows us two choices. We can alter our way of thinking (probably making it more complicated) to make it easier for the computer to deal with, or we can alter the computer's way of "thinking" (write more complicated programs) to make the data going in and the information coming out easier for us to deal with.

How to store data.

This leads us to two terms we shall use continually in describing data storage and many other aspects of this human–computer partnership. **Logical** refers to the human view of things, the way they appear to us. **Physical** refers to the way things are actually done inside the computer system.

For example, in shifting from neutral to drive in your car, logically you move the lever from N to D. Can you imagine having to physically get into the transmission and move all those little gears and valves to their proper positions? Fortunately, the automotive engineers have accommodated the physical requirements of shifting to an easy logical action.

Our problem, then, is to accommodate the computer's physical storage of the data to our logical view.

Files

A **file** is a collection of related data. This book is stored in a file, as are the listings in a phone book. A company will keep a file of employees' names, addresses, social security numbers, and so forth. It probably also keeps a file of the details of each sale. Typically, the data we think of as a logical file is also stored in the computer as a physical file, although the organization of those data may not fit our logical patterns.

Repetitive Files

Most of what we store on computers is repetitive data about some aspect of our business. For example, supermarket managers regularly order certain products and keep track of those orders in their computers. For each can of peas ordered, they must know the name of the item (canned peas, 14 oz.); the market's stock number (G403-7); the vendor (Libby's); the quantity ordered (63 cases); and the price ($15.26 per case). Actually, they need to know more, but we'll limit ourselves for demonstration purposes.

They keep this information in a **repetitive file,** a collection of data with details concerning a set of related transactions or entities. In this case it is an order file. The file consists of a number of individual **records,** data describing a single transaction or entity. In our example, each record is the data for each item ordered. Records are composed of **fields,** descriptions of characteristics of the record. Our records are composed of five fields describing the product name, stock number, vendor, quantity, and price. Each field is, in turn, composed of characters.

A Typical File

This is typical information that might be found in an order file. Each record has the same number of fields in the same order, and the same number of characters per field.

Product	Number	Vendor	Qty	Price	
CANNED PEAS, 14 OZ	G403-7	LIBBY'S	63	15.26	
BROCCOLI, FANCY		GRABNER	12	9.46	
BALL POINT PENS	R022-4	INTL INK, INC	1250	.22	Records
POTATOES, 5 LB	V331-6	CENTRAL GROWE	350	.74	
CAPTAIN SMASH	C370-0	GENERAL MILLS	92	30.72	

Fields

Another good example of a file is a phone book. The records are the individual listings, and each listing is made up of fields—name, address, and phone number. Each field is made up of characters.

In repetitive files, then, characters are combined to form fields which are combined to form records which are combined to form files. The figure below is a printout of our order file.

Consistency in Data Units

Someone once said, "Consistency is the hobgoblin of small minds." The computer has no mind at all, so it thrives on consistency. Remember, the computer operates on its own physical data units and not on our logical ones. It does not understand the end of a field or record, it simply stores the data as a long string of characters. In order for our programs to process logical units, we must identify them in the data. One way to do this, often used in large computers, is to put some kind of a code at the end of each field (like the spaces between words in a sentence) and another at the end of each record (like the period at the end of a sentence).

Another way, commonly used in smaller computers, is to consistently use the same number of characters in fields and records. In our example, we made each record the same number of characters, 52. By counting characters (which the computer can do very easily) we know that the second record starts at the 53d character, the third at the 105th, and so forth. If we want to print out the fourth record, we can program the computer to count to the 157th character ($3 \times 52 + 1$) and print the next 52.

We use the same technique to separate fields. The product field in our example is always twenty characters long, the stock number six characters, the vendor thirteen, and so forth. This does not mean that we can buy products only from vendors with thirteen-character names. If the name is too short, like Libby's, it is lengthened, or **padded,** with blanks to thirteen. If it is too long, like Central Growers, Incorporated, it is shortened, or **truncated,** to thirteen.

Because fancy broccoli is a new product for the supermarket, the company ordered it before assigning it a stock number. If we had tried to put it in the file without a stock number (left the stock number empty), our character count would be off and the data from that point on would make no sense. Therefore, that field was not left empty; it was filled with six blanks to maintain consistency.

Maintaining consistency sounds like a lot of trouble and a potential source of errors for the data-entry people. However, most data entry is controlled by programs which commonly take care of inserting end-of-field and end-of-record codes, or padding and truncating data. For example, at the supermarket when a data-entry operator types in a vendor, like LIBBY'S,

How a File is Stored

A file is not usually stored in the computer in the same way it appears on a printed report but rather as a continuous stream of characters. It is up to the programs that put the data onto and get it from the file to keep the logical units—records and fields—straight.

```
CANNED PEAS, 14 OZ   G403-7LIBBY'S          63      15.26BROCCO
LI, FANCY            GRABNER           12       9.46BALL POINT P
ENS       R022-4INTL INK, INC 1250        .22POTATOES, 5 LB
     V331-6CENTRAL GROWE     350          .74CAPTAIN SMASH          C370
-OGENERAL MILLS  92    30.72
```

If each record is the same number of characters, the computer can find a particular record by simply counting.

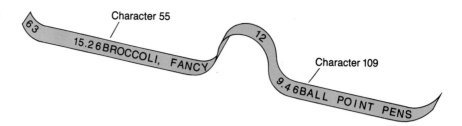

Character 55

Character 109

the program directs the computer to count the characters, seven in this case, subtract that from thirteen, and add six blanks. In this way, the computer is programmed to help maintain consistency.

Stream Files

Many files, such as the one containing this book, are not sets of repetitive data. They may be organized by human standards, but the organization is by thought and human logic rather than some mathematically predictable repeating sets of characters. Such a file is called a **stream file** or **text file.** Although these files are stored in the computer in many different ways, the typical method is simply by order of entry.

COMPUTERS IN THE BACK ROOMS

Different organizations use information differently but it would be valuable to take one company, Value Stores, Inc., and see where it uses computers to provide its information. We will look at only some representative samples of Value Stores' uses of hardware and software, because to look at all of them would require an entire library, not just this book.

Value Stores started as a corner grocery store in Oakland, Indiana, in 1922. Through expansion and acquisition of other companies, it has grown to a large retailing conglomerate with sales of about $7.2 billion per year. Its largest unit is still the retail food operation, with about 400 stores, but it has also branched into other areas such as the Olde England Pizza restaurant chain, MASco Auto Stores, DANCO discount department stores, and a number of chains of specialty stores. A company that large and diverse needs a staggering amount of information. Supplying most of it by computer is a necessity.

Each of Value's units operates essentially as a separate company, with its own information needs and computer systems to handle those needs. All units report to the Value Stores corporate headquarters in San Francisco, which assembles the data to provide total company information to corporate management. The corporate computers provide their users with a host of information, including accounting figures that are much the same as Brinkman's but on a larger scale.

One of the main functions of the corporate entity is financial— generating funds for expansion, acquisition, and ongoing operations, as well as investing excess funds that become available from time to time. Value's computers at the corporate headquarters provide information and

In many business networks data can be downloaded from a central mainframe computer to a PC.

projections on where funds will be needed in both the short and long range, and how much will be available from internal operations or will be required from outside to meet those needs. In making those projections, various factors, such as interest rates, profit expectations, and stock market conditions, are figured in. The computer allows Value's financial analysts to adjust those and other factors for simulations and "what-if" games (what if the stock market goes down, what if the prime interest rate goes above ten percent, and so forth).

Other financial information is hardly so exotic but equally valuable. The computer keeps track of all the stock and bond holders, writes and mails out dividend and interest checks, and monitors all of Value's investments. This last task sounds relatively simple but it isn't, because Value, like most large companies, moves millions of dollars in and out of various banks, financial institutions, and securities each day. Keeping track of all this activity without Value's computers would be extremely costly, if not impossible.

Other computer information provided at Value's corporate office is much the same as that required by most businesses—sales, expense, and profit figures; payroll data; government reports; and so forth. All this information is provided by each of the operating units and consolidated for the company as a whole.

The retail food unit uses typical accounting data but it also has its own unique set of information needs. One of these stems from the buying and distributing of food and sundry items. The unit is organized into twelve regions, each of which has about 30 to 35 stores. The buying is done on three levels. Much of the packaged and canned food is purchased by the national organization which directs shipment to the various regional warehouses. Most of the meats are ordered by the regions with shipment

specified to the various stores, and the stores themselves order their own produce.

Small computers at each store provide information on what items are needed by that store, generate orders for those items, and keep track of the status of those orders at all times. These orders are either handled by the staff at the store or are transmitted to the computers at the regional warehouses. The regional computers generate shipping bills and purchase orders, in addition to communicating order information to the headquarters computer.

In addition to the normal, ongoing information needs, there are always unique, short-term problems. For example, special sales require an inventory build-up closely coordinated with advertising, the time period of the sale, and the expected response to the sale. The computer is programmed so that even with all these variables it is very unlikely that any store would run out of Crispy Critters cereal.

Finally, there is the storage and delivery problem. Most items are stored in the regional warehouses. The local store's computer must transmit order information to the regional warehouse's computer. That system must provide information on which store needs what, and route deliveries of the right stuff to the right store. If a particular regional warehouse is out of an item, the regional computer must know at what other warehouse it is available.

Keeping all this straight without a computer, or in this case a network of computers, would be a nightmare. It is the individual store that needs the items but, since most of the buying and distributing are carried on farther up the line, the amount of data that must be passed between the store, the regions, and headquarters is mind boggling.

COMPUTERS ON THE DESKTOP

All of these large computers provide mountains of information, much of it used for management decision making. The information is produced quickly and relatively cheaply, but it is not terribly flexible. What you get is what you're given. Anything that varies from the standard reports is usually prohibitively expensive. Information-systems departments are set up for volume and not personalized service.

At Value Stores, if you want something different, and most executives do from time to time, you do it yourself—with the aid of a personal computer. Much of the data in the big computers is made available through

---

BOX 3-3

The Laptop Comes of Age

The fastest-growing segment of the PC business continues its climb.

The sun beams down, a soft breeze blows, the boat rocks gently as a waterskier glides by. On the deck, a sun worshipper drinks in the tanning rays while on the bridge under a Bimini top, this article is being written. Hold on! Can this be right?

It certainly is and it is just another example of the versatility of the laptop computer.

A laptop is a complete, light computer system with its own battery power supply. It contains a CPU, main memory, secondary storage (typically two floppies or a floppy and a hard disk), a keyboard, and a display (usually LCD). Most laptops weigh from 4 to 18 pounds and have all the power of a PC. Their biggest advantage is that they can go almost anywhere. And they do. You see them on airplanes, in waiting rooms, on commuter trains, and at the beaches.

The laptop industry is an outgrowth of the portable computers of the mid 1980s. These "luggables," as they were often called, had to be plugged in, often weighed 25 pounds, and looked like a sewing machine. Various advancements, such as more sophisticated ICs; small, low-power hard disk drives; high-resolution LCD screens; and better rechargeable batteries led to the transition from the portable to the laptop.

With their reduced size and increased capabilities, people are snapping up laptops like hotcakes. According to Dataquest, Inc., a marketing research firm, a little over 400,000 laptops were sold in 1987, about 700,000 in 1988, and an expected 1.1 million will be sold in 1989. Buyers parted with about $1 billion for them in 1988 and are expected to spend as much as $4 billion in 1992.

Oddly enough, the biggest sellers in this market were not the giants of the desktop

market. IBMs PC convertible was a flop, Compaq has only recently introduced its first entry, and Apple may have their competitor out by the time this book is published, but that is in doubt. The biggest sellers are Zenith Data Systems, with about 25 percent of the market in 1988, followed closely by Toshiba, and then Grid and NEC.

Laptops are not only a boon (or bane) to the workaholics who cannot have a nonproductive moment no matter where they are, but also to other, less obvious people. Consider the case of Orel Hershiser, star pitcher for the Los Angeles Dodgers and Most Valuable Player of the 1988 World Series. After each game he plays, he sits down with his laptop and enters in all of his pitches. Before his next game, he uses some specially designed database software to analyze the tendencies of the rival team, and plans his game accordingly.

data networking systems to personal computers on executives' and assistants' desks. These PCs are equipped with software and hardware that allows the user to ask questions of the big system and assemble information in almost whatever fashion the user wants. The software on both the large systems and the PCs allows for **downloading** data—transmitting blocks of data to the PCs—where the users can do what they want with it.

User Application Software

All of the PCs at Value Stores have at least three application software packages installed in them to allow the user to manipulate data. One is a **word processing** package, which allows the user to write letters, reports, memos, and such easily. It allows entering text, editing it, combining it with other text, changing its format or appearance, printing it out, and transmitting it to other PCs.

Another application package is a **spreadsheet,** which allows easy manipulation of numbers, especially those organized in rows and columns. With such a package, you can enter a few numbers into a few rows and columns, tell the computer how to figure the rest of the rows and columns, and let it complete the report for you. By using the spreadsheet, you can make changes in just a few numbers and the computer will figure out a completely new report incorporating your changes.

The third program that all of the PCs at Value Stores have is a **database** package. It allows the user to store (or download from the large system) lots of data and access them in almost any way the user wants. It also allows a user to organize the data into almost any desired report format. For example, you may have a database of customer information—such as name, address, purchasing volume, and such—on your PC. Using your database software, you could ask for an alphabetical mailing list of all customers in New York with purchasing volume over $200,000 per year.

A Spreadsheet

The income tax statement below is as it would be typed in by the user. On the left is the income statement completed by the spreadsheet program. To make next month's income statement, the user has only to change the numbers on the right and the spreadsheet software will figure out a new one.

INCOME STATEMENT		INCOME STATEMENT	
Sales	10,000[A]	Sales	10,000
Returns	1,000[B]	Returns	1,000
Net Sales	A+B[C]	Net Sales	9,000
Cost of Goods	5,000[D]	Cost of Goods	5,000
Gross Margin	C−D[E]	Gross Margin	4,000
Sales Expenses	1,000[E]	Sales Expenses	1,000
General Expenses	2,000[F]	General Expenses	2,000
Total Expenses	E+F[G]	Total Expenses	3,000
Net Income	E−G[H]	Net Income	1,000
Estimated Taxes	H*.2[I]	Estimated Taxes	200
Income after Tax	H−I[J]	Income after Tax	800

Business Focus BOX 3-4

The Transaction-Speed War

Who's got bragging rights?

Question: What cost $100,000, was over ten miles high and went 1300 miles per hour? Answer: Oracle Systems Corporation's bid to establish their bragging rights in transaction-processing speed.

Oracle hired a Concorde jet and invited a few dozen reporters and consultants aboard while the plane circled over the Atlantic at 55,000 feet. The guests in this brazen publicity stunt were supposed to relate the Concorde's 1300 mile per hour air speed to the speed and efficiency of Oracle's transaction-processing software. While this stunt may seem excessive, it is only the latest shot fired in an ongoing battle between both hardware and software companies to impress business computer buyers with the merits of their on-line transaction-processing (OLTP) systems.

IBM fired one of the first shots when it claimed to have the fastest system. Other companies, including Digital Equipment Corporation, cried foul. They said that not only did IBM perform the tests itself, but it also wrote the testing software and kept the coding a secret. After all, even a toothpaste company has its comparative tests performed by some independent firm.

But what is all the yelling about? Only one of the fastest-growing segments in information systems. Worldwide sales for on-line transaction-processing systems amounted to about $27 billion in 1987. By 1992, they are expected to top $51 billion—almost double in only five years. With stakes like that on the line, everyone is jumping into the fray.

Processing transactions is nothing new to the information systems industry. Computers have been doing that since their introduction to the business world. In the typical system of a few years ago, transactions such as sales, purchases, orders and so forth, were collected together, sent to the computer people and, through keyboards, put in a form that could be input into the computer in batches. This worked, but was not the ideal system because the data had to be handled twice—once when the transaction was made and again when it was put into the computer—and the computer did not have up-to-the-minute data. It might be a week or more until a batch of transactions was fed into the machine.

A more ideal solution was to have a transaction input into the computer as soon as it occurred. This required immediate, on-line access to the computer from all the locations where a transaction might occur. In an airline reservation system, for example, each ticket counter and travel agency must have access to the airline's computer. That computer would have to handle requests and transactions from thousands of different locations. Automatic teller machines, so common with banks these days, involve thousands of terminals which must access the same computer system.

New OLTP applications are arising all the time. J. C. Penney, for example, is test marketing a home shopper's service using cable television. Penney's will offer products ranging from luxury clothing to appliances and groceries to as many as 40,000 subscribers who can order using an ordinary touch-tone telephone.

With the decreasing costs and increasing capabilities of computers, these systems are not dreams any more but realities. The question is not "Who can do it?" but "Who can do it the fastest for the least amount of money?" Hence, the pitched battles between the suppliers of OLTP machines and software.

The combatants are not only a "Who's Who" of the computer industry—companies such as IBM, Unisys, Digital Equipment and Fujitsu—but also a "Who Might Be Who" of companies wanting to ride the OLTP bandwagon into wealth and prominence.

SUMMARY

The information industry is a huge and rapidly growing business, and we all contribute to its well-being by consuming information. Our government is the largest single consumer of information, and American business demands about as much information as all businesses in the rest of the world combined.

We, as businesses, need so much information now simply to be competitive with other businesses who also have similar information. The trick is to spend as much for information as is needed to make sound business decisions, but not so much that the cost of the information exceeds the value of the decision. The amount of information required to reach that point is constantly increasing. One of the principal reasons is that, because of computers, information is getting cheaper.

Data processing takes data, raw facts; collects and transforms them into information, immediately useful facts; and disseminates that information. Most of this activity follows the data processing cycle: input, process, and output.

While data processing does not necessarily demand the use of computers, modern information systems all use them. The computer, then, is a tool we use to make data processing more efficient and less expensive. It is only one part of a computer information system, however. A complete system includes the computer elements (hardware and software) and the human elements (people and procedures).

Data in an information system must be organized to make logical (human) sense. Often, this does not relate to the physical way it is stored in the computer. Logically, we organize data files in a simple data stream, usually in the order in which we input it; or in a repetitive file consisting of records made up of fields made up of characters. In a repetitive file, consistency is important. We either maintain it by marking the end of fields and records with special codes or keep the same number of characters in similar fields, and the same number and order of fields in each record. To find something, the computer does not have to understand the organization, just be able to recognize codes and count.

Businesses and other organizations use computers in many different ways. Large computers are centrally located and provide most of the information for the overall organization. Individuals or small groups in the organization often use personal computers, sometimes directly tied in to the main computers, to provide them with their own special information needs. Most of these personal computers are equipped with applications packages such as word processing, spreadsheet, and database management.

KEY WORDS

(in order of appearance in text)
Data
Information
Data processing
Information processing
Data-processing cycle
Input
Process
Output
Hardware
Software
People

User
Systems analyst
Programmer
Programmer-analyst
Operator
Data-entry operator
Manager
Procedures
Logical
Physical
File
Repetitive file

Record
Field
Pad
Truncate
Stream file
Text file
Download
Word processing
Spreadsheet
Database

REVIEW QUESTIONS

1. What organization is the largest single user of information in the world?
2. Does more information mean greater profit?
3. Why is information becoming less expensive?
4. Was there data processing before computers? Explain.
5. Explain the difference between data and information.
6. What is the main objective of a computer information system?
7. Outline the three steps in the data-processing cycle.
8. What are the four important elements in a computer data-processing system?
9. Compare and contrast the terms software and procedures.

10. Who are the most important people in any data-processing environment?

11. How does a system analyst's job differ from a programmer's?

12. Explain the difference between the terms "physical" and "logical."

13. What are the main elements of repetitive files?

14. Why is consistency important in repetitive files?

15. What are some of the things large computers are used for in an organization?

16. What are personal computers used for?

17. What are three typical applications packages used on personal computers?

THINK ABOUT IT

1. To what would you attribute the fantastic growth of the information industry?

2. A company with profits of $12 million per year spends $9 million per year on its information systems. Why don't they just eliminate that expense? Wouldn't their profits increase to $21 million per year?

3. Would our taxes increase or decrease if our government discontinued using computers?

4. If you were a president of a college, would the number of students in a single computer information-systems course be data or information? What would it be to the professor teaching the course? Why?

5. Why are people important in a data-processing system?

6. What might happen if a field in a record of a repetitive file were somehow left out?

CHALLENGES

1. Pick a local company and look at its data-processing efforts. What kinds of information do the people in the company use? Of this information, which is provided by computers and which is not? Can you identify manual tasks that might be done more efficiently using a computer? For one of the computerized tasks, what kinds of hardware does it use; in general terms, what does the software direct the hardware to do? What people are involved in the task and what written procedures do they follow? Identify operators, data entry people, users, and managers. Examine the data that go into the system and the information that comes out of it. How does the company use this information?

2. Set up a file to identify all the shirts or blouses you own. Set up fields to describe characteristics (size, brand, and so on) and decide how many characters should be in each field. Write or type the file on paper as the computer would store it (stretched out in a straight line without regard for field or record separations) and explain how you could find the beginning of any field in any record in your file.

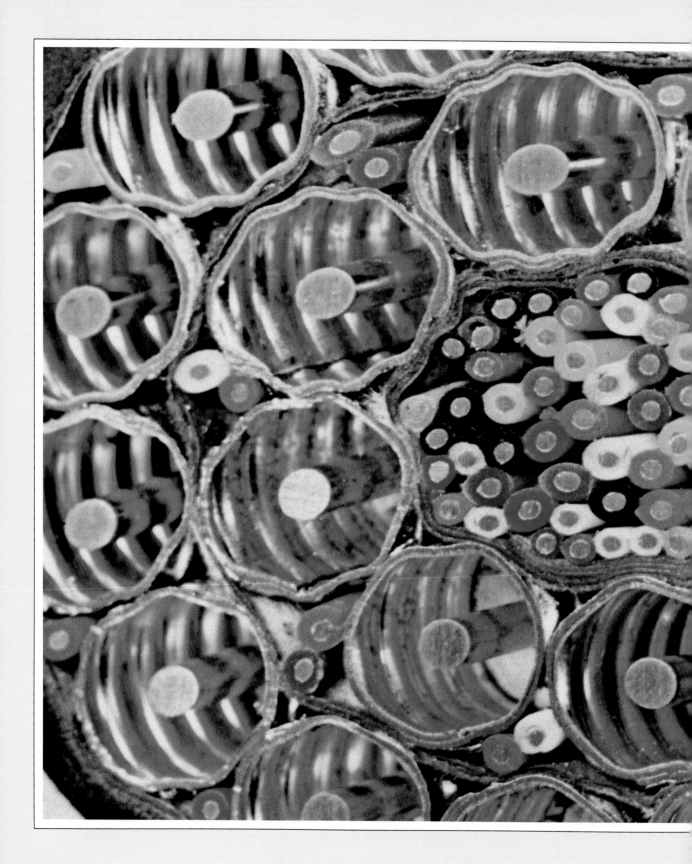

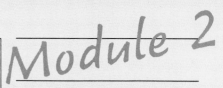

HARDWARE

The main processor, secondary storage, input, and output are all discussed in Module II. Specifically, in Chapter Four we look at such things as digital versus analog devices, binary numbers, encoding and decoding, data units, types of memory, and the central processing unit.

Chapter Five gives information on the physical principles of secondary storage and its various forms—sequential and direct access, magnetic and optical, and so forth.

Chapter Six addresses the human–computer interface and the different methods we use to put data into the computer, while Chapter Seven outlines the many ways that the computer can produce this information as output.

THE MAIN PROCESSOR

PREVIEW

At the center of the computer system is the main processor. In this chapter you will learn what it consists of and how it uses data. After reading this chapter you should know:

- How a digital device differs from an analog one and why we use digital devices.

- What the binary number system is and how it relates to our decimal system.

- How characters such as A, B, and C are represented in the computer.

- What the computer's principal physical units of data storage are.

- The types of data access used in computer systems.

- What the principal components of the main processor are and how they work together.

- The characteristics of main memory and some different types of main memory.

- The main components of the CPU and how the CPU follows instructions.

he **main processor** consists of the central processing unit (CPU) and main memory. All other devices in the computer system are referred to as **peripheral equipment** or simply peripherals. Because almost all computer information systems utilize digital computer technology, we will concentrate on that type of main processor; peripheral equipment will be covered in subsequent chapters.

THE DIGITAL COMPUTER

As we have seen, the principal component of a data-processing computer is a transistor. The transistor is used as a switch, performing about the same function as a light switch. In other words it can be in one of two states or conditions, either off or on. In order to operate with any degree of sophistication, a computer needs at least a million of these switches and most computers require many millions. All the data that we store and use in the computer are stored using switches. The processing of these data is a matter of detecting whether switches are off or on, and changing them from off to on and vice versa. In fact, our programs are really switch settings that tell the computer which other switches to switch.

switches
(1) on or off.

Digital versus Analog

Each of these switches can be in one of two easily recognizable states, off or on, which we show as the two digits, zero and one (0 and 1). They are totally separate, discrete states or digits representing specific, distinct values. There is nothing in between. No "half on," or "a little bit on," or "almost off." No 0.5 or 0.279 or 0.001. A **digital computer** works with data expressed in such discrete states, digits, or values. We can contrast that to an **analog computer** which works with data expressed in a continuous range of values. A light switch is a digital device, while a light dimmer is analog. The dimmer can make the light anything from off to bright.

example.

Another good example of the difference between digital and analog can be found in watches. A digital watch expresses time in discrete units. If the watch has digits for hours and minutes, it will always state some exact number of minutes, such as 4:53. An analog watch has hands that continuously sweep around a set of numbers and marks on its face. If it has hour and minute hands, you could read the time as almost exactly 4:53 (you can never really be sure if it is exact), a little past 4:53, or getting close to 4:54.

A Computer's Circuitry, Simplified

Operating a digital computer is a little like moving boxcars around a railroad yard. To perform a task, such as moving a boxcar from here to there, the correct switches must be thrown. In the railroad yard, it is the yard master in the tower who directs the changing of the switches. In the computer, the program performs this function.

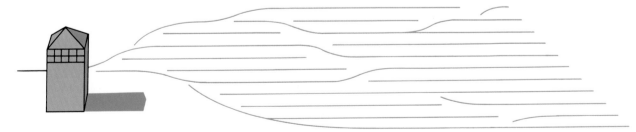

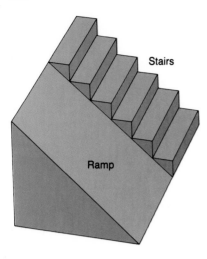

Stairs

Ramp

The Advantage of Digital Data

We store data in digital form principally because it can be reproduced more accurately. When we read data from a computer disk to main memory we must, and do, accomplish it with virtually no errors. We can copy the data back and forth time and time again without errors. Try copying the music from a phonograph record, which stores music in analog form, to a tape. It loses a little in the process. If you copy it from the tape to another tape, it loses a little more. With each copy some of the quality, or accuracy, is lost.

As we shall see, we can represent all of our data with series of ons and offs, discrete data units. In one data-communications scheme, for example, on is represented by transmitting a 12-volt signal and off by -12 volts. Actually, the receiver will interpret anything above 3 volts as on and below -3 volts as off, allowing a lot of leeway in voltages.

Let us use your paycheck as an example of the effects of digital versus analog reproduction. We can digitally represent your pay by a series of 12 and -12-volt signals. We could also represent your paycheck in analog fashion with a single signal using the voltage to represent the value, say 125.45 volts for $125.45.

Since your pay is determined in California but the check is actually written in New York, the amount of the check will have to be sent from California to New York. Over such a long distance, some voltage loss is bound to occur. The perhaps two-dozen 12-volt signals that combine to represent $125.45 all arrive at about 7 volts, well within the range to be interpreted correctly. The single 125.45-volt analog signal arrives at 73.62 volts. Would you rather have your check written by a digital or an analog system?

NUMBER SYSTEMS: OURS AND THE COMPUTER'S

Our decimal number system is based on ten number symbols, 0 through 9. (*Decem* means ten in Latin.) We have all grown up with numbers like 6 or 49 or 3017, which are combinations of our ten basic symbols. It would be hard for us to imagine those values expressed in any other way. Our ten-symbol system developed quite naturally because our earliest counting machinery had only ten different elements, the ten fingers on a human's hands.

Each of the values 0 through 9 can be expressed with one symbol. To express numbers greater than 9 in the decimal system, we use combinations of symbols and positional notation. A symbol's position determines its

Decimal Positional Notation

Positional notation determines a number's magnitude. Notice that in a decimal number system each higher position is ten times the position before it. One times ten is ten, ten times ten is one hundred, one hundred times ten is one thousand, and so forth.

The decimal number 468042:

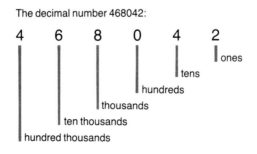

4 — hundred thousands
6 — ten thousands
8 — thousands
0 — hundreds
4 — tens
2 — ones

BOX 4-1

A Closer Look At the Superchip

The 80386 microprocessor has more going for it than just 32 bits. Its unique architecture marks machines made from it as mightier than most minicomputers while lightening the load on programmers.

The heart of any microprocessor is its registers, where actual computations take place. Previous PC microprocessors from the 8088 to 80286 have used 16-bit registers; eight registers of the 80386 are double that width, so they can work with twice the information in the same time.

In addition, these registers can function as pairs of 16-bit registers to copy perfectly the commands of earlier processors. Further, four of the 80386 registers can be manipulated 8 bits at a time, taking such compatibility down to the basest level.

Besides having a 32-bit data path, the 80386 has 32 bits of addressing so it can directly manipulate 2^{32} bytes of memory, a total of 4 gigabytes. In addition, it is designed to handle virtual memory—that is, it can swap bytes from RAM to disk to make programs think it has more RAM at its disposal than really exists—up to 64 terabytes, or 64 trillion (2^{46}) bytes.

The 80386 does not manage this virtual memory by itself. It must work together with a disk operating system, which, in turn, must be written to take advantage of this feature.

Incorporated into the design of the 80386 is a feature called pipelining, which allows different internal modules of the chip to operate concurrently to speed up its operations further. For instance, a special prefetch cache allows the microprocessor to hold 12 bytes of memory (such as the next three 32-bit instructions) in a special buffer that makes the code almost instantly available. This pipelining also allows the 80386 chip to address memory at the same time as it is executing an instruction.

Just as with the earlier 80286, which had two operating modes, real and protected, the 80386 has three modes. The first two are the same as those of the 80286, and the third is "virtual 86" mode in which the 80386 can act like one or more 8086 chips (or PCs based on them) that are independent and isolated from one another.

In addition, the 80386 has many internal features that

facilitate multitasking operations, including four levels of privilege, privileged instructions, a system of access rights, and the ability to segment tasks.

Unlike other Intel chips that break their address ranges into fixed segments, the 80386 allows dynamic segmenting unbound by the 64K-byte limit of the 8086 and 80286. Segments for the 80386 can be as large as 4 gigabytes or as small as a few bytes.

Most importantly, the instruction set of the 80386 is a superset of that of the 80286, so older code will run on the chip without a hitch. It also has its own powerful 32-bit instruction set.

All of these features are implemented with a special low-power, high-speed fabrication process called CHMOS, which helps the chip achieve its 12.5- or 16-MHz internal clock speed.

The net result of the combination of all of these features is that the 80386 does a whole lot more than its predecessor did, and it does it better and faster. So much so, in fact, that most PC users may not discover its true power for the next couple of years.

Source: Winn L. Rosch, PC Magazine, Sept. 29, 1987, p. 92.

magnitude. In decimal, the first (rightmost) position tells how many ones, the second (to the left) tells how many tens, and so forth. The value twenty-four is two tens and four ones—written 24. Similarly, 4680 means four thousands, six hundreds, eight tens, and no ones.

The Human's Versus the Computer's Counting Machinery
The computer's number system differs from the human's because of a fundamental difference in natural counting machinery. The human's has ten positions, while the computer's has only two.

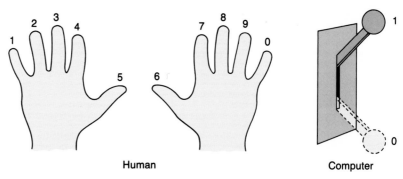

Human   Computer

Binary Numbers

As we have seen, the computer's basic counting machinery consists mainly of large sets or arrays of transistors on integrated circuits acting as switches. Since these switches have only two possible states, off and on, the computer is capable of working with only two possible symbols or digits, zero and one. This means that instead of using the decimal system, the computer must express numbers in a **binary** system—one with only two symbols, 0 and 1. Though humans express the value seven as 7, the computer must express it with a series of zeros and ones.

In decimal notation, the highest numeric value we can express with a single digit is nine (9). If we want to express the value ten, we have to start the current position over at zero (0), move to the next position, begin that with one (1), and write the value as 10. If we want to count beyond 99, we must start those two positions over and begin a third to give us 100.

In binary notation, the highest numeric value we can express with a single symbol is 1. To express values greater than 1, we also use positional notation, but we must use more number positions because we can express less numbers, only one of two, in each position. To express the value one, we would use the symbol 1, the same as in decimal, meaning one one. But since 1 is as high as we can go in binary notation, to express the decimal value two we would have to use the next binary position. Binary 10 (pronounced "one oh" or "one zero", never ten) means one decimal two and no ones, the equivalent of decimal 2.

Following this logic, we would express decimal three as binary 11, one two and one one. Decimal four would require yet another binary position, 100, meaning one four, no twos, and no ones. Decimal 9 would be 1001 (1 eight, no fours, no twos, 1 one) and decimal 87 would be binary 1010111. In the decimal system, each position is ten times the position

The binary number 1010111 (decimal 87):

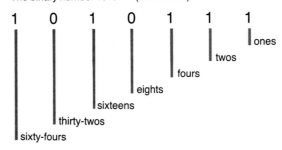

1   0   1   0   1   1   1

sixty-fours
thirty-twos
sixteens
eights
fours
twos
ones

Binary Positional Notation
Positional notation works the same in binary as it does in decimal, except that each succeeding position is two times the position before it rather than ten times as in decimal.

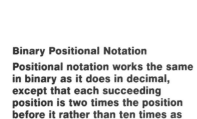

Computer expresses numbers in binary system — 0 or 1.

TABLE 4-1   Decimal-Binary Number Table

Decimal	Binary	Decimal	Binary
1	1	11	1011
2	10	12	1100
3	11	13	1101
4	100	14	1110
5	101	15	1111
6	110	16	10000
7	111	17	10001
8	1000	18	10010
9	1001	19	10011
10	1010	20	10100

Notice the extra digits it takes to express a number using only the two symbols available in the binary system.

before it because there are ten symbols to use in each position. There are only two symbols in the binary system; therefore, each position is only two times the position before.

To work with large numbers, computers use large combinations of zeros and ones. This takes a lot of transistor switching, but what the computer loses in numerical efficiency it more than makes up for in speed. A human can add 9 to 19 in perhaps half a second. The computer would have to add 1001 to 10011, but it can do it in about a millionth of a second.

Bits

Each symbol of a decimal number is a digit or, more properly, a decimal digit. The value 206 can be expressed with three decimal digits. We could store, or remember, that value by having three people, each representing a decimal digit, standing in a row with their hands extended. The first person would be holding up two fingers; the second, no fingers; and the third, six fingers.

Each symbol in a binary number is called a **bi**nary digi**t**, or **bit.** The number 11001110 (decimal 206) has eight bits (no ones, 1 two, 1 four, 1 eight, no sixteens, no thirty-twos, 1 sixty-four, and 1 one-hundred-twenty-eight). To store this value, the computer would use eight switches, the first two would be on; the second two off; the next three on; and the last one off.

CHARACTERS IN THE COMPUTER

A numeric value remains the same no matter which symbols we use to express it. A typical car has four wheels whether we call it 4 (decimal), 100 (binary), or IV (Roman). We saw that computers can handle numeric values easily with their two-symbol, binary system. However, we know that computers work with more than just numbers. We have seen bills, advertising letters, and grade reports with As, Bs, and Cs, on them. In fact, most computers can work with a set of at least 96 different printable characters.

> ## BOX 4-2
>
> ## *What's a K?*
>
> In computer ads and descriptions, we see the letter K tacked to the end of numbers all the time, such as 512K memory or 250K bits per second. In the decimal system, K stands for kilo, meaning 1,000—512K means 512,000. The number 1,000 is convenient for the decimal system because it is a one followed by three zeros, or 10^3.
>
> The same value in binary notation is 1111101000, not a very convenient number at all.
>
> The closest convenient binary number to decimal 1000 is 10000000000, 2^{10}, which is decimal 1,024. A computer K, then, is equivalent to decimal 1,024. A 512K memory would have a capacity of 524,288 characters, not 512,000.
>
> A decimal M, for mega, means 1,000,000, or 10^6. In other words, K times K. This last meaning holds true for computers also, except that a computer M is 1,024 times 1,024, or 1,048,576.

How can computers work with 96 different character symbols when they can only store and understand two? They use various **coding schemes** which combine bits in definite patterns to represent different characters. One such scheme is the **American Standard Code for Information Interchange (ASCII,** pronounced ask'-key), shown in Table 4-2. ASCII is a seven-bit code allowing 2^7 or 128 different combinations. It is used in almost all microcomputers and many minicomputers. An A in the ASCII coding scheme is 1000001, an N is 1001110.

The **Extended Binary Coded Decimal Interchange Code (EBCDIC,** pronounced eb'-see-dick) is an eight-bit coding scheme used on

---

TABLE 4-2   Some ASCII Codes

0	0110000	A	1000001	a	1100001
1	0110001	B	1000010	b	1100010
2	0110010	C	1000011	c	1100011
3	0110011	D	1000100	d	1100100
4	0110100	E	1000101	e	1100101
5	0110101	F	1000110	f	1100110
6	0110110	G	1000111	g	1100111
7	0110111	H	1001000	h	1101000
8	0111000	I	1001001	i	1101001
9	0111001	J	1001010	j	1101010
		K	1001011	k	1101011
Blank	0100000	L	1001100	l	1101100
.	0101110	M	1001101	m	1101101
,	0101100	N	1001110	n	1101110
;	0111011	O	1001111	o	1101111
?	0111111	P	1010000	p	1110000

The ASCII code is a seven-bit coding scheme used by most micro- and many minicomputers.

TABLE 4-3   Some EBCDIC Codes

0	11110000	A	11000001	a	10000001
1	11110001	B	11000010	b	10000010
2	11110010	C	11000011	c	10000011
3	11110011	D	11000100	d	10000100
4	11110100	E	11000101	e	10000101
5	11110101	F	11000110	f	10000110
6	11110110	G	11000111	g	10000111
7	11110111	H	11001000	h	10001000
8	11111000	I	11001001	i	10001001
9	11111001	J	11010001	j	10010001
		K	11010010	k	10010010
Blank	01000000	L	11010011	l	10010011
.	01001011	M	11010100	m	10010100
,	01101011	N	11010101	n	10010101
;	01011110	O	11010110	o	10010110
?	01101111	P	11010111	p	10010111

EBCDIC is an eight-bit code. Numeric characters are identified by the four zone bits, 1111, followed by four bits that represent the binary value of the decimal character.

many minicomputers and almost all mainframes. Eight bits allows 2^8 or 256 possible code combinations, about half of which are actually used. Most computers could use either coding scheme, the choice really depends on the scheme for which the software was written. Since both schemes represent essentially the same group of characters, other software is available to translate one code to the other so that ASCII computers can communicate with EBCDIC computers and vice versa.

The sets of bits that represent characters look to the computer just like binary numbers. For example, the characters A and N in ASCII are 1000001 and 1001110 which, if interpreted as binary numbers, would have the decimal values 65 and 78. If we could see inside the computer's memory, we would find only offs and ons and we could not tell whether they were supposed to represent numeric values or characters. If the computer were performing a mathematical operation, we would want the bits interpreted as numbers rather than as characters. If it were printing text, those bits should be interpreted as characters.

How does the computer know whether a given set of bits is a number or a character? It doesn't. Our program will tell the computer what to do with the bits and that will determine whether they are used as characters or numbers.

To use a human analogy, holding up a hand could mean "5," "Hi" or "Stop." It is up to us to tell the observer which interpretation to make.

Encoding and Decoding

When we put data into or take it out of a computer, we use familiar character symbols rather than a bunch of zeros and ones. We see and use these characters because the computer's input and output devices are built to automatically translate familiar characters into the proper bits, and vice versa.

We call the translation processes **encoding** (changing from characters to bits) and **decoding** (changing from bits to characters). They are

Character Encoding and Decoding

A character typed on a computer keyboard is encoded into a specific pattern of 0s and 1s and sent to the CPU. The CPU's output is, of course, a pattern of 0s and 1s that must be decoded into a readable character by the output device.

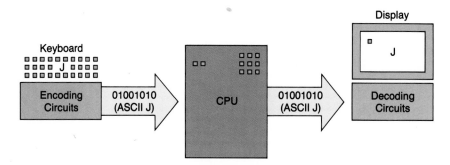

similar to translating between one language and another, say Japanese and English. Our set of characters, our alphabet, is much smaller than the Japanese set, so we must employ a number of English characters to represent one Japanese character. For example, " 馬 " in Japanese translates to "horse" in English. Similarly, "H" in English characters translates to 1001000 in ASCII.

The encoding process begins when we first communicate with the computer, usually through a keyboard. For example, when we want to send the name JONES to the computer, we start by typing a J on a keyboard. The instant the circuits behind the keyboard determine that the J key has been struck, they translate the J into the code 1001010 (J in ASCII) and then pass it to the computer. In all its internal operations, the computer will use the bits 1001010, not J. The computer does not know JONES from Adam, it only knows 1001010 1001111 1001110 1000101 1010011 (JONES, encoded).

After some processing we may want the computer to print out another name, 1010011 1001101 1001001 1010100 1001000, for example. The CPU will send these bits to the printer whose decoding circuits will print out SMITH.

Coding Schemes in Use at Value Stores

To illustrate the use of coding schemes, let's see what Value Stores does. The computers throughout the chain use various coding systems. As we said before, each store has a number of cash registers connected to its own

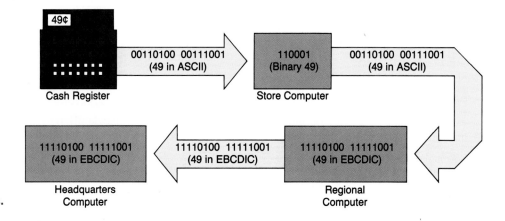

Coding in Value Stores' Computer System

Like many large systems, Value Stores uses a variety of computers, each with its own coding requirements.

minicomputer. The cash registers send their data in ASCII to each store's HP 840 computer where the numeric data are converted to binary and stored, while the character data remain in ASCII. Since communications between each store and the company's regional computers are all in ASCII rather than in a combination of ASCII and binary, the numeric data must be converted back to ASCII prior to transmission.

The regional computers are IBM 9370 mainframes which use EBCDIC as their internal character code. When the ASCII characters come in, they are immediately converted to EBCDIC and stored. Numeric values can remain in EBCDIC. The big Amdahl 5890 mainframe at the corporate headquarters also uses EBCDIC, so communications between the regional IBM 9730s and the Amdahl 5890 is carried on in EBCDIC.

HOW DATA ARE STORED

We know that the smallest unit of computer storage is the bit, the setting of one switch. However, bits never sit alone in the computer, but are grouped into larger units.

Bits → grouped into larger units.

Bytes

Having the computer process data one bit at a time would be like putting sugar in your coffee one grain at a time; it is easier to use lumps. The computer processes bits in lumps called bytes, which saves computer instructions and time. Think about directing someone to put sugar in your coffee. It is much easier and faster to say, "Put in one lump," than "Put in one grain, another grain, another grain, another grain . . . ."

The **byte** is the smallest unit of computer operation. If you instruct the computer to move data from here to there, it will move at least one byte at a time. If you instruct it to add, it will add at least one byte to another. The actual addition will be done a bit at a time, but the single instruction will direct the computer to add all the bits in each byte involved, with the final sum also expressed as a byte.

A character in either ASCII or EBCDIC will fit within eight bits. (EBCDIC is an eight-bit code. ASCII is seven bits, but by adding an extra, meaningless bit, it will fill an eight-bit space.) Since it makes sense to process data a character at a time, practically all computers use eight-bit bytes. We have already said that main memory is individually addressable; the computer can access any character, so each memory location must be one byte—eight bits. These characters are processed in small holding circuits called **registers** in the CPU; therefore, the registers also must hold at least one byte.

If our computer uses binary notation for numeric values, these binary values will be forced to fit within even bytes. It would take only one bit to express the binary value zero (0), but to store it in the computer we must use an entire one-byte memory location (00000000). Decimal 23 would be stored as 00010111. Numbers with values above 255 (eight bits, 11111111) require two or more bytes of storage and might take two or more sets of instructions to process.

BOX 4-3

Computer Word Sizes

Computer	Bits per Word
Apple II	8
Kaypro 4	8
IBM PC/XT	16 (processing), 8 (data transfer)
IBM PS/2	32
MacIntosh	32 (processing), 16 (data transfer)
Amiga	32 (processing), 16 (data transfer)
Cray	64

Words

Even a small computer processes eight bits simultaneously to save time and instructions. Larger machines process even more bits concurrently (16, 32, or 64, for example) for the same reasons. We call the number of bits a computer can process concurrently a **word.** Since each character occupies eight bits (one byte), words are often multiples of eight. Even though many word lengths are even bytes, they are always expressed in bits. We refer to a 32-bit rather than a 4-byte word.

Typically, microcomputers have 8- or 16-bit words (one or two bytes) with some getting into the 32-bit range; minis have 16- to 32-bit words with some higher; and mainframes 32 bits or more. Many mainframes allow a variable word length—meaning that, as part of the program, you can tell the machine the size of the word you want to process. The larger the word, the larger all the CPU registers and data paths between parts of the computer must be. Therefore, machines with larger word sizes are generally more expensive, but faster.

Physical versus Logical Data Units

In Chapter 3 we saw the logical data units typically used in computer information systems: the character, field, record, and file. Here you have been introduced to the first three of many physical data units used in computers: the bit, byte, and word.

Rarely will these physical and logical units match. A physical word, for example, is some given length, say 32 bits. If our logical words were limited to 32 bits, we would be forced to go through life speaking in only four-letter words. Similarly, there are no physical equivalents of the logical field or

A computer's memory is organized into fixed-length physical units like the 32-bit physical words shown above. Computers can easily story varying-length logical words in their physical words by simply overlapping them.

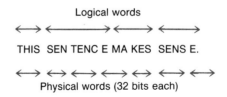

Logical words

THIS SEN TENC E MA KES SENS E.

Physical words (32 bits each)

logical record. There is only a single case where there is always a one-to-one correlation between the physical and logical: one character (logical) is always stored in one byte (physical).

Fortunately, the computer's fixed word length causes humans few problems because it determines only how much the computer processes with a single instruction. We can still store and process larger logical entities, like words and sentences, by storing them across many physical words and processing them a physical word at a time. The computer knows where its physical words end, and when the computer outputs logical entities, we know where those entities end by the spaces and periods.

ACCESS TO DATA

Remember that the computer is merely a series of switches representing data. When it operates, the computer detects the settings of some switches and changes the settings of others. It therefore has two types of access—detecting and changing. A **read** access is the detection of data. When a computer reads, it sees what is there but does not remove or destroy anything. Reading a book is a good analogy. When you read, you look at what is there; you don't change anything. The book can be reread any number of times.

Playing back an audio or video tape is another good example of reading. Again, the tape machine simply looks at what is there without destroying it.

A **write** access is the changing of data. When you write on paper, you cover up blank areas. When you write, or record, a tape, whatever was there is replaced by the new information.

Movement of data requires both operations. The computer reads from one place and writes to another. The end result is that some data have two copies (whatever was read and subsequently written), and other data are lost (whatever occupied the place in which the new data was written).

MAIN MEMORY

Main memory is working storage. It is here that we store the programs and data with which the computer is currently working. In Chapter 2 we mentioned the speed of main memory as a reason for this use. An even more important one is that main memory is individually accessible. The CPU can access, read from or write to, any location (one byte of space) in the memory. More specifically, main memory allows **random access,** which technically means that any individual location can be accessed in the same amount of time as any other.

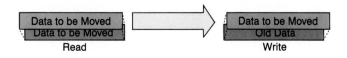

Read   Write

Movement of data requires both a read and a write.

Random-access memory is similar in concept to a pigeon-hole filing system.

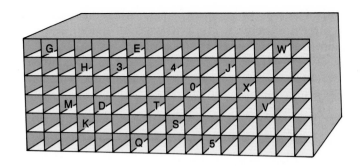

The pigeon-hole filing system, where the person using it can reach any box from one position, is probably the closest human analogy to random access. Searching for different items at the grocery store would not be random access, because the frozen peas might be right next to you while the hot dogs are at the other side of the store.

Although it is not really part of the definition, we assume that random access is also fast access. A typical memory circuit allows access of a word of data in perhaps 20 nanoseconds (20 billionths of a second). We shall see that access to data in other types of storage systems are often 10 to 1000 times slower.

Fast, random access is an advantage of using main memory for storage, but there are some disadvantages. Most main memory is **volatile,** meaning that when the power is turned off, the memory forgets. Main memory is also relatively expensive, perhaps 10 to 100 times as costly per character as some other storage devices.

Because of the capability of random access and, as a practical consideration, because of the speed, data stored in the computer must be

This main memory card can hold four megabytes of data.

in main memory before it can be used by the CPU. Because it is volatile and expensive, main memory is limited. Therefore, main memory is used as temporary, working storage for the computer. Only the program currently instructing the CPU and the data being used by the program reside in main memory. When that program finishes, it and the data will be moved elsewhere to make room for the next program and data.

RAM, ROM, PROM, EPROM, UVPROM

There are many kinds of main memory circuits. The usual is as described above, and referred to as **random-access memory,** or **RAM.** Many computers set aside a certain portion of their main memory for **read-only memory,** or **ROM.** Like RAM, ROM is random access but it allows only read access, not write access. Furthermore, the data (or program) is permanent. It does not disappear when the power is turned off. Whatever was built into the circuit can be read, but it can never be changed or erased.

Many home computers, like the Commodore 64 or Apple II, have the operating system and a programming language (typically BASIC) stored in ROM. The advantages of this technique are that the programs cannot be inadvertently erased, and when the computer is turned on it is ready to be *Advantages of Rom* used immediately. With other systems, you must load the operating system and a programming language from secondary storage as soon as you turn the computer on.

The game cartridge for a home video game contains ROM circuits that have the program for a particular game, Pac-Man or Frogger for example, permanently on them. When you change cartridges, you are actually changing part of the main memory.

PROM is **programmable read-only memory.** It is read-only memory that can be programmed, or written to. This may sound contradictory but it isn't. When installed in a normal computer, the PROM is read-only. In order to write to it, the PROM must be removed from the computer and inserted in a special programming machine.

EPROM, UVPROM, and any number of other acronyms ending in PROM refer to methods of erasing and writing to these specific types of programmable read-only memories. For example, EAPROM stands for electrically alterable PROM, meaning that it can be erased and written to electrically. UVPROM stands for ultraviolet PROM, meaning that it is erased by exposure to a strong ultraviolet light.

Nonvolatile Memories

One of the early main memories was a magnetic core memory which stored each bit by magnetizing a circle of iron in one direction or another. Since the storage was magnetic, the data remained even after the power was removed. It was **nonvolatile memory.** Core memories were large, expensive, and slow, and have been almost entirely replaced by modern, but volatile, semiconductor memories.

Some nonvolatile semiconductor RAMs exist, but they are expensive

and tend to be slow. The most common way to implement a nonvolatile RAM is to provide a small battery which takes over when the main power is turned off. Such circuits are used in small portable computers (often called **laptops**), which may not have secondary storage in them, or for the clock-calendar sections that exist in many PCs. Obviously, these parts must continue running even when the PC is shut off.

Cache Memories

Typically, the faster the memory, the more expensive it is. Most computers make their main memories out of relatively inexpensive, but slower memory circuits. Some larger machines, however, make a portion of their memories out of the super-fast, but expensive, memory circuits. This section is called a **cache memory** (pronounced cash). These computers have operating systems that determine which data are being used the most and that store those data in the cache section of the memory. Having the most-used data in the fast memory speeds up the overall processing.

MORE ON THE CPU

In Chapter 2 we established that the central processing unit (the CPU) directs the entire system. It has three principal functions: control, following the instructions given it by a program; arithmetic operations, performing calculations; and logical operations, making comparisons. Let us examine the CPU more closely to see how it performs these functions.

Registers

Inside the CPU are a number of registers or register sets, each capable of storing and/or working with a word of data. One of these, called the **instruction register,** holds the current instruction being executed (this is one of the possibly many thousand instructions that make up a program). Others, called **data registers,** hold data that are being worked on by current instructions. A CPU may have anywhere from two (for a small microcomputer) to two dozen (for a supercomputer) data registers. (Other registers also perform functions which we shall not discuss.) The CPU, then, is capable of holding one instruction and only a small amount of data at one time. All the rest of the instructions and data are stored in main memory or secondary storage.

The Machine Cycle

The set of operations that the CPU must go through to perform one instruction is called the **machine cycle** and it is controlled by an internal **clock.** Each tick or pulse of the clock (perhaps each ten millionth of a second) signals the CPU to perform the next operation in the machine cycle. The machine cycle for moving a word of data from main memory to a data register can be accomplished in five steps.

1. Fetch the next instruction (the one to move the data) from main memory to the instruction register.
2. Interpret the instruction. (The CPU discovers that the instruction is directing it to move data.)
3. Fetch the next part of the instruction, which is the address of the main memory location of the data to be moved.

BOX 4-4

New Coprocessors for a New Era

A coprocessor is aptly named. A cohort, companion, and coconspirator of the microprocessor, the coprocessor is designed to handle specialized duties with the utmost dispatch.

Unlike the microprocessor, which is designed to be a general-purpose device, the coprocessor is optimized for one particular task, such as crunching numbers or drawing pictures. This specialization earns the coprocessor a high speed rating. Once equipped with a coprocessor, a computer can complete its job much faster than it could with an ordinary microprocessor alone.

In general, coprocessors use their own microcode instructions (passed to them through the main processor), operate independently of the main processor, and only share raw data and results with the main processor.

Probably most famous is the numeric coprocessor, and the most popular of these in the Intel family are the 8087, 80287, and 80387. These chips are designed to carry out floating-point mathematical operations very quickly.

A numeric coprocessor best speeds up programs that rely on many mathematic calculations. Hardly coincidentally, these applications are generally those that make the best use of an 80386 computer—for instance, CAD, desktop publishing, high-resolution graphics, and scientific calculations.

The performance improvement won by adding a coprocessor to an 80386 system is so great and the cost so nominal (even at $795 for a coprocessor chip) that not adding a coprocessor is often foolish—provided, of course, that the software you plan on using is written to take advantage of a numeric coprocessor.

The 80386 microprocessor is compatible with both the 80287 and 80387 numeric coprocessor chips, and the new 80387 is generally compatible with the instructions used by 80287. Both coprocessors, for instance, have 80-bit registers to handle their mathematic operations. Either of the two chips can execute coprocessor code of most of today's DOS applications.

Although the two chips operate similarly, they are not directly compatible. An 80387 won't fit into an 80287 socket, and vice versa. When adding a coprocessor, you must use the chip that the computer was designed for.

Most early 80386-based PCs were designed for use with the 80287 coprocessor, primarily because that chip was available and the 80387 was not. In addition, 80287 chips, priced between $295 and $490, are cheaper than their 80387 rivals.

In the 80386 environment, however, the 80387 coprocessor is the best—and speediest—choice. The two chips were designed to work together, and the 80387 handles the same high speeds as the 80386, up to 16 MHz currently.

The 80287 comes in several speed ratings, from 5 to 12 MHz, with faster chips being more expensive. In any computer, the coprocessor you install must have a speed rating as high or higher than the clock frequency the computer circuitry uses for driving the coprocessor chip. Usually, this frequency is different from that clock frequency used by the main microprocessor.

Source: Winn L. Rosch, PC Magazine, Sept. 29, 1987, p. 93.

4. Request a word from that specific location in main memory.
5. Accept the word from main memory and put it into a specific data register.

This is quite a complicated set of operations just to move one word of data, but remember, our computer is performing them at the rate of perhaps 10 million a second. In the figure opposite we will look at what the computer has to go through to perform a simple addition operation.

Business Focus BOX 4-5

New Input Computers for TVSN

The Television Shoppers' Network (TVSN) is a relatively new unit of the DANCO division of Value Stores. TVSN is offered over many television cable systems as well as a few broadcast stations. The programming offers a steady parade of descriptions of bargain items offered for sale, and an 800 number to call to purchase the items. Buyers call in with the stock number of the item and their credit card numbers (or they can chose COD delivery) and a transaction is made.

The order-entry facility in Iowa started with 12 order-entry people (it now has 22 and is still growing) who wear a telephone headset and type orders into a personal computer. The PCs are all connected to a central computer which keeps track of inventory, generates shipping orders, and so forth. Each of the PCs runs order-entry software that confirms product availability with the central computer and sends the completed order there.

When TVSN went shopping for personal computers, it was faced with a dazzling array of choices. The options were immediately cut by about half, because the software TVSN had chosen ran on IBM-compatible machines. The problem now was to choose the type of processor, amount of memory, and a specific brand.

The TVSN computer people found that PC-compatibles (this includes the IBM PC and all the other machines that act just like it) were available in three distinct levels based on the type of CPU in them. The lowest (and first to be introduced) was based on the Intel 8088 processor, capable of processing 16-bit and transferring 8-bit words. The second was based on the 80286, with 16-bit processing and data transfer. The third was based on the 80386 with 32-bit processing and data transfer.

The levels varied principally in speed of operation, amount of memory addressed, and cost. The 80386 machines were almost five times as fast as the 8088s and the 80386s were about three times as fast as the 80286s. Both the 8088s and 80286s could easily address 640K of memory compared to the 80386s 4G bytes (4 giga or billion bytes). The 80386 computers cost about twice as much as 80286s, which cost about twice as much as 8088s.

At this point, the 80386 machines were heralded as the greatest thing since sliced bread—fast, massive memory capabilities, and a whole lot of other fancy features. The TVSN people were unimpressed. They opted for the plain vanilla, slow 8088s. Why? They examined the job that the computers would be required to do—principally handling keyboard input and sending data search requests to the main computer. Their software would easily run in 640K of memory and keyboard entry is slow. The only operation requiring speed was the data search and that was performed by the central computer with the results sent back to the PC. Why spend the extra money for capability they couldn't use?

TVSN's computers aren't fancy but they do the job.

Simple Addition Operation

The figures above represent a simplified version of what the main processor must do to perform a simple addition, 22 + 14. The three instructions are part of a larger program that, among other things, puts the data in main memory and will do something with the result of the addition. Everything—the numbers, memory addresses, and instructions—must be in binary notation for the computer to operate on them. The instructions are shown in characters for clarity.

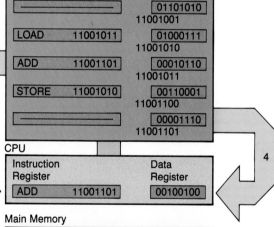

1. The control unit fetches the first instruction and memory location from main memory and writes them into the instruction register.
2. The instruction directs the CPU to read the number stored main memory location 11001011 (decimal 22) and write it to a data register in the CPU.

3. The CPU fetches the next instruction and memory address.
4. This instruction directs the CPU to read the number in location 11001101 (decimal 14), add it to the number in the data register, and write the result (decimal 36) into the data register.

5. The CPU fetches the next instruction and memory address.
6. This instruction directs the CPU to read the number in the data register and write it to memory location 11001010.

SUMMARY

The main processor of a computer system consists of the central processing unit and main memory. All other hardware is referred to as peripheral equipment.

Most data-processing computers are digital rather than analog because digital data is easier to reproduce accurately. Almost all digital computers are built of two-state (off or on) switches which requires them to represent all the data they store and process with series of bits, binary digits. The binary system of numbers is identical with the decimal system in all respects except the number of available number symbols. While the decimal system uses ten (0–9), only two (0 and 1) are available in the binary system.

Characters, too, must be represented by series of bits. A number of coding systems, the most popular of which are ASCII and EBCDIC, have been developed for characters. When a character is input (at a keyboard, for example) it is immediately encoded (translated to bits) by the input device and the binary code sent to the CPU. When the CPU sends something to an output device (a printer, perhaps), that device decodes the binary code and displays a character.

Bits are never processed individually. They are grouped together in bytes (eight bits) or larger groups called words. Processing a larger group of bits as a unit reduces the number of instructions needed and makes overall processing faster, but requires the individual components of the computer (such as registers and data paths) to be larger. The greater the word size, then, the more expensive the machine.

The heart of the computer system is the CPU. It contains one instruction register, which holds the single instruction being executed at the moment; and a number of data registers, which hold only the data being processed by current instructions. The CPU performs each of the instructions given it through a detailed process referred to as the machine cycle. In this cycle, the computer must perform many operations that we, as humans, would not be required to, nor would we even think of. However, the computer does each so rapidly that its overall speed far exceeds ours.

Main memory circuits are fast, random access devices that the CPU calls upon for program instructions and data to process. Most main memory is RAM, but some computers store programs in ROM so that they will be available as soon as the computer is turned on, and so that they cannot be erased. Most main memory is volatile, but a few types of nonvolatile main memory exist. Some computers have a section of extra-fast, but expensive, cache memory where the most-used data is stored.

KEY WORDS

(in order of appearance in text)
Main processor
Peripheral equipment
Digital computer
Analog computer
Binary
Bit
K
M
Coding scheme
American Standard Code for
  Information Interchange (ASCII)

Extended binary coded decimal
  interchange code (EBCDIC)
Encoding
Decoding
Byte
Register
Word
Read
Write
Random access
Volatile
Random-access memory (RAM)

Read-only memory (ROM)
Programmable read-only memory
  (PROM)
Nonvolatile memory
Laptop
Cache memory
Instruction register
Data register
Machine cycle
Clock

REVIEW QUESTIONS

1. What are the principal components of the main processor, and what do we call other hardware?

2. How does analog data differ from digital data? Why do we use digital?

3. Why do computers use the binary system?

4. Do decimal or binary numbers require more digits? Why?

5. What is the binary equivalent of the following decimal numbers?
   a. 4   b. 37   c. 63   d. 100

6. What is the decimal equivalent of the following binary numbers?
   a. 101   b. 1101   c. 101101   d. 10001101

7. What is a bit?

8. Explain the difference between a numeric value and a character.

9. Where in the computer system does encoding take place? Decoding?

10. How many bits are needed for a character in EBCDIC? ASCII?

11. Typically, how many bits are there in a byte?

12. Explain "word" in the physical (or computer) sense.

13. What is the smallest unit of data storage?

14. What is the smallest unit of data on which an instruction will act?

15. Explain the difference between a physical and a logical word.

16. List the characteristics of main memory.

17. Name some different kinds of main memory.

18. What kinds of registers are contained in the CPU?

19. What is the machine cycle?

THINK ABOUT IT

1. In binary, add 10011 to 1001. Subtract 1011 from 11001. Remember that except for the number of symbols, the binary and decimal systems work the same way. You must carry and borrow when adding or subtracting.

2. Why doesn't each computer manufacturer design its own coding system instead of using ASCII or EBCDIC?

3. In Table 000, ASCII codes are given for the characters A through P and a through p. Extend these charts to Z and z.

4. If your computer is a 32-bit machine, how many bits will be read from memory each time? How many bits long will each register be? Why?

CHALLENGES

1. If a computer is designed using tri-state switches (three different states instead of two), is there a number system that can accommodate it? Invent symbols and write a table translating decimal zero through twenty into your new system.

2. Investigate the computer system at your school or a local company. Find out what coding scheme(s) are used, the machine's word size, and its main memory capacity.

3. In both the ASCII and EBCDIC coding schemes a special relationship exists between each uppercase character and its lowercase counterpart (such as F and f). Discover what that is and see whether you can determine why it is important.

Computer
Hardware

1. An array of computers is evident in this view of NASA's Jet Propulsion Laboratory.

2. Computers have become indispensable in the making of sophisticated aerospace equipment.

3. A dancer's position is compared with that generated by the computer. The computer can record and play back a dance as needed to help the choreographer and the dancer improve their work.

4. Before a computerized simulation device was implanted in Carmen Scozzari's spine, she had little control of her muscles and was confined to a wheelchair.

5. After the operation, Scozzari could walk. The computerized radio transmitter at her waist controls muscle stimulation.

6. Honeywell's Manufacturing Automation System/Controller (MAS/C) for industrial use provides system administration, engineering, and plant-floor personnel with an interactive environment from which to develop and operate applications.

7. Special-purpose computers, such as the highly technical equipment used in this neonatal nursery, are designed for only one specific purpose.

2

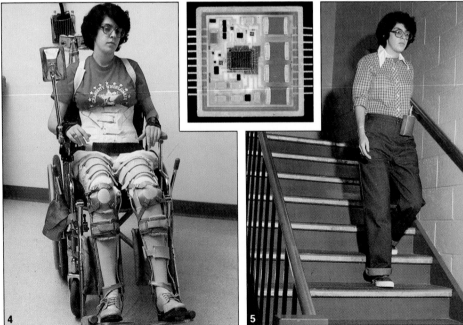

4

5

8. Documail generated by computers has become an alternative to more traditional forms of mail.

9. This Cray-2 supercomputer at NASA Ames does a quarter-billion computations per second and has an enormous 256 million-word internal memory — 16 times larger than those of previous supercomputers.

10. The Wang Freestyle personal computing system features an electronic pencil and tablet and a telephone-like handset for adding synchronized handwritten and spoken comments to information captured as an electronic piece of paper on the PC screen.

11. This 2500 MFlops/2500 Mips CM-2 provides access to 10 Gbytes of data.

12. Here we see the interior of the cab in a multiple-launch rocket system (MLRS), a high-tech battlefield rocket launcher used by field artillery personnel of the United States Army in Europe.

13. Hewlett Packard's quarter-inch cartridge autotape-changer subsystem can be integrated with a computer system into Hewlett Packard's Design Plus cabinet, as shown here.

8

9

10

11

5

SECONDARY STORAGE

PREVIEW
In this chapter we shall look more closely at secondary storage. After reading it you should understand:

■ Why a computer system needs secondary storage.

■ How magnetic storage media work and how data are accessed on them.

■ The difference between sequential- and direct-access storage.

■ The common media and devices for both sequential- and direct-access storage.

■ Common applications for both direct- and sequential-access devices.

■ What some of the new secondary-storage devices are and how they work.

■ How we make our use of storage both efficient and cost effective by using combinations of devices.

The scene opens on the glowing eyes and twisted smile of the evil Dr. Krinchov, the mad scientist who is about to push the button that will destroy the world. Behind him we see a number of machines with spinning reels and whirling disks. Because we are concerned that the fate of the world is hanging by the frayed threads of this man's brain, we probably do not focus on these machines as secondary-storage devices. But that is what they are. Since they are among the few pieces of computer hardware that actually move, they often find themselves in supporting roles in Hollywood films.

As we said in Chapter 2, the concept of a stored program (and stored data, too) is a principal characteristic that separates computers from other calculating machines. Computers cannot live on main memory alone, however. Main memory is temporary (when the power goes off everything in main memory is lost); and it is relatively expensive, many times the cost per byte as compared to secondary storage. Main memory is used only for programs that are currently executing on the computer and data being used by those programs. As soon as a program finishes, it is dumped from main memory so that another one can take its place.

Programs and data that are kept permanently (as most are) must be stored in secondary storage. Most computers have hundreds of times more secondary-storage capacity than main memory. In this chapter we shall look at the nature of secondary storage and how data are stored there.

PHYSICAL STORAGE PRINCIPLES
Magnetic Media

Almost all modern secondary storage is magnetic. Data are stored on some **medium** (such as a magnetic tape) consisting of a magnetic **coating,** which stores the data, on a **substrate,** some nonmagnetic underlying material like aluminum or plastic to give it strength. An ordinary audio-cassette tape is a good example of a magnetic medium and, in fact, is often used to store data. The dull side of the tape (facing out) is the coating.

When a magnetic medium is manufactured, it is totally blank, completely unmagnetized. When we record binary data on the medium, we magnetize regions of it in one direction (for a zero bit) or the opposite direction (for a one bit). Each individual region is extremely small and the regions are recorded extremely close together—perhaps as many as 25,000

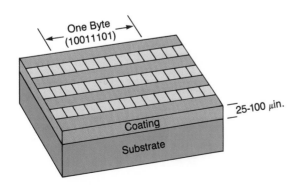

A top view of the magnetic medium depicting the magnetic regions.

of them per linear inch. A series of eight regions together forms a byte and sets of these, perhaps 80 to about 5000, form physical records.

Once we magnetize a given region, no power is required to hold the data there. We have created a permanent record of the data which will remain intact as long as we do not scratch, melt, distort, crack, or expose it to another magnetic field.

Reading and Writing

When you record an audio cassette, the recorder converts the sound to an electrical pattern and directs it to a recording **head.** As the tape moves past it, the head converts the electrical pattern to a magnetic pattern, which is stored in the magnetic coating of the tape. When you play back the tape, the same head (sometimes another one in audio equipment) senses that pattern, converts it to an electrical one, and back to sound.

Computer data go through the same processes when they are recorded (written) or played back (read). The machine that takes data from the computer and converts it to magnetic regions or vice versa is called a **drive.** The important functional parts of the drive are quite similar to those in an audio tape deck. They are:

1. A read/write head.
2. Electronic circuitry to convert data to electronic patterns for the head and vice versa.
3. A mechanism to move the magnetic medium past the head.

When you write data on a magnetic medium, any data that was there before will be replaced, just like rerecording an audio tape. When you read, the data on the medium will be detected, but not disturbed. Again like an audio tape, the data can be read any number of times.

Physical Records

As we learned earlier, main memory can access any single byte of data stored in its arrays of components. However, a secondary-storage drive cannot go to any byte of data stored on its magnetic medium. Remember, a secondary-storage drive works like a tape deck. Can you take one of your cassette tapes and play back just one note in a song? Hardly. You can, however, search around on the tape by fast forwarding and/or rewinding and listening every once in a while until you locate the general area of the

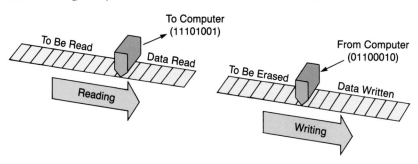

Reading and Writing Magnetic Media

A read/write head will either sense the magnetic regions and copy the data from the medium or erase the regions while recording new ones.

note. Then you can play the tape, listening for the desired note. Your mind can separate the one you want from the others around it.

A computer secondary-storage device works the same way. The drive must find the general area of the data on the medium, move it past the head, and transfer a whole section of data to main memory. The CPU, like your brain, can then separate the byte you want from the others. The term **physical record** refers to the data in the section transferred to main memory.

ACCESS TO STORED DATA

In a computer system, we can access data either sequentially or directly. **Sequential access** means starting at the beginning of the secondary-storage medium and reading each physical record, one after the other. You

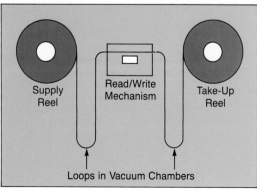

Supply Reel

Read/Write Mechanism

Take-Up Reel

Loops in Vacuum Chambers

Magnetic Tape Drive

In concept, a magnetic tape drive is similar to a reel-to-reel stereo tape deck.

read novels sequentially, starting at page one and reading page after page until the end.

Direct access means going immediately (or nearly so) to a particular physical record on the medium and reading only that record. You would access a dictionary directly. If you wanted to look up "migraine," you would not start with the *A*s and keep reading until you found it. Instead, you would open the dictionary somewhere in the middle and go as quickly as possible to "migraine."

We shall see how some storage devices are better suited for one type of access or the other, and that different applications work more efficiently with one or the other.

SEQUENTIAL STORAGE DEVICES

Magnetic tape is ideally suited for sequential access. Most tape drives work like audio or video tape recorders—tape runs from one reel across a head to another reel. The tape starts at the beginning and ends at the end, therefore the data (or music or video) is accessed sequentially.

Direct access on tape machines—either audio, video, or computer— is not so easy. If you wanted to hear just the ninth song on your audio tape, you would have to start at the beginning and move the tape past the first eight. Going from there back to the fourth song would be a real pain in the neck. With computer tape, if you wanted to access the 417th record, you would have to move the tape past the first 416 records. Some computer tape drives can fast forward and rewind, like audio tapes, but we shall see that jumping around from one physical record to another can be accomplished more easily with other secondary-storage devices.

Most audio tapes are one-eighth- or one-quarter-inch wide and allow four tracks, or lines of data (music in this case), to be recorded on them. Two tracks are used when the tape runs in one direction and the other two are used when the tape runs in the other direction. The head has two sections, or channels, so that it can play back both tracks simultaneously as the tape moves past. The output from these two channels is amplified separately and run through two speakers to create the stereo effect.

Computer magnetic tape comes in all sizes, shapes, and containers. Some are open reel, others are in cassettes. All types, however, are long, thin strips of flexible plastic covered with a magnetic coating which moves from one reel to another.

Stereo Cassette Tape

Stereo tapes have four lines or channels of data (music), two of which the head can read or play back in each direction.

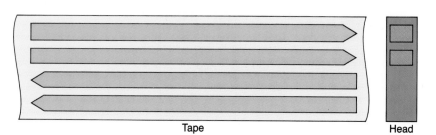

Tape

Head

Serial or Parallel Recording

There are many formats for data on tape. Some tape drives use **serial recording** of data, one bit after another. On such tapes the data appears like this:

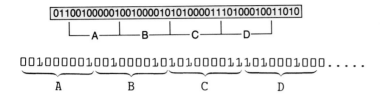

If the tape has more than one track (most do), then each track is recorded separately. It requires four complete passes of the tape (reeling the entire tape from one reel to the other) to record four tracks.

The most common computer tape is one-half-inch wide, runs in only one direction, and has nine tracks. Instead of serially recording data on one track at a time, the nine-track drives use **parallel recording,** accessing all nine tracks simultaneously with nine channels in the read/write head. The byte, instead of stretching lengthwise down each track on the tape, is written across the tape. ANSI (American National Standards Institute), an industrial association, has set standards for such tapes so that tapes and drives from one manufacturer will be compatible with those of other manufacturers.

Parity

Why nine bits per byte instead of eight? For accuracy. We learned earlier that computers are extremely accurate. This is no accident; it had to be designed into the system. You can imagine inaccuracies occurring when data is transferred from one part of the computer to another (such as from secondary storage to main memory), or perhaps between computers by long-distance telephone lines or satellites. With all those bits flying back and forth, it would seem easy to lose one. With today's highly efficient equipment, it isn't easy, but it is possible; so engineers have devised various error-checking schemes.

One of the most common is the **parity** check where the writing or transmitting device adds an extra bit, a **parity bit,** to a byte. Parity comes

HI THERE . . .

	Tape	
Bit 8	01010111	
Bit 7	00010000	
Bit 6	00000000	
Bit 5	11001111	
Bit 4	00000010	
Bit 3	00010000	
Bit 2	11111111	
Bit 1	11011111	
Parity	10111010	

Tape   Head

Nine-Track Computer Tape

ANSI-standard tapes have nine tracks or channels of data, all of which are read in one direction. Bytes of data are stored across the tape, and the read/write head with its nine channels accesses an entire byte at once. The characters HI THERE in EBCDIC code with even parity are recorded on the tape section above. Under the standard, the tracks are not in such neat order (1–8), but they are shown here that way for clarity.

in two flavors, even or odd. **Even parity** means that the number of one bits in the byte, including the parity bit, is an even number. **Odd parity** means that the number of one bits in the byte, including the parity bit, is an odd number. For example, to send or write the character *H* in EBCDIC (11001000—three 1 bits), an extra 1 bit (the parity bit) is added to achieve even parity (**1**11001000—four 1 bits). Since the character *I* (11001001) already has an even number of 1 bits, four, a zero parity bit is added (**0**11001001).

In the case of even parity, the machine on the reading or receiving end counts the number of 1 bits in each byte, including parity. If the result is not an even number, it recognizes that an error has been made.

The parity check is not infallible. If two bits were wrong instead of just one, they would cancel each other out and the error would go undetected. For example, if 011010010 were read as 0110**00**1**1**0, even parity would still exist. The chances of this happening are rather slim in a properly working system. If the system is not working properly, there will be lots of errors and many of them are bound to be detected. At that point, you should have the system fixed.

The parity check does not tell whether the error occurred on the transmitting or the receiving end, only that one exists. The software in the system determines what happens when a parity error is detected. Some systems are programmed to shut down, displaying a red light that says "parity error," while others will retransmit or reread sections that have had errors.

Physical Characteristics of Tapes and Tape Drives

Regardless of the type of computer system you use, you want to store as much as possible on a single tape. To do so requires high recording **density,** which refers to how tightly the drive can pack the data on the medium. Density depends on two things: the quality of the medium, and the ability of the drive to write and read small, close-together regions on the tape. We usually measure it in a linear fashion, bits per inch (**BPI**), rather than bits per some area like the square inch. As you might suspect, the more expensive tapes and drives are the higher-density ones.

Another important physical characteristic is **transfer rate,** the speed at which the drive can either read or write data. This is usually measured in bits per second (**BPS**). Again, the usual tradeoff is between price and transfer rate.

For an example of these characteristics, let us look at ANSI-standard nine-track tape. This usually comes on 10½-inch reels containing 2400 feet of tape and in standard densities of 800, 1600, and 6250 BPI. Since a byte of data is stored across the tape and densities are measured along the length of the tape, an inch of 6250 BPI tape holds nine tracks of 6250 bits each, or 6250 bytes per inch across the entire half inch of the tape.

A 2400-foot, 6250 BPI tape fully packed with data could hold 180,000,000 bytes (2400 × 12 × 6250), or about 100 copies of this book. We shall see, though, that we can realistically put only about 20 to 60 copies of this book on one tape. Not bad, though, for something that costs less than one book and can be erased and rerecorded.

The transfer rate depends on the tape's density and how fast the tape moves past the head, typically from 25 to 200 inches per second. The wide ranges in both densities and tape speeds give us a wide range in transfer rates, from about 100K BPS to 1.25M BPS.

Start/Stop Tapes

Computers are rarely programmed to access tapes all at once. Generally, the computer reads a physical record (called a **block**), stops the tape and processes the data, then reads another block, stops the tape and processes that data, and so on. While the tape is being read (or written) it must be going full speed. Anything else would give you erroneous data. (Try playing your stereo tape at half speed. It sounds terrible, doesn't it?)

While the data are being processed, the drive must stop the tape, and then start it again to read the next block, hence the name **start/stop tape.** The tape cannot be started and stopped instantly, so when the tape is recorded, the drive leaves some blank tape between each block, an **interblock gap (IBG),** which provides room to start and stop the tape. Depending on the amount of information in a block (usually between about 80 and 5000 bytes), the IBG may be longer than the block itself. In fact, a tape may have a block as small as a tenth of an inch and an IBG as large as seven tenths of an inch.

With start/stop tapes, the transfer rate alone does not tell us the full story of how fast the computer can access the data on a tape. The transfer rate is based on the tape moving full speed past the head. We must also consider the time it takes to start and stop the tape, typically one to five milliseconds (.001 to .005 seconds).

Assume your tape drive operates at a transfer rate of 200,000 BPS with a start/stop time of three milliseconds (3 ms). To read a 200-character block, it would take your drive 1 ms (200/200,000) plus the start/stop time of 3 ms or a total of 4 ms. This illustrates a problem we will frequently encounter with computers: electrical processes (such as reading data from a tape) are much faster than mechanical processes (such as starting and stopping the tape). A computer system with no moving parts could be incredibly fast.

Blocking Tapes

One way to allow faster access to data stored on tape is to put more than one complete logical record in each physical record or block. We call this **blocking** the tape. Using this scheme, you might take, say, four logical records, combine them together, and write them as one physical record on the tape. This way, you would have one fourth of the gaps (one gap for four logical records instead of one for each), using a greater portion of the tape for data and reducing the number of starts and stops.

**Blocks and Gaps
on Magnetic Tape**

Tape drives write to magnetic tapes in blocks with gaps in between to allow room for starting and stopping the tape. Often the gaps are larger than the blocks.

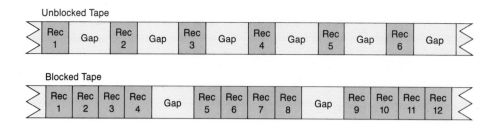

Unblocked Tape

| Rec 1 | Gap | Rec 2 | Gap | Rec 3 | Gap | Rec 4 | Gap | Rec 5 | Gap | Rec 6 | Gap |

Blocked Tape

| Rec 1 | Rec 2 | Rec 3 | Rec 4 | Gap | Rec 5 | Rec 6 | Rec 7 | Rec 8 | Gap | Rec 9 | Rec 10 | Rec 11 | Rec 12 |

Blocked Tape

More than one logical record may be combined in a single physical record to increase both the transfer speed and the amount of data on the tape.

Let us look at our earlier example (with a transfer rate of 200,000 BPS and start/stop time of 3 ms) in which it took 4 ms to read a 200 character record. If we blocked our logical records by a factor of four (four logical records to a block), all four could be read in 7 ms (3 ms for start/stop and 4 × 1 ms for transferring the data) versus 16 ms (4 × 4 ms) for unblocked data.

Increasing the physical record length by blocking the tape requires more memory space (remember it all has to be transferred to main memory to be used), and the program must be written such that it can handle many logical records instead of just one each time the tape is accessed.

Streaming Tape

Streaming tape is not meant to start and stop. It is meant to accept a continuous stream of data from the computer (or deliver one to the computer) without interruption. Since there is no need for starting and stopping, there is no need for gaps, except to signal the end of a block of data. Therefore, the gaps are extremely small, or in some cases nonexistent, allowing at least twice the amount of data to be stored on the same tape.

Streaming tapes with gaps can actually be started and stopped but, since the gap is so small, the tape will undoubtedly stop in the middle of the next data block. To start again, the tape will have to be rewound to well before the desired data block and restarted, resulting in delays of a second or more.

Streaming tape is most useful where there has to be almost no processing of the data, only high-speed transfer.

Changing Data on Magnetic Tape

Some tape drives will read and write data both forward and backward. Changing the data on these is relatively simple. The main processor reads a block, makes the appropriate changes to that block while it is in main

Making Changes in Tape Files

Making changes in tape files often requires two drives. The first drive reads a record, sends the data to the CPU to be checked or possibly changed, and the CPU then sends the data to the second drive, which writes the data on a new tape.

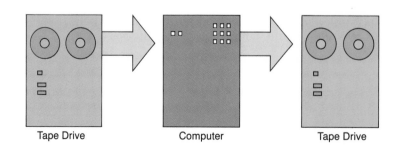

Tape Drive   Computer   Tape Drive

memory (directed by a program, of course), and then writes the block in the same place on the tape, erasing the old one.

Many tape drives will read and write in only one direction—forward. To go back to some previous point on the tape, you must rewind it to the beginning and start over. To make changes, then, you must use two tape drives (see Figure 000). Your program must direct the main processor to read a block from one drive to main memory and write it from there to the second drive. Any changes that you require are made while that block is in main memory. The process must continue to the end of the tape because the good data is now on the second tape. You can now take the first one, erase it, and use it for something else.

Tape Storage Applications

Magnetic tape is a sequential-access medium and should be used wherever sequential access to the data is at least as efficient as direct access. It is possible to use a direct-access device for sequential access by going directly to record one, then directly to record two, and continuing that way through the file. This is kind of like reading a novel by finding page one and reading it, closing the book, finding page two and reading it, closing the book, finding page three, and so forth; obviously not as efficient as turning from page one to page two to page three.

Value Stores uses sequential access and magnetic tape ("mag" tape for short) for a number of different purposes. The organization keeps currently used data **on line,** that is, electronically available to the CPU on direct-access secondary-storage hardware. Other data are kept **off line** on tapes on shelves in a storage room. If Value needs this off-line data, a computer operator will have to fetch the tapes and mount them on a tape drive.

why use sequential access?

For example, Value Stores, for certain of their operations, stores the payroll file containing pay rates, deductions, tax information, and such on tape. Once every two weeks when the checks are written, an operator mounts the tape on the system which writes checks for everyone sequentially (since everyone is being paid, there is no need to jump around in the file); then the operator removes the tape until the next time.

Value Stores, like any other business, considers its collection of data a valuable asset and takes good care of it. To protect the on-line data against loss, the company creates a **backup,** a copy of the data, and keeps it off line on mag tape. If anything should happen to the on-line data (such as a faulty circuit or an earthquake that wipes it out), when the problem is fixed, the operator can reload the data from the backup tape and be back in business.

Streaming tape is especially useful for backup since there is no need to process the data, only to transfer it. In fact, the eighth-inch cassette, which can hold up to 60 million characters, is becoming popular, especially in smaller computer systems.

DIRECT-ACCESS STORAGE DEVICES

Most direct-access storage is done on **magnetic disk,** which looks a bit like a phonograph record but plays more like magnetic tape. Like tape, the

**Magnetic Disk Versus
Phonograph Record**

A phonograph record has a single
groove or track of data. The
physical records, the songs, are
separated by wide-spaced grooves.
A magnetic disk has many tracks
and the physical records are
separated by gaps.

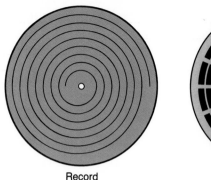
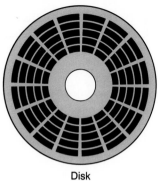

Record   Disk

disk has a magnetic coating over a substrate. The disk's coating is almost identical to the tape's, but the disk's substrate is usually aluminum or a heavier plastic. The shape and the method of data access are more similar to the phonograph record in that the disk is round and flat with data on both sides and it is "played" with a gadget similar to the arm on a record player.

A phonograph record's surface has a single groove or track beginning at the outside and spiraling toward the center. The record player spins the record at a fixed speed and the needle accesses, or plays, this groove. Normally, you position the needle at the beginning of the groove and it reads data (plays music) continuously until it reaches the end of the groove toward the center of the record. If you wanted to hear just one song on an album and had a steady enough hand, you could position the needle over the point of the record where that song began.

Disk Data Format

In contrast to a phonograph record, a disk surface has a magnetic coating, like a tape, instead of grooves. When the disk is manufactured, the magnetic coating is empty. When it is first put into use, the disk is **formatted,** meaning that a specific magnetic pattern consisting of blank spaces (that will eventually hold data) is recorded on it. The pattern is not a continuous line or track like the phonograph record's, but many separate, concentric tracks (sometimes more than 1,000). Each track is divided into a number of physical records, called **sectors,** separated by intersector gaps. Sectors contain from about 128 to over 5000 bytes depending on the disk, and typically they are of fixed length.

Like a phonograph, the disk drive spins a disk continuously (at 300 to 5000 revolutions per minute, depending on the disk drive). The phonograph's tone arm is replaced with an **access arm** and, instead of a needle, the disk drive accesses the disk with a read/write head similar in function to the one in a tape drive. The disk drive, under program control and with extremely accurate servos or motors, can position the head at any point across the surface of the disk.

The read/write head differs from a magnetic tape head in that the disk head needs only one channel because the data is serial; it is linear in one line or track. In order to read a byte of data (with parity) the head would have to pass nine magnetic regions.

A record player plays only one surface of the record at a time, while disk drives usually access both top and bottom surfaces. In fact, many disk drives are multiplatter systems with a separate head for each surface. Some drives have removable **disk packs** so that you can change the disks (and the data) on the drive.

Accessing the Disk

To find a physical record on a disk, the drive must know its track and sector. The drive can then position the head over the correct track and wait until the proper sector rotates beneath it. In a multisurface system, the drive must also know the surface that the physical record is on. Typically, these drives move all the heads simultaneously so that they are all in the same **cylinder** (the same track on each surface). To access a particular physical record, then, the drive must switch to the head above the proper surface and then find the right track and sector.

Hard Disks

We categorize magnetic disks according to their substrate material. The first disks were manufactured with a hard aluminum substrate and were consequently known as **hard** or **rigid** disks. These are now used as the principal secondary-storage media for mini and mainframe computers, and the more expensive microcomputers.

A typical hard disk might rotate at 3,600 revolutions per minute (which means that the data is cruising by the head at about 125 m.p.h.) and each track might hold 100,000 bits of data. At that speed, the head cannot actually contact the disk because the resulting friction would wipe out both the head and the disk. In order to read such tightly packed data, the heads must lie very close, about five millionths of an inch in some cases. Disks do not attempt to rigidly hold such tolerances. Their heads are mounted on flexible arms and shaped aerodynamically so that the spinning disk creates a cushion of air that keeps the head away from the disk. The head actually "flies" over the disk.

Disk Pack and Access Arms

A disk pack is made up of a number of hard disk platters all connected to the same spindle and rotating together. Access arms holding read/write heads move in and out of the disk pack together. Also shown is a close-up of an access arm, head, and single disk platter.

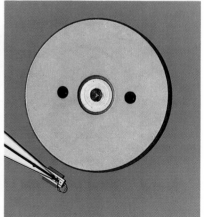

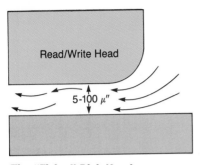

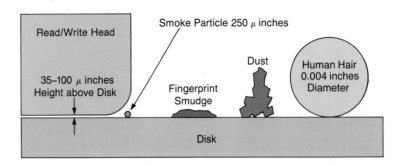

The "Flying" Disk Head

Hard disk heads are not held rigidly above the disk but are aerodynamically designed to "fly" on a cushion of air just 5 to 100 microinches thick. Debris that is microscopic to us becomes very significant to a disk drive.

The number-one enemy of disk-stored data is dirt. Even a fingerprint smudge looks like a mountain range at these tolerances. Therefore, organizations keep their disk drives in super-clean rooms and the disk packs themselves in sealed plastic cases whenever they are not mounted on a drive. One type of disk known as a **Winchester disk**, has practically all of the moving parts—the disk platters, the spindle on which they rotate, and the access-arm assemblies—sealed in a dust-free **disk module**. If the disk pack is removable, the entire module—access arms and all—is taken off.

Hard disks range in size from 3 1/2 to 14 inches in diameter, from single to 16-platter packs, and from about 2M bytes to hundreds of megabytes in capacity. The IBM 3380, for example has a 2.5 gigabyte (2.5 billion byte) capacity, while the TRS-80 model III/I hard disk has only 5M bytes.

Floppy Disks

Disks made using a plastic or Mylar substrate only a few thousandths of an inch thick are flexible, hence the name **flexible** or **floppy disks**. Floppies

A Disk Pack

A normal disk pack is stored in a protective plastic case but is exposed to the elements when it is loaded on or unloaded from a drive, as here.

BOX 5-1

Crash

Imagine a Boeing 747 flying at 500 m.p.h. only six inches off the ground and you have a pretty good idea what a disk head has to do. Normally, the head zooms along effortlessly, unless something gets in its way. When that happens, disaster!

The typical scenario goes like this: A head flying at 120 m.p.h. at an altitude of 20 microinches meets a gigantic dust particle about 75 microinches tall. The particle forces the head up and over it. No problem—yet. However, when the head comes back down, its momentum breaks through the cushion of air and it *crashes* onto the disk surface itself.

The result is a damaged head and a lot of magnetic coating, data included, scraped off the disk. When a head crashes, you have to shut down the drive, replace both the disk and the head, and then, if you can, replace the data.

Below we see a head crash as the head (left) rips the surface—and the data—from the disk (right).

are meant to be handled. They are sent through the mail, stored in filing cabinets, and constantly put into and taken out of drives. Therefore, they must be more tolerant of dirt and other destructive elements.

The disk itself is protected in a stiff paper jacket with a hole for the spindle and a slot through which the head can access the disk. The drive holds the jacket in one position and spins the disk inside the jacket. Because the disk is flexible, it would be impossible to maintain any constant head-to-disk distance, so the head actually rides on the disk. Floppies cannot be rotated as fast as hard disks because of the friction

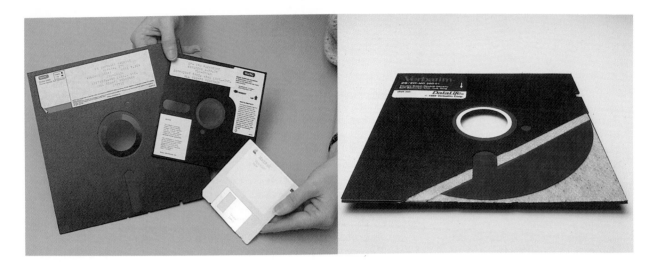

A Floppy Disk

Floppy disks are shown here, along with a cut-away of a floppy disk in its protective jacket. When the floppy is inserted in the drive, the disk rotates inside the stationary jacket and the head accesses the disk through the slot at the bottom.

between the head and the disk, and between the disk and the inside of the jacket. A typical floppy might rotate at 360 r.p.m.

Unlike hard disks, floppies are always mounted on a drive singly, never in a pack. Some have data recorded on only one side, but most are two-sided (where a two-headed drive reads both sides).

Floppies come in lots of sizes and capacities. The standard-sized floppy, which is eight inches in diameter, holds from about 250K bytes to 1.2M bytes. The most popular variety now is the minidiskette or minifloppy. It is 5 1/4 inches in diameter and holds from about 116K to 1.2M bytes. Many current systems are now using a 3 1/2 inch disk cartridge holding up to 2M bytes.

Access Time

 Direct access is fast but not instant. As with magnetic tape, a number of characteristics affect access time:

1. **Seek time:** The time it takes for the head to be positioned over the correct track. Average seek times vary from about 10 to 150 milliseconds for hard disks, and 50 to 200 milliseconds for floppies.
2. **Rotational delay:** The time it takes for the desired sector to rotate under the head after the drive positions the head over the right track. It ranges from about 5 to 15 milliseconds for hard disks, and about 80 to 100 milliseconds for floppies.
3. **Transfer rate:** The time it takes for the drive to actually read or write data. As with tape, the transfer rate depends on both the density of the data on the medium and the speed of the medium. For hard disks the transfer rate ranges from about 500K to 3M bytes per second, for floppies from 30K to 250K bytes per second.

OPTICAL STORAGE

Most of us have seen the video laser-disc players available for home televisions or the compact digital disc for stereo systems. These same technologies, and in some cases the same discs, are being applied to secondary storage for data. These **laser** or **optical discs** (in this case, disc is spelled with a *c* instead of a *k*) so far have a very small share of the total secondary-storage market, but use of them is growing rapidly.

Instead of a magnetic coating on the substrate, the most common type of optical disc uses a thin metallic polymer coating that is highly reflective. To write on the disc, a laser at relatively high power (at perhaps .02 watts, about 1/5,000 the power of an ordinary light bulb, this is hardly a death ray) makes small imperfections (either pits or bubbles) in the surface. A pit indicates a one bit, no pit is a zero. To read the disc, the laser power is turned down and light sensors detect its reflection off the disc's surface. Where there are pits, one bits, the reflection is scattered, otherwise it is strong.

The greatest advantage of optical disc is that the pits or bubbles may be made very small and close together, allowing a great deal more data on the same surface. Currently available, 12-inch optical discs can store as much as 3.6 gigabytes (3,600,000,000 characters, about 7,000 of these textbooks) compared with 500 megabytes on a comparable magnetic disk.

The greatest disadvantage is that the current strictly optical discs (we will look at another related technology in a moment) are nonerasable. No process will smooth over and polish up the pits so that they may be rerecorded.

CD-ROMs and WORMs

Current optical discs fall into two different categories—CD-ROM and WORM. **Compact disc read-only memory (CD-ROM)**, like video discs and compact audio discs, are manufactured with the data already on them. These are useful for reference materials—such as dictionaries and phone books—and are finding their way into the home- and personal-computer markets.

WORMs do not sound like anything you would like in your computer system, but they are catching on rapidly. These are **write-once, read-many** discs that allow you to write your own data and read it any number of times, but they still cannot be erased and rewritten. They are useful for archival storage—for example, the Library of Congress stores books and catalogs on them—and some organizations are using them in places where they once used magnetic disks. Because of their huge capacity, it is practical to make changes by canceling out old data and finding a clean place on the disc for the new data.

CDROMs are currently available for home and personal computers.

Erasable Optical Disks

Another technology, closely related to strictly optical storage, is finding its way into the marketplace because the disks are erasable. **Thermo-magneto-optical (TMO)** disks are written and read using a laser beam,

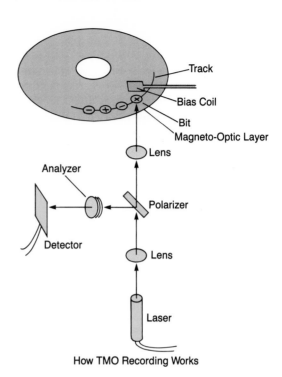

How TMO Recording Works

In thermo-magneto-optic technology, an optical head writes on the disk by focusing a laser beam on a magneto-optic recording layer while, opposite, a coil exerts a magnetic field. The absorbed light heats the layer's film at the point of focus, lowering the amount of magnetic force required to change its magnetic orientation. This permits the coil to magnetize that spot on the disk.

How TMO Recording Works

but the storage process is really magnetic rather than optical. TMO disks are made with a thin layer of transparent magnetic material on them. At normal room temperatures, it requires a large magnetic field to change its magnetic orientation. When the temperature is raised to about 150°C, however, a very slight magnetic field will change the material's magnetic orientation.

During the writing process the disk spins in a constant magnetic field. A relatively high-power laser beam is focused on the disk and turned on when a one bit is desired. This laser heats the material in a very small region to the required temperature and its magnetic orientation changes. To erase an area, the magnetic field is reversed, the laser is kept on, and that area becomes all zero bits.

When light is reflected off the magneto-optical material, the reflected light is polarized according to the material's magnetic orientation. To read the disk, then, the laser power is turned down, and the drive detects the polarization of the reflected light.

Magnetic versus Optical Disks

Are erasable optical disks the secondary storage of the future? Probably, but let us look at the current state of the art and compare the advantages of both.

Optical disks take the prize for storage density. Current models can store about 300 million bits per square inch versus only about 43 million for the magnetic variety. Optical disks are more reliable and less subject to damage. Since optical disks are read and written by laser beams, head-to-disk distances are not critical and tend to be in tenths of an inch rather than millionths. While high-capacity hard disks must be housed in heavy drives, optical disks can be handled more like floppies.

BOX 5-2

From Mozart to Megabytes

Compact discs now offer a symphony of knowledge too.

Millions of music lovers have become addicted to the crisp, clear sound of the compact disc, which is rapidly replacing the records and cassette tapes in their collections. Now the CD seems destined to win the affection of computer buffs too. Inserted into a special disc drive connected to a personal computer, a single CD can deliver to the screen as much information as can be stored on 1,500 floppy disks. That is music to the ears of software manufacturers. Says Microsoft Chairman Bill Gates, who has spearheaded U.S. research in CD technology for computers: "The key is that the CD enables individuals to use a lot of information fast."

Microsoft underscored that point last week at an international CD conference in Seattle, where it introduced a $295 compact disc called Bookshelf. The title is most appropriate. The disc contains digitized versions of ten popular reference volumes, including *Bartlett's Familiar Quotations,* Roget's *Thesaurus,* the *World Almanac* and the *U.S. Zip Code Directory.* Equipped with a copy of the Bookshelf, the special disc drive and a personal computer, a writer can have instant access to a wealth of reference material without interrupting word processing. With the push of a button, an individual can call up synonyms and quotations—which pop up in "windows" on the screen—and then, with another tap on the keyboard, insert them into the text.

The disc that stores music and data with equal ease is a technological marvel. Molded out of the same durable plastic used in bulletproof windows, the discs are engraved by laser beam, leaving microscopic "pits" and "lands" (flat areas) representing streams of binary digits. Each pit is no larger than a bacterium; some 2 billion fit on a 4.72-in. disc, laid down in a continuous spiral nearly three miles long. With this capacity, a single 4.72-in. disc can store up to 250,000 pages of text. And a CD surface area 6 ft. long and 6 ft. wide would be sufficient to store the words in every book ever written.

Book publishers were among the first to tap the CD's vast capacity. Two years ago, Grolier fit all 9 million words of its 20-volume *Academic American Encyclopedia* onto one-fifth of the surface of a single disc. Now some 130 different discs are available, including CD editions of such voluminous tomes as the *Oxford English Dictionary, Books in Print* and the *Reader's Guide to Periodical Literature.* The CD version of Census Bureau data enables anyone with a properly equipped personal computer to conduct demographic searches that once required a mainframe computer.

Despite their enormous potential, compact discs have some drawbacks. Unlike floppy disks, which can be erased and rerecorded at will, the compact discs now generally available are "read only" and cannot be altered outside the factory. Thus computer owners are unable to use the CDs to store their own data and programs or to alter those prerecorded on the disc. The same limitation affects software producers. Instead of updating it's *One Source* disc of Wall Street data electronically, for example, Lotus must mail subscribers a new CD every week.

Price too has inhibited the spread of the discs. Computer CD drives cost about $800, and software publishers are charging up to $50,000 for CD versions of especially valuable data. But strangely enough, audio CDs may be coming to the rescue. Says David Davies of Minnesota's 3M company, which produces about half of the world's compact discs for computers: "Without the CD music market, data CDs would not exist. The hardware would be too expensive." The intense competition to produce music CDs, he explains, will spill over to the CD data field, forcing down the costs of both discs and their computer drives. Donald McLagan, a Lotus vice president, agrees. "Every time Bruce Springsteen and Stevie Wonder sell a compact disc," he says, "it's good news for the data side."

Source: Philip Elmer-DeWitt, Time, Mar. 16, 1987, p. 71.

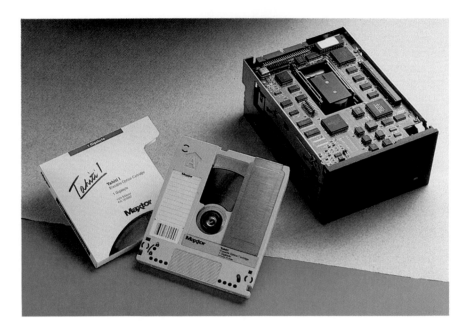

Magnetic disks are expensive. It costs about $1,200 for removable Winchester disk packs totaling 600 Mbytes. A 600 Mbyte optical disk in a cartridge now costs about $100 and the price is expected to drop to between $25 and $50.

Magnetic hard disks are faster, however. Transfer rates are roughly comparable, but access times are currently about a quarter to half that of optical disks. Both the transfer rates and access times of optical disks are improving at a greater rate than those of magnetic disks, so the near future will probably reverse this situation.

The least-expensive erasable optical drives are currently about three times as expensive as comparable magnetic ones. This, too, will change as optical prices come down.

Magnetic disks will certainly be here for years to come. Too many of them are in use to disappear overnight. As optical disks become faster, cheaper, and better accepted, though, we should see them replacing magnetic disks.

OTHER TYPES OF SECONDARY STORAGE

The earliest popular secondary-storage method was punching the data on cards ("IBM cards," see Chapter 6) and putting them on a shelf. To access the data, an operator would load the cards into a reader and transfer the data to main memory. Compared to any of today's methods, punched cards were extremely inefficient and a mess. Almost nobody uses punched cards as a storage medium any more.

Other Magnetic Storage

The **magnetic drum** works something like a magnetic disk except that the data is stored on the outside of a cylinder, called a drum, which the drive accesses with fixed (nonmovable) heads, one for each track (some drums have hundreds of tracks). The advantages are the same as for the fixed-head disk—eliminating the seek time.

Mass storage devices like the Masstor M860 work like a magnetic tape drive except that the tape is not on reels but in cartridges stored in honeycomblike cells. The drive itself, rather than an operator, pulls the cartridges out of the cells, mounts them, and replaces them after use. Total access time can be as long as 15 seconds, but that is still much faster than having an operator mount and unmount tapes. The capacity of this particular device can be as high as 440 billion characters, significantly more than most other secondary-storage devices.

Serial Access:
Bubbles and Charge-Coupled Devices

A magnetic bubble is a minute magnetic region in a thin crystal layer on a silicon chip. The film holds thousands or millions of possible bubble sites and the presence or absence of a bubble in a site represents a one or zero bit. This is similar to a region on a magnetic tape, except that the bubble is much smaller and can be moved across the film at high, electronic speeds.

A **bubble memory** accesses bubble sites using either a read or write station on the chip. In function, these stations are analogous to a read/write head on a magnetic tape, but instead of physically moving the medium (the tape) past the head, the bubble medium (the chip) remains stationary and the bubbles themselves are moved past the read and write stations. We call this technique serial access because the moving bubbles parade past the access stations one by one, in serial fashion, and the computer must wait until the correct set of bubbles comes by.

Bubble memories are slow by semiconductor main-memory standards

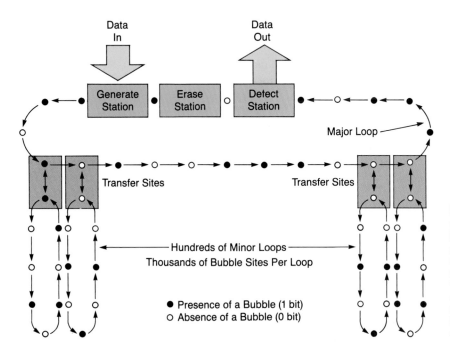

Bubble Memory

In a magnetic bubble memory, bubbles are stored in minor loops and transferred to a major loop when needed. There they pass by read and write areas for access. The bubbles move at high electronic speed but the computer still must wait for the proper bubbles to march past the access areas.

but are many times faster than other secondary-storage devices. In addition, their data density far exceeds that of other secondary-storage devices (some having in excess of 2.5 million bits per square inch). As required for secondary storage, they are nonvolatile (they don't forget when the power is turned off).

In the late seventies, many analysts thought that bubbles would take over the world, at least the world of secondary storage. So far that hasn't happened. Why? Bubble memories still are too expensive. Much of the anticipated lowering of manufacturing cost failed to materialize and the prices of the alternatives, principally disks, have declined rapidly. Still, bubble memories are used in situations with strict power consumption and space limitations, such as in portable terminals and military weapons systems.

Charge-coupled devices (CCDs) are similar to bubbles in that they circulate data past access areas and are made on semiconductor chips. CCDs are faster and may prove in the long run to be less expensive to manufacture. However, they are more a threat to semiconductor main memory than secondary storage because they are volatile; they forget when the power goes off.

RAM Disk

To us, accessing data from secondary storage in a matter of a thousandth of a second or so seems incredibly fast. To main memory, which works in fractions of millionths of seconds, it is incredibly slow. Many systems use

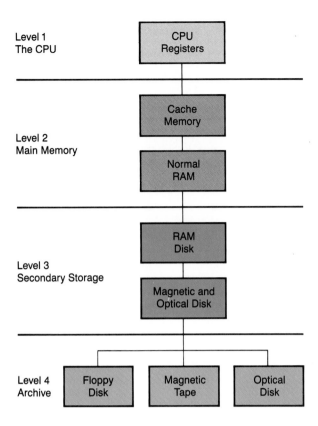

RAM disk, extra main-memory circuits that the operating system accesses as if it were a magnetic disk. The main advantage is fast access, typically 100 to 200 times as fast. The offsetting disadvantage is that RAM is volatile; it forgets when the power goes off. To use a RAM disk, then, the most frequently accessed data and/or programs are loaded on it from conventional magnetic disk when the computer is turned on, and any changed data is transferred back to magnetic disk before the power is shut off.

STORAGE HIERARCHY

Computers, like life, involve many trade-offs—you gain in one area only at the expense of some other. In computer storage, the principle trade-off is between speed and cost. The faster a storage device is, the more expensive it is. We try to establish a mix of storage devices to give us acceptable speed at an acceptable price by setting up a hierarchy of devices ranging from the slow but cheap to the fast but expensive.

All of the computer's work must be done in the registers in the CPU. This is the highest level of the storage hierarchy. We do not usually classify registers as storage devices, but they really are. Data, however, stay there only a few microseconds at the longest because a CPU has very few registers and they must constantly be cleared to make way for other data. To make a faster computer, we can base it around a larger, more expensive CPU with more registers.

BOX 5-3 PC Focus

What Kind of Secondary Storage?

"What kind of secondary storage should I buy for my personal computer?"

This question always comes up when anyone is considering a purchase or an upgrade of a PC. The answer is not so simple because of the wide variety of options available for PCs and the range of costs for these options. Almost anything available for mainframes is now available for PCs in a scaled-down version.

The main consideration is the use to which you will put your PC and how much data you will have to store. Another consideration is the status of your wallet. If almost all your use is playing computer games, a simple cassette tape drive and the ROM cartridges on which

many games are distributed should suffice. Cassette setups are available for computers such as the Commodore 64 for about $30 to $50.

For normal home use—writing checks, the greeting card list, occasional programming—the floppy-disk drives that come with most PCs or are available for a few hundred dollars extra should do. If the PC is for a very small business, be sure that the disks are in the higher-capacity range, 360K to 1.2M bytes, and that you have two drives. Otherwise, most of your time will be spent swapping disks, taking this one out and putting that one in.

For larger businesses or applications that require ready access to large amounts of data, a hard disk becomes

imperative. Many newer PCs are now sold with a hard disk built in, but for those that aren't, add-on disks with capacities from 5M to over 100M bytes are available for prices ranging from $500 to $5,000.

Part of your secondary-storage configuration should be a provision for backup. With a floppy-based system, backup can be copies of floppies. With a hard-disk-based system, backing up a 40M byte disk on 120, 360K-byte floppies could become tedious. A hard-disk user should seriously consider a cartridge streaming tape or a removable hard-disk cartridge for backup. These are available in capacities up to 60M bytes for about $300 to $3,000.

The second level is main memory where we store the data that go into the registers and those which come out. This level can be subdivided into expensive-but-fast cache memory and cheaper-but-slower normal memory. Larger main memories (especially cache) allow us to store more data at the CPU's fingertips, so to speak. If all the data for our current job does not fit into main memory (and it typically doesn't for big jobs), we will have to trade data back and forth between main memory and secondary storage, a relatively slow process.

The third level is secondary storage where we can store things permanently. RAM disk can be used in conjunction with secondary storage allowing super-high speed but requiring transfer to and from conventional secondary storage. Hard disk is on the fast end of secondary storage, with tape in the middle, and floppy disk at the slow end.

Most systems do not store all the data in on-line secondary storage; it is not worth it to buy drives for seldom-used data. These data are stored in the fourth level, the **archive** level, that is, on some removable medium packed away in a closet. Typical archive media are magnetic tape, floppy disk, or optical disk.

SUMMARY

Secondary storage is necessary for modern computer systems because it is permanent and cheaper than main memory. Most secondary storage utilizes a magnetic medium, consisting of a magnetic coating on a substrate, which a drive accesses by moving the medium past a read/write head. The CPU cannot access the data on the media a byte at a time, instead, an entire physical record must be transferred to main memory where the CPU can process it. Access to data in secondary storage is either sequential, beginning at the beginning of the data and accessing each record in turn, or direct, going immediately to a desired record.

Magnetic tape is the most common sequential access medium. The data may be stored on the tape in either serial or parallel fashion, whereas disks use serial storage almost exclusively. Most tapes, as well as most other storage and data-transfer schemes, use nine bits per byte, the extra being the parity bit.

Tapes are either start/stop or streaming. Start/stop tapes are meant to be accessed a physical record at a time and have large interblock gaps. ANSI-standard nine-track tape is the most common example. Streaming tapes have little or no gaps and are meant to be accessed continuously, such as for backup applications. The speed of access to data on tape depends on transfer rate and start/stop time. Naturally, access is faster for streaming tapes because they are not started and stopped, but access to individual records is difficult. Logical records may be blocked into physical records to save space on start/stop tape and to speed access.

Typical magnetic tape applications are off-line storage of data, backup, and storage of data that can be processed sequentially.

Magnetic disks are the most common direct-access storage medium. Disks are made either rigid or floppy, and hard disks often combine many platters into a disk pack. A disk drive directly accesses a disk pack by positioning the heads in the correct cylinder, switching to the head over the right surface, and waiting until the proper sector rotates by.

Disk access time depends on seek time, rotational delay, and transfer rate. Hard disks access data much faster than floppies.

Optical storage devices, which use lasers to read and write on special disk surfaces, are starting to be used. These disks have tremendous storage capacity and are tougher than hard magnetic disks. Most present optical disks are either CD-ROMs, which have the data imprinted on them at the factory; or WORMs, which can be written by the user, but only once. Erasable optical disks, using the thermo-magneto-optical technology, are now finding their way into the market place.

Other types of secondary-storage devices that enjoy some degree of popularity are bubble memory, which offers faster access but higher cost at present, and RAM disk, which uses main memory circuits to store frequently used data.

The various storage systems in a computer follow a hierarchy from relatively slow but inexpensive to fast but expensive storage. The processing must be done in the registers in the CPU, which are fast, but the data that are eventually used in the registers reside at one of the lower levels—main memory, secondary storage, or archive—and are passed up or down, depending on the immediacy of their processing and the capacity at the various levels.

KEY WORDS

(in order of appearance in text)

Medium	Block	Flexible disk
Coating	Start/stop tape	Floppy disk
Substrate	Interblock gap (IBG)	Seek time
Head	Blocking	Rotational delay
Drive	Streaming tape	Transfer rate
Physical record	On line	Laser disc
Sequential access	Off line	Optical disc
Direct access	Backup	Compact disc read-only memory
Serial recording	Magnetic disk	(CD-ROM)
Parallel recording	Formatted	Write-once, read-many (WORM)
Parity	Sector	Thermo-magneto-optical (TMO)
Parity bit	Access arm	Magnetic drum
Even parity	Disk pack	Mass-storage device
Odd parity	Cylinder	Bubble memory
Density	Hard disk	Charge-coupled device (CCD)
BPI	Rigid disk	RAM disk
Transfer rate	Winchester disk	Archive
BPS	Disk module	
	Crash	

REVIEW QUESTIONS

1. Why is secondary storage necessary?

2. Magnetic media are made of two layers. What are they called and what is the function of each?

3. Explain the difference between a physical and a logical record.

4. Explain the difference between sequential and direct access.

5. How is a computer tape and drive similar to a stereo tape and drive and how do they differ?

6. Why does a parallel computer tape have nine tracks?

7. What is parity?

8. Why are interblock gaps needed on magnetic tape? What kind of tapes do not have them (or have small ones)?

9. What factors determine access time in magnetic tape?

10. Explain blocking of tapes. What are the advantages?

11. How are changes made on magnetic tape?

12. What is meant by backup?

13. Describe the similarities and differences between a record player and a disk drive.

14. What terms are used to locate a physical record on a multiplatter disk drive?

15. How do hard and floppy disks differ?

16. What determines the access time for disks?

17. What is the principle advantage of optical over magnetic storage? A disadvantage?

18. How do CD-ROM and WORM differ?

19. What is an advantage of bubble memory over magnetic storage? A disadvantage?

20. How is RAM disk used in a computer system?

21. What are the four levels of the storage hierarchy and what types of devices belong to each level?

THINK ABOUT IT

1. If you could have only one type of secondary-storage device (tape or disk) on your computer system, which would you specify? Why?

2. Refer to the EBCDIC chart in Chapter 4. What parity bits would you have to add to the bytes in the word "Apple" for odd parity?

3. If your hard disk had a seek time of 50 milliseconds, rotational delay of 10 milliseconds, and transfer rate of 1M bytes per second, how long would it take to read a 500-byte physical record?

4. You have last year's sales data stored on a computer tape on a shelf, but you discover that the price for one item sold should have been $9.98 instead of $9.89. Describe the path, and the devices in the path, that the data would have to take to make the change and end up back on the shelf.

CHALLENGES

1. Look into the secondary storage on the computer at your school or at a local company. See what types of devices they are using, the capacities of those devices, and what types of data are kept on each device.

2. You are the computer-systems consultant for a local retail store (pick any one you want). Decide on the types and capacities of devices that the store should have at the lower three levels of the storage hierarchy. Be careful not to make it too expensive or you will lose a client.

6

INPUT

PREVIEW

This chapter will introduce you to the various ways in which we get data into the computer. From your reading you should learn:

■ Why data input is important.

■ The differences between and advantages and disadvantages of batch and on-line processing.

■ How accuracy is maintained in input.

■ How a computer can aid the input process.

■ Methods for automating the input process.

■ Some of the graphic input devices and how they work.

"**H**ey Frank [I always call my computer Frank], run me off a report that shows how I did last month versus the same month last year. By the way, I knocked 'em dead in the Eastern region this week—$148,000 worth of trinary bangfeezers. Put that in your memory banks, old buddy."

Talking to your computer is usually not the way to convince people of your sanity. Although some computers can understand a few words of human speech, and others can understand even more word patterns from a specific person, a casual conversation with your computer is not likely to occur in the near future. Still, it is our data that the computer must process, and, since we just don't seem to speak the same language, some accommodation has to be made between us.

The media computers use to communicate with one another— streams of bits, magnetic tape, floppy disks, and so forth—we refer to as **machine readable,** able to be used directly by the computer. The media we use—writing and talking—we refer to as **human readable.** Many of our input problems revolve around making human-readable data machine readable.

THE HUMAN–COMPUTER INTERFACE

In the world of computers, we say, "garbage in, garbage out" (GIGO). In other words, what you get out of your computer strictly depends on what you put into it. Therefore, input plays a crucial role in any data-processing system. The cost of input usually runs high, not because input devices are expensive but because it usually requires people, and people are more expensive than computers. Likewise, since people function more slowly than machines, input consumes a lot of time; and since people make more mistakes than their computers, input can lead to lots of errors.

It seems that people are the major problem with input. Why not just sidestep the issue and let computers talk with computers? When it is possible, we do. However, we stressed earlier that our world is, and should be, centered around people and not computers. Computers are tools for people's use; therefore, people must communicate with them to provide them with both data and direction.

If the machine is too hard to communicate with effectively, then it is not worthwhile. Therefore, our objectives are to make input as accurate, easy, and inexpensive as possible. Of the three, accuracy is by far the most important.

DATA COLLECTION AND PROCESSING SYSTEMS

Practically all data-processing efforts follow a basic pattern: input, process, and output. How we get from input to output differs.

Batch Processing

In **batch processing,** we put all the data for a particular task in machine-readable form, usually off line (separate from the main comput-

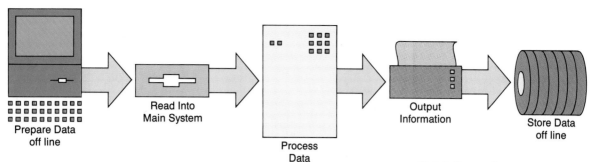

Prepare Data off line — Read Into Main System — Process Data — Output Information — Store Data off line

Batch Processing

In a batch-processing system, we prepare the data off line, load it on the main system all at once, process it, and then store it off line.

er). When we want to process the data, we put the entire batch of data into the computer, process it, and output information. Then we take the data off line again.

A typical batch-processing method is **key and verify,** where each piece of data is keyed twice, once for the initial input and the second time to see whether the first was correct. It works like this:

1. Data comes to the data-entry operators in human-readable form on **source documents.** These could be sales slips, time logs, order forms, or whatever people use to write down transactions.
2. The data-entry people type the significant data on keyboards into a machine that produces some machine-readable medium. For us old-timers, that machine might be a **keypunch** machine that produces **punched cards,** or "IBM cards." More modern systems use **key-to-tape** or **key-to-disk** machines that produce magnetic tape or disk.
3. Both the source documents and the media are given to another operator who rekeys the data using an identical machine. Instead of putting data onto the medium, this machine is set to verify—compare the second operator's keystrokes with the data on the medium. If the machine detects a difference, bells go off, lights flash, lightning strikes, or whatever the machine is programmed to do. The second operator then must examine the character that caused the problem, determine what is right, and key it again.
4. Often, the last part of the process is to print out an **edit report,** a document that goes back to the person originating the data—the salesperson, for example—to allow the originator to check it for accuracy and make any needed changes.

At Value Stores, a central purchasing department purchases major equipment. When a buyer generates a purchase order, he fills out the people-oriented form with some general information such as the name of the supplier, the date of the order, desired delivery date, his own name, and the name of the supplier's sales contact. For each item ordered, the buyer fills in the quantity, the catalog number, the description, the price per unit, the total price for each item, and the grand total for all the items. One copy of this document goes to the data-entry department, another to the supplier.

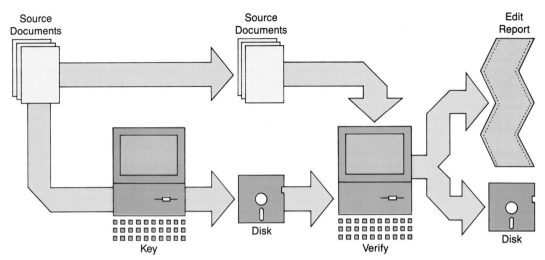

Key and verify is an accurate but expensive input method often used in batch processes.

The data-entry operator must organize the data in field and record format. The fields in each record are the supplier's name, order date, expected delivery date, quantity, catalog number, description, and price per unit. Notice that a lot of the data on the source document do not go into the computer. Much of the supplier data must appear on the form, but they are not used in the Value Stores's computer system, so there is no reason to spend time and money keying them. Also, because each computer record must consist of complete fields, the operator duplicates some of the data. With most data-entry systems, one button will duplicate an entire field.

Value Stores has replaced their punched cards with key-to-disk equipment, but we will show the data as they would appear on the old punched cards because we can read them and we can't read the disks.

Source Document versus Punched Card

Notice the differences in the data on the source document and the punched cards. Some data are omitted, others duplicated, but all are in precise fields.

Value Stores Purchase Order

Vendor: Wilshire Equipment, Inc.
        4006 East Blvd.
        Harftown, IL 31025

Order Date: 3/2/89
Delivery: 6/1/88
Buyer: Harry Flep
Contact: Phyllis Grebbis

Quantity	Cat No	Description	Unit Price	Total
3	102A4	Freezer displays	12,622.48	37,867.44
1	3315TL	Meat packing station	4,180.00	4,180.00
26 sets	1141-YN	Display shelves	387.40	10,072.40

WILSHIRE EQUIPMENT INC	890302890601	3102A4	FREEZER DISPLAYS	12622.48
WILSHIRE EQUIPMENT INC	890302890601	11315TL	MEAT PACKING STATION	4180.00
WILSHIRE EQUIPMENT INC	890302890601	261141-YN	DISPLAY SHELVES	387.40

Supplier   Order   Catalog No.   Description   Price

Delivery   Quantity

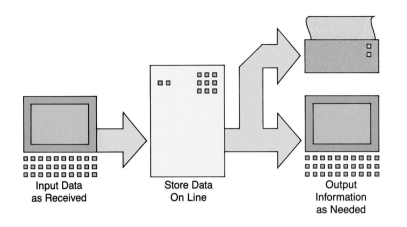

On-Line Processing

Using on-line processing, we input data directly into the main computer where it is stored in secondary storage, immediately available for use.

On-Line Processing

In **on-line** or **transaction processing,** we put our data directly into the main computer system, usually as individual transactions occur, rather than waiting to gather up a batch of them. These data are stored on line for immediate access by users or programs running on the system.

Most on-line input systems use CRT terminals as the input device. Because the input goes directly into the computer, no input media are involved. In a typical input configuration, the operator runs a specific program for the type of input being performed (payroll, sales, purchases, inventory). Sometimes the operator selects this program from a **menu,** a list of choices which appears on the screen.

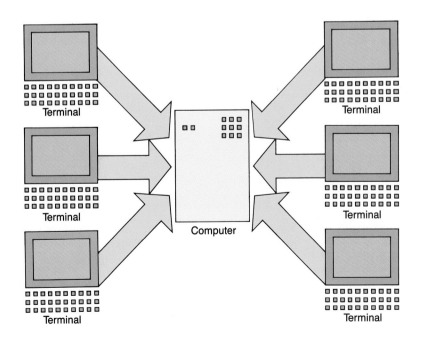

System Using On-Line Input

A typical system using on-line input connects a number of terminals to the main computer. As data is generated (perhaps a sale occurs), it is input through the terminals into the main computer for on-line storage, generally on disk. Often these same terminals can immediately access the data for the latest, most up-to-date information.

136

A CRT Menu

```
  Select one of the following:
    ■ Input sales data
    _ Input order data
    _ Input shipping data
    _ Input receiving data
    _ Query database
    _ Other
```

Commonly the input program will produce a form on the screen that the operator fills in, much as it would be done with pencil and paper. The operator hits a special key when the blanks are filled correctly and the data are sent to the computer.

A good example of an on-line input system is the order-processing methods used by the Television Shoppers' Network division of Value Stores's DANCO discount stores. Cable-television viewers tune in TVSN to find bargains on everything from jewelry to clothes to kitchen appliances. When they see something they like, they phone a toll-free, 800 number and place an order.

TVSN's order taker sits in front of an on-line terminal and fills in a screen form. The system takes the data, flags any out-of-stock items, fills in the prices and figures the total (including tax and shipping), charges the customer's credit card, prints out the customer's invoice (including item descriptions), prints out the shipping order, and adjusts TVSN's inventory figures.

Computer-Assisted Input

Whether we use batch or on-line input methods, the computer or input machine can do a lot of things to make input easier and more accurate.

Example: order form on screen.

```
Name:    Emile Goldfarb_____      Order date:_4/25/89
Address: 402 Yankton Way_____     Ship by: UPS_____
         Valve City, NH_00276_____    Sold by: PRS
Credit card: M Number: 4165 1228 3004 1162 ____ Exp:_7/31/89

Cat Number  Qty  Size  Color  Description        Price
485-23      2__  14__  blue__ overhanger_____   ____6.98
253-78      10_  2___  orange underhanger_____   ____2.75
229-00      6__  60__  red___ sidebottom_____   ___14.59
___-__      ___  ____  _____ _____     _____.__
___-__      ___  ____  _____ _____     _____.__
```

An On-Line Input Screen

Earlier, we stressed consistency in data—each record having the same number of fields and like fields having the same number of characters. Virtually all input machines enforce this for the operator. If a field is omitted, the machine adds blanks. If a field is too long or too short, the machine adjusts it to size. Duplicating fields is usually a matter of pressing one button.

Our input machine may also have access to **look-up tables,** data stored in the machine that allow the operator to abbreviate the input and have the machine fill in the rest. For example, if the input requires a customer name and address, the operator may have to type in only the customer number or a few characters of the customer name, and the machine will look up the rest and fill it in.

Error Checking

Our input machine, typically the kind used for on-line input, may perform error checking for us. Following are some of the usual types of error checks:

- *Look-up Checks.* By using look-ups, the machine can ensure that the data input is valid. For example, it can tell us that a customer we input does not exist. This error check will not help if we simply input the wrong customer.
- *Type Checks.* An input computer can check fields and characters in fields to see whether the data is of a specific type; alpha (*A* through *Z*), numeric (0 through 9), or something else (special characters such as $, # or &). For example, if a part number always contains an alpha character followed by three numbers, say X508, part of an input program could easily spot a mistake like 508X. It could not spot X507 as an error, however, because the characters are in the right positions.
- *Range Checks.* We can program an input computer to determine whether the values of various fields fall within ranges we have set up for them. For example, the program could signal us if we typed in a zip code with more or less than five digits or if we entered $1000 for a part that should be between $8 and $12. Unfortunately, the program would not catch errors that fall within proper ranges (an incorrect five-digit zip code or a $9.88 price instead of $9.98).
- *Check Figures.* We may request that the people who submit data to us for input give us a check figure for those data, some number that the computer itself can calculate from the data after input. For example, a total-sales figure calculated on an adding machine may accompany a bunch of sales invoices. If that figure does not agree with the total-sales figure the computer calculates, an error must have occurred. This check does not tell us where the error was made, but it does tell us that we must correct something before using the data.

These error-checking schemes are often used in systems to avoid the double keying and high cost of key and verify.

Batch or On-Line?

Since both systems exist and are in common use, each must have its advantages and disadvantages. As in most things, both human and computer, we have a series of trade-offs. Let us examine them:

- *Accuracy.* The key-and-verify technique usually used with batch input takes the prize for accuracy. It is highly unlikely that two different input operators will make the same mistake at the same time. If a data error makes it through the key-and-verify process, it is usually a mistake in the source document that was keyed accurately.

batch.

- *Personnel Costs.* On-line input is usually done by people who have some other function in the organization—shipping personnel, sales people, accountants, various managers, and so forth. Batch data entry requires a separate department with people dedicated to nothing but keying data. Are personnel costs cheaper using the on-line or batch scheme? It depends upon how often the data are handled.

on-line → cheaper.

Often personnel costs are lower using batch input and a separate data-entry department. Data-entry operators are specialists. They spend the whole day keyboarding and they are good at it. A sales manager may be able to sell refrigerators in the Arctic, but probably types at about six words an hour with 50 percent accuracy. Not only that, sales managers earn considerably more than data-entry operators.

If, however, the person creating the source data would have to significantly handle the data anyway, perhaps filling out and totaling a sales slip, on-line input may be cheaper. This would eliminate the second handling of the data by the data-entry operators.

The full key-and-verify process often drives the cost of batch input up because each item must be keyed twice. It is, however, the most accurate input method.

Batch → cheaper

- *Equipment Costs.* Batch processing is usually cheaper. Batch data-entry equipment is in constant use, sometimes twenty-four hours a day. On-line terminals sit on a desk until someone who usually does something else wants to communicate with the computer.

In addition, batch systems require much less secondary storage because batch-input data typically reside in the main computer only temporarily while they are being processed and output. On-line input data usually reside on line all the time.

- *Computer Resources.* In a completely on-line environment, the computer must constantly shift from one job to another. It might be running an accounting report while receiving input from sales, shipping, and fourteen other departments. Though a large, modern computer can handle this, it does take computer time to shift from the accounting-report program to the sales-input program, back to the accounting-report program, to the shipping-input program, back to accounting, and on and on.

It is much more efficient to batch input, process, and output the entire accounting job, then do the same for sales, then shipping, and so forth.

■ *Accountability.* Who is responsible for the validity of the data? The person who originates it. Since batch input is usually done by a special group of people whose only function is to input data, they are usually accurate and effective but they seldom understand or even read the data they input. Therefore, they cannot be held responsible for the data itself, only for their keystrokes matching the data on the source document.

On-line systems usually have the originator of the data also input them on a terminal, which makes the originator fully accountable for the accuracy of the data. Too often with batch systems, we find an originator, who writes on source documents like a four-year-old, mumbling things like: "Those &*%$#@ input operators can't do anything right."

■ *Data Currency.* In batch systems, data are held until, say, the end of the week before they are input into the computer. Therefore, those data, and information based on those data, are not available until then. On-line input of data usually occurs as soon as the transaction takes place, making those data immediately available.

■ *Convenience.* You can perform on-line input anywhere you can put a terminal. The warehouse may have one for inputting inventory data, the production department for manufacturing data, the buyers for purchasing data, and so forth. Many retail establishments have **point-of-sale** terminals that act as both cash register and input terminal.

Banks have automatic bank-teller machines which give customers cash while posting the transaction to the customer's account. Some banks have a system whereby, using your touch-tone telephone, you can pay your bills over the phone. In this case the telephone is your "terminal," you are the "input operator," and you are "on-line" with the bank's computer.

Many organizations use both batch and on-line input for different tasks. Batch jobs are often run at night and on weekends when on-line demand for system resources is minimal. With hardware becoming cheaper and more powerful, and with users becoming more sophisticated, the trend is toward more on-line systems.

TABLE 6-1   Batch vs. On-Line Processing

Batch Advantages	On-line Advantages
Accuracy	Accountability for data
Fewer expensive personnel	Handling data only once
Lower equipment costs	Currency of data
Less computer resources	Convenience

BOX 6-1

How Scanners Scan

Scanners are based on a simple physical principle: black absorbs light and white reflects it. Each scanner contains a light sensor of some kind—in most cases a special kind of chip called a charge-coupled device (CCD) or an array of photodiodes, each sensitive to light. In fact, each CCD is itself a rectangular array of microscopic light sensors, side by side.

The light that falls on each sensor is converted into an electrical voltage. The more light that falls on a particular sensor, the higher the voltage from that sensor. Light that reflects from the object or document to be scanned is directed at the CCD. If one sensor on that CCD is struck by light from a white area, it will have a high voltage. A sensor struck by the smaller amount of light that does manage to bounce off a dark area of the object or document will have a low voltage.

The various voltages from all the CCD sensor elements can then be read by an electronic circuit and stored as a collection of numbers, each number representing a position on the CCD and a particular voltage. (This same scheme with CCDs, incidentally, is employed in some of today's giant telescopes to see distant objects far too faint to be discerned by the human eye.)

The values from an array of photodiodes can be treated the same way. Most of today's scanners pick up values for 300 points or dots per inch—90,000 dots per square inch of a document. Most also offer the ability to scan at a lower resolution, picking up fewer points but getting the job done faster.

The electronics within the scanner can then interpret the voltage values from the photosensor. Some scanners understand only "continuous-tone" information—black and white. They decide if each point is dark enough to be black or light enough to be called white and store the information that way. Gray-scale scanners can interpret the voltage values with more precision, assigning a variety of gray levels to the assorted intensities of light that strike the photosensor.

Color scanners have even more information to work with, scanning a document through various filters to determine the intensity of each component color, working with the equivalent of several

Source: Deborah Asbrand, PC Computing, Nov., 1988, p. 168.

SOURCE-DATA AUTOMATION

Each of the input processes we have been discussing requires a person to keyboard data. If the computer is so smart, why can't it type the data by itself, or better yet, eliminate the keyboard altogether? First of all, the computer is not smart. Next, our eyes, ears, and brains allow us humans to make sense out of a hodgepodge of inputs. The computer is not nearly so flexible. It must have its streams of zeros and ones.

To get normal human data into the computer, we must devise schemes to translate human symbols into the machine's internal codes. The obvious scheme involves having a human look at the symbols—words on a paper, for example—typing these on a keyboard which translates them into codes. Another involves the computer "looking" at the symbols directly, through some kind of sensing device, and proceeding with the coding by itself. We call this approach **source-data automation.**

gray-level values for each point. The collection of scanned values is converted into bits that make up an image. The image can then be stored, manipulated by software, displayed (showing black and white, gray intensities, or colors on a screen), and printed.

Just how do you bounce the light off the scanned object and onto the sensor? You can use background light, but that may not be bright enough to adequately and quickly energize the CCD or other light sensor, so most scanners have their own bright light source to shine on the scanned object.

And how do you focus the image of the object or document on the CCD or sensor? You can use lenses and various optics to send the entire image to the chip at once. Or you can cut down on optics costs and use a smaller photosensor that scans only part of a document at a time. The typical way to do this is to scan horizontal lines of the document, storing the light and dark information from a single line, then moving to the next line down and scanning it. Handheld scanners depend on their users' muscle power to move the photosensor across a document.

Finally, there's the software angle. Many scanners let you adjust the brightness, contrast, resolution, and some other aspects of a scan, either through hardware switches or through software commands from an attached PC. But most image manipulation is done by the computer, not by the scanner.

Optical Sensing

The human eye is amazing. We can register a constantly changing set of images without thinking about it. We can see in color, in a wide variety of light conditions, pick out small details, focus near or far, and spot a good-looking member of the opposite sex on the beach at 200 yards. Computers are not nearly so good, but a number of light-sensing devices are available.

Most of them work on the same principles. They have some type of light source, which illuminates an object, and a light detector, which picks up the light reflected from the object. The optical-sensing device can tell the difference between light and dark surfaces by whether light is reflected or not.

The simplest type of optical sensing is used for **mark sense** reading. Here, cards or sheets are preprinted using some reflecting ink (so these areas do not look dark) with specific areas to be filled in with a dark pencil.

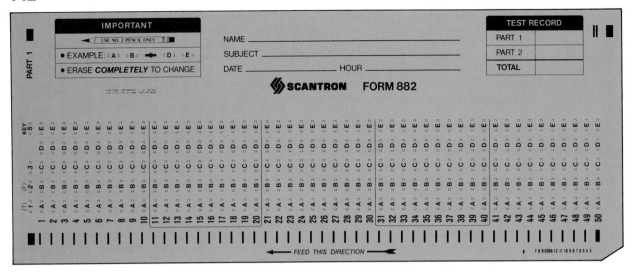

Mark-Sense Input

Many students are familiar with the ScanTron testing sheets. To indicate your answers, you darken the appropriate areas on the paper. The sheets are then put into a reader which transfers the data to a computer.

The reader checks each of these areas to see whether they are marked or not.

Detecting a pattern rather than just a blob of dark requires movement of the surface in relation to the light-sensing device. Let us take a bar code, for example. **Bar codes** are sets of parallel lines of varying thicknesses. The **Universal Product Code (UPC)** that we find on every package of potato chips or canned peas in the grocery store is an example of a type of bar code.

One type of reader for bar codes is the **wand,** a combination light emitter-sensor shaped like a pen. When the wand is moved across the bar code, the computer registers the lines in terms of the percentages of time the wand sees light or dark. The computer compares this pattern with ones stored in its memory and comes up with a corresponding code.

The bar-code reader built into the checkout stand at the supermarket is a little more complicated but works on the same principle. Instead of a wand, it has up to three lasers constantly moving back and forth. As a package is moved across, one (or maybe all three) of the lasers will find the bar code. The pattern-recognition software and hardware must be extremely fast and accurate to see a potato chip package and tell the difference between the bar code and the picture of Granny Goose.

Bar codes have many other uses, from identifying railroad cars to marking business reply mail so that the post office can separate it easily.

Each bar code, though it may be an inch high, is just one line of data. **Optical character recognition (OCR)** devices which read characters on

Product Category
(Grocery)   0   4

41500 02215

Manufacturer   Product
(R.T. French) (Scalloped Potatoes)

The Universal Product Code is a type of bar code found on many products, especially groceries. Using the UPC enhances the efficiency and reduces the cost of checkout.

a printed line must divide each horizontal line, perhaps 1/8 inch tall, into 5 to 24 or more individual lines. These lines, or "scans," must be assembled by the computer into two-dimensional character patterns, which then must be compared to stored patterns to determine the characters.

Specific type styles, such as OCR-A and OCR-B, are fairly standard to OCR readers. Some readers, however, have enough patterns stored and are flexible enough to recognize almost any style of typewritten characters. Others can even read human printing (as long as you don't write like Granny Goose).

Pictures and graphics can be stored in the computer using **image scanning.** Here, the image is scanned, usually one horizontal line at a time, and the spots of dark and light on each line are stored. A common standard of **resolution** (the amount of detail that can be recognized and stored) is 300 dots per inch (DPI) both vertically and horizontally. On an 8 1/2-by-11-inch page, that is 8,415,000 dots. If each requires one bit, each page could take up over 1M bytes of storage.

Point-of-sale terminals enter product codes directly onto the computer.

Magnetic Ink Character Recognition

If you look at the bottom of a check, you will see some funny-looking script designed to be read by another piece of computer equipment. Those

Bar Codes

The Universal Product Code is not the only type of bar code in existence. Here are some other types used in various applications.

OCR Characters
**The characters here look strange
to us but not to an optical
character reader.**

ABCD 0123

characters are printed in magnetic ink and read by a technique called
magnetic ink character recognition (MICR). Each check has a bank
identification code and your account number printed on the bottom in
magnetic ink. After you write a check, the first bank that receives it types the
amount of the check on the bottom, also in magnetic ink. From that point
on, machines called MICR reader-sorter units handle the checks automatically.

Use of MICR has reduced the cost of check handling considerably. A
check usually goes through several hands on its journey from the writer
back to the writer. Three different banks—the one serving the recipient of
the check, a Federal Reserve Bank, and the writer's own bank—must
process it. Once the first bank codes the check, machines do the sorting
and organizing at 2,600 checks per minute (instead of people at 50 checks
per minute).

Humans as well as machines can read OCR and MICR, a definite
advantage over other machine-readable forms. Magnetic ink has the edge
over optical characters because the magnetic ink can be read despite
stamps, smudges, grape jelly, and a limited degree of mutilation. MICR,
though, uses only fourteen symbols (the numbers 0 through 9 and four
other codes) while OCR can use hundreds.

Magnetic Stripe Readers

On the back of most bank credit cards is a brownish stripe that looks like
the coating on a recording tape, and indeed it is. These are **magnetic**

MICR Characters on a Check

**The characters on the bottom of a
check are read magnetically using
a process called MICR.**

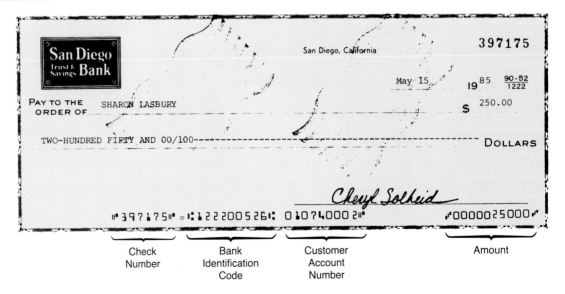

Check Number · Bank Identification Code · Customer Account Number · Amount

BOX 6-2

Portable Computer Runs on Handwriting

The distinction between a laptop computer and a notepad grew fuzzier with the introduction . . . of the Write-Top, a portable computer that replaces the keyboard with a glass screen and electronic pen.

"Other systems may recognize handwriting, but ours is the only one on the market where data is entered by writing directly on the display screen," says Jim Dondero, a spokesman for Linus Technologies, Inc., creator of the Write-Top, which converts handwriting into typed text that can be printed out or dumped into another computer.

Available for $2,800 to $3,600 depending on options and software, the system is advanced enough to read even sloppy penmanship, once it has been programmed to recognize the user's style. The stylus must be picked up between characters, though, says Dondero. Linus expects the prime customers for the 9-pound notepad will be industries that send inspectors out to collect information or that require forms to be filed on a routine basis.

In its first test of the system, the Reston, Va., company has teamed up with Baxter Healthcare Corp. to develop software for nurses to record patient data and track medical supplies.

Source: Susan Dillingham, Insight, Aug. 22, 1988, p. 48.

*Stripes on the back of credit cards.

stripes and have your account code recorded on them. Some stores have readers connected to telephones that directly read the account code from the card and automatically call the credit-authorizing computer for a purchase authorization. Airlines have ticket-vending machines in some airports that will sell you an airplane ticket and charge it to your credit card.

A variation on the automatically read credit card is the **smart card** that the United States Department of Defense and other groups are testing as identification cards. These cards contain small computer memory chips in them which hold special codes that certain computer-controlled locks can read. If your card doesn't have the right code, you can't open the door. Smart card codes can be much more complicated, and therefore safer than keys; and the lock computers can change the codes on the cards if someone's right to access has been denied.

Talking to your Computer

In science fiction movies, we often see people having a casual chat with a computer. Pure science fiction? Not really. **Speech recognition** devices in use today can pick up human speech which is analog in character, translate it into digital data patterns, then compare those patterns with ones in memory, thereby recognizing words. As when reading characters, the computer does not have flexible "ears" like ours. Therefore, speech recognition vocabularies are severely limited, as is the computer's ability to understand different dialects and accents. A speech recognition device that was "trained" by a New Yorker would never understand a Texan.

Below, we see a machine reading an account number on the back of a credit card and a key card, such as many businesses and hotels use to control access.

Still, input by speech recognition has found quite a few applications. In some stores, employees take inventory by talking into a recorder. The tape is then put through a speech recognition device, and the data goes directly into the computer. At some of its distribution locations, United Parcel Service has systems that direct packages to the proper trucks as the employees call out the destinations. Some frequent air travelers swear that some airlines have automated equipment such that when a baggage handler calls out "Atlanta," your luggage is automatically routed to Seattle.

NASA is experimenting with speech recognition to allow pilots to work some of the secondary controls on helicopters without taking their hands off the main controls or their eyes off what is going on outside.

In about ten years or so, a few companies expect to have word processors that take dictation. The stenographer's pads and old-fashioned shorthand will follow the slide rules to the graveyard of obsolescence.

GRAPHICS INPUT DEVICES

Producing pictures, diagrams, charts, and graphs has become commonplace with many computers today. Trying to draw a picture with a keyboard, however, is difficult at best. Fortunately, a number of devices are made especially for graphic input. Many of these devices also have applications for nongraphic input.

With straight character input, characters you type appear at the position of the **cursor,** a line or block on the screen whose function it is to show where the next character goes. The cursor, then, moves one position to the right, the next character goes there, and so forth. You have limited say in where that cursor moves. You may be able to press the "return" or "enter" keys to drop it to the next line, or with some software you may even use the arrow keys (pointing up, down, right, and left) to move it in those directions.

With graphics input, you must be able to move anywhere on the drawing surface and in any direction. The computer keeps track of your position on the screen with a smaller cursor of a different shape, like a cross or an **x**; or an **icon,** a picture-symbol such as an arrow or a pointing hand.

Graphics input devices allow two types of movement: absolute and relative. **Absolute positioning** is being able to point directly to a specific position on the surface. When you draw with a pencil and paper, you position absolutely, picking up your pencil and putting it down exactly where you want to draw your line.

Using **relative positioning,** you move in a direction relative to your current position. You drive a car using relative positioning. You can't just pick up your car and place it downtown, you must go north on Slosh Blvd., east on Burble, and northwest on Mellman Expressway.

Relatively Speaking

When you play "Zoldar, Hero of the Universe," on a video game, you move Zoldar around the screen by pushing a stick in one direction or another. Push the stick forward and Zoldar moves forward, right and he moves right,

A Joy Stick

Joy sticks are often used to move images or icons around on a computer screen.

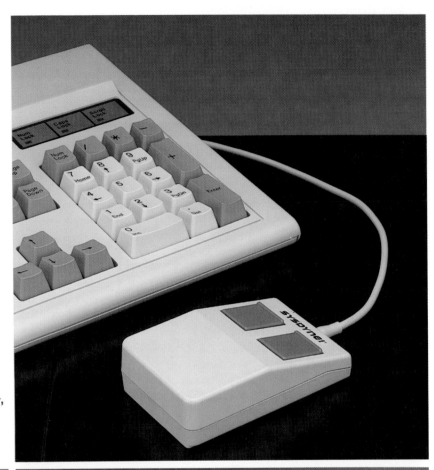

Mice

Mice come in three varieties: furry, mechanical, and optical. The furry ones we shall not be concerned with, but the other two are quite effective at graphics input.

and so forth. The stick is called a **joy stick** (named after the control stick used to fly many fighter aircraft), and it is a relative positioning device.

Joy sticks are fairly inexpensive, and are especially useful when moving "objects," like Zoldar, around on a screen. They are less efficient at drawing lines or precise positioning on the screen.

A welcome addition to your computer, though not very popular in your pantry, is a **mouse.** This device is shaped to fit easily under your hand, and moves the cursor in the same direction and for the same distance as you move the mouse.

There are two types of mice—mechanical and optical. Mechanical mice contain a rolling ball exposed at the bottom of the mouse. As you roll this ball against a surface, sensors in the mouse detect the motion and send these data to the computer. Optical mice require a special surface covered with dots. Light emitters and sensors detect the movement of the mouse over the dots and send the data to the computer. The two types are equivalently priced and equally efficient. The optical one has no moving parts, is almost maintenance free, but requires a special pad to move on, while you must periodically clean the lint out of the mechanical one.

Take a mechanical mouse, turn it up side down, and you have a **trackball.** With a trackball, the ball is in a stationary position but the surface, your hand, moves. It is advantageous because it requires almost no desk space.

Joy sticks, mice, and trackballs typically contain one to three buttons which can serve various purposes, depending on the software. One, for example, may allow Zoldar to fire the photon that wipes the evil Mergazoid off the face of the universe.

Absolutely

"I want the cursor there" you say as you touch the screen with your finger. You are, of course, using a **touch screen.** These sense the position of your finger or other object, typically using a grid of light emitters and sensors.

A Touch Screen

Touch screens do not offer high resolution, but the natural way in which they are used makes them very convenient.

150

A Light Pen

Light pens, like touch screens, allow you to define a specific point directly on the screen.

Digitizers

Digitizers provide a natural working surface and high resolution, and are used by most designers.

The computer knows your position by which sets of lights on the grid you interrupt.

Touch screens are wonderfully easy to use, but they have disadvantages. They are not very precise; the end of your finger is huge compared to a pencil point. For example, even a simple graphics screen is capable of producing 64,000 dots, while a typical touch screen, the HP 150, can detect only 1080 touch zones. (Besides, it takes a lot of Windex to keep the screen clean.)

Touch screens are rarely used in graphics applications, but make picking items from menus so easy it puts the fun back in using the computer.

A **light pen** is a device that looks like a pen with a wire sticking out of it. You touch the pen to the screen, push a small button on the pen, and the computer senses its position against the screen. With the right software, you can move the pen and draw a line on the screen.

Light pens are inexpensive, $20 to $100, and seem quite natural because you can draw directly on the screen. However, they are not very precise and users tire quickly because it is uncomfortable to draw on a vertical screen.

Graphics pads or, as they call the more precise and expensive versions, **digitizers,** provide a surface and a penlike thing called a **stylus** or a mouselike thing called a **puck** to move over the surface. Electronics in the surface detect the absolute location of the stylus or puck and send this to the computer.

You can draw on the surface, just as you would with a pencil and paper, or you can "digitize"—translate to computer storage—an existing drawing by taping it to the surface and tracing it with the stylus. These gadgets are expensive, from one hundred to thousands of dollars, depending on the size and resolution; but they provide a natural drawing surface and easy working situation, and so are the device of choice for most architects, engineers, and designers (and some of us authors, too).

Some digitizers even allow three-dimensional work. You can put an object on the pad, trace its corners and edges, and store a 3-D image in the computer.

Video Input

We mentioned optical image scanners above, but **video scanners** are another kind of image scanning. Here we take a video image, from any video source like a television camera, video-tape recorder, or on-the-air signal, and translate it to computer storage. This technique requires a video source, special hardware in the computer, and a bunch of added software, so it tends to be expensive, from about $1,500 to $50,000. However, such setups are available for most computers from all but the simplest PCs to large, dedicated graphics systems.

SUMMARY

Data input is so important to the data processing cycle because it is one of the most expensive parts, and because the end product, the information produced, can only be as good as the data put in. Input is made more difficult because we humans do not speak the same languages as our computers. Our input processes form the bridge between humans and computers.

We can divide computer operations into batch (where data for an entire task are assembled, input off line, read into the computer, processed, and stored off line) and on line (where data are continually input as they occur and are stored on line for immediate access).

A typical batch-input process starts with a source document, data from which is keyed onto some machine-readable medium. In a full key-and-verify process, those data are rekeyed and compared for accuracy. The data on the input medium are then read into the main computer for processing and generation of output. The data are then usually stored off line.

On-line inputs typically do not go through the key-and-verify process but are often subjected to various types of error checking by the computer, including lookups, type and range checks, and check figures.

Batch systems are usually less expensive in personnel, equipment, and computer resources, and more accurate because of the key-and-verify process. On-line systems ensure more accountability for the data, more convenience for the users, and more current available data.

Source-data automation techniques can cut the cost of input by eliminating the keyboard and operator from the input process. Some of the commonly used methods are optical (including mark sense, bar codes—such as the UPC—OCR, and image scanning); magnetic; and speech recognition.

Various, specialized graphics-input devices are available. Some—such as mice, joy sticks, and trackballs—use relative positioning within the image area, while others—such as touch screens, light pens, and digitizers—use absolute positioning. Video scanning takes a television picture of an image and translates it to digital form for computer storage.

Business Focus   BOX 6-3

Input Systems at Sounds Abound

Several years ago, Sounds Abound stereo stores used a batch input system. When a salesperson sold a component, he or she wrote the data pertaining to the transaction on a sales receipt form (a "sales slip"). At the end of each day, the forms from all the stores went to the central headquarters to be punched on cards. After the cards were read into the computer, a program produced reports for each store showing daily sales, sales and commissions for the salespeople, and adjusted inventory reflecting the items sold.

The King's Gate store manager, Kathy Laffer, was going nuts because of what she termed "data inaccuracies." Whe she added up the totals on the day's sales receipts it rarely agreed with what the computer

report said, the inventory reports often showed things in stock that simply were not there, and sometimes these reports showed "out of stock" on items that were there.

After checking with some of the other store managers, Kathy found that she was not alone. Her solution was to "shoot all the keypunch operators and the DP manager, too." Gary Ortiz, the DP manager, not looking forward to being shot, assigned systems analyst Fred Albert, "Al" to his friends, to look into it.

What Al discovered was a system that people were expected to feed but did not give much in return. The keypunch operators were accurate enough but the source documents (the sales slips) they were given often were not. They were not familiar

enough with the material to spot these mistakes, nor were they expected too. The sales people were primarily concerned with selling hi-fi gear, that's where their income comes from. Looking up inventories and stock numbers, filling out sales slips, and adding up totals were a nuisance.

Kathy and the other store managers were stuck in the middle. They wanted to encourage their salespeople to sell more, but since they needed accurate reports, they were constantly fighting with the salespeople to take more time to fill out the sales slips.

Al's solution cost a bundle in hardware and software, but it made him a lot of friends, a smooth running system, and a computer that the salespeople thought of as a help rather

KEY WORDS

(in order of appearance in text)	Type check	Smart card
Machine readable	Range check	Speech recognition
Human readable	Check figure	Cursor
Batch processing	Point-of-sale	Icon
Key and verify	Source-data automation	Absolute positioning
Source document	Mark sense	Relative positioning
Keypunch	Bar code	Joy stick
Punched card	Universal Product Code (UPC)	Mouse
Key-to-tape	Wand	Trackball
Key-to-disk	Optical character recognition	Touch screen
Edit report	(OCR)	Light pen
On-line processing	Image scanning	Graphics pad
Transaction processing	Resolution	Digitizer
Menu	Magnetic ink character recognition	Stylus
Look-up table	(MICR)	Puck
Look-up check	Magnetic stripe	Video Scanner

than a hindrance. Best of all from the company's viewpoint, it actually saved money in the long run. He converted from a batch to an on-line input system. At each store he took out the conventional cash registers and installed point-of-sale terminals with bar code readers.

Small items, such as cassette tapes and cables, are on the shelves in the store. Customers pick these up and bring them to the sales station. Large items, such as stereo components and speakers, are stored in the back room. Customers see the samples in the showroom and tell the salespeople what they want.

All items, large and small, are bar coded. When small items are purchased, the salesperson passes the wand over the codes on the packages,

entering the item into the computer. For large items, the salesperson either types in the stock number or looks up the item by name in a book. The book contains listings with the item name, description, stock number and the bar code for the stock number. The salesperson can move the wand over the appropriate bar code and the item is entered.

As each item is entered, the terminal displays the description and price, and tells whether it is in stock. After all the items are input, the computer figures out the total bill including tax. If the display seems to be complete and correct, the salesperson touches a button, the sales slip prints out, he takes the money, and goes on to the next customer. For large items the order appears on a screen in

the back room so that the stock people can find the appropriate items and bring them to the front.

In addition to filling out the sales slip, the computer adds the amount of the sale to the store's daily sales total, posts the appropriate credit to the salesperson's commission, subtracts the sold items from the store's inventory, and, if the inventory of an item falls below a predetermined level, reminds the store manager to order more.

Now, Sounds Abound's data are always up to date and about as accurate as they can get because the people who depend on them are also the originators of them and are accountable for them.

REVIEW QUESTIONS

1. Why is input usually the most expensive operation connected with computer systems?
2. Explain the difference between batch and on-line processing.
3. Typically, data that are entered in batch processes are keyed twice. Why?
4. In an input system that uses the key-and-verify process, where do most of the errors enter the system?
5. What are some of the error checks that can be made by computers?
6. What are the advantages of batch input over on-line input?
7. What are the advantages of on-line input over batch?
8. Why is source-data automation important?
9. What are some of the techniques used for source-data automation?
10. How does optical sensing work?
11. How are the data on checks read?
12. Speech recognition would seem to solve most of our input problems. What are some of its difficulties?
13. What is the difference between relative and absolute positioning?
14. What are some relative-positioning input devices? Some absolute-positioning ones?

THINK ABOUT IT

1. Why are many systems that were previously batch oriented now switching to on-line processing?

2. If you were to set up a computer-assisted library where the computer kept track of the card catalog, which of the books were checked out, when they would be back, would you use a batch or an on-line input system? What kinds of procedures would you set up? Why?

3. Assume that your school wanted a grade-tracking system that would allow a student number and grade to be input, and the results posted for the students to see. Would you use a key-and-verify input system or a computer-assisted system without a verification step? Why? If your boss didn't even look at your recommendation and said that you had to use a computer-assisted system, what kinds of error checks would you use?

4. In the system in #3 above, would an on-line system be more efficient than a batch system? Why or why not?

5. Mark-sense reading is really a primitive ancestor of optical character recognition. Why can OCR read so much more detail?

6. Why is a casual chat with your computer not feasible today? How can speech-recognition techniques be improved?

7. If your job was to modify designs that had been made some years ago, before the computer, what type(s) of input device(s) would you use? Why?

CHALLENGES

1. The shipping department of your company needs a new input system so that they can use the computer. Currently, they get a shipping order, start pulling items from the shelves, and put them in a box. If they are out of stock in a particular item, they mark it on the shipping order. After pulling all the items, they check their records to see when the out-of-stock items are due in. If none will take more than a couple of days, they set the box aside; otherwise they ship what they have and include a back-order notice. Figure out what data they should have in their computer and how they should input the data. In designing your input system, be sure to address hardware, software, people, and procedures.

2. How does your school input class-registration information? If they use a computer, examine their input systems. If they don't, suggest how they might use one.

3. Look closely at some system that uses source-data automation (UPC codes, automatic bank tellers, computer grading of tests, or whatever). Find out: what hardware is used; in general terms, the route the data takes from source into computer storage; what, if anything, is immediately done with the data; and where the possible sources of error are.

7
OUTPUT

PREVIEW

The final part of the input, process, output cycle is information output—providing data to satisfy the needs of the users. Here we will examine in some detail the kinds of output commonly produced with a data-processing system, and the hardware and software that produce it. You should be sure you understand the following by the time you have finished the chapter:

■ The importance of output in information systems and what criteria we use to measure output.

■ The difference between character and graphic output.

■ Representative types of printing devices and their characteristics.

■ Representative types of display devices and their characteristics.

■ How graphic output devices form images.

■ What types of machines produce graphic output.

■ The importance of software in graphic output.

■ How computers speak.

■ How data are output for other machines instead of humans.

The objective or "final product" of data processing is information. To be useful it must be readable, understandable, accurate, available, and presented in an attractive manner. If this book were scrawled in crayon on the backs of used napkins, the information might be the same, but you would be less likely to read it. Unless our output is well planned, our data processing effort will be wasted.

CRITERIA

Choosing the right output device for a particular application is important. As we examine various output devices and methods, we will always keep a number of criteria in mind. First, the suitability for the job at hand, but beyond that three other important considerations: speed, quality, and cost.

Output speed is important because in computers, as with most other things, time is money. As we shall see, output is terribly slow compared to processing speed. It is usually the output device that limits the speed of the entire project, not the computer. Computers often have to wait until the output device is ready to accept more information.

Think about having two computers tied up printing out two reports. If you could double the speed of the output device, you might be able to run both reports with one computer in the same time, thereby halving your investment in computers. The cost of your output device would be somewhat more, but probably not as much as the second computer.

The quality of the output—whether the characters or images are well formed and it is physically attractive—usually relates to cost. Generally speaking, higher-quality output requires higher-priced and slower-running equipment. Many things, such as most reports circulated only within the organization, do not demand high quality. They must be legible but need not be pretty. Others, such as correspondence and things that must represent the organization to the outside world, must be much more attractive.

The need for cost consideration is obvious. We must weigh our requirements and desires for speed and quality against the cost of the equipment and its operation.

TYPES OF OUTPUT

Literally hundreds of different kinds of computer-output devices have found particular niches in the market place. Some are quite specialized, others somewhat ordinary, but all have their uses. We will examine a number of examples of various types of devices and compare them to see why one is chosen over another for a particular application.

Characters

We can divide our output into characters (letters, numbers, and symbols) or graphics (pictures, designs, or technical drawings). Characters come in two basic types: solid font or matrix. **Solid-font characters** are always printed

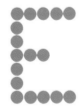

Solid Font   Matrix

**Solid-Font versus
Matrix Characters**

**Solid-font characters are formed in
one stroke, such as from a
typewriter. Matrix characters are
built up from patterns of dots.**

(rather than displayed) and are formed in one stroke from a fully formed character pattern. A typewriter produces solid-font characters.

Matrix characters are formed from a series of dots. The dots are placed in such a way that they look like a character. Generally speaking, the solid-font characters look better than matrix characters, although if you use enough dots and they are small enough, matrix characters can be of excellent quality. For example, the typesetting process used on this book builds each character from very small, very closely packed dots.

Graphics

Computer output devices produce pictures and images in one of two ways. **Vector graphics** refers to images that are drawn much as you would with pencil and paper. A pen (or stylus or point of light or whatever) starts at a certain point and moves in whatever direction is necessary to produce the desired line.

Raster graphics refers to images that are produced by scanning an area with horizontal lines as a television set does. The device begins by moving in a horizontal line at the top of the area and producing either light or dark spots as the image requires. It then moves down a bit and scans the next line and so forth until the entire area is scanned. The pattern of light and dark spots forms the image.

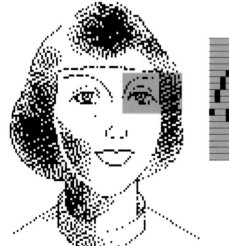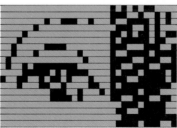

Enlargement

A Raster-Scanned Image

**This picture was formed using a
series of horizontal lines. Within
each line, light and dark spots
form the points of the image.**

Copy: Hard versus Soft

Some devices—**printers,** which produce principally characters, and **plotters,** which produce principally graphics—produce **hard copy,** permanent images on paper. Others, **displays,** produce **soft copy,** temporary images on a screen.

IMPACT PRINTERS

Impact printers work by pounding, or impacting, a character on paper. A typewriter is an impact printer. The necessary elements are:

(1) ■ *Something to form the character.* On a typewriter it is the hammer with the character formed on the end, or a ball-shaped printing element with a number of characters formed on it.
(2) ■ *A ribbon.* This is soaked in ink or coated with carbon to give the color.
(3) ■ *Paper.* To receive the character.
(4) ■ *A backing.* Something to pound against.
(5) ■ *A striker or hammer.* Something to force the whole thing together so that the ink will come off on the paper in a character pattern.

We can separate impact printers into two categories: single-character and line printers. **Single-character printers** print a single character at a time, like typewriters. Normally they print characters across the paper until they get to the end of a line, then they drop down to the next line and do the same thing. That sounds reasonable, how could it be done differently?

Line printers do it differently. **Line printers** print an entire line at a time instead of just one character. The obvious advantage is speed.

Single-Character, Solid-Font Printers

Single-character, solid-font printers use an assortment of gadgets such as daisies, thimbles, and balls, to form characters. A **daisy wheel** printer carries its character patterns on the ends of the spokes (called petals,) of a

The Anatomy of an Impact Printer

This type of impact printer uses a magnet-driven striker to force the character into the ribbon and onto the paper. Since it pushes against the backing, there is enough pressure between the character pattern and the backing to force the ink from the ribbon onto the paper.

Paper

Ribbon

Backing

Striker

Character

Single-Character, Solid-font, Impact Printing Elements

The daisy wheel, thimble, and ball produce comparable quality, although the ball is somewhat slower.

wheel (the daisy wheel). This printer looks somewhat like a typewriter except for the printing mechanism itself, which consists of the rotating daisy wheel and a hammer to strike it.

When the computer sends a character code to the printer, the entire print mechanism moves to the next character position, the proper character is rotated in front of the hammer, and the hammer strikes the character pattern through the ribbon onto the paper. This process is repeated for each character.

Most daisy printers produce **correspondence-quality** or **letter-quality** output, meaning that you would be proud to send out a business letter printed by one of these. This is about the best quality available from computer printers, and in fact, manufacturers of other types of printers will advertise "Almost as good as a daisy wheel" or **near-letter-quality (NLQ)** output.

Daisy-Wheel Printer
The daisy-wheel printer uses solid-font characters on the end of the "petals" of a "daisy" wheel. The output is relatively slow, but the quality is exceptionally high.

Speed is fairly slow by serial printer standards, about 25 to 80 characters per second (CPS). (Some of the inexpensive, home-computer daisy printers operate as slowly as 10 CPS.) This is far from slow; a good typist types at about 6 CPS not including coffee breaks, but we shall see that other printers are much faster. The speed of daisy printers (and most other serial printers) is often optimized by printing bidirectionally. The printer prints a line and, rather than taking the time to return the print mechanism to the beginning of the line, it prints the next line backwards. (Of course, the characters are also printed in reverse order so that the line looks normal after it is printed.)

Cost is relatively high for a single-character printer, from about $1000 to $3500. (Home-computer daisy printers are available for less than $700.)

A **thimble** printer is quite similar to a daisy printer in all respects except for the shape of the print element. The thimble looks like a daisy wheel with the petals permanently bent. Quality, speed, cost, and method of operation are all about the same.

The **ball** printer is similar to the daisy and the thimble in cost and quality, but it works slightly differently. The character patterns are formed on a ball which is rotated to the proper position in front of the ribbon and paper. Instead of being hit with a striker, the printer throws the entire ball against the paper. The ball is heavier than the daisy, and moving and striking it requires more force and time than does rotating the daisy wheel and firing the much-lighter hammer. Therefore, the ball printers are much slower than the daisies, usually about 15 CPS. The IBM Selectric typewriter is a ball printer, and there is a computer printer version of this machine.

Matrix, Single-Character Printers

All of the printers discussed above print solid-font characters, but there are also matrix, single-character impact printers. Matrix printers form their dot characters by firing wires against the ribbon, paper, and backing. The printing mechanism, or **print head,** has wires that can be fired by electromagnets. When the computer sends out a character code, the printer decodes it and fires the proper wires to form the character pattern.

Like any matrix process, each character is made from an array of dot positions arranged in rows and columns. A typical printer might have 63 dot positions per character—nine rows by seven columns. The print head does not have 63 wires, however; it has only nine in one column, one wire for each row. The printer forms a character by moving the print head continuously across the paper, firing selected wires seven times for each character. Matrix printers are much faster than daisy printers because the print head does not have to start and stop. Typically, matrix printers operate from about 50 to over 400 CPS.

Matrix character quality and readability is usually considerably less than that of solid-font characters. Disconnected dots simply do not look as good as a filled-in character. However, there is a trend toward near-letter-quality, "high density" matrix printers with quality approaching that of the daisies. The quality is achieved by using many, closely packed dots for each character. While the print head on a less-expensive matrix printer has nine wires allowing a character made up of nine dots vertically (and perhaps five to seven horizontally), some more expensive printers have up to 24 wires and dot densities of 64,800 dots per square inch or higher.

Modern typesetting is a good example of the quality that character matrices can produce. A typical typesetter (such as the one that this book is produced on) makes up a single character from about 800 by 600 (480,000) dot positions. With such a high density, the individual dots are indistinguishable and the character looks just like a solid-font character.

The images produced by a solid-font printer are limited to just the images, usually only characters, carried on the printing element. Since matrix printers produce their characters from series of dots, many are capable of producing different character fonts (styles) and even raster graphics. Anything that can be produced by dot patterns can, if the correct software exists, be produced by a matrix printer.

Matrix printers are usually somewhat cheaper than daisies because the mechanical parts are much simpler. Prices vary from about $800 to $3,500 with some home-computer versions priced at below $300.

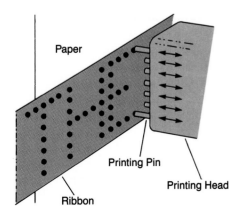

Paper

Printing Pin

Printing Head

Ribbon

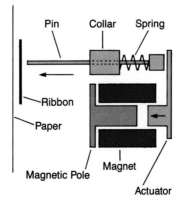

Pin   Collar   Spring

Ribbon

Paper

Magnetic Pole

Magnet

Actuator

Matrix Impact Printer

Matrix impact printers produce a character by firing selected wires into a ribbon with the paper behind. The pattern of dots formed by the wires determines the character. These printers are faster than daisies, thimbles, or balls, but the quality is usually not as good.

More Dots, Better Characters
As more dots are used to make a matrix character, the quality increases. The first set of characters shows the outline of dots as they would be printed on an impact printer. The second shows them as they are actually printed. More, overlapping dots are used in the characters to the left. The lower line shows dots as they might be made by a CRT typesetter. As the dots become smaller and more numerous, the quality of the character becomes better.

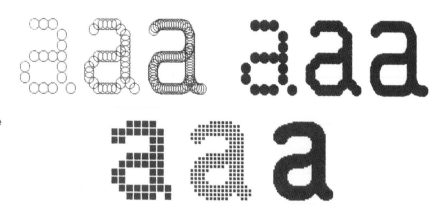

Line Printers

Most line printers are similar in operation; almost all of them use solid-font characters and the standard impact procedure of smashing together character pattern, ribbon, and paper. Since line printers print an entire line at once, there must be one striker for each character position on the line. If your printer prints 132 columns (as many do), it must have 132 strikers and magnets to fire the strikers.

The difference in line printers is in how the character patterns are carried. One popular type is the **chain** (or **train, belt,** or **band**) printer. These printers carry sets of characters (usually two or more of each character) on a continuous chain or belt mounted between two pulleys on either side of the print area. The chain is always moving, which means that a particular character (an *A* for example) will pass a particular striker position many times a second. The circuitry in the printer keeps track of where each character is at any time, and if an *A* is called for in a particular position, the printer will fire the proper striker at exactly the right time. The printer does not print a whole line at precisely the same time; each striker is fired when the proper character passes it. Within one pass of a full character set, the entire line is printed.

A **drum** printer is similar, except that the characters are carried on a cylindrical drum. A complete set of characters (typically 48) is embossed around the drum in each character position. If the printer prints 132 columns, there will be 132 character sets around the drum.

The quality of line printers is not nearly as good as the daisies because the characters are printed on the fly (without the character actually stopping) and the character set is not as complete. Most daisies have at least 88 characters available, whereas line printers usually have from 48 to 64 characters available.

Line printers operate at much higher speeds than serial printers, from about 300 to 3000 lines per minute (LPM). Line printers are not rated in characters per second, but if a 2500 LPM printer were printing 132-character lines, it would be operating at 5500 characters per second.

As you might suspect, line printers cost more than serial printers. The prices range from about $10,000 to $50,000. In applications where speed and volume are more important than quality, such as printing the company's periodic sales or accounting reports, line printers make sense.

Daisy vs. Line

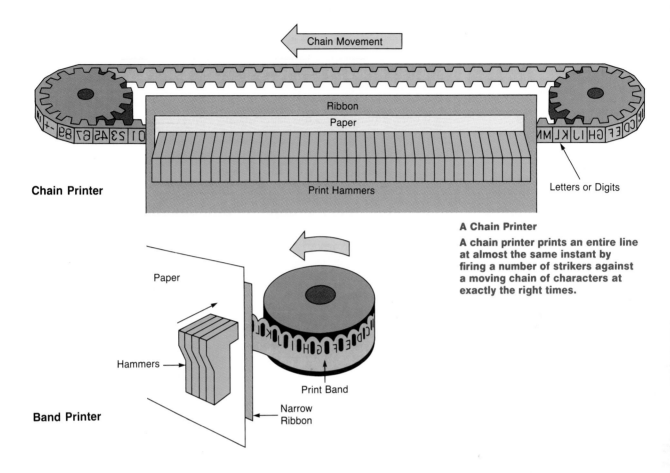

Chain Printer

Band Printer

A Chain Printer

A chain printer prints an entire line at almost the same instant by firing a number of strikers against a moving chain of characters at exactly the right times.

NONIMPACT PRINTERS

Nonimpact printers must form characters in some way other than squeezing a gooey ribbon against paper. Many techniques exist, but they all have a few qualities in common. First, they are usually quieter; there are no hammers constantly making noise. Second, you can't make carbon copies. The same hammer that squeezes the ink off the ribbon in an impact printer squeezes the carbon off the carbon paper. Some nonimpact printers operate so fast, however, it is much cheaper and quicker to print six originals, one after the other, than one original and five carbons simultaneously.

Thermal Printers

Thermal printers use a matrix of small heaters and heat sensitive paper. Like the impact matrix printer, the character is formed by selectively using some of the heaters. The traditional thermal printers form each dot by either burning the coating from the special paper, or changing its color by applying the heat. The relatively new **thermal-transfer** process uses a special, multicolored, heat-sensitive ribbon and normal paper to produce color output.

Thermal printers are slow (from about 10 to 300 CPS), and the quality has been the worst (some border on unreadable after they have been used for a while), but the new color printers are now producing relatively high-quality output. With such a range in quality one would anticipate the wide price range—from $200 for a black-and-white model to $300 to $10,000 for the color versions. The low-quality, black-and-white equipment is simple and light, and the paper usually comes in rolls, so it is often used in portable equipment.

Ink-Jet Printers

The **ink-jet printer** is a highly sophisticated squirt gun. Droplets of ink are discharged from a nozzle and thrown against the paper to form matrix characters. The first ink-jet printers were expensive (from about $3000 to $20,000), relatively fast (90 to 200 CPS) and produced output quality rivaling the daisy wheel. Not many were sold, however, because of their cost and maintenance problems—the ink was always gumming up the nozzles.

Lately, ink-jet printers have been resurrected in less-expensive, slower, but still relatively high-quality form with self-cleaning nozzles. The biggest difference, however, has been multiple nozzles and color inks, allowing full-color printing. Many of these models are priced from $500 to $1500 and print at 20 to 300 CPS.

Page Printers

A **page printer** is similar to a high-quality Xerox copier except that the image is not formed by optically copying an existing one; it is made, raster fashion, by computer-controlled dots of light. The light source puts an electrostatic image on a moving belt or drum. This image is invisible, but it attracts ink (called toner) and becomes visible. The toner is then transferred to paper, fixed by heat, and the process is finished. The light source can be very accurately controlled, so the quality is excellent—typical

The Anatomy of an Ink-Jet Printer
Many ink-jet printers can produce good-quality, color printing or graphics at a reasonable price.

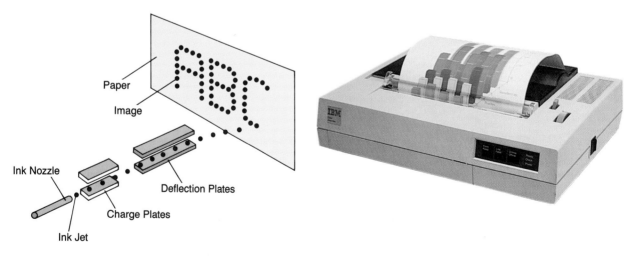

Paper

Image

Ink Nozzle

Deflection Plates

Charge Plates

Ink Jet

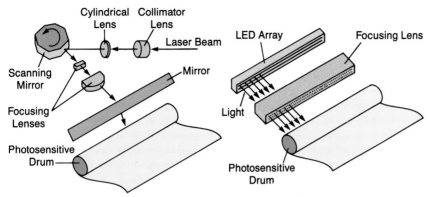

Laser Technology

In the typical laser printer, a single laser beam is focused on a rotating polygon mirror. As the mirror spins, the beam is deflected through a focusing lens and scans across the rotating drum, which accepts the image line by line.

LED Array Technology

In an LED array printer, a linear array of 2,400 light-emitting diodes is positioned to transmit light through a focusing lens to the rotating drum. These LEDs are turned on and off, creating the image on the drum line by line.

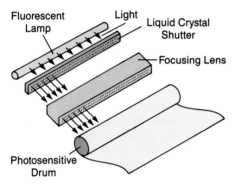

Liquid Crystal Shutter Technology

In an LCS printer, a fluorescent lamp provides illumination for the liquid crystal element, which consists of more than 2,000 tiny "shutters," 1/300 inch in diameter. Light passes through the shutters, through the focusing lens, and onto the drum to form the image by line.

Page Printers

Shown here are three methods page printers use to form their images.

resolution is 300 by 300 dots per inch. In fact, most page printers can print not only characters but also graphic patterns—pictures, diagrams, company logos, and so forth.

Three different types of light sources are currently used for page printers. The first and most common is the laser. In fact, most page printers, no matter what the light source, are often referred to (no matter how incorrectly) as **laser printers.** To produce the electrostatic image, the laser beam scans across the drum much like an electron beam in a television picture. The other two technologies use individual light sources for each dot across a single scan line. A typical eight-inch scan area at 300 DPI requires 2400 light sources. The **LED printer** uses light-emitting diodes as the light sources. The **LCS printer** uses a single flourescent light

Source: *Business Week*, Feb. 8, 1988, p. 88.

BOX 7-1

'Dumb' Terminals Are Getting A Lot Smarter

Woe is the lowly computer terminal that can't do much beyond displaying data generated by a powerful remote minicomputer. Lately, that kind of "dumb" terminal has been looking a bit dumber, thanks to personal computers that can do all sorts of tasks without relying on another computer. But makers of computer terminals don't see this as an irreversible trend.

One way they are fighting back is by adding some personal computer features to their terminals. For example, Palo Alto (Calif.) startup Cumulus Technology has built several PC-like software programs into chips in its new terminals. The programs include an on-screen calculator, an appointment calendar, an alarm clock, and a self-alphabetizing name-and-address file. Designed for use with Hewlett-Packard Co. minicomputers, the Cumulus terminal sells for $795. Esprit Systems, based in Hauppauge, N. Y., has begun selling an upgraded terminal that uses a special microprocessor to display information in separate boxes, or windows, on its screen. Such "windowing" features are usually found only on more expensive personal computers such as Apple Computer Inc.'s Macintosh.

bulb but controls the light through 2400 liquid-crystal shutters. Liquid crystals are used in digital watches among other things. When they are electrically activated, they turn black or opaque, creating either a numeral on your watch or a closed shutter in the printer.

The speed of page printers, especially laser printers, is incredible—up to 21,000 lines or about 350 pages per minute. Assuming an 80-character line, that is 28,000 characters per second. One of these printers could turn out about 504,000 complete pages in a 24-hour day, or one book like this in about a minute and a half. Almost as incredible as the speed is the price for such machines—from $50,000 to about $300,000.

A whole new market for slower but cheaper page printers is gaining momentum. These printers have the full 300 DPI resolution, (that is equal to 90,000 dots per square inch) but print slower, about 8 to 12 pages per minute, and cost from $1,500 to $5,000. This brings them within the range of personal computer buyers and desktop applications.

DISPLAYS

All of the output devices we have looked at so far produce hard copy, something that you can carry away with you. Quite often, hard copy is not needed. You may want to ask the computer for some data to answer a question, or the availability of a certain product, or some piece of information that you do not need written down. In that case, why waste the paper? Use a video display instead.

Most video displays are **cathode-ray tube (CRT)** devices. Characters

Flat-Panel Displays
Flat-panel displays, such as the LCD and gas-plasma, are becoming popular.

are produced by means of a dot matrix, and a typical character-oriented CRT display can produce at least 96 different characters and symbols in 24 lines of 80 characters each. The CRT display is really a kind of television screen with decoding circuits to change the computer's codes into characters on the screen.

The CRT has the corner on the market for displays and will have for some time to come, but it has some competition. Various types of **flat-panel displays** are coming into vogue. The **liquid-crystal display,** or **LCD,** (the same as a digital watch display) is becoming quite popular in portable computers because it is flat, light, and requires very little power. The LCD has relatively large dots, meaning very few for a given display area, and the display is slow in changing while the CRT is almost instant. Faster, higher-resolution, color versions are being produced, however.

Other types of flat panels such as the **gas-plasma display** and the **electro-luminescent display** have dot densities equivalent to the CRTs, change as rapidly, and are now being manufactured to display in full color. They are still quite expensive, about ten times the cost of a CRT, but prices are coming down and soon we will see them being used not only in computer applications but possibly also in television sets.

GRAPHICS OUTPUT

In the information business, it is not the quantity of information produced that counts but how well it serves the user. The more concise and understandable it is, the better it serves and, as the saying goes, sometimes a picture is worth a thousand words. Therefore, more and more time and money is spent getting the computer to draw pictures.

Graphics Display

In this graphics display, individual colored pixels make up the image.

Graphics Displays

Your television at home is a graphic display. It is capable of showing characters, like a CRT terminal, but it can also show pictures. Any CRT, then, is capable of graphics, all it needs is the proper software to put images on the screen rather than just characters. Most graphic displays are **dot addressable,** that is, the screen is made up of a number of dots (called **picture elements** or **pixels**), each of which can be addressed, or made to light up. By lighting up the correct dots on the screen, you can make a picture.

The more dots a screen has, the higher the resolution—the detail the screen is capable of producing. A reasonably standard CRT display screen might have over a million pixels in 16 colors each, which produces a very clear picture with sharp detail (about twice as sharp as a standard television set). Some on the market have over four million pixels and others can produce up to 4,096 colors.

Until recently, the use of such high-resolution graphics has been limited by the high demand for memory in the display device. Each one-color pixel requires one bit of memory. Each additional color requires more memory. Four colors requires twice as much memory, eight colors requires three times as much, and so forth. A 1024 × 1024 pixel screen (referring to the number of rows and columns of dots, a total of 1,048,576 dots) in 256 colors would require 8,388,608 bits of memory. Recently, however, the cost and physical size of memory have dropped considerably, making such machines commercially viable.

Plotters

Plotters print the pictures that graphic terminals display. One type of graphics printer is a modification of a matrix-character impact printer. Instead of using the dots just to form characters, though, it is dot addressable like the graphics display. Common resolutions vary from 5,184

Drum Plotter

A drum plotter achieves horizontal movement by moving the pen across the paper and vertical movement by rolling the paper one way or another. A typical machine might draw a four-color diagram 36 inches wide by 120 feet long with an accuracy of 0.001 inch.

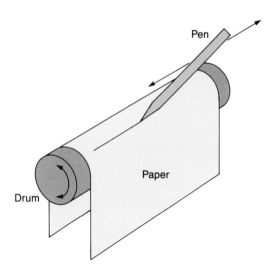

to over 90,000 dots per square inch. Some even use multicolored ribbons for a color printout.

The more sophisticated plotters print continuous lines in all directions. A **bed plotter** holds the paper on a drawing board and has a mechanism over the bed that holds a pen which it can move both horizontally and vertically, or diagonally by combining both horizontal and vertical movement. In this way it can draw a line in any direction, much like you would if you were drawing a picture.

A variation on this is the **drum plotter** which can move the pen only horizontally but rolls the paper over a drum both forward and backward for the vertical movement. Many of these plotters can print in a number of colors by carrying different colored pens and writing only with the one your program calls for at the time.

Graphics Software and Applications

The secret of good graphics is good software to produce them. You could sit in front of a graphics display and say: "Let's light up this dot and this dot but we'll leave this one dark" and so forth. After you defined a million dots, you might have a picture that looked like something. A better way is to have the computer programmed to help you define the dots. For example, many programs will allow you to define two points and then have the computer

---

BOX 7-2

Fast Moves in Computer Graphics

Source: *New Scientist Magazine*, Feb. 11, 1988, p. 34.

An American company has developed a novel computer graphics system that visualises a calculation in three dimensions as it is carried out. The idea is that engineers and scientists working out how air flows around an aircraft, or simulating a chemical reaction, for example, can immediately see the effect of a change in parameters.

They can view the changes in real time. The wave moving along on the right-angled shape below changes as different parameters describing it are fed into the computer.

In modelling everyday objects, the software can translate a design from a wire-frame version into smoothed, coloured and shaded images in less than a fifteenth of a second. The maker, Ardent Computer, combines the number crunching of a supercomputer with graphics.

Translating data from a number cruncher to a machine optimised for sophisticated graphics causes a bottleneck in the design process. Ardent is about to launch a machine which links the two. It bases the system on a very wide bus—an internal structure that can transfer data at speeds of 100s of megabytes per second.

There will also be versions of the software, sold separately, that can be tailored to run on Cray supercomputers and on some commonly used workstations. However, the software (called Dore) will work best on the Ardent machine.

In one deal, Ardent will licence the software to universities for £200, as long as they return to the company any features they develop to be included in future versions of the software. Companies will have to pay £10 500 for the software licence, and almost £100 000 for the whole system.

170

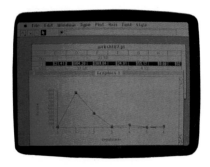

Using Graphics Software
With a very few instructions from the user, the figures in the background on the screen produced the graph in the foreground.

figure out the correct dots to connect the points. Others will allow you to take a predefined shape, like an oval, and place it anywhere on the screen, even make it larger or smaller or rotate it.

Business users now use graphics displays where they once just printed out numbers. For example, a ten-year trend in sales could be presented as ten numbers, but using a graphics display or plotter, those numbers can carry a lot more visual impact as a bar chart or line graph. Many software packages now exist that will take a set of numbers and automatically create a graph, including the axes, and correctly size it to fit the paper. We will discuss such packages later in the book.

The entire field of **computer-aided design (CAD)** depends on graphics. Where a draftsperson once worked for a month on a particular design, the same person, with the aid of a computer, might produce the same drawings in three days. For example, computers are used extensively in laying out the components on integrated circuits. With somewhere in the neighborhood of 1,000,000 components on a chip a lot of drawing must be done, and the space must be used efficiently. Some design software will allow the engineer to describe the characteristics of the design, and the computer will figure out the most efficient layout and make the drawing.

With other software, an engineer can design a structure and have the computer help him draw it. Then the computer will tell the engineer how much stress the structure will withstand and how much it will cost to build.

VOICE OUTPUT

Talking to your computer is bad enough, but can you imagine having one talk back? Many computers use **voice synthesizers** to do just that. Some synthesizers can take ASCII- (or EBCDIC-) coded words and pronounce them phonetically. You could type a letter into a terminal, ask the computer to read it back to you, and it would. Most synthesizers take letter combinations, match them with similar patterns in their memories, and emit the codes that will cause sounds to come from a speaker. It is kind of the reverse of a child learning phonetic spelling.

Voice synthesis is a relatively new field and is progressing quickly; however, it does have some disadvantages. Synthesized voices tend to sound somewhat flat; it is hard for an emotionless computer "mouthing" things it does not understand to say anything with feeling. Also, the English language often does not make phonetic sense. Take the letter combination *ough*. Is it pronounced as in rough, trough, through, bough, or though?

Still, voice synthesis is used in many applications. For example, a bank will let you pay bills over the phone by punching in some codes on the touch-tone dial. It confirms your order by repeating it in synthesized speech.

MACHINE-READABLE OUTPUT

The output we have been discussing has all been human readable. This is fine for us but if the data had to be put back into a computer (perhaps a different one) we would be faced with that slow, manual keyboarding operation which is both expensive and error prone. If the data are destined for another computer, we should make the output machine readable.

Business Focus   BOX 7-3

Fewer Printers, Greater Output

"Regina, where the %#!& is my *&#@ materials requirements report?!" Regina Colby, data-processing manager at Graybill Manufacturing, could still remember Fred Ignoffo's kindly voice over the phone practically every week. She usually told Fred he could take his *&#@ report and . . . , but it was rapidly becoming apparent that, even with her tight budget, she was going to have to buy another line printer at a cost of about $46,000.

The company currently had four line printers: one that was loaded with various forms (which constantly had to be changed for different runs), another that always had 15-inch paper in it for wide reports, and two that were used for everything else. She really didn't have the floor space for another printer nor the operator time to man it—change paper, ribbons, character trains, and so forth.

Her solution to the problem was to sell three of the line printers and buy a laser printer. Her boss, Clement Graybill himself, was not too happy about buying a $103,000 laser printer but softened considerably when she convinced him that it would actually save money.

As it turned out, Regina was right. They got a total of $51,000 for the three used printers, making the incremental cost of the laser printer only $52,000, and the laser printer, at 18,000 lines per minute, was considerably faster than the combined speed of 4,000 LPM for the three line printers. She did not have to hire another operator either, because changes in character sets are all performed by software (the laser is dot matrix instead of a solid-font print train), and when the laser printer prints forms, it prints not only the information on the form but also the form itself so they never have to change paper.

The new laser printer does not print carbon copies but it prints so fast that it can produce multiple originals faster than the old printers could turn out carbons. As a side benefit, the company reduced its paper costs (carbon paper is expensive) and eliminated the messy and expensive process of removing the carbon paper and separating the copies.

The one line printer was retained specifically to print on 15-inch paper. (The laser printer would also handle 15-inch paper but she decided that it would be more efficient to never change its paper type.) She found out that most of the users reduced the 15-inch paper on copy machines to 8 1/2 by 11 so that it would store easier. To save them the trouble, she had the laser printer output many of the wide reports in reduced form on 8 1/2 by 11 paper. Now, she finds that the remaining line printer gets very little use.

The story has a reasonably happy ending. Fred still swears a lot, but usually not at Regina.

Punched cards are often used to print out something that requires a response, with the card coming back to the computer. The local utility may send out its bill in the form of a punched card. Your name, account number, and amount owed are printed in human-readable form, but the same information is also punched into the card. When you send the bill back with a check, the operator will simply put the card into a reader, and your account will be credited.

Magnetic tape and disk, both hard and floppy, are used to send data from computer to computer. This cannot be read by people at all but that is not the point. The other computer can read it very rapidly and accurately.

SUMMARY

Information is the final product of a data-processing system and, if the information is not presented effectively, it will not be used. Hundreds of types of output devices are available to choose from. As our criteria, we look at the suitability of the device for the job and at speed, quality, and cost.

Output hardware can be divided between character versus graphic devices (although some can do both), printers versus displays, machine-readable output devices, and voice synthesizers. Characters are either solid font or matrix. Printers can be either impact or nonimpact, single character or line.

Impact printers all work on the same general principle, transferring ink to paper by hitting a ribbon with a character pattern against the paper. Single-character, solid-font, impact printers include the daisy, thimble, and ball devices, which all produce high-quality characters fairly slowly at a relatively high cost for their speed. Matrix printers run faster, are somewhat cheaper, but do not produce quite as good character quality.

Line printers all produce solid-font characters at a fairly high speed with quality not as good as a daisy printer. Line printers are expensive, but can actually be run at a lower cost per character because of their speed.

There are a number of types of nonimpact printers. Thermal printers work with various heat processes that are slow and produce poor to reasonably good character quality depending on the process. They are inexpensive, however. Ink-jet printers throw droplets of ink on paper in precise patterns, producing a high-quality character faster than a daisy. Using a laser or other light source beam, page printers form images which are transferred to paper by a xerographic process. These printers produce high-quality images, both character and graphic. Some operate at incredible speeds and cost a fortune; others are slower, but more reasonably priced.

The CRT is the most popular display, although it is getting some competition from flat-panel displays—including liquid crystal, gas plasma, and electro-luminescent displays. Most displays will produce both characters and graphics, depending on the software that drives them.

Graphics output is produced on display screens or plotters that use either dot-matrix techniques or actually use pens to draw patterns. One of the most significant aspects of graphics is the software that is available to aid the user. In many cases, the software provides basic patterns that can be placed, rotated, enlarged, or reduced, and combined into a drawing. Other software can be given the characteristics of a drawing, such as the points on a graph, and produce the finished graph, for example. The entire field of computer-aided design depends on such software.

If the output is to go to another computer, it should be made machine readable using punched cards, magnetic tape, or disks.

We now have computer output devices that will even talk to us. Voice synthesis, although just an emerging technology, is now being used in some specialized applications.

KEY WORDS

(in order of appearance in text)

Solid-font character	Letter quality	LED printer
Matrix character	Near letter quality (NLQ)	LCS printer
Vector graphics	Thimble	Cathode-ray tube (CRT)
Raster graphics	Ball	Flat-panel display
Printer	Print head	Liquid-crystal display (LCD)
Plotter	Chain	Gas-plasma display
Hard copy	Train	Electro-luminescent display
Display	Belt	Dot addressable
Soft copy	Band	Picture element
Impact printer	Drum	Pixel
Single-character printer	Thermal printer	Bed plotter
Line printer	Thermal transfer	Drum plotter
Daisy wheel	Ink-jet printer	Computer-aided design (CAD)
Correspondence quality	Page printer	Voice synthesizer
	Laser printer	

REVIEW QUESTIONS

1. By what four characteristics do we usually judge our output devices?

2. What is the difference between a solid-font and a matrix character?

3. What is the difference between raster and vector graphics?

4. What is hard copy? Soft copy?

5. Which type of single-character, impact printer produces the highest-quality characters? Which is fastest? Which is least expensive?

6. What do we mean by correspondence quality? By NLQ?

7. Why is there such a wide variation in the character quality available from matrix printers?

8. Does a typical line printer produce all the characters in an entire line at the same instant? Explain.

9. How does a drum printer differ from a chain printer?

10. Of the various types of nonimpact printers discussed, which produces the lowest-quality characters? Which is the fastest? Which is the most expensive?

11. What can a line printer do that a laser printer cannot? What can a laser printer do that a line printer cannot?

12. What is the most popular display device? What other kinds of display devices are there?

13. Why are high-resolution graphics displays enjoying greater use now than previously?

14. Which types of character printers might also be used to produce graphics?

15. Compare and contrast dot-addressable matrix, bed, and drum plotters.

16. Why is software so important to graphics output and what kinds of things does software allow a user to do?

17. What are some of the problems of phonetic voice synthesis?

18. If you were to prepare output for use by another computer, what types of media might you use?

THINK ABOUT IT

1. If you had a personal computer used mainly for writing business letters, what type of printer would you choose for low volume (a few letters per day)? For high volume (hundreds of letters per day)?

2. If yours was a high-volume application and you needed multiple copies of reports of quality good enough for circulation only within the company, what type(s) of printers might you use?

3. What types of printers might you use if your application required high quality in both character and graphic output?

4. What type of display would you most likely find on a computer built into a tie clip?

5. A plotter can produce characters, but why is it inefficient to use one for straight character output?

6. If you were designing automobiles using a computer, think of some of the ways software could make your task easier.

CHALLENGES

1. Look at the output devices used by your school or a local company. Why did they choose those particular devices? If you were to replace all their output devices with ones currently available, which would you choose?

2. Analyze your current situation now. If you had the type of personal computer you feel would be most appropriate, what kind of display would you buy for it, and what kind of hard-copy output device? Why?

3. Many graphics software packages are on the market today. Investigate one of these packages and outline what the software will do for the user, what kind(s) of equipment it runs with, and how much the software package costs.

Computer
Graphics
and Art

1. Carl Rosendahl, president of
   Pacific Data Images, creating
   computer graphics.

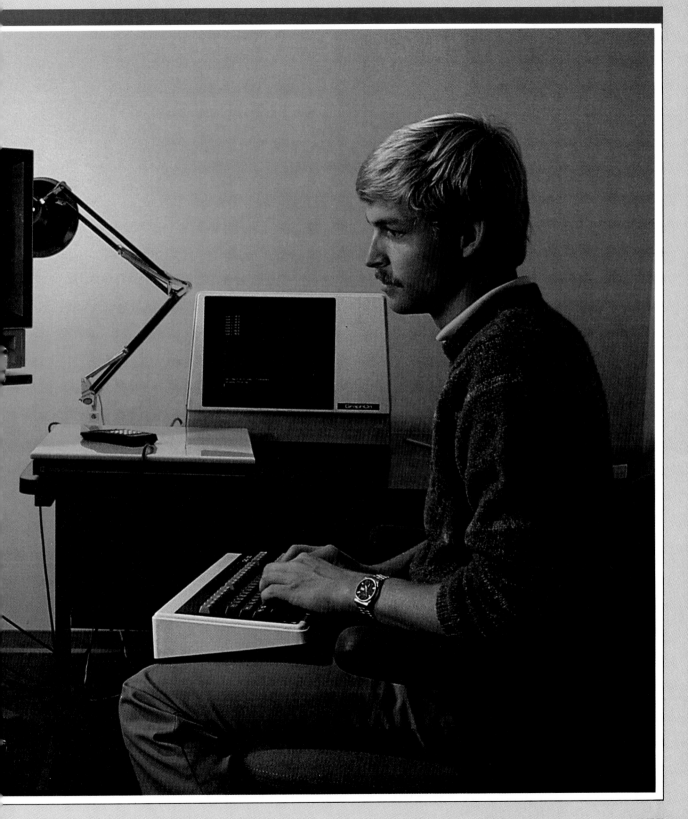

2. The first computer-generated figure to have authentic human motion, known as "Sexy Robot."

3. Computer-aided design (CAD) set up.

4. This is entitled *Line*.

5-6. These two graphics show how CAD can be used in architecture.

7-9. These three illustrations were all created on the Genigraphics artist workstation with Design Plus software. Each piece was imaged on the Genigraphics film recorder at 8192 x 8192 lines of resolution.

10. Computer simulation of DNA molecule.

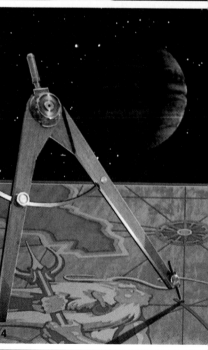

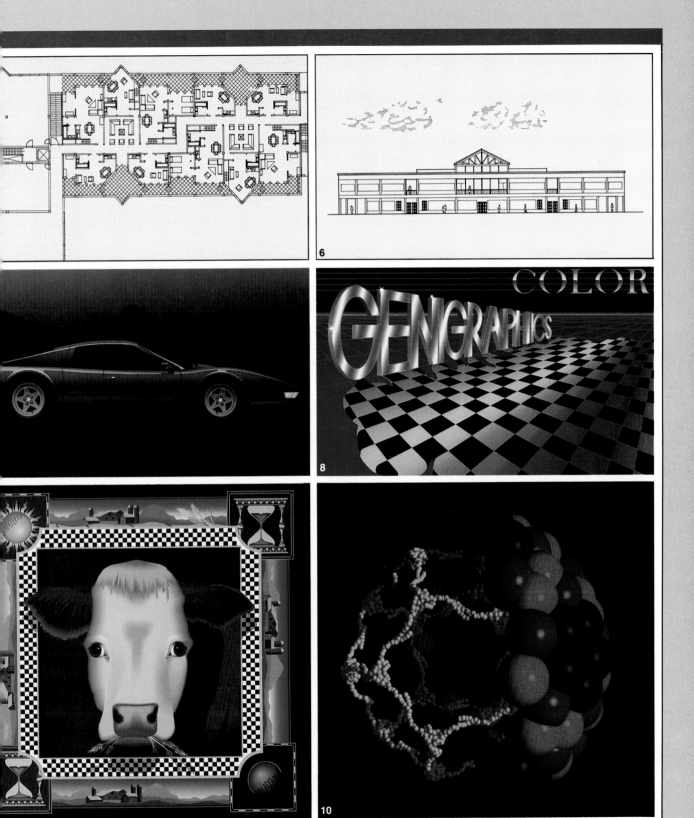

11. This piece of computer art is entitled *Ripple.*

12-13. These two examples of computer graphics are both from Commodore.

14. An example of computer-generated art.

15. This example from the film, *Return of the Jedi,* shows how computer-generated art is used in movies.

16. The migration of hot gases through NASA's space shuttle main-engine fuel turbine is shown in this computational simulation. Red signifies a region of high pressure, and blue of low pressure.

17. Computational fluid dynamics give a full three-dimensional solution for the unsteady flow field of counter-rotation propellers, from NASA. Blue areas represent lowest pressure contours, and pink the highest.

18. A Cray-2 simulation of the flow of gaseous hydrogen around posts in NASA's space shuttle main engine.

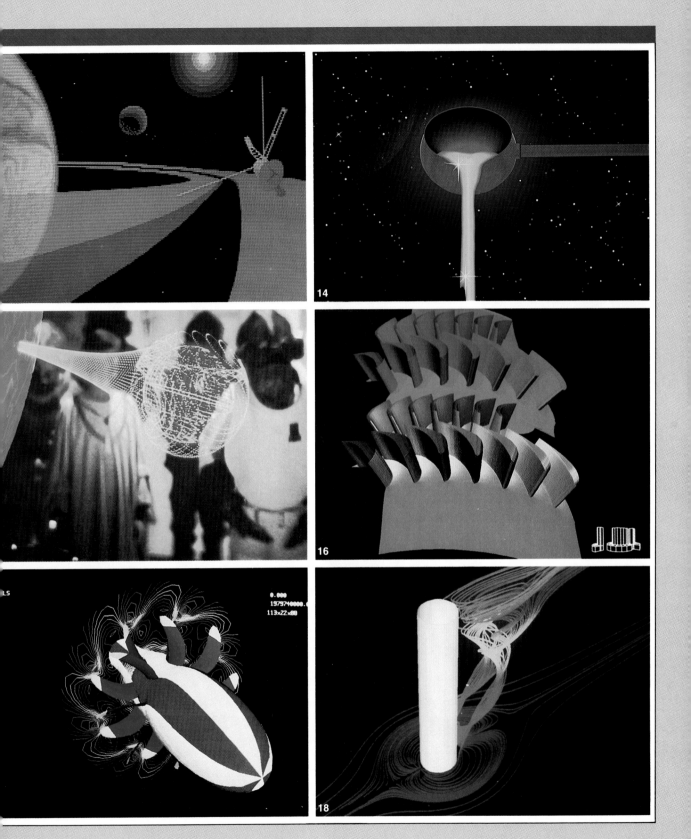

14

16

18

Module 3

SOFTWARE

Without software, hardware is of no use, so in Module III we discuss system software, programming, and languages. The components of system software and various operating systems—single user, multiuser, multiprocessing, and fault tolerant—are discussed in Chapter Eight.

Since software is made up of programs, Chapter Nine deals with the ways programs are written—from initial specifications to final testing.

The languages in which programs are written range from low-level machine and assembly languages to high-level ones such as BASIC and C. These are reviewed in Chapter Ten.

8
SYSTEM SOFTWARE

PREVIEW

We usually use system software without really thinking about it. We rarely change it, don't question it, and almost treat it as part of the hardware. This chapter will be devoted to gaining an understanding of system software and what it does for us. You should end up with a good grasp of these concepts:

■ The importance of system software to the entire system.

■ The types of programs that make up system software.

■ Features of common system software for single-user and multiuser computers.

■ How multitasking operating systems control the running of many programs concurrently.

■ How operating systems work to make computers more efficient.

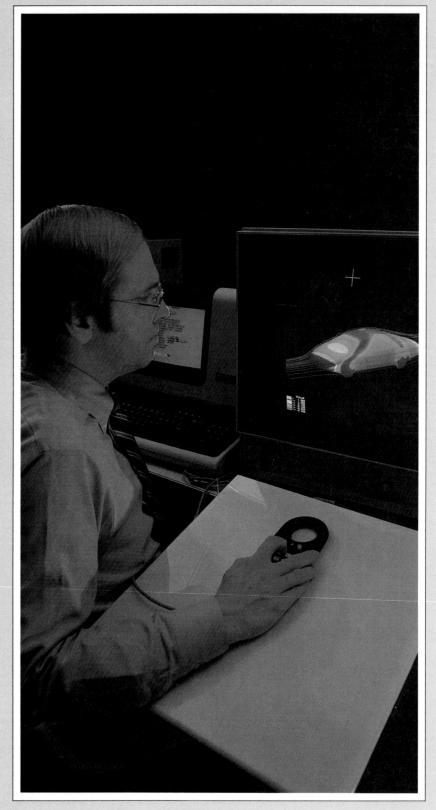

The automatic transmission in your car is a complicated collection of hydraulic pumps, oil lines, valves, shafts, gears, and miscellaneous parts. When you shift from neutral to drive, pumps start pumping, oil flows, valves open and close, parts slide from one position to another, and gears engage. You don't see all that is happening, you just move the shift lever from "N" to "D." The control mechanisms inside the transmission take care of all the rest.

You could, conceivably, perform all those actions inside the transmission yourself. Since shifting from neutral to drive is a common occurrence, however, the makers of automatic transmissions designed the control mechanisms and connected them to a simple shift lever. Those mechanisms are our assistant inside the transmission to help us perform the routine task of shifting.

System software performs a similar function for us in relation to computer hardware. It allows us to give the computer relatively simple commands for routine tasks, and directs the hardware in the required detail to perform those tasks. More specifically, **system software** is a collection of programs that manages and delivers system resources. We could give the computer the detailed instructions that would manage and deliver those resources, but having system software makes it more efficient for us.

Another purpose of system software is to provide some measure of compatibility for computer software on different hardware. Users and applications software deal mainly with the system software. We often refer to this as the "front end" of the system software. The "back end" of the system software directs the hardware in response to our directions on the front end. By keeping the front end of the system software the same but changing the back end to fit different hardware configurations, the same instructions from us will do similar things with different computers. System software developers often write different versions of their packages. They

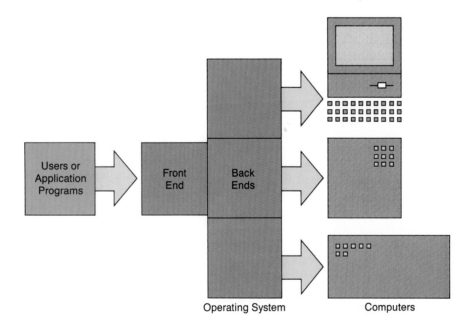

System Software Compatibility

System software can provide compatibility for applications by accepting the same commands from the applications on the front end but having different back ends, giving different hardware instructions to different computers.

have the same front end, but the back ends are written for various machines. A program that uses the XYZ operating system on an ABC computer should also run with little or no modification on a DEF computer using the same operating system.

When you buy a computer, it typically comes with a collection of system software. To this you could add other system software packages, depending on your needs. Since system software is very specialized and complicated, users purchase virtually all of it, practically never writing any of it themselves.

COMPONENTS

Most computers use a number of system programs. Some of these run concurrently with application programs, others perform specific tasks on the computer between executions of applications. Those system programs which are frequently used are typically **resident** in the system. In other words, they stay (reside) in the system's main memory. Those used less frequently are typically **transient.** They are stored in secondary storage until their functions are specifically called for.

The various types of system programs fall in these categories:

1. Operating system.
2. Utilities.
3. Language translators.

The Operating System

The core program of a system software package is the **operating system,** often called the **supervisor, monitor,** or **executive.** This program provides services to our applications programs. Depending upon the specific operating system, the services may be limited to simple tasks, such as finding files in secondary storage or sending characters down the proper wires to the printer; or they may be more complicated, such as controlling the operations of twelve application programs running concurrently or deciding whether the guy behind the terminal in Festus, Missouri, should have access to our Swiss bank-account numbers. As you might suspect, the larger the computer, the more complicated its operating system is likely to be.

✳ The operating system is always resident. The first operation to occur after a computer is turned on is to load the operating system from secondary storage, referred to as **booting** the computer or the **initial program load (IPL).** The term booting comes from the expression, "Pulling yourself up by your own bootstraps." In other words, the computer does it for itself. Most computers have a small boot program, usually stored in ROM, whose only function is to get the operating system from secondary storage and load it into main memory. Turning the computer on starts the boot program which loads the operating system and then turns control of the computer over to the operating system. From that point on, the operating system remains in main memory.

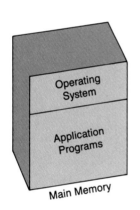

Resident System Software

Resident system software, principally the operating system, stays in main memory while various applications programs move in and out.

BOX 8-1

Stress Shutdown

Data processing people are sure this is true but are not well enough versed in solid-state physics to prove it.

There is a property of silicon crystal (from which virtually all integrated circuits are made) that reacts to atmospheric vibrations, particularly bad vibes caused by stress in human beings. Whenever the situation is tense—work is behind time, things aren't going right, the reports *must* be finished by 2 P.M., and the boss is all over your case—silicon crystal tends to break down and the computer crashes.

It happens all the time. Everybody seems to know about it. But nobody can do anything about it.

Some smaller computers—the Apple II for example—have their entire operating systems built into ROM, so that as soon as the computer is turned on, the operating system begins running.

Utilities

System **utilities** exist to provide services principally to the users of the computer, although many operating systems also allow these utilities to be accessed by applications programs. The selection of utility programs can be few or many, depending on the system software package and the user's needs. Some are packaged with the operating system, while others may be purchased elsewhere. The services they provide run the gamut from telling the user the names of the files stored in secondary storage to setting up the computer for specific types of input and output devices.

Most utilities are transient programs, called into main memory from secondary storage only if need for them arises. Some of the larger systems, however, make many of these utilities resident along with the supervisor.

Language Translators

As we shall see in Chapter 10, a computer understands only one language, its **machine language** that was built into the CPU at the time of its manufacture. A machine language program is a long series (perhaps millions) of offs and ons, zeros and ones, that may mean something to the CPU but is virtually unreadable to a human. We communicate to the computer in other languages, such as BASIC and COBOL, that are made up of characters and words that we humans can understand.

Since the computer cannot understand programs in our languages, they must be converted into the computer's machine language by yet other

186

System Software

System software helps the user, or the user's applications programs, control the hardware. The operating system performs most of the routine jobs, while other utilities and language translators are called upon when needed.

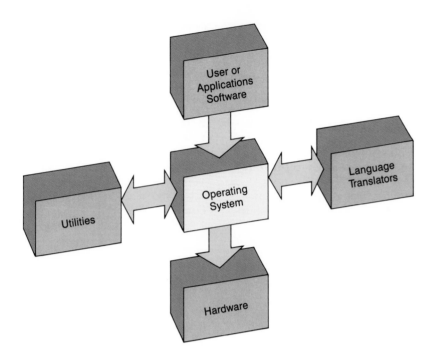

programs called **language translators.** We write a program in BASIC, for example, then we run a BASIC language translation program that converts our program into machine language which can be executed by the computer.

Language translators—except with some of the less expensive, home computers—are always transient programs and are usually purchased separately from the operating system.

SINGLE-USER OPERATING SYSTEMS

Almost all home and personal computers are used by one person at a time. They usually have only one keyboard and one screen, and run only one application program at a time. There are over a hundred different single-user operating systems, but only a few have gained any measure of popularity and we shall only mention a select few of those as examples.

CP/M (control program for microcomputers) is the most popular operating system for eight-bit microcomputers used in business environments. Use of CP/M has fallen off sharply along with the decline of eight-bit machines.

MS-DOS (Microsoft disk operating system) and PC-DOS (personal computer disk operating system) were both developed by the Microsoft Corporation. They are essentially the same system, but PC-DOS is sold with all IBM PCs and MS-DOS with all of the **PC-compatible** machines—those that will run all the software and accept the same add-on hardware that works with IBM PCs. These computers are often referred to as PC **clones.**

PC- and MS-DOS are the most popular operating systems for 16-bit microcomputers.

The reigning 32-bit microcomputers are the Apple Macintosh and the high end of the IBM PS/2 product line along with its clones. The Macintosh uses its own Macintosh operating system and the PS/2 uses either PC-DOS or OS/2, also developed by Microsoft.

We shall examine some of the representative functions of single-user operating systems and make a general comparison between the various systems mentioned above.

Disk Control

To a computer, accessing a file on a disk is much more complicated than just asking for it by name. The computer must know which drive, surface, track, and sector each part of the data occupies; set up space in main memory to hold one or more physical records of the data; and transfer the proper data to that space. These are just a few of the disk services provided by an operating system. Others include deleting and creating files, and finding out other information about files.

More complicated operating systems—such as MS-DOS, OS/2, and Macintosh—allow more sophisticated file access, such as paths and environments. These say, in essence, "If you don't find it here, try there, or there, or there." All of these services allow the user or application program to refer to the file simply by a name.

Other Input and Output

When we work with a computer, it seems that it accepts our keystrokes, displays things on the screen, and prints things out with no effort at all. All of these, however, are quite complicated operations. Even a simple operating system like CP/M has 256 different I/O connection possibilities ("ports"); and keyboards, screens, and printers may be attached to any of them. The operating system keeps track of where all these peripheral devices are attached.

Communicating with these devices is still another matter. To send characters to the printer, for example, the CPU carries on a running dialogue with that I/O port that goes something like this: CPU: "Ready?" Printer: "No." CPU: "Ready?" Printer: "No." "Ready?" "No." "Ready?" "No." This goes on for perhaps hundreds of times until the printer is finally ready to accept another character. Now the CPU sends the character to the printer and the process starts all over for the next character.

Other I/O services allow the user to edit keyboard input, control the display screen, and use various output devices. The more sophisticated systems allow many extra features, such as setting or getting today's date and time, or running more than one application concurrently.

Utilities

The depth and breadth of utilities for use with almost any operating system is limited only by the depth of the wallet. You can purchase utilities that will play Brahms while printing out a report. Almost all single-user operating systems include the following:

- Formatting new floppy disks.
- Displaying a **directory,** a list of the names of the files stored in secondary storage.
- Changing the name of or erasing files in secondary storage.
- Copying files from one place to another.
- Displaying file contents on the screen.
- Changing input and output devices.
- Allowing the user to set up command files—a series of user commands that the computer will execute without the user being present.

File Directory
A file directory shows information about each file in secondary storage.

More sophisticated operating systems, such as MS-DOS and OS/2, allow more flexibility in controlling input and output devices and in

Directory of C:\YFC on September 15, 1988 at 9:35 AM

```
DEPOSIT .SCR    2k   9-25-87  12:12:22a ¦ SALE8710.DAT  409k  11-12-87   5:55:22p
INVOICE .SCR    1k   9-17-87   2:51:03p ¦ SALE9011.DAT    1k  11-12-87   4:14:06p
JNVENTUR.WKS    5k  10-16-87   9:35:13a ¦ SALES   .BAS   61k  11-12-87   5:55:27p
MANUAL  .YFC   10k   9-25-87   3:12:29p ¦ SALES   .EXE   82k  11-12-87   6:04:15p
MOUSEMAN.YFC    2k   2-11-87   0:25:17a ¦ SALES   .OBJ   57k  11-12-87   6:03:20p
ORGCHART.YFC    3k  10-16-87  12:11:07a ¦ SCREEN  .BAS   21k   9-18-87  10:09:20p
QB      .INI    1k   3-11-87  12:31:01a ¦ SCREEN  .SCR    2k   9-18-87   9:18:15p
REM             1k   2-07-87  10:56:18a ¦ SPECS   .YFC   14k   9-25-87   3:18:18p
RETL2902.DAT    0k   2-22-87   8:50:19p ¦ TOYFC   .BAT    1k   2-22-87  10:09:15p
RETL8701.DAT    1k   9-18-87   4:21:08p ¦

27 files, Disk: 674K/32678K - 9386K free.   Memory: 192K/640K - 448K free.
```

command files, including "command languages" for writing small programs made up of all operating system commands. These operating systems also use "subdirectories" which allow you to put all your accounting data in one place, marketing in another, and the Christmas card list in a third. Other handy utilities are available, such as being able to sort data files, recover data from bad disks, change directory search paths, and so forth.

One very significant feature of these operating systems is the capability of allowing a program to add itself to the resident operating system. Application programs can now take advantage of the services offered by this **memory-resident program.** One simple but popular example of such a program is SuperKey, in which you can define various keys to generate keystrokes other than the one typed. If you found yourself typing "the party of the first part" over and over again, you could tell SuperKey that every time you hit a combination of the "Alt" and "P" keys, it should type "the party of the first part."

Operating Environments

Macintosh and OS/2 go beyond the usual definitions of operating systems. They are really **operating environments.** They are easy for the casual user to use, allow data sharing between programs (combining text from one program with graphics from another, for example), and provide added support for graphics presentations and output to different types of devices.

Both of these environments are **window** oriented. An application program can run in a window, a specific section on the screen. This application program can be interrupted and another run in a separate window alongside or perhaps partially overlapping the previous window. Several programs may be suspended in such windows, and the user may shift from window to window (program to program), or even transfer data from window to window.

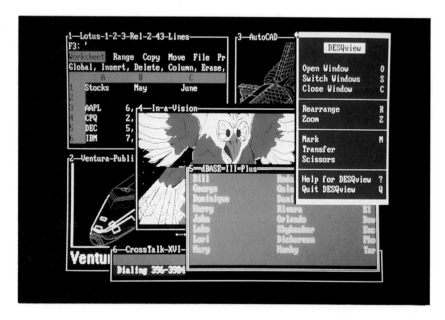

Windows

Windowing allows programs to be suspended while other programs in other windows are executed.

Pull-Down Menu

Instead of typing commands on the keyboard, many programs provide on-screen menus. When you point to a menu item, the program executes that function.

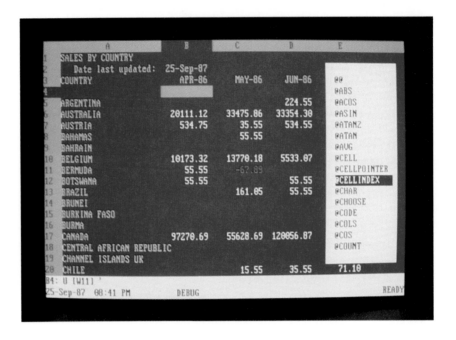

These operating environments are also **point-and-click** oriented. They use mice (electronic, not furry) and on-screen menus. The mouse is used to point to a specific menu item. When you click the button on the mouse, whatever you pointed to starts happening. Often this operation activates a secondary menu called a **pull-down menu** which superimposes itself on the screen under the initial item you pointed to. For example, you may have clicked an item labeled "FILE" and underneath four more choices—"SAVE," "LOAD," "NAME," and "EXIT"—appear. Now you move your pointer to one of those and click again.

Using a memory-resident program, you may add an operating environment to MS-DOS. Popular ones are Microsoft's Windows and Quarterdeck's DesqView, which act similarly to those described above.

MULTIUSER OPERATING SYSTEMS

Larger computers (minis and mainframes) allow more than one user to access them at the same time. They have far greater capacity and operate at higher speeds, and consequently would become "bored" at the prospect of handling only one person's work at a time. In addition to the functions already described for single-user operating systems, most multiuser operating systems provide some or all of the following:

1. Multitasking.
2. Job control.
3. Time sharing.
4. Data security.

As with single-user operating systems, a number of different multiuser operating systems are available. Some of the common ones are the

IBM-compatible MVS (multiple virtual storage) and VM (virtual machine), and Unix, a popular system for minicomputers.

Speed: Human, Mechanical, and Electronic

Remember, a computer information system—a system which accepts data and delivers information—is made of four elements: hardware, software, people, and procedures. Involved in the four elements are three kinds of processes and mechanisms: human, mechanical, and electronic. People are friendly, good to talk to, and the only thing to take out on a date. However, they are slow. The average trained typist, for example, can transfer data (type) at about 6 CPS (characters per second)—not including coffee breaks, chatting at the water cooler, lunch, sleeping, and ten paid holidays per year.

A computer printer (essentially a mechanical device) can transfer data (print) from about 30 CPS to many thousand CPS. Within the main processor (all electronic, no moving parts) data can be transferred at many million CPS. This discrepancy in speeds can cause problems for the computer system.

Serial Processing

Most microcomputers are limited to **serial processing,** that is, working on only one task until it is finished, then completely doing the next, and so forth. This sounds quite reasonable, but let's see what it really means to the efficiency of the computer system.

Suppose that you are typing into the computer at 5 CPS (200,000 microseconds per character), and the computer is capable of handling characters at 1,000,000 CPS (1 microsecond per character). When you type a character, the computer will handle it in 1 microsecond and then wait

192

199,999 microseconds for you to type the next one. During this input process, 99.9995 percent of the computer's time is spent waiting for the next character, a waste of expensive computer equipment.

When the computer has processed the data and is ready to output, it will be sending characters to a printer that can handle, say, 1,000 CPS (1,000 microseconds per character). The computer will send out a character in one microsecond and then have to wait 999 microseconds until the printer is ready for the next, wasting 99.9 percent of the computer's valuable time.

But how else?

You yourself don't operate your life in a serial processing mode. You manage your tasks so that you are performing more than one at a time. For example, if you are doing a project for a computer class that requires that you use one of the school's computer terminals and they will all be busy for the next hour, you won't stare at the ceiling for that hour (we hope). You may start writing the term paper for art history due in two weeks. If the term paper depends on something that the professor will be discussing in lecture next Tuesday, you will certainly do something else between now and then.

We call this **concurrent processing**—having more than one project going at a time. This is not simultaneous processing. That would be actually doing more than one thing at the same instant—like typing in the computer project with the left hand while writing the art history paper with the right. Most humans are capable of a certain amount of simultaneous processing, such as walking and chewing gum at the same time. Most computers are not. They would have to walk one step, chew once, walk another step, chew again, and so forth—concurrent processing.

Multitasking

One objective of an operating system is to make the computer run more efficiently. Obviously, one of the biggest inefficiencies is the disparate speed problem and the associated waiting time usually involved in serial processing. A **multitasking** operating system allows more than one program to run concurrently, addressing the speed problem as well as some others we shall examine.

We said before that an executing program and the data it is working with must be in main memory. In a multitasking system, main memory is usually **partitioned,** divided between the various sets of programs and data working concurrently. One of the partitions is for the operating system itself and the others are for applications programs.

The CPU can still handle only one instruction at a time, but that one instruction can come from any of the memory partitions. It is the operating system that will decide from which partition to take the next instruction. The operating system must also make sure the correct data goes into the correct partition.

With a multitasking system, each program gets its turn. After the CPU performs some operations for program #1, the operating system will direct the CPU to take the next instruction from another partition, perhaps that of program #2. (Shortly, we will discuss the reasons for switching.) Then it

Memory Partitions

In a multitasking environment, main memory is partitioned into separate areas for each program (with its data) running concurrently.

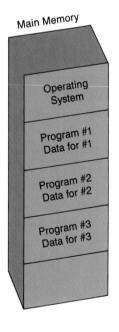

Main Memory

Operating System

Program #1 Data for #1

Program #2 Data for #2

Program #3 Data for #3

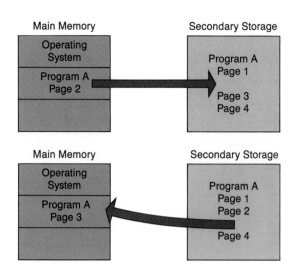

**Swapping in a
Virtual Memory System**

**In a paging virtual-memory system,
pages of programs or data are
swapped in from secondary
storage as they are needed. In the
example above, the computer is
currently working in page two of
program A but needs data from
page three. The operating system
will direct it to put page two back
in secondary storage and bring
page three into main memory.**

will move on to the next program, and the next, and so forth, until it gets back to #1 and the process repeats.

Virtual Memory

Partitioning main memory solves the problem of having more than one program executing concurrently, but it requires lots of main memory, more than is available on many computers. Some computers overcome this by using **virtual memory,** substituting some secondary storage for some main memory. The most common virtual-memory technique is **paging,** dividing the program (and data) up into equal-sized chunks, or pages (perhaps a few thousand bytes long), and keeping one or more pages in main memory while the others are in secondary storage. When the program needs a page that is not in main memory, the new page is **swapped** in from secondary storage. In other words, a current page is written to secondary storage and the new page is brought to main memory. The program always runs from main memory, but only a portion of it is there at any one time.

Virtual memory is not found exclusively in multitasking environments; a serial-processing system may also take advantage of the larger effective main-memory size made available by virtual memory. However, the greater demand for main memory when more than one program must reside there makes virtual memory common with multitasking operating systems.

Input and Output Channels

Since input and output are the slowest of computer operations, many multitasking systems provide for more efficient and faster communications channels. A **channel** is a path data take when going from one place to another. In everyday terms, the route that a phone call takes from one telephone to another—through wires, amplifiers, switching circuits, and perhaps even satellites—is a channel.

A computer input or output channel has the CPU at one end and

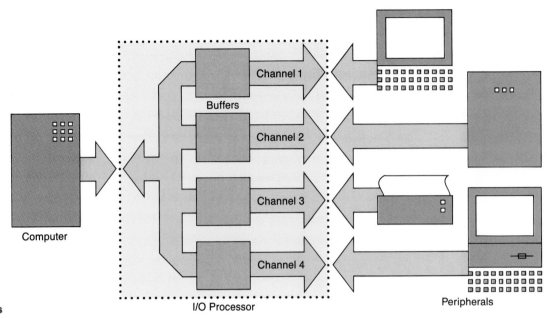

Computer

Buffers

Channel 1

Channel 2

Channel 3

Channel 4

I/O Processor

Peripherals

I/O Channels

Multitasking computers use input and output channels, often utilizing a separate processor called an I/O processor, to collect data going between the main CPU and slower input, output, or storage devices, allowing the CPU to operate at maximum speed.

some other device—say a printer, display, keyboard, or a disk drive—at the other. Most channels are capable of going both ways and are called input/output or simply I/O channels. The operating system must know which devices are connected to which channels, and access those channels accordingly.

A **buffer** is a small memory (or a small section of main memory) of perhaps a few hundred to a few thousand bytes used for temporary accumulation and storage of data. Often a buffer is put in the middle of an input or output channel to coordinate disparate speeds at either end.

For example, when the CPU has some data to send to the printer, those data are put on the channel at CPU speeds, say a million bytes per second. Instead of going directly to the printer, which could not possibly handle them at that speed, they are stored in a buffer and sent to the printer at printer speed, say a hundred BPS. This way, the CPU can send out 1000 bytes in one thousandth of a second, which will take the printer ten seconds to print. In the 9.999 seconds left over, the CPU is free to do other widow things.

Buffered channels can work both ways. If a person is typing at a keyboard at five characters or bytes per second, those bytes can be saved in a buffer and, when there are enough of them, sent to the CPU at a million BPS.

Shifting From One Program to Another

A number of reasons exist to change from one program to another in a concurrent multitasking operating system. Many have to do with making the most efficient use of the CPU and other computer resources, but some are just to keep humans happy. We shall examine the following change criteria:

1. CPU idle time.
2. Priorities.
3. Interrupts.
4. Time slicing.

Idle time is the time that the CPU does nothing productive. Perhaps no one has instructed it to do anything. More likely it is waiting for a slower input or output device. Most multitasking operating systems will move to the next program during what would otherwise be idle time.

The simplest change would be from program #1 to #2 to #3 and so forth. Many operating systems allow us to set **priorities** to define how the changes will take place. For example, we may prioritize our programs to put #2 highest, #1 next, and #3 last. When there is reason to change from #2 (perhaps idle time coming up) the CPU would shift to #1, then back to #2. It would only work on #3 if both #2 and #1 were hung up.

One simple priority system is to put jobs in either the foreground (high priority) or background (low priority). **Foreground** processes allow the user to interact with the computer and treat it as if he or she were the only user (even though there are probably many users). **Background** processes typically run by themselves, not allowing user interaction unless foreground processes are halted (which usually only happens in an emergency). Often, in a system where batch and transaction processing are done together, transaction processing is done in the foreground while the batch jobs are relegated to the background.

Interrupts are special signals sent to the CPU saying that one part of the system, usually an I/O channel, needs attention. An interrupt system works like an orderly class. If a student has something to say, the student raises a hand and is called on by the teacher. Without interrupts, the teacher periodically would have to go around the class and ask each student in turn whether he or she had something to say. Most multitasking systems use interrupts.

Most interrupt systems allow the interrupts to be prioritized. If two interrupts are sent to the CPU, the higher priority one will be handled first. If two hands are raised in the class, the one in the front of the room may be called upon first.

Many multitasking systems are set up for **time sharing,** use of the system by many, nonrelated users. In an ideal time-sharing system, each user should be made to feel that he or she is the only user. This will rarely be true, but if the **response time** (the time between when the user gives a command to the system and when the system reacts to the command) is kept low, hopefully less than a second, that single-user feel will be maintained.

If only idle time, priorities, and interrupts were used as change criteria, one user would be allowed to dominate the system at the expense of the others. For example, suppose Sally Serious is typing in figures for the company's annual report, a process that creates lots of idle time because most of it comes from the keyboard. Harold Hacker is calculating pi to the nearest million digits, which will take even a very fast CPU hours or even days to complete with no idle time.

Sally types an *A,* beginning the word *Annual.* The next character is probably a fifth of a second away, practically an eternity to a computer, so the operating system changes to Harold's job. Since Harold has finagled high priority for himself and his process generates no idle time, Sally has to wait seventeen hours before the CPU will accept her n. This is unacceptable response time.

Most time-sharing systems cure this problem with **time slicing,** allowing each user a maximum slice of time, perhaps a few milliseconds, before moving on to the next. The CPU will eventually get back to the unfinished programs, but others will be worked on in between. This way, the elapsed time between when Harold started his program and when it finished is longer, but the response time for all the users is reasonably short.

Job Control

In a batch-processing system, or the batch applications on a combination batch and on-line system, the computer will run many jobs over a period of time. Each of these jobs requires some special set-up of the system. Channels must be assigned to input, output, and secondary-storage devices, and the correct programs must be loaded into the main processor. As one job finishes, the computer operator could load the first program for the next job and type in the instructions required to set up the I/O channels, but that takes a lot of time and requires that the operator wait for the CPU to finish a job, and the CPU to wait while the operator types in the particulars for the next job.

It would be much better if the operator could have a number of jobs lined up (or "queued") and the computer could start on the next one as soon as it finished the current one. Most operating systems have **job-control programs** that allow this to be done. Inserted in front of each job in the queue are a few instructions in a special **job-control language (JCL)** that tell the operating system such things as the name of the job; who it is for; input, output, and storage devices needed; and the programs to be run.

When the current job is finished, the job-control program will read and follow the next set of JCL instructions and set up for the next job.

In conjunction with—or in addition to—the job-control program, many operating systems have a scheduling program that looks at the various jobs and schedules them according to criteria that the CIS people have set up. Some things that this program might take into consideration are the priority of the job, the length of time it will take to complete the job, and the efficient use of the systems resources. For example, a very short job might be scheduled before a much longer one. Or, two jobs that use an optical scanner, a relatively slow device, would not be scheduled to run concurrently.

Data Security

On a single-user computer, you can keep prying eyes out of your data by taking out your floppy disk, locking your computer, or barring your office

BOX 8-2 Industry Focus

DOS-Easy

Putting on a friendly interface

During the last six years, since the introduction of PC/DOS from IBM Corp. on personal microcomputers, users have become accustomed to computer terms like files, directories, backups, data and programs. They have also become willing to work at a level of complexity that I call "DOS-Easy." That is, they have the ability to execute programs, manipulate data and perform tasks using C: as a signal indicating that the computer is awaiting information.

The complexity of a single-user operating system, like PC-DOS, is rudimentary compared to a multitasking and multiuser operating system like UNIX or AIX. The complexity that the user is willing to accept and deal with has not changed. If we expect to reach the mass computing market with sophisticated operating environments, like work group processing, we must achieve the same level of a DOS-Easy user interface.

Friendly and easy

Successful resellers in the UNIX market have for years developed easy-to-use front-end shells for users. These shells have been limited in functionality to accommodate the computing tasks provided by the reseller and their specific vertical software application. In order to appeal to the DOS mentality of computing, the user interface must be broadened to encompass general functionality of file system management, program selection and user customization. All of these features have been provided in the DOS environment, and the user will accept nothing less.

The successful user environment must be "user-friendly;" it must be almost intuitively usable without extensive manuals. User friendly is a necessary condition, but not sufficient. The interface must also be "user-easy." User easy means that, once the user becomes accustomed to the interface, functions can be accessed

directly or through hierarchies of menus, and that the user interface can be completely bypassed by the experienced user.

The functionality of the interface addresses all of the needs of the system, from application program access to day-to-day administration and maintenance functions. The user-easy feature of the interface becomes even more important in the complex multitasking and multiuser environment of UNIX and AIX than in either the single-user or multitasking environments of PC-DOS and OS/2.

A user-friendly and user-easy interface is going to be the key to mass market acceptance of the newer sophisticated operating environments being introduced to the computing public. Complex workgroup computers, which can be made DOS-Easy, will provide the next generation of computing expected by the DOS user.

Source: Terry Keene, *Mini-Micro Systems*, Aug. 1988, p. 49.

door. On a multitasking, multiuser computer, where everyone's data is on the same set of hard disks, security becomes a more complicated matter.

Most multiuser operating systems provide some measure of security by requiring all users to have a unique identification code, often with a secret password. Unless some specific action is taken, other users are not allowed access to one user's files. Some more sophisticated systems set up various levels of security for files or even different types of data. Individual users may have read/write, read only, or no access to selected data.

BOX 8-3   Business Focus

Unix: The Soul of a Lot of New Machines

AT&T's operating system is gaining popularity fast

Sporadically, over the past decade, practically every major computer maker has tried to convince Gary D. Handler that its machines were the answer to his every problem. But Handler, the executive in charge of computer systems for Shearson Lehman Brothers' trading floor, didn't believe it. He knew that committing himself to just one brand of computer might make it harder to buy the best products in the future.

So when Handler saw the chance to avoid this trap, he took it. In 1986, just after arriving at Shearson from Merrill Lynch & Co., he decided to base its trading operations on Unix. Unix is an operating system, a piece of software that controls the basic functions of a computer and has to be in place before the machine can run applications software that does useful work, such as financial analysis or text editing.

Unix was obscure and a bit hard to use, but it had one huge advantage: Unlike the proprietary operating systems of IBM, DEC, or Apple, it was available on many different machines. Now Handler is confident that he can mix

brands and sizes of computers to build any network he needs. "I'm prepared for the future," he says.

Suddenly, Unix is catching on everywhere. In just the past year, it has become available on scores of machines, from personal computers to supercomputers. Unisys Corp., an old-line mainframe maker, says its sales of Unix systems topped $500 million last year. International Business Machines Corp. says it now spends as much on the development of Unix-based systems as it does on PCs. And last month, Apple began shipping Unix for its Macintosh. International Data Corp. predicts that by 1991, Unix will be the main operating system for a quarter of the worldwide computer market.

As the popularity of Unix grows, it will threaten the proprietary operating systems that have produced huge profits for companies such as IBM and Digital Equipment Corp. "The industry powerhouses don't want Unix," says William N. Joy, chief technologist at Sun Microsystems Inc. Indeed, nonproprietary systems such as Unix "put more bargaining power in the buyer's hands," comments Melvyn E. Bergstein,

a managing partner at Arthur Andersen & Co.'s $1 billion computer consulting practice. "The marketplace is getting a lot smarter."

Unix has come a long way since Bell Laboratories developed it in the 1970s for AT&T's internal use. Prohibited as a regulated company from selling Unix, AT&T licensed it to universities, and eventually to computer makers, on the understanding that it wouldn't support the product. As its use spread, an entire generation of programmers became fans of Unix. But producers of applications software were not about to tailor their programs to it, since not many business customers used Unix.

This began to change in 1983. AT&T had already signed the consent decree leading to its 1984 breakup, which let the company enter the computer business through a separate subsidiary. It began promoting Unix and by 1987 had licensed it to some 225 computer makers. By then, Unix' main drawback was a multiplicity of versions. The original program essentially was a nugget that every licensee embellished. By late 1986 there were perhaps a dozen major varieties, all slightly different. The question that confronted customers and producers of applications

Source: Richard Brandt and John W. Verity, *Business Week*, Mar. 14, 1988, pp. 94–95.

software was which version to bet on.

AT&T started trying last year to answer that question. Aiming to create a single dominant Unix version, it decided to pluck the best features from the three most widely used varieties: Its own, called System V; Microsoft Corp.'s Xenix, for personal computers; and Berkeley 4.2, used by Sun Microsystems on its engineering workstations. Now, AT&T, Microsoft, and Sun are working together on a new version of Unix, to be released later this year.

The biggest worry of rivals is AT&T's increasingly cozy relationship with Sun, currently one of the fastest-growing computer makers. Last year Sun licensed its basic computer design to AT&T, and the two are implying that Sun's design plus Unix equals superior machines, from personal computers to supercomputers. Then in January, AT&T announced plans to buy 20% of Sun. Now other Unix licensees fear that Unix will be tailored to run best with the Sun architecture, giving AT&T a lever for improving its disappointing computer sales.

Despite the controversy, Unix' reputation continues to grow. "I've been at it for three years, and I still don't know everything about Unix," says D. Brent Chapman, a 19-year old Unix whiz who has left college to write currency-hedging programs. "But once you learn it, you're more productive on Unix than on any other operating system." Tom Love, chairman of Stepstone Corp. in Sandy Hook, Conn., says it takes a few weeks at most to convert a major program from one Unix machine to another. That's a long changeover that AT&T and others are still working to shorten. But it compares with months or even years on systems without Unix.

Major commercial demand for Unix is being led by the U.S. government, the biggest computer customer in the world. The Air Force has specified Unix as a requirement on a $4 billion contract for which it is taking bids. Amdahl Corp. and National Advanced Systems are selling mainframes that run Unix, while Italy's Olivetti is aiming Unix systems at law firms. Unix is a key selling point for Hewlett-Packard Co.'s new Spectrum minicomputers. And Datapoint Corp. in San Antonio finds Unix demand particularly strong in Europe, says Chief Executive Robert J. Potter.

Cost is a big selling point for Unix. Because it is available on a wide range of machines, makers of those computers have had to compete on price. Indeed, Unix systems frequently deliver two to three times as much performance as comparably priced machines using proprietary operating systems, notes Richard R. Janssen, president of Delphi Systems Inc. in Westlake Village, Calif. Delphi is a supplier of Unix systems to insurance brokers. Adding to Unix' appeal, says Janssen, are the 2,000 applications programs now available for it, a number that's growing fast.

Many customers also see Unix as the one major alternative to IBM. The No. 1 computer maker is promoting a concept called Systems Application Architecture, a set of software standards that will let a customer transport programs between different types of computers. But as currently envisioned, SAA would only work on IBM machines. So many customers view it as a sophisticated attempt to lock them in. Bergstein, who keeps up on product developments for Arthur Andersen, says "SAA is driving people to consider Unix." That may be all the endorsement Unix needs.

MULTIPROCESSING

In order to increase processing speed, some computers have more than one CPU to share the workload. These are **multiprocessing** systems and exist in many different configurations. Some, principally scientific "number crunchers," are single-user systems that use **parallel processing.** They break down a program so that many parts of it can run simultaneously.

Others, principally business-oriented computers, are multitasking systems. Scheduling many programs on the same CPU is a difficult enough task, but scheduling even more programs on multiple CPUs can be a nightmare! Needless to say, multiprocessing operating systems must be complicated, sophisticated, and large. (Some of them require a few million bytes of main memory for just the operating system.)

How the work is divided among the CPUs depends upon the system. In some, all the CPUs are more or less equal and the operating system divides jobs among them. In others, a single job might be split between more than one CPU. Still others have CPUs dedicated to special tasks like controlling inputs from various sources, or handling batch or on-line jobs. Some multiprocessing systems share the same main memory among the CPUs, some have separate memories for each CPU, and some have separate memories but can access data from the separate memories of the other CPUs.

FAULT-TOLERANT SYSTEMS

Eighty-six people are using the computer system, batch jobs are running in the background, and management is screaming for results. A normal

enough situation. What is not normal, but happens anyway, is that an integrated circuit cooks itself to a cinder and the system shuts down. Aside from all those people who are inconvenienced, the data that were currently being worked on may be lost.

To combat this situation, some systems are designed to be **fault tolerant.** They have redundant parts—many CPUs, duplicate secondary storage, identical sets of input/output channels—and an operating system that will shift tasks from a section with a failure to a similar section that is still working. For example, if your program is running on CPU #3 and that CPU shuts down, the operating system will shift your work to CPU #5 and you will not know the difference.

The system monitor will show a failure in the system, and if too many failures occur, work on the system will slow down, but no single failure will stop the system.

SUMMARY

System software is a group of programs that act as our assistants inside the computer system. The programs are either resident (remaining in main memory while the computer is functioning) or transient (remaining in secondary storage until their functions are called for).

The supervisor program is always resident and provides services principally to our applications programs. Utilities provide services primarily to the users, although applications programs often take advantage of them. The supervisor and utilities are referred to as the operating system. Language-translator programs convert programs written in people-oriented languages into machine language so that the computer can execute them.

Single-user operating systems such as CP/M, MS-DOS, Macintosh, and OS/2 provide a measure of compatibility between different hardware with the same operating system, and give the user and/or applications program easy control over disk and input/output functions, as well as many basic utilities. Some of these operating systems have or can be extended into more complete operating environments, allowing the user easier access to and control of the computer.

Multitasking operating systems allow the computer to run more than one applications program concurrently. Usually main memory is partitioned between the various jobs. Since a single CPU can handle only one job at a time, the operating system must determine when to change from one job to another. Some criteria for switching are CPU idle time, priorities, interrupts, and time slicing.

In addition to multiprogramming, many of these operating systems provide for job-control programming, time sharing, data security, multiprocessing, and fault tolerance.

KEY WORDS

(in order of appearance in text)

System software	Directory	Buffer
Resident program	Memory resident	Idle time
Transient program	Operating environment	Priority
Operating system	Window	Foreground
Supervisor	Point and click	Background
Monitor	Pull-down menu	Interrupt
Executive	Serial processing	Time sharing
Booting	Concurrent processing	Response time
Initial program load (IPL)	Multitasking	Time slicing
Utility	Partition	Job-control program
Machine language	Virtual memory	Job-control language (JCL)
Language translator	Paging	Multiprocessing
PC-compatible	Swap	Parallel processing
Clone	Channel	Fault tolerant

REVIEW QUESTIONS

1. What is the purpose of system software?
2. How does system software differ from applications software?
3. What is the difference between a resident and a transient system program?
4. Name the three main categories of system programs.
5. What kinds of functions does the supervisor program perform?
6. What happens when you boot a computer?
7. What types of functions are considered utilities in system software?
8. Name a few single-user operating systems.
9. What does the memory-resident feature allow you to do?
10. How does an operating environment differ from an operating system?
11. What four additional main functions do most multitasking operating systems provide?
12. In executing many programs, how does serial processing differ from multitasking?
13. What is the purpose of virtual memory?
14. How do buffered I/O channels match the speed of the CPU to that of the slower peripheral devices?
15. In a multitasking system, what are four criteria the operating system might use to switch from program to program?
16. What are background and foreground processing?
17. How does time slicing control response time for time-sharing computer users?
18. What is multiprocessing?
19. How do most fault-tolerant systems tolerate faults?

THINK ABOUT IT

1. Could you write applications programs for a computer without an operating system? If so, how would it differ?
2. Could all the resident, supervisor functions of an operating system be made transient to save memory? What effect would that have on applications program execution?
3. If you had five programs to run and idle time was not a factor (perhaps very little use was made of peripheral devices), could you complete all five programs faster using serial processing or concurrent multitasking?
4. What type of a computer system would be capable of both concurrent and simultaneous processing?
5. Would time slicing be necessary in a batch-processing system? Why or why not?

CHALLENGES

1. Investigate two single-user, personal-computer operating systems. Compare them feature for feature. Which would you rather use in a business situation? Why?
2. Investigate a multitasking operating system, perhaps the one at your school or business, or one of the few available for personal computers. See how they handle (if they do) job control, time sharing, security, and fault tolerance.

9
PROGRAMMING

PREVIEW
We have seen the importance of software in the overall computer system. Now we will look at some of the techniques used to write programs that make up the software. After reading this chapter, you should have an understanding of:

■ Where programming fits into the total development of a computer system.

■ What elements make up a program specification.

■ Flowcharts: what they are, the standard symbols and their meanings, and how to construct them.

■ Pseudocode: what it is, the key words used, and how to use pseudocode to design programs.

■ How structured programming techniques are used to make programming easier.

■ Some common programming applications.

■ How modular programming techniques are used.

■ The importance of testing and documenting programs.

In the last chapter we examined system software, programs that go hand in hand with a particular computer system and make commonly used functions available to whoever or whatever uses the system. We also mentioned applications software, programs written to solve the specific problems of a particular user or set of users. In this chapter we will look at the process of writing application software, common design methods, and some of the tools used.

PROGRAMS AS PART OF A SYSTEM

Remember, the computer is simply a tool that we use to help us perform some task. The use of the computer is not an end in itself. Therefore, when we create the program that directs the computer, we must keep the task, and the user who needs the task done, firmly in mind. This requires careful planning and effective human communication. A programmer who works only with the computer may write super programs (they work well), but they usually fall short of satisfying the user.

A great deal of research and planning must be done before an actual program is even thought of. Most organizations follow a formal, step-by-step process in information-systems development and only a part of one stage is the actual writing of the programs. It is an important part, but it must be viewed in its proper prospective. We will look at the entire systems-development process in detail in Chapter 11.

Developing an efficient and useful program must follow a regular pattern, just like the development of a whole system. Patterns vary from organization to organization, but most contain some common elements. Let us assume that you are the programmer and examine what you must go through to write a program.

PROGRAM SPECIFICATIONS

First, you must be sure that the program specifications have been properly defined. If you are working with a systems analyst, the analyst should have done this. If there are questions or ambiguities, be sure to clear them up before proceeding. "Write a program to print paychecks." is not an adequate program specification. You should know exactly what a completed check should look like, where the raw data are coming from, how to figure the amount of the check, what other uses there are for the data, and so forth.

If you are working by yourself, then you—in consultation with the users, of course—must define the program specifications. When you do, follow the golden rule—do for yourself what you would have others do for you. In other words, don't cheat yourself. Treat yourself to a complete description of the program before you write it.

At this and many other points in the process, you should check your specification with the users to solicit their comments and to make sure that your interpretation of their needs is correct. In some organizations this is done informally, but in others it requires a formal signing-off at each step.

Output Design Worksheet

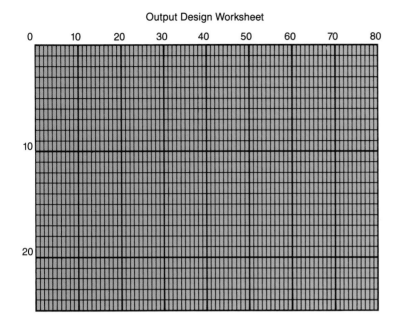

Output Design Sheet

Programmers and systems analysts often use output design sheets to format reports. These sheets come in pads and have spaces on them for all the rows and columns that would be found on an output page or screen.

Output

Remember, we said that most programs follow the input, process, output pattern. The most important factor is the final result, the output, so that is where you direct your attention first.

For example, producing a payroll is much more complicated than printing the paychecks. Most payroll systems produce a number of outputs for different groups, inside the company and out. Some examples are:

Your program specifications should include the designs for all these reports. Each proposed report should be laid out on a video display or paper (there are output coding sheets for this purpose) showing what the

Recipient	*Document*
Employee	Paycheck
	Pay details—gross pay, deductions, and so on.
Management	Summary reports showing total pay by department, average pay, labor cost by project, overtime by department and project, and so on.
Personnel dept.	Detail report showing pay details for each employee.
	Detail reports showing deductions for taxes and insurance.
Insurance company	Detail report showing insurance contributions by both company and employee.
Internal revenue	Deposit checks for taxes withheld.
	Detail reports of taxes.
State tax board	Deposit checks for taxes withheld.
	Detail reports of taxes.

Provider	Input
Employees	Timecards.
Personnel	New employee data—wage rate, exemptions, extra deductions, and so on.
	Terminations.
	Raises, changes in deductions, and so on.
IRS and state	Tax and unemployment insurance changes.

headings should be, how many characters go in which columns in the body of the report, and what all the total and subtotal lines should look like.

Input

Once you have determined the output, you must decide on exactly what data must be input in order for the computer to produce that output. In our payroll example, the inputs might be as follows:

If these inputs do not already exist, you must design them in much the same way as you did the output. For batch inputs, you must create the documents that go to the input operators. For on-line inputs, you must design the CRT screen formats that the people who input will be using.

Process

Now that you know what goes in and what should come out, you can define the process to get from input to output. You must be sure you understand the calculations that must be made along the way. In our paycheck example, you must know how to figure gross pay, taxes and other deductions, and the paycheck amount among other things. You must also know what kinds of stored data (files) you will be working with.

Just like input and output, the files must be precisely designed. You should specify what fields are in each record and the number of characters in each field. The companies that print coding sheets have provided for this also.

File	Data
Employee	Name, address, exemptions, pay rate, other deductions, hire date, cumulative pay and taxes, and so on.
Tax tables	Tax rates for both state and IRS.
IRS information	Payments and associated data for IRS reports.
State tax information	Payments and associated data for state reports.
Insurance	Insurance tables and payments to the insurance company.

DESIGNING THE PROGRAM

Writing even a simple computer program is always a two-step process. First you must understand the entire task in human terms, then you can translate it into a computer language. Beginning programmers often try to combine the steps—they see the program specifications and immediately sit down at a computer terminal and start typing. Writing a program without careful planning is a hit-or-miss proposition. There is too much guesswork. It may be successful on simple programs, but as the requirements get more complicated, programmers find out that the time devoted to careful planning is well spent.

Most programmers use, and most companies require the use of, some relatively formalized program design tools—"languages," so to speak, that are easy to write, easy to understand, and clearly show the logical patterns of the task being designed. The two most popular tools are flowcharts and pseudocode. Normally, a programmer will "write" a program using one of those, review it by himself or with the help of other programmers, and then translate it into an actual computer language.

FLOWCHARTS

If you drove your car from New York to Los Angeles you would most likely follow a road map. The map would show various points along the way—Hoboken, New Jersey; Pagosa Springs, Colorado; and Cucamonga, California—and roads connecting those points. It would be much easier to follow the map than to follow some written directions like, "Turn left at Bayonne, New Jersey, proceed to King of Prussia, Pennsylvania," and so forth.

A **flowchart** is similar to a road map. It is a visual representation of a task made of symbols (like cities) and lines (like roads). The symbols indicate operations such as adding values or displaying things at a terminal. The lines connect the symbols, specifying in which order the operations are executed.

In flowcharting, we use different symbols to represent different types of operations. The symbols shown here are some of the generally accepted ANSI symbols. Although the symbol shapes are standard, the situations in which they are used by programmers sometimes differ. We shall attempt to present the most accepted uses of the symbols.

The Terminal Symbol

The **terminal symbol,** an oval, signifies the beginning or end of a job. The words START or STOP inside the symbol tell you which end of the job it is. Each job must have one and only one START symbol.

Theoretically, a job might stop as a result of a number of different conditions, or it might never stop. For example, perhaps you have planned a buying trip looking for a gold-plated widget. Part of your plan says that if you find one in any of the cities you had originally planned to visit, you will

BOX 9-1

Bad Language

All the software tools in the world won't bail out an inarticulate programmer.

All too frequently, we hear the lament "Johnny can't read." Neither can he write. Nor code.

To write software, you have to communicate through language—the English language. You do not have to do square roots in your head or be able to give the day of the week for any arbitrary date. You do have to be able to express an action in terms of subject and predicate and properly use nouns, verbs and clauses.

Sound far-fetched? Think about this: Programming is nothing more than the practical ability to communicate with an obtuse, literal machine. Those who cannot write well cannot program well.

Many programmers, undereducated in basic English and writing skills and consequently unable to keep up with the technology, typically find themselves in one of two predicaments.

They either develop programs aimed at solving programming flaws that really lie with themselves, or they shelve good programming tools because they lack the skills that are necessary to use them.

Ada resulted from conclusions reached by a panel of programmers that determined, among other things, that the problem with programming lay not with the programmers themselves but with their tools.

The truth is that products such as Ada, APL and IBM's PL/I have failed to prove their superiority over even the most basic Cobol language.

There is no reason to believe that other so-called "super languages" will be any more capable of improving the lot of programmers. Nor will SQL, artifical intelligence and other such concepts that would replace real intelligence with purchased expertise eradicate poor programming.

At this point, it is not at all reasonable to assume that further technical advances alone will rescue the programming community. An organization will be better served by providing training to overcome practical shortcomings.

You would think that tools such as relational data base management systems and high-level fourth-generation languages would let programmers deliver simple up-stream applications sooner and cheaper than a decade ago.

The sad reality is that many programmers, lacking basic language skills for whatever reason are unable to use these tools effectively. The new tools bewilder the underskilled programmer,

leading him to come up with all kinds of excuses for project delays. One of the more popular cop-outs is the old whine heard during the Fortran and RPG days that "the language is not up to the problem."

Actually the language can more than handle the problem. The first fully relational DBMS/fourth-generation language pair, Adabas and Natural from Software AG of North America, Inc., could produce applications hundreds of times better, faster and more reliable than any competing product.

Regrettably, the products were often assigned to those who were accustomed to being towed along by a computer rather than driving it.

Freed from the constraints of primitive languages and DBMSs, many programmers introduced to the Adabas/Natural combination found themselves confronting their own shortcomings —shortcomings that stemmed from their lack of training in the King's English, inadequacies caused by an educational system that failed to teach students the basics.

So when you hear the often-used excuse that "the language was not up to the problem," you should examine the various skills of the staff. Better yet, have them explain the situation—in writing.

Source: Dan Nolan, *Computerworld*, July 25, 1988, p. 67.

stop. Also, if you run out of gas, you will stop. Your plan, then, will show a number of different possible stopping points. You will only hit one of those points depending upon where you find the widget (or run out of gas), but all of them are part of the plan.

Also, theoretically, you could design a job that never stops. The sun comes up in the morning and goes down at night, day after day. We hope that this process never stops, at least in the foreseeable future. So your flowchart might have a lot of STOPs or no STOPs.

We shall see, however, that designing a job for the computer with no end or more than one end is not good form. We may do so in the early stages for the sake of demonstration, but once you have learned enough techniques of programming, your flowcharts should all have one STOP symbol.

A terminal symbol, either START or STOP, can have only one line attached to it. The START symbol has one line going out of it to the first actual operation of the job. Naturally, it has no line going into it because that is where you start. The STOP symbol has one line going into it from the last actual operation of the job. No lines go out because once you hit the STOP you don't go anywhere else.

The Input/Output Symbol

The **input/output symbol,** a parallelogram, represents data moving between the main processor and some other part of the computer system. It might be data coming in from a keyboard or card or tape reader, data being read from or written to a file, or data being displayed on a CRT screen or printed at a printer.

Like most symbols, the input/output symbol has two lines, one coming in and one going out. The program comes from some operation, does the input or output, and goes on to the next operation.

A description of the operation, in plain English, is written inside the symbol. It must be brief to fit, but it should also be specific. "Print results" is not as acceptable as "Print gross pay, total deductions, and net pay." Remember, the object of flowcharting is to make a job easily understandable to us ordinary humans.

The Process Symbol

The **process symbol,** a rectangle, is used to represent most operations that occur within the main processor. (The input/output symbol represented operations that involved the main processor and some other part of the computer system.) Arithmetic calculations fall in this category, as does moving data from one main memory area to another. Like the input/output symbol, there are two lines, one in and one out, and a description of the process within the symbol.

We prefer that the description be written in plain English instead of mathematical formulae. The actual formula must be used when the program is written in computer language, but the flowchart is usually more readable when long formulae are avoided. We would prefer "Compute net

A Very Simple Flowchart (Using Terminal Symbols)

This is a correctly formed flowchart using the terminal symbols. Unfortunately, it doesn't do anything because there are no actual operations between the start and stop.

Another Flowchart (Using Input/Output symbols)

This program allows a name to be entered at a keyboard and printed by a printer. It is still somewhat dull, but at least we're getting somewhere.

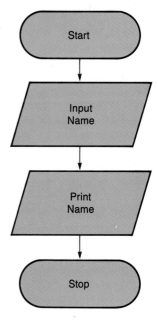

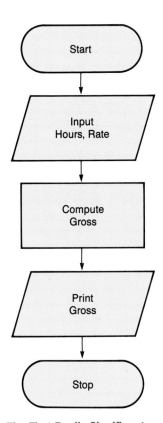

The First Really Significant Flowchart (Process Symbol)

Using this program, the person at the terminal types in the number of hours worked and the wage rate; the computer figures the gross pay, and prints it out.

pay" rather than "Net pay = gross pay − income tax − FICA tax − disability insurance − retirement − union dues − life insurance." Others would prefer to see the formula written out. To each his own.

The Connector

The **connector** is a small round circle used to indicate a connection between lines in a flowchart. If it is impossible to draw a line from one symbol to another (such as between two pages of a flowchart or across the middle of a flowchart), you can put a letter in a connector just after the line leaves one symbol and the same letter in another connector that goes into the other symbol, indicating that the line extends from one to the other.

The connector is also used to bring two lines into one, like bringing together two branches of a process. In this case you use just the circle with no letter inside it.

The Decision Symbol

Computers do not really make decisions as we think of decisions; they cannot exercise judgement. However, they can be programmed to react to certain conditions and, depending upon whether those conditions exist or not, do one thing or another. This is called a program **branch,** and the **decision symbol,** a diamond, represents the point at which the branch takes place.

Testing for the existence of the condition makes use of the logical capability of the CPU—a comparison is made. When faced with the question "Is it raining?" we would look outside and compare the conditions there to what we know rain looks like. If it were raining we would take the branch that says "Put on a raincoat." Otherwise, we would take the branch that says "Wear sunglasses."

In a computer system we might program for the condition "Are sales greater than $1000?" In response to this condition, the computer would go to its main memory, see what is stored in the location for sales, and compare it to $1000. The true or "yes" branch following this decision might have the computer print out "Bonus earned." The false or "no" branch might print out "Normal commission."

The description in the decision symbol is always in the form of a question that can be answered by "yes" or "no." The symbol has one line

Using Connectors

The point labeled A on page 1 is connected to point A on page 4. The third connector shows a horizontal line intersecting and joining a vertical line. The last shows two lines coming together into one.

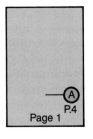
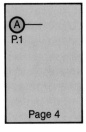
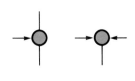

coming in and two lines, labeled "yes" and "no," going out. By tradition, the line going in enters at the top point of the diamond. The yes and no branches going out may exit at any two of the other three points.

Some Rules for Flowcharting

1. Use symbols for proper operations with the correct number of lines in and lines out.
2. Use plain English rather than some esoteric, unreadable code or shorthand.
3. If there is any doubt as to which way a line is going, use arrows.
4. Be consistent in your language, especially when referring to specific quantities. If you call it GROSS in one part of your flowchart, don't call it TOTAL somewhere else.
5. Be neat, please!

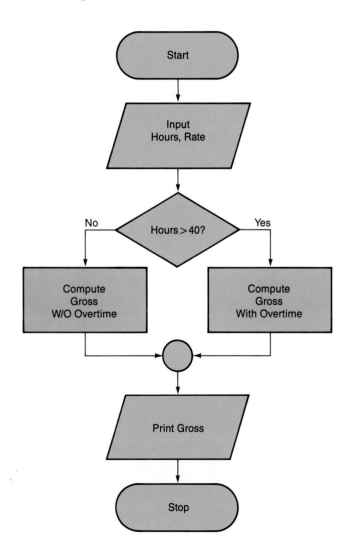

An Even Better Flowchart (Decision Symbol)

This process will figure out gross pay with overtime for anything over 40 hours.

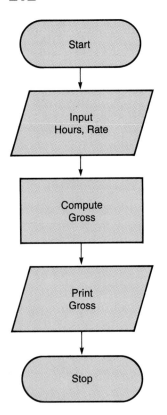

The Sequence Structure
Pseudocode

```
Input Hours, Rate
Compute Gross
Print Gross
```

The sequence structure is a simple list of instructions requiring no special pseudocode language.

STRUCTURED PROGRAMMING AND PSEUDOCODE

Another common program-design tool is **pseudocode,** literally meaning false code, which allows you to outline a process in fairly simple but consistent human terms. Inherent in pseudocode is the concept of **structured programming,** which says that any computer process—no matter how complicated—can be described using various combinations of just three simple patterns called **control structures.** The more complicated the program, the more of these patterns you link together, but the whole thing is still made up of combinations of those three basic patterns.

Pseudocode is implemented in various ways in various organizations. We shall use it in its most basic and straightforward form. Most other implementations are simply embellishments on this.

Pseudocode instructions (called **statements**) are written in outline form using indentation to indicate subordinate parts of the process. Most of the statements are in plain English, except those that indicate the beginning and/or end of one of the control structures. These statements require more formalized language.

The Sequence Structure

The simplest of the three, the **sequence structure,** requires no special language at all. It is simply a list of instructions to be performed in order.

The Selection Structure

The **selection structure** requires that the computer evaluate some condition and follow one of two paths, depending upon whether or not the condition exists. We flowcharted such a structure using the decision symbol. To pseudocode this structure, we use special language and indenting. The pattern is:

In the selection structure, the capitalized words (**IF, THEN, ELSE,** and **END IF**) show the required parts of the pattern. Between IF and THEN is a condition or question that can be either true or false (Are sales greater than $1000?). If it is true (sales are greater than $1000), then the computer

The Selection Structure
Pseudocode

```
IF condition(s) THEN
    do one thing
ELSE
do another
END IF
```

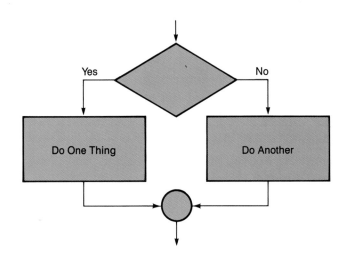

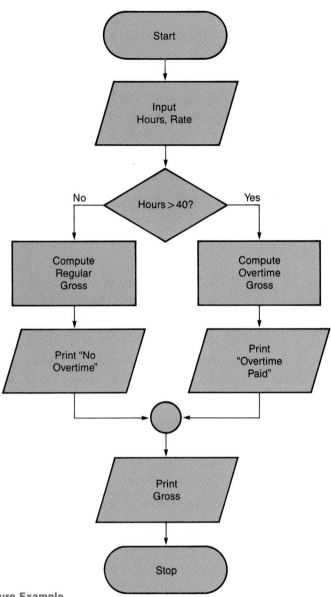

Selection Structure Example
Pseudocode

```
Input Hours, Rate
If Hours > 40 THEN
    Compute Gross using
     overtime formula
    Print "Overtime paid"
ELSE
    Compute Gross using regular formula
    Print "No overtime"
END IF
Print Gross
```

This example illustrates the selection structure. Note the capitalized words and the indenting.

The Iteration Structure

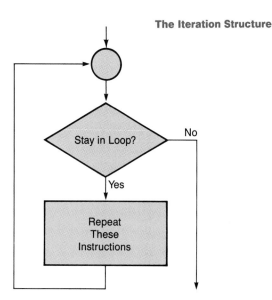

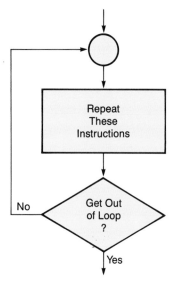

DO WHILE
Pseudocode

```
DO WHILE conditions for looping
    do these instructions
END DO
```

DO UNTIL
Pseudocode

```
DO UNTIL conditions for exiting
    do these instructions
END DO
```

will perform the instructions just below IF . . . THEN (pay the bonus). If it is not true (sales are less than or equal to $1000), the computer will perform the instructions below ELSE (pay normal commission). In either case, the two branches will come back together at END IF and go on to the next operation.

The Iteration Structure

Suppose that we had a simple program that took hours and pay rate and figured gross pay. That would work fine for one employee, but if we had a lot of them, we would want that set of instructions to repeat until we had paid all the employees. This is possible using the **iteration structure** or **loop,** which performs a single set of instructions more than once. Those instructions will iterate (repeat) or stop, depending on some conditions we have established.

There are two ways of stating the conditions. One, **DO WHILE,** states conditions for continuing the loop, performing the set of instructions again. These conditions are always tested for at the beginning of the loop, before the instructions in the loop are executed. The other, **DO UNTIL,** states the conditions for getting out of the loop and going on to the rest of the program. They are always tested for at the end of the loop. In either case, the words **END DO** signal the last statement of the loop. When the conditions for getting out of the loop have been met (or the conditions for

Iteration Structure Example

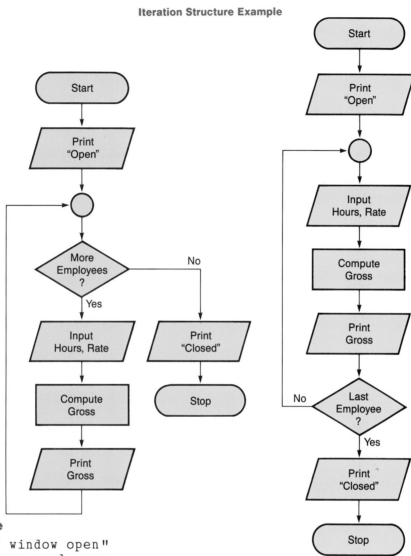

Pseudocode

```
Print "Pay window open"
DO WHILE more employees
     Input Name, Hours, Rate
     Compute Gross
     Print Name, Gross
END DO
Print "Pay window closed"

Print "Pay window open"
DO UNTIL last employee
     Input Name, Hours,
      Rate
     Compute Gross
     Print Name, Gross
END DO
Print "Pay window closed"
```

This shows both forms of the iteration structure. Notice the capitalized words, the indenting, and the difference in the flowcharts for the two processes.

staying in the loop are no longer met) the process should proceed with the statement following END DO.

Notice that if the iteration is set up by DO WHILE, the statements within the loop will never execute if the condition is not initially met. Since the test in the DO UNTIL loop is at the end of the structure, it will perform at least once, no matter what the conditions are.

Some Rules for Pseudocode

1. Use (and capitalize) special words for showing the selection and iteration structures.
2. Use plain English otherwise.

BOX 9-2

Will NEXT Usher In the Software of the Future?

The problem with computers is programming them: It always takes longer than planned, and the results rarely live up to expectations. That's because even after four decades of electronic computing, there is still no easy way to add major functions to a working program, nor to reuse pieces of it to build a new one. Instead, most programs get written from scratch, line by line, which takes time and tends to produce flimsy software that collapses under the weight of its own complexity. So the computer industry for years has longed for a way to build big programs the way bridges and skyscrapers are built—from small, prefabricated building blocks that can be trusted to work the first time, every time.

Now a major step is being taken toward that ideal. Software is beginning to be written in components, or "objects," that can be reused ad infinitum. So-called object-oriented programming promises not only to boost programmers' productivity but also to put powerful computing capabilities in the hands of non-techies. The success of Next Inc.'s new computer will be a key test and possibly a strong advertisement for the technique, since Next's primary software, or operating system, is largely object-oriented.

To make its programming easier, the Next machine comes with a starter set of about 30 software objects, or prewritten chunks of software, that customers can use as the foundations of their own programs. One Next object creates "windows" to display information on the screen. Bruce M. Blumberg, Next's man in charge of helping outsiders develop software for the new computer, says the window object can slash programming time from months to a matter of minutes. Another Next object provides text-editing facilities. All the Next objects can be tailored to new uses and "built into" many different programs at once.

Customers can create their own objects, too, and gain many benefits. Objects greatly simplify the task of building big programs by hiding complexity. The process is analogous to hardware engineers creating powerful machines from a few standard microchips. Programmers can use objects without knowing their internal workings, only the specific function that they perform. Object-oriented programs also can be modified quickly, which makes them useful for building prototypes of graphically complex programs.

Next itself is encouraging

Source: John W. Verity with Karen Frenkel, *Businessweek*, Oct. 24, 1988, p. 78.

3. Indent properly. It should be easy to tell which statements are part of which structure.
4. Be consistent in your language, especially when referring to specific quantities. If you call it GROSS in one part of your pseudocode, don't call it TOTAL somewhere else.
5. Be neat, please!

Some Rules for Structured Programming

1. Use only the structures outlined above. (Don't make up your own. Nobody will understand a DO DURING MAYBE THIS OR THAT.)

the creation of objects by specialist companies, at first in the educational field. For instance, says Blumberg, a set of objects could be created to help students build and watch simulated physics experiments. The objects might represent weights, springs, and simple machines.

This power and flexibility carries a price, though. Object-oriented programs consume more processing power than do traditional programs. More troublesome is that the new method requires software designers to analyze problems in a radically different manner. "It's a true paradigm shift," says Jeff McKenna, a software consultant in Tualatin, Ore. Those accustomed to traditional methods take up to six months to catch on to the object-oriented way. "About 10% of the people," McKenna adds, "just don't get it."

Yet the technology is catching on. Arthur Andersen & Co. is using it for financial accounting programs, while McDonnell Douglas Corp. is applying it to manufacturing systems. It is central to much work in artificial intelligence and advanced office automation. September saw 1,500 object-oriented fans meet at the third annual OOPSLA conference, which is dedicated to the subject. IBM seems convinced, too: It has licensed Next's software and the Objective-C language it's written in, and will soon convene 300 of its own software engineers for a private OOPSLA. Speaking there will be Alan Kay, the technology's leading advocate and a top scientist at IBM's archrival, Apple Computer Inc. Evidently, when it comes to software, IBM can be as objective as the next company.

2. Be sure that each structure has only one entry and one exit. Pseudocoding takes care of that for you, but when flowcharting, you might be tempted to exit a selection structure from both branches. Don't.
3. There are no limits on how structures may be combined. Any one may follow any other or be contained within any other. In fact, you may have structures within structures within structures and so forth.
4. Be sure your process fits the structures. You may have to alter your thinking a bit to make it fit.

SOME STRUCTURED-PROGRAM APPLICATIONS

The objective of structured programming is to make programs easier to read and write by making them simpler. Individual instructions for the computer are relatively easy to learn. Combining those instructions in some logical pattern makes programming difficult. By limiting the possible patterns to only the three control structures, you have less to learn and others you communicate with have less to try to figure out. Extremely complicated processes may still be designed, but they will all be combinations of the three basic structures.

In this section we will look at some typical programming applications and design processes for them.

Accumulating

Accumulating is the process of keeping a running total. The **accumulator** is kind of like a wishing well—every time someone walks past, they drop a coin in the well, increasing the total amount in the well. In the physical terms of the computer, the accumulator is a location in main memory, and every time the computer executes an accumulation instruction, another value is thrown in, adding to the value already there.

Accumulators are used constantly in programming. For example, let us say that we are writing a program for the local office of the March of Quarters (inflation has struck) fund-raising drive. At the end of the day, they would like to know the total of all the donations taken in by all their volunteers. As each volunteer comes in, the amount collected is put into the computer. After they have all reported, the total is printed out.

Notice that there are really three structures here, each nested inside another. The innermost one is a sequence, inputting and accumulating the collections; the next is an iteration, doing that sequence while there are more volunteers; and the overall one is another sequence, starting with a zero total, doing all the inputting and accumulating, and finally printing the results.

Counting

A counter is really a specialized type of accumulator. Instead of putting any old number into the accumulator, every time the computer executes a

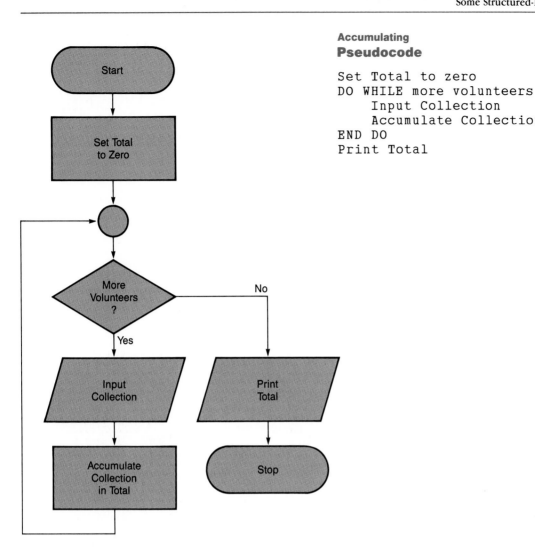

```
Set Total to zero
DO WHILE more volunteers
    Input Collection
    Accumulate Collection into Total
END DO
Print Total
```

counting statement, the same number is put in—one if you are counting by ones, five if you are counting by fives, and so forth.

Let us modify the program for the March of Quarters so that we not only print out the total collected but also the average collected per volunteer.

Multiple Selection

Our factory pays workers a basic hourly wage plus a piece rate of $2 each, if they assemble up to 100 widgets; $2.10 each, if they assemble up to 150; or $2.20 each, if they assemble over 150. Our program must figure out each employee's gross pay.

We can figure the base pay using a sequence structure. To figure the bonus, we must have a selection structure, but one with three possible branches. Since the selection structure only permits two branches, we must use more than one selection.

A selection structure allows only two branches. If more are needed,

Counting
Pseudocode

```
Set Total, Counter to zero
DO WHILE more volunteers
    Input Collection
    Accumulate Collection into Total
    Add one to Counter
END DO
Compute Average
Print Total and Average
```

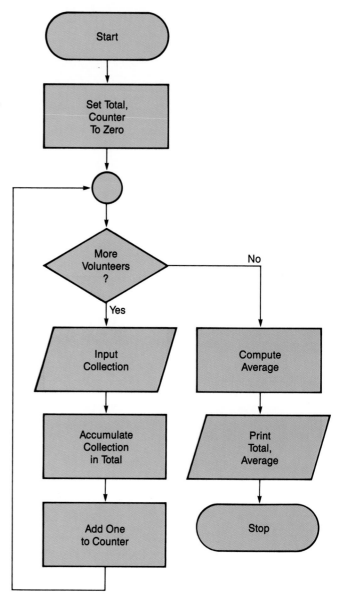

more selection structures will have to be used. You will need one less selection than there are possible branches. In this case, there are three possible branches, so two selections are used. If it is not the first or the second, it must be the third, so there is no need to test for it.

Notice again the combinations of structures. The overall structure is an iteration. Within that, there is a sequence. Within that, a selection. And within the THEN branch of the selection, another selection.

MODULAR PROGRAMMING

Two old sayings are, "Don't bite off more than you can chew" and "Divide and conquer." We can combine those into one and say, "Divide it and you

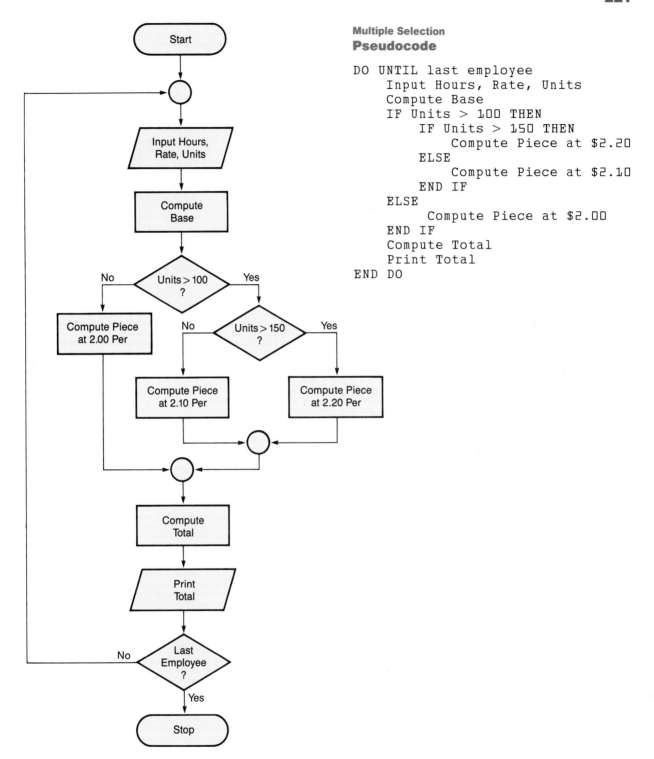

Pseudocode

```
DO UNTIL last employee
    Input Hours, Rate, Units
    Compute Base
    IF Units > 100 THEN
        IF Units > 150 THEN
            Compute Piece at $2.20
        ELSE
            Compute Piece at $2.10
        END IF
    ELSE
        Compute Piece at $2.00
    END IF
    Compute Total
    Print Total
END DO
```

Top-Down Programming

This program was written in modular, top-down fashion. The first macroprogram contains only a brief overview of the major steps involved. Each of the statements is really a module, covering large chunks of the process. Each of these modules is refined into more detailed modules (here we have shown only the breakdown of one module at each level) until the last breakdown yields a detailed microprogram.

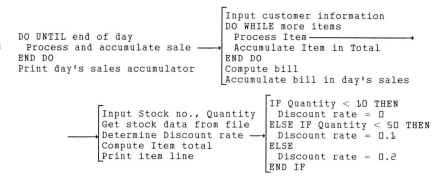

```
DO UNTIL end of day
  Process and accumulate sale ——→
END DO
Print day's sales accumulator
```

```
⌈ Input customer information
| DO WHILE more items
|   Process Item ——————————→
|   Accumulate Item in Total
| END DO
| Compute bill
⌊ Accumulate bill in day's sales
```

```
⌈ Input Stock no., Quantity
| Get stock data from file
→ Determine Discount rate ——→
| Compute Item total
⌊ Print item line
```

```
⌈ IF Quantity < 10 THEN
|   Discount rate = 0
| ELSE IF Quantity < 50 THEN
|   Discount rate = 0.1
| ELSE
|   Discount rate = 0.2
⌊ END IF
```

can chew it better." If we are assigned some massive computer task, we can take heart in the knowledge that all computer processes can be designed using only the three control structures, and that a complicated process is made up of a lot of simple processes. All we have to do is to divide our massive task into a number of small, easy tasks. Easier said than done, you say. Perhaps, but there are some techniques that will help.

One way is to initially state a computer task in its simplest terms, using only general processes and not worrying about the detail that must fill in those processes. For example, suppose that we had an on-line sales system that asked the salesperson for stock numbers and quantities sold, looked up and printed the names and list prices of each item, figured the total price of each item less some quantity discount, printed out the total price, subtracted a trade discount, added tax, and printed the final total. At the end of the day, the computer would print out total sales for the day.

We could approach this task by initially writing a **macroprogram** or **modular** description of the task. Each **module** is a major portion of the task that will be broken down into submodules, those into sub-sub-modules, and so forth until the last breakdown results in the actual or **microprogram** showing all the instructions that have to be performed. We refer to this process as **top-down programming.** The figure above shows a pseudocode example of modular, top-down programming.

WRITING THE PROGRAM

Once the design is completed using flowcharts and/or pseudocode, it is translated into whatever programming language is to be used on your computer. Programming using the BASIC language is discussed in the supplement *Introducing BASIC.*

TESTING

A program is not completed until you convince both yourself and the users that it works. The more complicated it is, the greater the opportunity for "bugs"—little insidious problems that always seem to arise. This means that you must test it extensively, find any problems that may exist, and

---

BOX 9-3

BUGS!

Grace Hopper was one of the pioneers of the electronic computer and contributed much in the area of software development (see the essay on history). She also added some color to computer terminology with the term "debug." According to Captain Hopper, "In 1945, while working in a World War I–vintage, non-air-conditioned building on a hot, humid summer day, the computer stopped. We searched for the problem and found a failing relay—one of the big signal relays."

"Inside, we found a moth that had been beaten to death. We pulled it out with tweezers and taped it to the log book. From then on, when the officer came in to ask if we were accomplishing anything, we told him we were 'debugging' the computer."

"debug" it. In testing, you must anticipate every condition or situation that could arise in the use of your program and make sure that it will perform correctly in any combination of these. If a program is designed in modules, it is a good idea to do **modular testing**—wringing out each module separately before assembling them into a complete program.

In any case, the program should work under all foreseeable conditions before delivering it to a user.

DOCUMENTATION

Writing documentation is like eating your spinach. "It's good for you." But it usually isn't much fun. **Documentation** is all those things that explain your program and its functions to humans, both yourself and others. You may think that writing documentation for yourself is a waste of time—after all, you wrote the program. However, it is easy to forget why you did certain things, or how individual parts fit into the entire task.

We have put documentation at this late point in the text, but it is really something that should be done continuously as the program is designed and written. If writing all the documentation is left until the program is completed, first, you will not have it to refer to while writing, and next, you won't remember the program well enough to write the documentation.

Program Documentation

Program documentation exists for two sets of people: the programmer who wrote the program, and other data-processing people who must understand the program. These other DP people might have to change or finish the

BOX 9-4   People Focus

Programmers: <u>Not</u> a Breed Apart

Stereotyped personality defects are far from unique to the field.

Proponents of robopsychology warn that computers can be hazardous to our mental health and emotional well-being. They tell us that programmers who spend long hours at their terminals learn to respond to the world as they do on line.

Do programmers expect instant gratification in all things? Are they impatient, uncompromisingly logical and, as a result, uncreative?

I am an intensive computer user and do have some of the personality traits mentioned, such as an occasional shortage of patience and less-than-ideal social skills. However, I had these traits long before I first touched fingers to a keyboard, which wasn't until I was in graduate school. My self-analysis may not be accurate, but I see no sign that my computer experience has exaggerated these behaviors.

Computing is not a very old field. I suspect that most programmers who have been in the field for several years were adults at the time of their first encounter with a computer, and I seriously doubt that their exposures to programming have been at all responsible for any radical change in their personalities.

I suspect that programming just happens to attract people who already feel a large amount of frustration in social situations. They find they can withdraw into an environment in which they have a great deal of control —control they lack in their social lives.

Certainly this running away is not the healthiest approach to the problem, but you cannot lay the blame for fleeing on the destination.

If computers did not exist, then surely these individuals would withdraw into something else. Would they become mechanics and work under the hood of a car? Sheepherders in the mountains? Night watchmen?

Some people in those professions probably chose their occupations for unhealthy reasons, but the occupation itself is not at fault. The worst you could say about these jobs is that they serve as attractive havens for social misfits.

I see computers as having the power and flexibility to enhance creativity, not stifle it. There is plenty of opportunity in programming for flashes of insight and creative problem solving. It is no less creative to analyze a problem for a computer solution than to analyze one for any other type of solution.

Debate, trial law and mathematics also require a disciplined, logical approach to problem solving. Do lawyers or mathematicians lack creativity?

Creativity is determined by the purposes for which a tool is used, not by the method of applying the tool. Have you ever seen nail art? Is the hammer used differently for this purpose than for the purpose of fastening shingles to a roof? Certainly not, yet very different amounts of creativity are involved.

Let me provide some examples of real-life problem solving.

Case A: Joe is a good professional programmer. When he wants to work with a new software package, the first thing he does is sit down and read the manual or at least browse through it extensively. When he gets an error message, he collects all pertinent information—with great attention to detail—and thinks the problem out before taking action. He often spends hours poring over obscure hexadecimal printouts in order to find the source of a bug.

Frankly, there aren't very many people out there like Joe—people who can correctly solve a problem in the least amount of time without making things worse first.

But his ability in this area does not come out of an expectation of instant gratification. On the contrary, it is because of his sheer patience in working things through. Joe may appear to get results quickly, but only because he handles a situation with a minimal amount of hysteria and wasted motion.

Case B: Fred is an ordinary business user of computers, a typical manager.

Now here is a guy who really expects instant gratification. He won't take the time to pick up the manual for any reason, because he has to have an answer *right now*. Looking in the manual would take too much time. Instead, Fred will usually just call Joe. Fred has a thousand excuses for doing so, such as, "I can't find the information I want in these gobbledygook manuals," which means that he never learned to use an index and table of contents.

Of course, Fred is in such a tearing hurry for instant solutions that he can't take time to figure out exactly what it is that he needs to know. So Joe has to patiently tease the information out of him by asking a number of questions to define the problem clearly. Joe knows that Fred will often only read half of the error message to him over the phone, because Fred is in too much of a rush to really see the screen that he's looking at.

Fred also has a number of other interesting habits. For example, if a command produces an error, he will often issue the same command again in the same way, sometimes repeatedly. His intuitive, nonlogical, "human" thought process seems to tell him that the command will work if he insists on it.

Even worse, sometimes Fred feels that he doesn't have time to even call Joe, much less pick up the manual. So he begins to play word association games, entering any and every command that pops into his mind. Surely one of them will get him the quick results he needs. When he finally has things totally hashed, then he'll holler for Joe to come fix it. By that time, he's created hours of work for Joe, but he's still in a rush, so he relieves his frustration by hovering over Joe and chewing him out.

Funny thing, but Fred seems to be treating poor Joe like an extension of the machine. Oh well, after all, Joe is supposed to be an expert in this stuff, right? We expect miracles from the shamans who understand the machines, even when they protest that what they do isn't magic.

But Joe had better not so much as hint that Fred has been proceeding in an unreasonable or irrational manner, because Fred is nobody's dummy, and no snotty programmer is going to tell him that he's being careless, hasty or unobservant.

In my experience, there are at least 10 "Freds" in the world for every "Joe." I can give you dozens of real-life horror stories of just this kind of Fred behavior. If computers really do change their users, training them to think before acting and to consider several possibilities and alternatives, then more power to them. But the skills involved in programming are the same skills needed to do library research.

Source: Brett Middleton, *Computerworld*, April 4, 1988, p. 63.

program after the original programmer has left the job, or the program might be part of a system of programs and other programmers must refer to it.

The program documentation should consist of a prose description of the purposes and functions of the program, flowcharts and/or pseudocode, and the program itself. The actual program should be thoroughly commented. Each language has a type of statement that is not really an instruction to the computer but serves to include comments or notations in the program. Each module or subsection should have a comment that tells what that section does. For example, "This section figures out the discount percentage." When either the programmer or someone else reads the program, he or she will not have to spend time deciphering programming language to find out what is going on. Anything that might not be understood should be commented on.

User Documentation

Since programs are written for users, the analyst or programmer must tell the user what the capabilities of the program are and how to get information from it. This documentation might consist of a few paragraphs, in layman's language, about what the program can do for the user, what data the program needs from the user, and what buttons to push or forms to fill out to get information from the program.

THE WALL STREET JOURNAL

"I program, therefore I am. . . ."

SUMMARY

Writing programs is important, but it is only a part of a detailed procedure for developing computer information systems. As part of the overall procedure, program specifications are developed. These must include detailed descriptions of the outputs the programs are to produce, the inputs needed to provide the data, and the processes the computer must perform to get from input to output.

Programmers often use (or are often required to use) various design tools to make programming easier, more standard, and more understandable to others. One design tool is the flowchart, which is made up of symbols—indicating various operations—and lines connecting the symbols. Some important symbols are the terminal, input/output, process, decision, and connector symbols.

Using the techniques of structured programming, a programmer can design complicated programs using combinations of only three control structures: sequence, selection, and iteration.

Pseudocode is a design tool that specifically uses the principles of structured programming. It consists of written statements, some key words to specify the various control structures, and indenting to indicate how the structures are combined in the program. The common sets of key words are IF THEN ELSE and END IF for a selection structure, and DO WHILE or DO UNTIL and END DO for an iteration structure.

There are a number of routines that show up in many different programs. We looked at the processes of accumulating; keeping running totals; counting; and multiple selection—having many branches in a program.

Using modular programming, a programmer can view a task in simple, macroprogram modules, then break down each module into more complicated submodules and so on until a complete microprogram, with all the required instructions in it, is made.

Before being used, a program must be tested and documented for other programmers and for users. Documentation is an ongoing process; it should be done at all stages of program development, not left to the end of the process.

KEY WORDS

(in order of appearance in text)
Flowchart
Terminal symbol
Input/output symbol
Process symbol
Connector
Branch
Decision symbol
Pseudocode
Structured programming
Control structure

Statement
Sequence structure
Selection structure
IF
THEN
ELSE
END IF
Iteration structure
Loop
DO WHILE

DO UNTIL
END DO
Accumulator
Macroprogram
Modular programming
Module
Microprogram
Top-down programming
Modular testing
Documentation

REVIEW QUESTIONS

1. What kinds of things must be done before a program is written in computer language?

2. In developing program specifications, which part of the data-processing cycle should be considered first? Second? Third?

3. Draw the flowchart symbols used for arithmetic operations, for printing information, for stopping a program, for creating branches in a program, and for connecting two lines together.

4. How many lines may a decision symbol have going into it? Coming out of it?

5. How many lines may a terminal symbol have going in or out of it?

6. How many lines may an input/output symbol or a process symbol have going into it? Coming out of it?

7. Name the three control structures and describe the functions of each.

8. Show the proper form for a simple selection structure using flowchart symbols and lines. Do the same using pseudocode key words.

9. Show the proper form for an iteration structure where the conditions are tested for at the beginning in both flowchart symbols and pseudocode key words.

10. Show the proper form for an iteration structure where the conditions are tested for at the end in both flowchart symbols and pseudocode key words.

11. How many ways can there be into an entire selection structure? Out of it?

12. Which kind(s) of structure(s) may not be nested within other structures?

13. Describe the process of accumulation. Counting.

14. Name and describe the process for branching in more than two ways in a program.

15. Why do we use top-down programming? Describe the process.

16. What kinds of documentation should a program have and when should it be written?

THINK ABOUT IT

1. Adams County has a 7 percent sales tax rate while the rest of the state has 6. Flowchart and pseudocode a program to print out the amount owed on a purchase including sales tax given the amount of the purchase and the county.

2. Flowchart and pseudocode a program to compare two strings. The program should print out which string is greater than which or that they are equal.

3. Good people all have last names that begin with the letters G through L, all the others are bad. Flowchart and pseudocode a program that differentiates the good people from the bad.

4. Flowchart and pseudocode a program that will figure the average of any number of values input into the computer. The value zero should be used to signal the end of input.

5. Flowchart and pseudocode a program that converts feet to meters. Use a FOR loop. It should go from one to ten feet in half foot steps. One meter equals 3.28083 feet.

6. Flowchart and pseudocode a program to assign letter grades given numeric scores. A score of 90 or above is a A; 80, B; 70, C; 60, D; and below 60, F. The program should stop when a score of −1 in input.

CHALLENGES

1. Find out from your school or a local company what kind(s) of design tools they use in developing programs. Why did they choose those particular ones?

2. Salespeople at Sagacious Systems, Inc., are paid monthly on a salary plus graduated commission plan. They receive $1000 plus 6 percent of the first $10,000 they sell, 8 percent of the next $10,000, and 10 percent of anything over $20,000. At the end of each month, sales orders for each of the salespeople are sent to data processing where the sales amounts are input and gross pay for each salesperson is figured. At the end of the process, the computer prints out total sales and total commissions paid. Flowchart and pseudocode the program to perform this task. Do it in top-down, modular fashion, showing the initial macroprogram and each step in breaking down the modules into submodules.

10 PROGRAMMING LANGUAGES

PREVIEW

In the last chapter we talked about the process of programming. Here we will look at some of the more popular programming languages and comparisons between them. From this chapter you should gain knowledge of:

■ Language levels and why they exist.

■ Some characteristics of machine languages.

■ What assembly languages are and how they relate to machine language.

■ Some of the general characteristics of high-level languages.

■ The programs that translate assembly and high-level languages into machine language.

■ Some of the high-level languages, their characteristics, and comparisons between them.

Wouldn't it be nice if all computers spoke the same language? Wouldn't it be nice if all people spoke the same language? People speak different languages because various groups developed their languages separately from the other groups. There was no need or even a mechanism for standardization. To a small extent this same phenomenon occurred with computer languages. Principally, however, different computer languages developed because different people had different uses for the computer, or they thought that they had some better way of communicating with it. Some new languages were improvements on old ones, some were just different.

We shall see that the variety of languages causes us some difficulty—we would probably have to learn more than one to be effective in the computer world. We shall also see that some of the differences are quite meaningful. Some languages are especially good at certain applications and others better at other ones. If you continue in the computer field, you will find that, once you learn one language, you have passed the greatest barrier—learning how to program—and you will learn other languages much more easily.

LANGUAGE LEVELS

Computers don't understand English. In fact, they don't "understand" anything at all, they simply react to instructions. Remember, a computer is nothing but a huge mass of switches. Early computer "programming," such as on the ENIAC, consisted of flipping switches and plugging in wires, not a very satisfactory way of communicating with the computer. Subsequent computers were programmed by loading the switch settings into the computer from some outside source like a keyboard or punched cards.

We saw in Chapter 4 that the CPU is only capable of working with zeros and ones, for both data and programs. Some very early experimental computer programs were written in zeros and ones. The instructions to direct the computer to perform a calculation might look like this:

0010010100100101011100111101001011010100101011101011010101

That was not a very satisfactory way of communicating with the computer either. Unfortunately, the CPU must have zeros and ones to work with, so ultimately that is what it must get.

In 1951, the UNIVAC I became the first major computer to accept a language other than zeros and ones. The programmer could write a program using **alphanumeric** (alphabetic and numeric) characters and the computer would translate it into the zeros and ones that it needed to function. This led to the development of various levels of computer language; from machine language—the actual zeros and ones that the CPU works with—to high-level languages that look almost like English.

MACHINE LANGUAGE

The native, or **machine language,** of a computer is still zeros and ones. Each kind of CPU has an instruction set built into it—patterns of zeros and

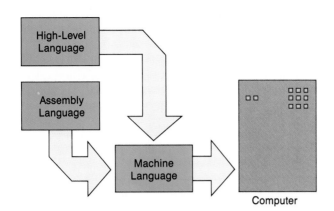

Language Levels
At higher levels, computer languages become more humanlike and deal less with the detail of the computer hardware. All computer programs must be translated into machine language to be executed, however, because that is the only language the computer understands.

ones that it recognizes and reacts to. These instructions are for very basic and elementary functions within the CPU, such as moving a word of data from a memory location to a data register or subtracting one value from another. They are the types of instructions we looked at in our simple addition example in Chapter 4. To do anything worthwhile, like the simple addition, it takes many machine-language instructions. Machine-language programs tend to become quite long, complicated, and unreadable.

We use the term machine language to define a class of languages. There are many different machine languages because each type of CPU has its own, which may differ significantly from that of another CPU. This means that a program that works on one type of CPU, say an Intel 80486, will not work on another, say a Motorola 88000.

every CPU has different language.

It simply is not practical to program in straight machine language. Humans do not think naturally in zeros and ones, and the programming would not be efficient. Also, since each different model of machine has a different language, you would probably end up having to learn many of them to be versatile and employable. Besides, there are easier ways to program.

ASSEMBLY LANGUAGE

Assembly languages use the same instruction sets as machine languages. The principal difference is that assembly languages use alphanumeric characters instead of zeros and ones. The instructions are given **mnemonic** (pronounced ne-mon'-ik and meaning memory aid) codes that give some indication of the instruction to be performed. For example, the instruction to add a value to one in a register may be ADD (instead of some machine language instruction like 10001011); comparing one value to another might be CMP.

CMP = compare

Memory locations are given symbolic addresses like NETPAY (instead of 001010010100101110011011), or HOURS. Using an assembly rather than a machine language reduces programming time because it is more readable; you can look at your own program and make some sense out of it, and the instructions are easier to remember. However, since assembly language is nothing more than machine language written with characters, the programs must be just as long and complicated. In fact, they must be slightly longer in assembly language because many of the symbolic names you use must be equated to actual numeric values, requiring more instructions.

Both assembly- and machine-language instructions are made up of **operators** (the actual instructions) and **operands** (the values, registers, or memory locations that the instruction will affect). Assembly-language instructions also have a column for **labels,** symbolic names for memory locations. For example, in one assembly language, an instruction might look like this:

TOTAL	ADD	NET, TAX
Label	Operator	Operands

The label—TOTAL, in this case—refers to the location of the program instruction in memory. If you wanted to go to this section of the program from some other, you could instruct the computer to perform the instruction at TOTAL next. The ADD operator instructs the computer to take the value stored at the memory location referred to by the second operand, TAX, and add it to the value at NET, leaving the result in NET.

With certain assembly languages, the number of instructions can be reduced by using **macros** (macro-instructions), single labels that refer to a series of instructions. For example, if your program printed something at the printer many times, you could write the printing instructions (perhaps a dozen or more) as a macro and assign the label PRINT to them. Every time you wanted to print, you would tell the computer to execute the PRINT macro instead of writing the instructions all over again. Using a macro-assembly language can reduce the number of instructions to many less than that of machine language.

Assemblers

Computers can run only machine language, so assembly language is translated into machine language by another program called an **assembler.** Each type of computer must have a different assembler program because the machine (and possibly the assembly) languages are different.

When you write an assembly language program, you first write the instructions in your assembly language (called **source code**) and then you assemble it—run it through the assembler program to translate it to machine language (called **object code**). This leaves you with two programs, one in source code that you can read and one in object code that the computer can run. During the assembly step, the assembler may detect errors such as incorrect symbols used or labels referred to that have not been defined. It will print out these errors and you will have to correct them in the source code and reassemble the program.

Many assemblers allow you to combine the object code you have developed with object code that has been developed before. Perhaps you

```
        LXI   H,NUMBERS   ;SET MEMORY LOCATION COUNTER TO
                          ;LOCATION OF VALUES TO BE COMPARED
        MOV   B,M         ;FIRST VALUE IS NUMBER OF VALUES TO
                          ;BE COMPARED. PUT IN REGISTER B
        SUB   A           ;SET REGISTER A TO ZERO
NEXT    INX   H           ;INCREMENT MEMORY COUNTER (NEXT VALUE)
        CMP   M           ;COMPARE VALUE IN A WITH VALUE IN MEMORY
        JNC   COUNT       ;IF A GREATER, DO COUNT INSTRUCTION NEXT
        MOV   A,M         ;M GREATER, MOVE TO A
COUNT   DCR   B           ;DECREMENT (SUBTRACT ONE FROM) B
        JNZ   NEXT        ;IF COUNTER NOT ZERO, DO NEXT VALUE
        STA   MAXIMUM     ;ALL DONE, PUT A IN MEMORY LOCATION FOR
                          ;MAXIMUM NUMBER
        JMP   0           ;END PROGRAM
MAXIMUM DS    1           ;LOCATION WHERE MAXIMUM WILL BE PUT
NUMBERS DS    1           ;NUMBER OF VALUES TO COMPARE
        DS    100         ;RESERVE ROOM FOR UP TO 100 VALUES HERE
```

Assembly Language Program

These assembly-language instructions direct the computer to find the maximum of a series of values. Symbolic labels for memory locations are in the first column. The second column contains the operators, and the third, the operands. Anything after a semicolon on a line is not part of the instruction; it is only a comment. These instructions are only a part of an actual program; notice that there are no inputs or outputs.

are using common routines that you have already written for some other program or that came from some other programmer. At this stage you will use a program called a **linker** to link, or combine, your new object code with any other object code that you need.

When the program assembles and links error free, you now have **executable code** that may be loaded in the computer's main memory and run. An error-free assembly and link does not mean that the program is perfect, however, only that the individual instructions are valid. It still may have run-time errors—when the program is run, the computer is unable to accomplish an instruction, such as trying to send data to a channel that does not exist—or logical errors—the program runs but does the wrong thing. These errors are more difficult to debug than are assembler errors.

HIGH-LEVEL LANGUAGES

High-level languages make the computer even easier to communicate with. They simplify programming by making instructions more English-like and by making one instruction in the high-level language substitute for several machine-language instructions. For example, in one high-level language, the instruction

ADD MIDTERM TO FINAL GIVING GRADE

moves two values from main memory, adds them together, and puts the result in another place in main memory, much like the simple addition we did in Chapter 4. The statement looks like ordinary English, and it performs the job of several machine-language instructions.

As we said before, computers can only run machine language, so we have other programs—compilers or interpreters—to translate the high-level languages into the proper machine language. As with assembly language, there must be one compiler or interpreter for each combination of high-level language and computer type.

Compilers

A **compiler** works somewhat like an assembler. You write your program in the high-level language (the source code), compile it (translate it into machine-language object code), link the object code into an executable program, and run it. The compiler, of course, may detect errors just like the assembler, and these errors must be corrected in the source code before recompiling, linking, and running the program.

Again, just because the program compiles correctly does not mean that it will run correctly; it only means that the statements are valid, that you have followed the basic rules for each statement type. It still may not do the right thing. Commonly, programs are tested, modified, recompiled, re-linked, retested, remodified, and so forth until they produce the right results.

Industry Focus   BOX 10-1

Computer Viruses

The idea of a computer picking up some wandering microbe and coughing, sneezing, and acting sick is ludicrous . . . or is it? The latest thing to hit the computer industry is the computer virus, an illness of the computer that acts much like its biological counterpart. Both biological and electronic varieties are essentially information disorders. Biological viruses attack living cells by attaching scraps of genetic code—RNA and DNA—to the cells which trick the cells into reproducing the virus, thereby spreading it.

Electronic viruses attach scraps of computer code to the computer's memory which tricks the computer into making copies of the code and passing it on. Typically, a computer virus strikes when a user runs a program containing one. Like the biological variety, the virus is hidden, buried in the machine-language code of the executable program. The user doesn't know it is there. The virus replicates by attaching itself to the computer's disk-operating system. From then on, any other program that is run on the infected computer is also infected. If this program is passed on to another computer, the infection spreads.

There is a major difference between the biological and the electronic virus. The biological variety is a fact of nature. These viruses existed long before the existence of human beings. Computer viruses, on the other hand, were invented by humans. They are created for "sport," to demonstrate the programming prowess of the inventor, and to feed the inventor's ego.

The symptoms of computer viruses are as varied as those of the biological type. Some are relatively harmless. The "peace virus," for example, spread quietly until March 2, 1988. On that date, several thousand Macintosh owners, when they turned on their machines, were greeted by a drawing of the earth and a "universal message of peace." The message was cleared from the screen, the virus erased itself from the computer, and it disappeared without a trace.

Some, which were meant to be harmless, turned out not to be so. The "Christmas virus" of 1987 infected a world-wide, 350,000-terminal network operated by IBM. This happy creature flashed a Christmas message on the user's computer screen and then sent a copy of itself to every name on the user's electronic mailing list. The problem became serious when the network became clogged with Christmas messages and users could not get their work done.

Other viruses were specifically designed to be malicious. One was spread by

Interpreters

The result of a compilation and link is three programs—one in the source code that you wrote, one in object code, and the third in executable code which the computer runs. The source code is generally stored off line somewhere, the object code generally dumped, and the executable code kept in secondary storage where it can be easily loaded into main memory and run.

An **interpreter** does not produce three programs. This program does a run-time translation and execution of each line of source code. In other words, you load the source code into main memory and "run" it. The interpreter takes each source code instruction in turn, translates it into machine language, and executes it. The translation is not saved. Instead, each time the program is run it is retranslated.

two brothers from their computer store in Lahore, Pakistan, to "punish" computer owners for pirating (making unauthorized and un-paid-for copies of) commercial software. The brothers made bootleg copies of popular software packages such as WordStar and Lotus 1-2-3, which cost several hundred dollars in their authorized versions, and sold them for as little as $1.50 each. These bargain disks contained a virus which was spread to other software and machines and, in many cases, wiped out all the data on the infected computers.

It is estimated that this so-called "brain" virus (after the brothers' shop, Brain Computer Services) infected at least 100,000 floppy disks, most of them in the United States, almost none in Pakistan. Pakistanis were sold uninfected disks. According to the brothers somewhat confused reasoning, since Pakistani copyright protection does not extend to software, Pakistanis were doing nothing wrong. But foreigners, especially Americans, "must be punished."

That was, unfortunately, but one of the malicious viruses going around. Another deletes everything on the computer's disk and prints GOTCHA! on the screen. Still another produces an animation featuring the singer Madonna, erases all the files on the disks, and then prints, "You're stupid to download a video about rock stars."

The list of harmful viruses gets longer all the time. The problem has become so serious that many companies pay "virus doctors," special consultants, $100 per hour or more to detect and rid them of infections. Software companies have jumped into the fray by writing and selling "vaccine" programs which reside in the computer and detect and eliminate viruses before they have a chance to attack. Like its biological counterpart, however, as vaccines kill off the current viral strains, new ones appear.

What is the best protection against computer viruses? Abstinence! Don't download programs from networks and bulletin boards, don't trade disks with other users, and don't use bootleg software. Even those measures don't offer 100 percent protection. It is to be hoped that the misguided minds that produce the computer viruses, like those that gave us poison Tylenol and razor blades in Halloween candy, will tire of their games. It will probably get worse, however, before it gets better. As one industry sage predicts, "We ain't seen nothing yet."

A Sample Program

We will use this program to illustrate various high-level programming languages.

Pseudocode

```
Set Total sales to zero
Open Sales file
Print report heading
DO WHILE more records in Sales
   Read Name, Qrtrly sales from Sales
   Compute Yearly sales
   Print Name, Yearly sales
   IF Yearly sales > 1000000 THEN
      Print "Exceptional"
   ELSE
      IF Yearly sales > 500000 THEN
         Print "Average"
      ELSE
         Print "Poor"
      ENDIF
   ENDIF
   Accumulate Yearly in Total sales
END DO
Print Total sales
```

File

```
MAYNARD JONES,225435,415062,
   173380,122027
EULALIA SMITH,430048,209653,
   322112,235408
and so forth
```

Output

```
SALESPERSON          SALES      PERFORMANCE

MAYNARD JONES        935922     AVERAGE
EULALIA SMITH       1197221     EXCEPTIONAL
and so forth

TOTAL SALES = $  30482129
```

Most interpreters are **interactive,** they carry on a dialog with the programmer. When the programmer types in a statement, the interpreter immediately checks it to see whether it makes sense. If it does, it is stored in main memory with the other program statements. If it does not, it is rejected and a diagnostic-error message is sent back to the programmer's terminal. At any time, the programmer may list his program (see what statements are stored in main memory) or run it (have the computer actually execute those instructions). This interaction makes programming easier because the programmer gets instant feedback on some errors (statements that don't make sense) and the program may be continually reviewed and tested as it is written.

Both types of translation programs have their advantages. Once the testing phase is completed, the compiled program never has to be translated again, but the interpreter must make a translation each time the

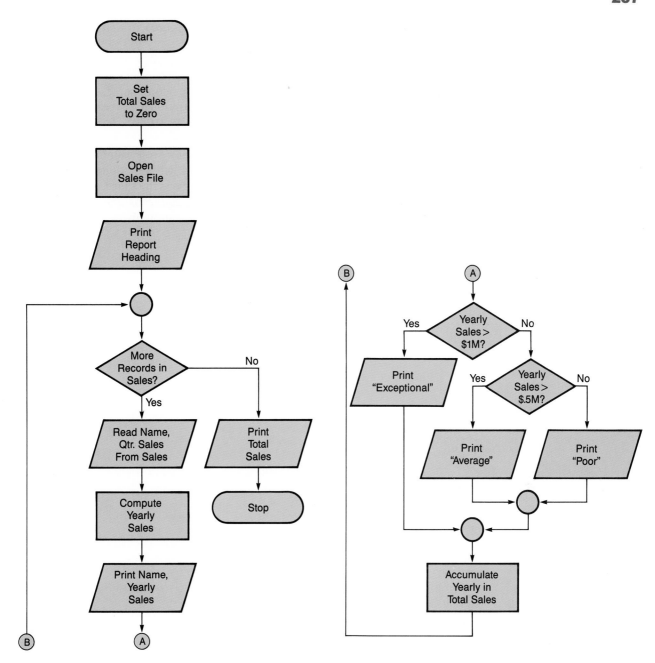

program is run. Therefore, programs that are compiled run much faster. However, it is easier to write programs using an interpreter because you can test run your program any time without compiling and linking it, and, with an interactive interpreter, you get instant feedback on many kinds of errors as soon as you type in a statement.

There are hundreds of different high-level languages—everyone seems to want to invent their own—but we shall limit our discussion to some of the more popular ones. To illustrate the various languages, we shall use the same program (as shown in the figure) written in each.

The program prints a report showing the sales and performance for each of the company's sales force. The data comes from a file called "SALSDATA" which contains each of the four quarter's sales for each salesperson. The program prints out each salesperson's name, total sales for the year, and whether their sales were exceptional (over $1,000,000), average (over $500,000), or poor (less than $500,000). At the end, the program prints the total sales for all salespeople.

We shall write this program in the various programming languages discussed in this chapter. The actual programs will look quite different in the different languages, even though the process is the same. In each case, we have chosen the simplest way to write the program, occasionally sacrificing some sophistication in technique or output form, but showing a direct solution to the task.

Basic

If you count the number of computers using a particular language, you would probably find that **BASIC** (Beginner's All-purpose Symbolic Instruction Code) is the most popular. Most microcomputers are sold with the BASIC language packaged with them, and many minicomputers, and some mainframes "speak" BASIC.

Our Program in BASIC

The program here was written using a minimal, interpreted BASIC. Following structured-programming guidelines is difficult and, at best, clumsy with such a BASIC.

Unstructured "Normal" BASIC

```
10   REM    PRINTS SALES AND PERFORMANCE REPORT FOR SALES FORCE
20   TOTAL=0
30   OPEN "SALES" FOR INPUT AS #1
40   PRINT "SALESPERSON     SALES              PERFORMANCE"
50   PRINT
60   REM  PRINT SALESPERSON LINES UNTIL AT END OF FILE
70   IF EOF(1) THEN 220
80   INPUT #1,NAME$,QTR1,QTR2,QTR3,QTR4
90   LET YEARLY=QTR1+QTR2+QTR3+QTR4
100  PRINT NAME$,YEARLY,
110  REM   DETERMINE PERFORMANCE RATING
120  IF T>1000000 THEN 180
130  IF T>500000 THEN 160
140  PRINT "POOR"
150  GOTO 190
160  PRINT "AVERAGE"
170  GOTO 190
180  PRINT "EXCEPTIONAL"
190  REM  ACCUMULATE TOTAL SALES FOR END OF REPORT
200  TOTAL=TOTAL+YEARLY
210  GOTO 70
220  REM  FINISH OFF REPORT
220  PRINT
230  PRINT "TOTAL SALES = $";TOTAL
240  END
```

BASIC was first invented at Dartmouth College way back in 1964. It was meant to fulfill three requirements.

1. Be easy to learn.
2. Encourage people to use the computer.
3. Handle most types of programming. (In those days, languages were classified as either scientific—they handled numbers and formulae well—or business—they handled character data and files well.)

BASIC succeeded on all three counts so well that it became adopted by many computer manufacturers and many companies that leased time on computers. Now, it is available for almost every general-purpose computer made.

Its success has also spawned one of its problems—its lack of standards. The original BASIC was a well-defined language; but as other people adopted it, they added enhancements to it to increase its performance and to make it do new things. Most of the enhancements were worthwhile, but instead of one set of enhancements and one expanded language, each company offering BASIC made essentially the same improvements in different ways. Now, we have many different dialects of BASIC, all doing just about the same things, but doing them slightly differently. For example, to put data from a file into a location in main memory, some BASICS use the statement INPUT #1,DATA while others require READ #1;DATA. The process is the same but the language is slightly different.

This program uses a structured, compiled BASIC, which allows the pseudocode to be directly translated into the program.

Structured, Compiled BASIC

```
REM    PRINTS SALES AND PERFORMANCE REPORT FOR SALES FORCE
DEFDBL A-Z                           'Allow for large numbers
Total = 0           'Accumulator for all sales at end of report
OPEN "SALES" FOR INPUT AS #1
PRINT "SALESPERSON     SALES           PERFORMANCE"
PRINT
DO WHILE NOT EOF(1)  '*******PRINT LINES UNTIL AT END OF FILE
   INPUT #1, Name$, Qtr1, Qtr2, Qtr3, Qtr4
   Yearly = Qtr1 + Qtr2 + Qtr3 + Qtr4   'Figure yearly totals
   PRINT Name$, Yearly,
   IF T > 1000000 THEN               'Determine performance rating
      PRINT "EXCEPTIONAL"
   ELSE
      IF T > 500000 THEN
         PRINT "AVERAGE"
      ELSE
         PRINT "POOR"
      END IF
   END IF
   Total = Total + Yearly 'Accumulate total for end of report
LOOP
PRINT
PRINT "TOTAL SALES = $"; Total
END
```

The American National Standards Institute (ANSI) published standards for what they termed "minimal BASIC," which are fine as far as they go; but they are, as the title states, minimal. They do not cover the newer enhancements, and so those are still up to the suppliers of the language. As a consequence, the standards have been less than widely implemented.

BASIC is meant to be a "free-form" language where the programmer can write statements without having to conform to a lot of restrictive rules. We shall see that other languages require some groundwork to be done (such as exactly what the output should look like or how the files are constructed) before actually writing instructions.

Most versions of BASIC are also interpreted and interactive, which means that the final program executes relatively slowly but that the programs are easier to write.

Another disadvantage of BASIC is that most implementations do not directly address the control structures (DO WHILE or IF THEN ELSE) that we discussed in the last chapter. These processes can, of course, be done, but somewhat clumsily in terms of structured programming.

Cobol

Before the early 1960s, no language was specifically suited to business (as opposed to scientific) tasks. In 1959, the United States Department of Defense, recognizing this and their need for such a language, sanctioned a group of users, manufacturers, and educational institutions called **CODASYL** (COnference on DAta SYstems Languages) to create an appropriate language. In 1960, that group came up with **COBOL** (COmmon Business-Oriented Language).

COBOL was a great success. In fact, more business programs are run using COBOL than any other language. The reason for the success is twofold. First, it directly and competently addressed the need for a business language. Second, the United States government would not buy a nonscientific computer without a COBOL compiler.

ANSI first published COBOL standards in 1960 and updated them in 1968, 1974, and 1985. One of the great advantages of COBOL is that the standards are generally adhered to.

A COBOL program is organized like the English language. Instructions are **sentences** that look almost like written English, with verbs (like READ, ADD, or DISPLAY) to tell the computer the operation to be performed. A number of sentences dealing with the same function are grouped together into a **paragraph.**

Although the individual statements (or sentences) look like plain English, COBOL is a very formalized language. Unlike BASIC, which you can almost write as you think, a COBOL program is divided into four divisions, each of which must be dealt with in order. The first, the **identification division,** shows the name of the program and may give any other documentation deemed necessary. This often includes the name of the programmer, the date the program was completed and/or last updated, and perhaps a few paragraphs about what the program does.

The **environment** or **configuration division** describes the specific hardware that is to be used with the program. This is the only machine-dependent part of the program. You should be able to take a program, and by making a few changes in this section, have it run on another, completely different computer.

The **data division,** as the title indicates, describes the data used in the program. You must detail the field and record formats of each file to be used in the program, the names of the main memory locations you will be using (like GROSSPAY or TAXRATE), and the formats of any output files you will be producing (what goes in which column in each report).

The last COBOL division is where a BASIC program starts. This is the **procedure division** that contains the actual instructions.

In addition to the formality of the four divisions, each sentence must be written to follow specific formats. Certain columns must contain certain types of information, and main memory and report parameters must be defined exactly in terms of number of characters allowed, where decimal points fall, and so forth.

Because COBOL is written in Englishlike form, using common terms and actual names for memory locations, it tends to be easy to read. You don't have to decipher a lot of esoteric code to make sense of it. It is somewhat **self documenting**—the statements explain themselves. This English-like property also tends to make programs quite long and wordy, and, although it reads like English, you cannot write it like English. COBOL requires very precise "sentence" structure and limited, exact vocabulary. You can get away with a little casualness in English, but not in COBOL.

```
IDENTIFICATION DIVISION.
    PROGRAM-ID.   COBOL-EXAMPLE.
    AUTHOR. ERIC R. STIETZEL.


ENVIRONMENT DIVISION.

CONFIGURATION SECTION.
    SOURCE-COMPUTER. FOOTHILL TANDEM.
    OBJECT-COMPUTER. FOOTHILL TANDEM.

INPUT-OUTPUT SECTION.
    FILE CONTROL.
        SELECT INPUT-FILE ASSIGN TO SALES.
        SELECT OUTPUT-FILE ASSIGN TO $S.

DATA DIVISION.

FILE SECTION.

FD'INPUT-FILE
    LABEL RECORDS ARE OMITTED
    RECORD CONTAINS 37 CHARACTERS
    DATA RECORD IS INPUT-RECORD.
01 INPUT-RECORD.
    05 INPUT-NAME            PIC X(13).
    05 FILLER               PIC X(01).
    05 FIRST-QUARTER        PIC 9(05).
    05 FILLER               PIC X(01).
```

Our Program in COBOL

```
        05  SECOND-QUARTER          PIC 9(05).
        05  FILLER                  PIC X(01).
        05  THIRD-QUARTER           PIC 9(05).
        05  FILLER                  PIC X(01).
        05  FOURTH-QUARTER          PIC 9(05).

    FD  OUTPUT-FILE
        LABEL RECORDS ARE OMITTED
        RECORD CONTAINS 36 CHARACTERS
        DATA RECORD IS OUTPUT-RECORD.
    01  OUTPUT-RECORD.
        05  OUTPUT-NAME             PIC X(16).
        05  YEARLY-SALES            PIC 9(06).
            88  POOR-PERFORMANCE                VALUE 0 THRU 500000.
            88  AVERAGE-PERFORMANCE             VALUE 500001 THRU 1000000.
            88  EXCEPTIONAL-PERFORMANCE         VALUE 1000001 THRU 10000000.
        05  FILLER                  PIC X(03).
        05  PERFORMANCE-LEVEL       PIC X(11).

    WORKING-STORAGE SECTION.

    01  HEADER                      PIC X(36)  VALUE.
              "SALESPERSON       SALES          PERFORMANCE".

    01  LINE-SKIP                   PIC S9(02) VALUE ZERO

    01  TOTAL-SALES-TEMP            PIC 9(08).

    01  TOTALS-OUTPUT.
        05  FILLER                  PIC X(14)  VALUE
              "TOTAL SALES =".
        05  TOTAL-SALES             PIC $ZZZZZZZZ9.

    PROCEDURE DIVISION.

    A00-MAIN-CONTROL.
        PERFORM A10-INITIALIZE.
        PERFORM B00-MAIN-PROCESS.
        PERFORM A50-FINALIZE.
        STOP RUN.

    A10-INITIALIZE.
        OPEN INPUT INPUT-FILE.
        OPEN OUTPUT OUTPUT-FILE.
        PERFORM R00-READ-INPUT-FILE.
        MOVE SPACES TO OUTPUT RECORD.

    A50-FINALIZE.
        CLOSE INPUT-FILE.
        CLOSE OUTPUT-FILE.

    B00-MAIN-PROCESS.
        PERFORM C00-PRINT-HEADER.
        PERFORM C10-PROCESS SALESPERSONS UNTIL INPUT-RECORD = HIGH VALUE.
        PERFORM C20-OUTPUT-TOTALS.
```

```
C00-PRINT-HEADER.
    MOVE HEADER TO OUTPUT-RECORD.
    MOVE -1 TO LINE-SKIP.
    PERFORM W00-WRITE-OUTPUT-RECORD.
    MOVE 1 to LINE-SKIP.
    PERFORM W00-WRITE-OUTPUT-RECORD.

C10-PROCESS-SALESPERSONS.
    MOVE INPUT-NAME TO OUTPUT-NAME.
    COMPUTE YEARLY-SALES = FIRST-QUARTER +
                           SECOND-QUARTER +
                           THIRD QUARTER +
                           FOURTH-QUARTER.
    ADD YEARLY-SALES TO TOTAL-SALES-TEMP.
    IF YEARLY-SALES = POOR-PERFORMANCE
    THEN
        MOVE "POOR" TO PERFORMANCE-LEVEL.
    IF YEARLY-SALES = AVERAGE-PERFORMANCE
    THEN
        MOVE "AVERAGE" TO PERFORMANCE-LEVEL.
    IF YEARLY-SALES = EXCEPTIONAL-PERFORMANCE
    THEN
        MOVE "EXCEPTIONAL" TO PERFORMANCE-LEVEL.
    MOVE 1 TO LINE-SKIP.
    PERFORM W00-WRITE-OUTPUT-RECORD.
    PERFORM R00-READ-INPUT-FILE.

C20-OUTPUT TOTALS.
    MOVE TOTAL-SALES-TEMP TO TOTAL-SALES.
    MOVE TOTALS-OUTPUT TO OUTPUT-RECORD.
    MOVE 2 TO LINE-SKIP.
    PERFORM W00-WRITE-OUTPUT-RECORD.

R00-READ-INPUT-FILE.
    MOVE SPACES TO INPUT-RECORD.
    READ INPUT-FILE
        AT END MOVE HIGH-VALUE TO INPUT-RECORD.

W00-WRITE-OUTPUT-RECORD.
    WRITE OUTPUT-RECORD AFTER LINE-SKIP.
    MOVE SPACES TO OUTPUT-RECORD.
    MOVE 0 TO LINE-SKIP.
```

NOTE: The program varies slightly from the flowchart and pseudocode because of the special requirements of the language and the program author's preferences.

Pascal

Pascal is one of the few language names that is not an acronym. It was named in honor of Blaise Pascal, a French mathematician, inventor, and philosopher who lived in the 1600s. It is also the first major language to be developed outside the United States. It was originally conceived by Professor Niklaus Wirth at the Swiss Federal Institute of Technology.

BOX 10-2

The Language of Languages

The community of Oblivion, Nevada, is about 100 miles away from anything you would want to call a town. To say it was isolated would be an overwhelming understatement. The residents had cause to be proud, though, because Luther Prescott, Del and Mary's boy, had been accepted at the university and was just now spending his first few days there.

Luther knew it would be strange among all these city folk, what with him not up on the latest lingo and all. Howsomever, what he found truly surprised him. While waiting in the registration line, he was surrounded by computer students and was picking up snatches of their conversations.

"Have you had MUMPS yet?" (Was there an epidemic going 'round?) "No, I'm going to try to get it next term from Professor Marks." (You sign up to have a teacher give you a disease?)

"I bought an Apple last week for seventeen hundred bucks." (I heard about inflation and a bad fruit harvest, but this is ridiculous. I'm glad Aunt Martha has a couple trees behind her barn.) "It came with AppleSoft [soft apples?] but I'm going to stuff Pascal in it and grind out some neat stuff." (Pascal is probably something like parsley, but what is she cooking?)

"How's your LISP coming?" "It's getting easier as I use it more." (These folk are tetched. This guy practices saying esses funny?) "I'm getting more Jovial next term." (It's nice to be happy.) "Are you rolling in SNOBOL yet?" (What?) "I'm going to try Ada this term." (Does he mean that he's going to get a date?)

The more Luther heard, the more confused he got. How was a poor country boy ever going to catch on to this new way of talking?

Most importantly, it was the first major language to be developed after the dissemination and acceptance of structured programming concepts. The DO WHILE (or WHILE DO as it is said in Pascal) and IF THEN ELSE structures are part of the language, and the language is modular. A Pascal program is composed of statements organized into blocks, which facilitates modular programming.

Like BASIC, Pascal is an all-purpose language, handling both scientific and business applications. It is only slightly more difficult to learn and write than BASIC, but often programs can be written in Pascal that execute more efficiently than if they were written in BASIC. It is somewhat more formal than BASIC, variables and other things must be declared at the beginning of the program before they can be used, but not as formal as COBOL with its four separate divisions and column restrictions.

Pascal has gained solid acceptance, especially in the academic world. Like BASIC, it was originally developed for use as a teaching language, but it has branched out far beyond the academic environment. Now it is available for almost all kinds of computers.

C

The programming language **C** is kind of an in-between language—either a low, high-level language or a high, low-level language. It consists of very

```
Program Sales (input, output);                    Our Program in Pascal

{Program is used to compute each person's total sales and
performance ranking}

Type persondata = record
                        name : string;
                         q1 : integer;
                         q2 : integer;
                         q3 : integer;
                         q4 : integer;
                    end;

Var  totalsales, yearlysales : integer;
                     person : persondata;
                     datafile : file of persondata;

begin
     totalsales := 0;
     assign(datafile,'diskfilename');
     reset(datafile);
     writeln('SALESPERSON      SALES        PERFORMANCE');
     writeln;
     while not eof(datafile) do begin
         read(datafile,person);
         yearlysales := person.q1+person.q2+person.q3
                        +person.q4;
         write (person, name, yearly sales);
         if yearlysales 1000000
             then writeln('EXCEPTIONAL')
             else begin
                     if yearlysales 500000
                         then writeln('AVERAGE')
                         else writeln('POOR')
                  end;
         totalsales := totalsales+yearlysales;
     end;
     writeln('TOTAL SALES=$',totalsales);
     close(datafile);
end.
```

few statements, mainly those dealing with storing values in main memory and the control structures. The rest of the language consists of functions, small subprograms that perform certain operations such as displaying a line of text on the screen. Many of these functions are supplied with the language, while with others you are expected to write them yourself. Functions may be written in C or in assembly language, allowing you access to the advantages of low-level programming.

C is becoming quite popular because it has a number of advantages over purely high-level languages. Structured and modular programming are not only allowed but demanded. The control structures are part of the language, and an entire program is made up of functions which are essentially modules. Low-level programming, control of individual areas of

246

Our Program in C

```
/* Prints sales and performance report for sales force */

#include "stdio.h"

FILE *sales_file;
double total=0; /* accumulator for sales for all employees */

main()
{   int x;
    double yearly;
    struct
    {   char name[14];
        double quarterly[4];
    } sales_rec;

    sales_file=fopen("SALES","r");
    printf("SALESPERSON         SALES       PERFORMANCE\n\n");
    while (read_struct(sales_file,&sales_rec,sizeof(sales_rec))
      != EOF) /* Print salesperson lines till at end of file */
    {   yearly=0;
        for (x=0;x<=3;++x)                  /* Figure yearly sales */
            yearly+=sales_rec.quarterly[x];
        printf("%13s    %9.0f",sales_rec.name,yearly);
        if (yearly > 1000000) /* Determine performance rating*/
            printf("EXCEPTIONAL\n");
        else if (yearly > 500000)
            printf("AVERAGE\n");
        else
            printf("POOR\n");
        total+=yearly; /* Accumulate total for end of report */


    }printf("\nTOTAL SALES = $ %f",total);
}

read_struct(file,strct,bytes) /* Reads structure from file */
    FILE *file;                     /* File to be read from */
    char *strct;                    /* Address of structure */
    int bytes;                      /*   Bytes in structure */

{   for (;bytes>0;--bytes,++strct)
    {   *strct=fgetc(file);
        if (*strct == EOF)
            if (feof(file) != 0) return (EOF);
    }
    return(0);
}
```

the computer, is possible with C where it is not with most high-level languages. With C, you can write programs that will execute about as efficiently as the computer will allow. Lastly, C will allow you to do just about anything.

That last advantage is also a disadvantage of C. Because it will allow you to do almost anything, it is very difficult to debug and very easy to get yourself in trouble. For example, the language does nothing to prevent you from writing over (and wiping out) parts of your own program or values stored in main memory.

Generally, it takes more lines of source code to write a program in C than in other languages. C programs, if not written very carefully, can be unreadable. Many programming shortcuts available that are "neat" to a dedicated nerd become indecipherable to us mere mortals.

Fortran

FORTRAN (for FORmula TRANslator), introduced in 1957, is one of the oldest programming languages in common use today. In 1966, ANSI released two sets of standards (one minimal and the other "full" or "extended"), making it the first standardized language. The standards were last revised in 1978. Although the standards exist and are often used, many companies have tried to improve on the standard FORTRAN, creating a lot of nonstandard versions. Unfortunately, many of the nonstandard versions are quite good and are heavily used, which means that, like BASIC, you constantly run into different language dialects in different installations.

FORTRAN was originally designed as a mathematical or scientific language and is still best suited for those purposes. It handles numbers and complicated formulae quite well, but does not do as well on file manipulation or character data as BASIC, COBOL, or many other languages. Some nonstandard enhancements of the language have added many BASIC-like features that make it more suitable to data-processing applications. Like BASIC, it is a compact, relatively easy-to-write language, but slightly more formal than BASIC. For example, before printing, you must set up an exact format for the print line. (You can also do this in BASIC, but it is not required.)

FORTRAN is now and will probably remain a popular language. It can be supplied for practically any machine, from micros to mainframes, and there is a great deal of software available in FORTRAN.

Ada

The language **Ada** was named after Lady Ada Augusta Lovelace (see the essay on history). To a certain extent, the development of Ada parallels that of COBOL. In this case, the United States Department of Defense, faced with thousands of computer programs in many different languages including COBOL and FORTRAN (as well as Jovial, TACPOL, and a bunch of others), has decided to shepherd the development of a single language, Ada, that will be both state of the art and satisfy the programming requirements of almost any task the department undertakes.

Business Focus   BOX 10-3

Steady as She Goes

With the aid of an improved standard and new maintenance tools, COBOL is keeping a steady grip on dp shops despite the incursion of 4 GLs.

As COBOL celebrates its 28th birthday this year, it is a language marked by both change and continuity. With an estimated 70 billion lines of code in use worldwide, COBOL is the premier programming language in today's dp shops, controlling areas like manufacturing, distribution, and finance. Even as other development tools such as fourth generation languages have emerged over the last decade to challenge COBOL, it continues to thrive. "No one is tired of talking about COBOL, because it never goes away," observes one vendor in the COBOL world.

There's plenty to talk about these days. Recent events are changing COBOL and having a big impact on users. The establishment of a new standard by the American National Standards Committee (ANSI), the emergence of new products and restructuring tools that promise to automate the costly process of maintaining code, and the development of pc-based tools are giving COBOL a long-overdue shot in the arm. Though the effect of these developments has only begun to be felt by users, in the long run it is likely to shake up an otherwise staid corner of the dp industry.

In September 1985, ANSI adopted a new standard for COBOL, called COBOL 85. It introduces structured programming to the language and allows it to be migrated more easily from one piece of hardware to another. The new standard eliminates certain language elements that were deemed obsolete, such as double character substitution and enter statements. The first products to implement this standard, notably compilers, began appearing on the market this past summer.

While observers in the COBOL world say the new standard is long overdue and its features advantageous for users, COBOL 85 has met with concern among users because its implementation would require the huge task of rewriting programs that were written under COBOL 68 or COBOL 74, the previous standards. Those programs won't run if they are recompiled on a compiler that conforms to COBOL 85. After October of this year, products sold to the government must embrace the new standard.

Consternation over COBOL 85 began several years ago when it was just beginning to be formulated. Today, with the standard in place, the concern has not lessened. COBOL 85 "scares me," says Jim Doyle, manager of programming support at Raytheon Co., Waltham, Mass. "I haven't looked at it in depth, so we're not sure how it will affect us. We'll eventually have to rewrite our programs, but we'll do it as late as possible." Several vendors now offer COBOL compilers that adhere to the new standard. Among them are

Source: Karen Gullo, *Datamation*, Jan. 15, 1987, p. 37.

Ada's development has been going on since the midseventies and, as of 1987, the preliminary language has been defined and some Ada compilers are being produced. If all goes as planned, within the next few years the Department of Defense will have all its new programs written in Ada and, as happened with COBOL, the rest of the government may follow. If the United States government, the largest buyer of computer programs, specifies Ada for all of its purchases, the rest of the industry may follow and we will have another standard language. Only time will tell.

Ada is a formal language and somewhat complicated to learn, but it is ideally suited to modular and structured programming and has modern facilities, such as the ability to program parallel processes (processes that execute simultaneously in the computer rather than one after the other).

California companies Ryan McFarland, Rolling Hills Estate; Micro Focus, Palo Alto; Tandem Computers, Cupertino; and Hewlett-Packard. Mike Saccomanno, director of product marketing at Ryan McFarland, says the company's compiler eliminates the need to rewrite code by including a "switch" that enables users to alternate between existing COBOL 74 features and COBOL 85. Programs can be compiled under either standard.

The feature certainly makes life easier for users who have previous versions of Ryan McFarland COBOL compilers. Ed Fisher, systems analyst at the Apollo Services group at United Airlines in Austin, says conversion to COBOL 85 was "relatively painless. When we wrote our code, we knew another version of COBOL would come out." Fisher started out using the switch, but now has converted almost all his code to the new standard. He acknowledges, however, that conversion may not be so easy for users who have used compilers from vendors other

than Ryan McFarland. Furthermore, continuing to compile programs under COBOL 74, he points out, only prolongs, not solves, the problem of rewriting programs.

Saccomanno agrees, saying that compiling in both standards could prove to be a problem in the maintenance cycle of the code when programmers have to be aware of the existence of two different standards. But, he says, "We support [COBOL 85] and believe that's what the world wants." Meanwhile, "a lot of the user base is not concerned about COBOL 85 yet and is not in a hurry to convert."

Do the features of COBOL 85 make it a more viable programming alternative to so-called advanced programming languages? COBOL has come under siege in the last decade from a variety of 4GLs on the market that have been particularly successful in dp shops for development of new applications. According to Vaughan Merlyn of Merlyn

Consulting, Atlanta, the new standard does not make COBOL any more competitive, but it gives the language more "wind."

"COBOL 85 is simply a long-overdue update of the standard to reflect modern methods. It should have been done 15 years ago," Merlyn says. He points out that there are two schools of thought concerning the use of COBOL vs. 4GLs for development. "There are those who feel it's important to preserve COBOL, that COBOL generators are the way to go, and there are those who say COBOL is worthless, let's get rid of it, 4GLs are the way to go. The more COBOL code you generate, the more COBOL code you have to maintain," Merlyn says, "but people want to use a language that's tried and true."

"Ten years ago we thought COBOL had a 10-year life span," says Paul O'Grady, cofounder and vp of worldwide sales at Micro Focus. "Now, with the new standard, the language has at least another 10 years."

SUMMARY

There are three levels of computer languages. The lowest is the actual language that the processor understands, machine language. This language is strictly binary and we rarely write in it directly because there are a number of other, easier languages that we can have the computer translate into machine language.

Assembly languages are similar to machine languages in concept, but the instructions are written in more easily remembered symbols rather than in binary. Assemblers translate assembly languages into machine language.

Macroassemblers allow us to make a single term, the macro, equivalent to a number of individual instructions. We can cut down programming time by using macros for repeated routines.

High-level languages make programming easier because the statements are written in more English-like code and one statement translates to a number of machine-language statements. The translations are performed by compilers, which translate the entire source code program into runnable object code, or interpreters, which take each statement in turn, translate it into object code, and execute it.

BASIC, found on the majority of microcomputers, is probably the most popular programming language. It is relatively easy to learn and handles most types of programming, but does not lend itself to structured programming.

COBOL, used on the majority of mainframes, is probably the most popular commercial programming language. It is quite formalized and more difficult to learn, but is the only fairly standard language and is very efficient for business applications.

Pascal is not really a new language, but it is becoming quite popular. It is a formal language and somewhat more difficult to learn than BASIC, but it directly addresses structured programming.

C is a midlevel language. It has many high-level features but allows access to the machine-level computer environment. It supports structured programming and, because it is written using many modular functions, forces modular programming.

FORTRAN is an old but still quite popular language with reasonably good standards. It is more formal than BASIC but far less than COBOL, and is quite efficient in mathematical applications.

Ada is one of the newest languages and may become the required language for programs for the Department of Defense. It is a very formal, all-purpose language which lends itself to structured and especially to modular programming.

KEY WORDS

(in order of appearance in text)	Object code	Paragraph
Alphanumeric	Linker	Identification division
Machine language	Executable code	Environment/configuration division
Assembly language	High-level language	Data division
Mnemonic	Compiler	Procedure division
Operator	Interpreter	Self documenting
Operand	Interactive	Pascal
Label	BASIC	C
Macro	CODASYL	FORTRAN
Assembler	COBOL	Ada
Source code	Sentence	

REVIEW QUESTIONS

1. What are the three levels of computer languages called?

2. In what type of language does the CPU always work?

3. Compare machine and assembly languages.

4. What type of program translates an assembly-language program into machine language?

5. What is the difference between source, object, and executable code?

6. What is a macroassembler?

7. What characteristics of high-level languages differentiate them from machine and assembly languages?

8. How do interpreters differ from compilers?

9. State the main advantages and disadvantages of BASIC, COBOL, FORTRAN, Pascal, Ada, and C.

10. Which of the languages discussed is the most standard from machine to machine?

11. Which language(s) can directly make use of structured programming?

12. Which languages are all-purpose? Which are business oriented? Which are science oriented?

THINK ABOUT IT

1. Why would you use an assembly language instead of a high-level language?

2. If you were in a situation where you were writing many programs that would be used only a few times each, would you prefer an interpreter or a compiler? Why?

3. Why is it important for a language to have standards?

4. Which language would you recommend to a casual microcomputer user? Why?

CHALLENGES

1. Find out which language(s) your school or a local company uses and why. If they were just getting into computers now, which language(s) would you recommend to them? Why?

2. Hundreds of computer languages were not discussed in this chapter. Pick one and compare it to some of the languages discussed.

History of Computers

1. Before computers there were calculators. One of the earliest successful calculators was the Chinese abacus, the modern version of which was developed in about 150 A.D.

2. Blaise Pascal developed the first successful mechanical calculator, the Pascaline, around 1650.

3. One of the first examples of a stored program was not a computer at all but a loom used for weaving cloth. Joseph-Marie Jacquard's invention (1801) used punched cards to store weaving patterns and control the loom.

4. Charles Babbage designed and built a "difference engine" (1834), which he used to compute mathematical tables. His conception for an "analytical engine," which would compute under the control of a stored program, was never built for lack of financial backing.

5. Lady Ada Augusta Lovelace (c. 1835) — daughter of the English poet, Lord Byron — is known as the first computer programmer. She worked with Charles Babbage on his analytical engine and described the loop and the subroutine.

6. The first United States census was done by hand and took seven and a half years. Herman Hollerith's punched-card tabulating machine did the 1890 census in two and a half years and saved the government 5 million dollars.

1

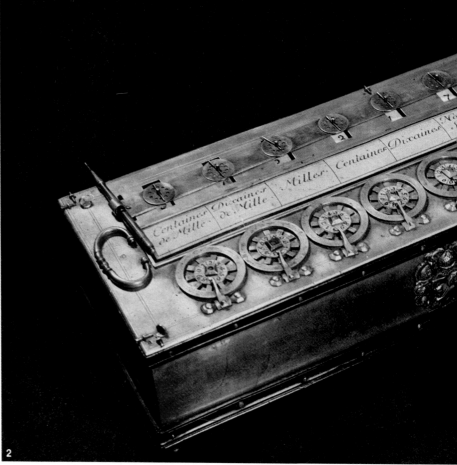

2

5

6

7. These machines (1925–1960) used data on punched cards and could count, summarize, and print out reports. "Programming," or changing jobs, was done by plugging in different, prewired control panels.

8. The Atanosoff-Berry Computer, or ABC (1942), set the trend for modern-day computers with its electronic nature, logic circuits, memory, and binary number system.

9. The Mark I Automatic Sequence Controlled Calculator (1944) — a joint effort by IBM and Dr. Howard Aiken, of Harvard — was a collection of electromechanical calculators in series.

10. J. Presper Eckert and John W. Mauchly designed and built ENIAC (Electronic Numerical Integrator and Computer) during WWII to calculate trajectory tables. With 18,000 vacuum tubes, it was huge and used a decimal rather than a binary number system.

11. Eckert and Mauchly, along with John Von Neumann, designed EDVAC (Electronic Discrete Variable Automatic Computer). Put into operation in 1951, it could store a program in the same way it stored data — unlike the ENIAC, where "programming" was done by switching switches and changing plugs.

11

12. **UNIVAC I (UNIVersal Automatic Computer)**, designed by Eckert and Mauchly for the United States census bureau, was the first computer (1951) built specifically for information systems, as opposed to military or scientific use.

13. The success of UNIVAC convinced IBM that computers were the wave of the future, and they brought out the IBM 701 in 1953 and the IBM 650 in 1954.

14. Though the transistor was developed some years earlier, it was only integrated into the computer by IBM in 1959 with its 1401 computer.

15. Grace Hopper helped design COBOL (Common Business-Oriented Language) as a common information systems language that could run on many different computers (1959).

16. Telstar, the first communications satellite, was launched in 1963.

12

13

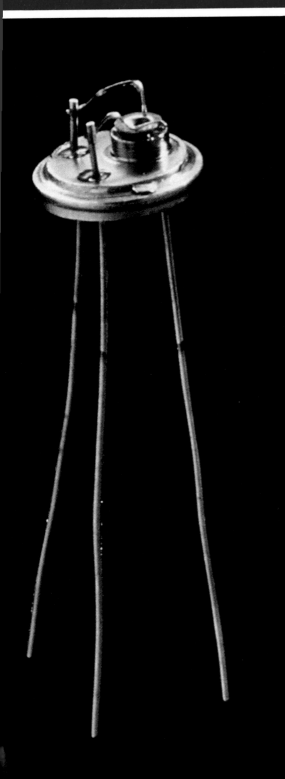

15

16

257

17. **IBM introduced their System 360 line of computers, which utilized integrated circuits, in 1964.**

18. **In 1971, large-scale integration ICs were introduced in IBM's 370 series — as well as in computers from CDC and DEC.**

19. **MITS, Inc., developed the Altair, the first commercially successful microcomputer (1971). It used the Intel 8080 microprocessor as its CPU.**

20. **Adam Osborne introduced the Osborne 1, a portable computer, in 1981.**

17

19

20

18

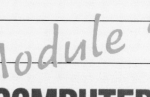

COMPUTER INFORMATION SYSTEMS

A computer information system exists to process various kinds of information for business. Its creation is a cooperative effort involving many people who design it, bringing together the hardware, software, people, and procedures needed to implement it. Chapter Eleven explores the development of such a system.

Chapter Twelve examines how data are transferred between parts of the system—the means, methods, and criteria for sending and receiving computer data.

How these data are accessed—stored and retrieved—is the subject of Chapter Thirteen with a look at the features of a database management system.

11

INFORMATION SYSTEMS DEVELOPMENT

PREVIEW
We have looked at some of the various components of information systems; now we will look at how those components are drawn together into a working unit. We will examine:

■ The reasons for developing new information systems.

■ What types of people are involved in the development.

■ The formalized process for information systems development.

■ Structured design methodology.

■ Some of the tools commonly used in designing information systems.

■ The individual steps in designing an information system.

Change. Nothing ever stays the same. What ever happened to the "good old days"?

If we really examined the "good old days," whenever they were, most of us would agree that we are probably better off now. We humans grumble a lot, but if, as a group, we didn't want things to change, they wouldn't. People, like us, cause most of the changes.

When it comes to information systems, we are changing extremely rapidly. As the saying goes, "Whatever you design today is already obsolete." The reasons for the fast pace are:

1. Information technology is advancing at an astonishing rate. Faster, more capable, and less expensive hardware is constantly being introduced. And the developments in software are more than keeping up.
2. Needs of individual businesses change. Some businesses grow, others shrink. They enter new marketplaces, offer new products and services, reorganize and hire new personnel, and react to their competition. Information is essential in effecting these changes.

We who cause the changes must also keep up with them. Information systems are services to the business. They allow it to transact business more efficiently. When the business changes, the information systems must also change. However, they are also expenses to the business. These changes cost money and must be made carefully.

THE PEOPLE

As we have said before, computers exist for the benefit of people. A computer information system is developed by people to satisfy people's needs. People are its most important ingredient. Let us examine some of the types of people involved in the systems-development process.

① Since the general objective must be to solve some user's problem, the user must be involved. In fact, we shall see that the user is involved in all facets of the project and is the most important class of person in any project.

② The user, however, is not expected to be a technical person, so a systems-development project must also involve people from the computer department. A systems analyst or systems designer will be involved throughout the project. This person is the bridge between the nontechnical user who has problems to attend to, and the computer system and its ability to solve those problems.

The systems analyst must not only understand the technical aspects of computer information systems but also be a people person—able to communicate with people, understand their needs and requirements, and help them to smoothly adapt to the new information system that is about to be developed. Much more of the analyst's time will be spent with people than with the machines.

③ Another technical person is the programmer. He or she will be involved in those projects that require programs to be written or modified,

The systems analyst provides the link between the user and the information-systems group.

and will spend the majority of time with the machine. Not that the programmer should speak only computerese. There will be times when he or she must talk directly to the user about the best way to approach some system problem.

(4)   Another class of people involved in systems development are managers. They are ultimately responsible for the success of the enterprise and so must be involved in the information system's contribution to its smooth running. The approval of management, both computer department and user department, will be required at various steps along the way.

People should use the system and derive its benefits, but in order to do so they must be committed to it. The best way to gain people's support is to involve them in its development. The biggest invitation to disaster is to have the computer folks huddle in the back room for months at a time and then announce that they have devised a system that will solve all the users' problems. The system will be greeted with suspicions that it won't do the job and will be more trouble than it's worth. And the suspicions will probably be right, because the computer people didn't spend enough time with the users to find out exactly what would do the job.

The Project Team

A project team monitors development of a new system.

At least two departments within the organization will be involved in the systems development, the computer department and at least one user department. This means involving more than one person in the development. Generally, organizations set up a **project team** to monitor each development project from its inception to its conclusion. Typically, a manager and a directly affected user or two will represent the users' views and one or more systems analysts will represent the computer department.

Who should lead the team is a hotly debated topic. Some feel that the leader should be from the users' area, because it is they who will eventually have to be satisfied by the system. Others feel that the systems analyst should be the leader, since he or she understands information systems and is the users' representative in the computer department.

STRUCTURED DESIGN CONCEPTS

In Chapter 9 we talked about tools for designing programs. We said that these tools made the task of programming easier and also facilitated communication between the programmer and anyone else who might have to work with the program. Some of these same tools, or slight modifications of them, are also used with designing information systems. We will examine various tools as they apply to different phases of the systems-development cycle. The objectives of all the tools are the same: To make the overall design job easier and to facilitate communication of the design.

Almost all of the tools used to design systems implement an overall **structured design** methodology. Structured programming, which we discussed in Chapter 9, is an example of one of these tools and follows the methodology.

In the structured development of a program we proceeded in modules from the top down. We use that same top-down, modular approach in all structured design. The top layer is a single, concise statement (just a very few words) of the overall objective of the system. In the second layer, the objective is broken down into a few major modules, perhaps two to five, which define the parts of the system needed to achieve the objective. Further layers break down each of these modules into the submodules needed to perform that module, and so forth until the whole system is described.

THE SYSTEMS DEVELOPMENT CYCLE

A computer-information system does not just appear out of thin air. It is developed from a bud of an idea to a fully-grown system—with hardware, software, people, and procedures—in a process we refer to as the **systems development cycle.** The terminology of the steps in the cycle, and the emphasis attached to each step, may vary from organization to organization, but the concepts of the process are similar no matter who is developing the system.

The Systems Development Cycle

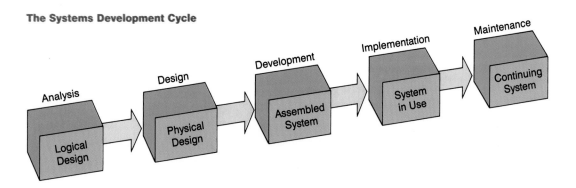

BOX 11-1

Following Successful Project Management Steps

Before insurance marketer AmCom undertook its major rearchitecture, it studied how other firms had negotiated systems transformations and emulated the practices that were instrumental in their successes. This is what AmCom found.

Keep the ceo and top management involved. Top management involvement is essential for success. But beyond the personal commitment of the chairman, the formation of a steering committee (made up of the chairman, the CIO, the project manager, and the head of each major business unit) makes clear to the whole organization top management's commitment and involvement throughout the project and forges organizational politics into the open.

Forge a business/technical partnership. In the course of a long-term project, complete control falls to technical management for about a third of the time—the time spent coding. For the balance of the schedule, technical management depends on the capabilities and cooperation of the user organization to help specify requirements and prototypes, perform functional testing, train users to use the new systems, and develop and implement modified procedures and practices. Ultimately, success depends not on the elegance of the technical implementation, but on whether the users and technical community break down the barriers between them and organize the project unconventionally. Users become full-time participants, just as the technical participants are. Users gain a deeper understanding of technical opportunities and constraints, and technical staff gain understanding of the business objectives underlying the specifications. By staying involved for the duration of the project, users can provide the business perspective to help decide the technical trade-offs that emerge in later stages, and help spearhead planning and management of the implementation effort.

Such a partnership also ensures broad support. Problems become the responsibility of the whole business to solve, not just the MIS manager operating without support or authority. And, after working together for months with a common purpose, users and systems developers have been known to actually trust each other.

Bring the best people into the project. Bring in the top achievers from all areas of the organization—from users to technical personnel. To get specific skills, supplement the team with outside hires. The

Source: *Datamation*, Oct. 15, 1988, p. 36.

In this book we shall divide the cycle into five steps. At each step we will look at the objective of that step, the people most involved with the system at that stage, and the end products of the step.

Systems Analysis

Objectives	Define the system from the user's viewpoint. See whether the system is feasible and practical.
People	Users and systems analysts.
End Products	Feasibility study and logical design.

Systems Design

Objective	Define the system from a technical and computer viewpoint.

overall project manager should be respected companywide and come from the business side of the organization.

Continue to develop the initial vision. While the initial vision serves to get a project chartered, it is too abstract to guide the project as it develops the details of the new strategies and systems. Instead of jumping directly to specifications, the project team should have time to focus on the underlying rationale and business strategies motivating the systems development. When the project views itself as the "keeper of the vision" (even after informal specs are developed and committed to code) and continues to develop that vision, it provides the organization with a reason and motivation for the extraordinary effort required.

The vision also becomes an essential management tool for controlling scope. There is a natural tendency, once the constraints of the existing installed base are removed, to attempt every possible systems improvement, which leads to disaster. Development initiatives, however attractive on a standalone basis, should be undertaken only if they implement an essential component of the vision. Additional capabilities can be implemented later, after the essential architecture and capabilities are up and running. Keeping the vision also ensures consistency between top management's objectives and what is actually implemented. Large projects sometimes lose sight of the forest for the trees. The vision serves in essence as a contract between the project and top management, ensuring that the investment actually achieves what is intended.

Empower the project team to make decisions.

A rearchitecture entails literally thousands of decisions about a huge range of issues: from fundamental issues of business strategy to simple issues of placing data on a screen. These have to be made quickly because time is the enemy of success. Conventional decision mechanisms are usually too slow, and more than one project has entered a death spiral, whereby requirements become obsolete before implementation, staff turns over, and management commitment weakens. One source of delay triggers additional delays, so that the project never finishes. The project team must have the authority to proceed without requiring sign-offs from line organizations. The steering committee should have the final authority in handling disagreements.

People	Systems analysts and users.
End Product	A system design.

Systems Development

Objectives	Purchase hardware and software, write software, and assemble and test the system.
People	Systems analysts, programmers, and users.
End Products	An information system ready to be put in operation. Users' manuals and technical manuals.

Systems Implementation

Objectives	Convert to new system. Train people in its use.
People	Systems analysts, programmers, and users.
End Product	An operational system.

Systems Maintenance

Objective	Keep the system operating smoothly. React to minor changes in requirements.
People	Users, systems analysts, and programmers.
End Product	A system that continues to provide for the company's needs.

SYSTEMS ANALYSIS

Four things must be accomplished during the **systems analysis** stage.

1. **Problem definition.** Determine the user's needs.
2. **Project definition.** Define the objectives and scope of the project.
3. **Feasibility study.** See whether solving the problem is practical.
4. **Logical design.** Design the system in human terms.

Defining the Problem

Jocylen Staud had a problem. Her salespeople sold items that the warehouses didn't have, they told customers that they were out of stock on items that the warehouses were full of, and they quoted delivery dates that were completely unrealistic. So she called a meeting.

Flying sixteen people in from all parts of the United States and Canada for three days of conference, coffee, and donuts was expensive, but Ms. Staud could do that because she was national sales manager for Starboard Marine Products, a wholesaler of parts and supplies for pleasure boats. Besides, their customers—major retailers and retail chains—were getting upset and ordering from other wholesalers.

Joe Kalua, whose territory is Hawaii and the South Pacific, was not at all pleased about having to go back to the home office in Massachusetts in February. "It's not our fault, Jock." Practically everybody in the company called her Jock. "We just go by the computer inventory reports we get each week. If they say the stuff is there, that's what we tell the customer."

Systems Analysis

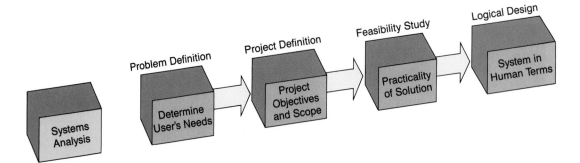

Wayne Bostrom, who handles the Pacific Northwest, was one of the most successful salespeople. Jock asked him how he handled the problem. "Simple, I just call the warehouses to check the stock before I write up a customer order." That explained why his telephone expenses were double what the rest turned in. "Occasionally, though, I get fooled when one of these other guys sells the same thing as I do and their order hits the warehouse before mine."

The purchasing and inventory computer system, which the warehouses used, gave up-to-date information on what currently existed in each warehouse, and what purchasing had ordered and when it was to arrive. The system could not give information on what was to happen to that inventory—whether it was committed to a customer, when it was to be delivered, and so forth. Even the information that was available lost its timeliness to the salespeople because the printouts were mailed to the sales offices.

After more discussion, more coffee, and an extraordinary number of donuts, they came to two conclusions. First, as a short-term measure, they would follow Wayne's example. Since the sales force's inventory printouts were at least a week out of date by the time they were received, they would not be relied upon. The salespeople would call the nearest warehouse instead. The warehouse people would consult their computer terminals and relay the information to the salesperson.

Second, their competition was forcing them to deliver fast and to quote accurate delivery dates. To do this, the salespeople would have to know exactly what was in stock and not sold by someone else, and purchasing would have to know what was being sold to allow them to order ahead. This, they felt, would require an expansion of the computer system as well as access to it and participation in it by the sales force.

Jock sent the salespeople back out into the field and called Ray Silva, the director of Information Services. Ray said, "What's the problem?" To Ray, this was not just friendly repartee but a technical question. After some discussion, Jock and Ray decided that the problem was not just giving bad delivery quotes to customers; that was a symptom. The problem was:

"Lack of sales force visibility into current inventory status."

The problem definition, then, is a statement of the underlying problem that is causing the symptoms that the users feel.

Defining the Project

Once a problem has been identified and a computer solution seems likely, a project team is formed to define the project and carry it to its conclusion. The project definition will include stating the objectives of the system, its benefits to the organization, and its scope—which areas of the organization will be benefited and/or affected. During this time, alternatives will be discussed and a reasonable solution, in general terms, decided upon. It is imperative that the project team agree on the definition, and that they communicate it to and get confirmation from those who will be affected by the system.

The project definition should be written up in a report and submitted to management, both user and computer, for approval. If the approval is granted, the project will move forward and the project definition will become the first part of the paperwork that constitutes the formal documentation of the system.

In the case of Starboard Marine, the project team consisted of Jock Staud; Robert Estevez, the New England salesman; Tom Oliver, the Boston warehouse supervisor; and Clarence "Call me Clancy, please!" O'Rourke, a systems analyst.

After a number of discussions among themselves and with their peers, they presented a project definition to management. It was six pages long and included such things as estimated lost sales and wasted personnel hours under the current system, and more detail about the proposed

---

BOX 11-2

Project Definition

> **To:** Director of Marketing, Information Systems Manager, distribution list below.
> **From:** Sales Information Project Team
> **Re:** Definition of the Sales Information Project

Abstract

It is estimated that we lose approximately $900,000 per year in sales and generate an inestimable amount of customer ill will because we are unable to provide our salespeople with adequate stock and delivery information. We propose to design and implement an addition to our computer-information systems that will allow our salespeople to quote accurate delivery dates.

The proposed system would include computer terminals in each sales office. The terminals would be connected to the central computer system in the home office, which is already part of the warehouse and purchasing system. Current warehouse stock and estimated arrival time of purchased items are presently in the system. The new addition would allow the sales people to query the system as to the status of items in our product line and enter orders directly into the system (instead of mailing them in).

This new addition to the system would make the information from the warehouses completely up to date. Not only would we know what was in the warehouses and when more was due but also how much of it was scheduled to be shipped and when.

The sales force would benefit by being able to confidently quote delivery times to the customers. Purchasing would be able to plan inventory levels better because they would know immediately which items were sold rather than waiting until the warehouse shelves were empty. The customer would benefit by having his order shipped faster (the order is entered directly rather than by mail) and by receiving things when they were promised.

The areas affected would be purchasing, the warehouses, and sales. There would be negligible differences in operations in purchasing and the warehouses. They already use the computer system and the data would not be different, just more up-to-date. The sales offices would have to be trained in the use of their part of the system, but their workload should not be increased. Indeed, with automatic printing of orders and less mailing and telephone requirements, their workload should be reduced.

interaction of the warehouse and the sales force using the computer. An abstract appears in Box 11-2.

It was signed by the director of marketing and the information systems manager, and had received the approval of the purchasing and warehouse departments, so the project team marched on to the next step.

The Feasibility Study

Defining a project does not mean that it can be accomplished. This is determined in a feasibility study. Three areas of feasibility must be examined:

1. Technical. Can we actually develop the system we have defined? The computer hardware, communications devices, software techniques, and skilled people must exist for the proposed system to become reality.
2. Time. Can the system be developed in time for it to do some good? If the problem must be solved within six months but the proposed system will take two years to develop, it is not practical.
3. Economic. Will the benefits from the system exceed the costs of the system? A detailed **cost/benefit analysis** must be done to predict whether the costs of developing and operating the system are less than the added revenues and/or reduced costs attributable to the system.

The first two questions can usually be answered with a straightforward yes or no. The economic feasibility is more difficult to assess but just as important to the project. The system is defined in general terms, but we do not know the exact hardware or software needed, precisely how many man-hours (usually stated in terms of man-months) it will take to complete it, or the the man-hours it will require to operate and maintain it.

The benefits are even harder to state in concrete terms. We can assign some dollar value to probable increased sales or the salaries saved by the system, but how do we quantify better-informed management or happier customers?

Like the project definition, the feasibility study is written up and submitted to management for approval.

The Starboard Marine team submitted their feasibility study to management. The director of marketing wanted clarification and refinement on some of the costs, but after some minor study and rewriting, it was approved. The abstract appears in Box 11-3.

The Logical Design

Before we even think about buying computers and writing software, we must have a clear idea of what the system is to accomplish and how our people will interact with it. So we create a logical design, or set of **system requirements,** a complete description of the new information system as it will appear to the user. This forms the foundation for the entire project. If we pay too little attention to this phase, the final outcome will suffer.

In order to design a new system, the project team must first understand the current system, computerized or not, with all its strong points and weaknesses. Much of this groundwork has been done in earlier steps, but now it must be formalized. The place to start gathering data is with the current users. Through a combination of interviews, questionnaires, and perhaps diaries—where people keep a written record of what

---

BOX 11-3

Feasibility Study

To: Director of Marketing, Information Systems Manager, distribution list below.
From: Sales Information Project Team
Re: Feasibility Study Sales Information Project

Abstract

The Sales Information Project, as outlined in the previous project definition, appears to be feasible and practical.

Technically, the new hardware would consist of terminals and communications devices for each of the sales offices, standard WATS telephone service, and an upgrade of the communications processor on the home–office computer system. All of these are standard, off-the-shelf items. The main system has enough CPU capacity to handle the extra load, and there should be almost no extra storage requirement.

There would be two main software packages. First is a communications package that would allow the sales offices to communicate with the home office. There are several choices of software that we could buy that would be compatible with the warehouse communication software. The other software would be programs for stock query and order entry. Since our way of doing business seems to be significantly different from other wholesaling organizations, this software would have to be specially written.

The sooner we can get on line with the new system, the better off we will be. The fact that we will be doing some of the proposed query functions manually, however, will reduce the time pressure. The estimated time to implementation of 11 to 14 months should suit our purposes.

The estimated cost of the entire system, including hardware, purchased software, programming, conversion, training, and miscellaneous, is $270,000. Additional continuing costs (over what we are doing now) including telephone, maintenance, finance costs, and others will be $65,000 per year beginning at the time of implementation.

The most tangible benefit would be regaining the $900,000 per year worth of lost business, of which about $180,000 is our margin. Purchasing also feels that with better visibility into sales demands on our warehouse stocks, they will save about $25,000 per year in taking greater advantage of quantity discounts and so forth. Intangible benefits include better customer satisfaction, faster shipping, and a slightly lighter work load at the sales offices.

Using only the $205,000 per year tangible savings against the $270,000 one-time cost plus the $65,000 annual cost, the system should pay for itself early in its third year.

Logical Design

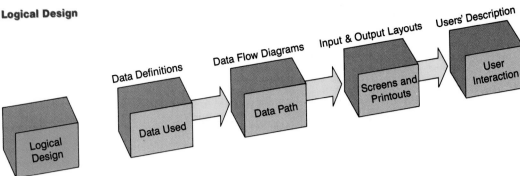

they do—the team will glean this information from the users. This extensive user contact serves two purposes. First, it gives the team intimate knowledge of the current system and how the users feel about it. Second, it involves the users in the process and tends to make them more committed to a successful outcome.

Once this information has been gathered, the team can create the actual design. The logical design will consist of a number of parts, but practically all designs contain the following:

1. **Data definitions.** A document describing the data that the system will use and manipulate.
2. **Data-flow diagrams.** Shows the paths data take through the system.

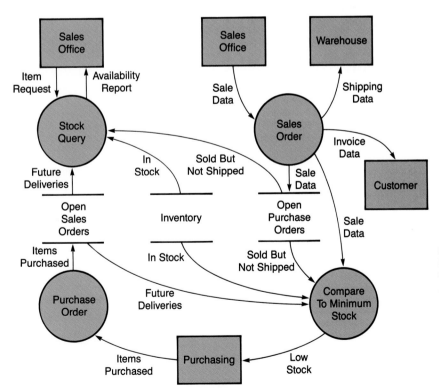

Starboard Marine's Data-Flow Diagram

The data-flow diagram is concerned with the movement of data (identified next to the lines) used with certain activities (in the circles) as it goes between the files (in the open lines) and people (in the rectangles). This one is a shortened version of Starboard Marine's.

3. **Input and output layouts.** Designs of the video screens and/or input forms, and the reports that are produced.
4. **Users' description.** How the user can get the system to perform for him or her. This will actually be the basis for the users' manual.

During this stage of the system's development, the most important class of people is the user. <u>There should be a constant dialog between the project team and the users, and the design should not be considered complete until the users have had a chance to review and comment on it.</u>

Once the logical design is complete, the project team should update the feasibility study, especially the cost/benefit analysis, and submit the whole thing to management.

SYSTEMS DESIGN

During the systems analysis, we developed the logical design that defined how the users would interact with the system. During the **systems design** phase, we will develop a **physical design,** a description of the hardware and software needed to implement the logical design. Systems analysts are the most active people at this stage.

In this stage we must produce these things:

1. **Data descriptions.** What data are used and how they are organized.
2. **System flowchart.** A diagram of the components of the system and how they interconnect.
3. **Hardware specifications.** The hardware needed for the system.
4. **Software specifications.** What programs are needed and what they should do.

Systems Design

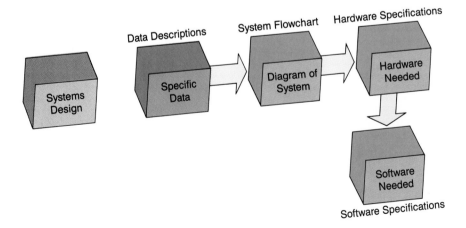

Data Descriptions

During the logical design, we identified all the data items that the user will see. Our data descriptions will specify the data in computer terms. We will organize these data into files and define the exact form in which the data

---

BOX 11-4

British Telecom Starts from Scratch

British Telecom has just completed rolling out an ambitious new customer service system (CSS) to roughly half of its 29 districts, with the other half expected to be completed in 1989. Developed from scratch, CSS is part of a fundamental reorientation of British Telecom's business: from a centrally driven, functionally organized government monopoly to a locally managed, customer-focused, competitive enterprise. Supporting the management discretion and entrepreneurship of the newly created 29 districts was a major part of the strategy.

CSS—which currently has 3 million lines of code—replaces, with a single data-base-driven architecture, all or most of the functions of six major and separate systems. The old systems ran on more than three different vendor's hardware, five different operating systems, and three different database managers. The original systems had been specified by a functionally organized headquarters management, and existed more to funnel reports up to headquarters than they did to help deliver customer service.

Improved customer service was the immediate design objective of the systems, and very much reflects the vision of how British Telecom needed to change. CSS supports the creation of a front office, where a single group of customer service personnel—reachable from a single telephone number—can answer customer questions, make repair or installation appointments, or adjust problems with billing, repairs, or new service orders. The systems then drive the actual operations of these activities, establishing schedules and assigning resources.

Integrated management reporting fundamentally changes the role of middle and senior management. Instead of working from summaries of what did happen, filtered by successive layers of the organization, management can see what is happening, view on-line summaries of current status, and then move at will to successively greater detail—ultimately to the same information available to the frontline supervisor. Nationally, the system supports more than 45,000 terminals for use by the frontline operators.

CSS had unusually high levels of organizational commitment and user involvement from the beginning. The project was championed at the highest management level, both within the organization and to the outside world. High-level user specifications were developed by committees chaired by the newly appointed district general managers. These were further developed by teams of full-time users—many on the project for 18 months—working closely with IS personnel.

The project did experience some major problems, however. The scope of the project increased beyond the original charter, and proved too unwieldy to deliver. This caused some delays, and disappointment after the scope was cut back nearer to the original specification. In addition, the effort required for pilot implementation was badly underestimated, and schedules slipped. Nevertheless, British Telecom persevered through these problems, which might have killed a less important project.

Source: *Datamation*, Oct. 15, 1988, p. 37.

Starboard Marine's System Flowchart

The diagram above is a somewhat abbreviated version of Starboard Marine's system flowchart for the sales-information system. Hardware input and output are shown as terminals in the sales offices, warehouse, and purchasing; and printers in those locations for customer invoices, shipping orders, and low-stock warnings. Files, open purchase orders, open sales orders, and inventory, are in the center. Activities, in the rectangles, show what events cause data to be moved from one place to another.

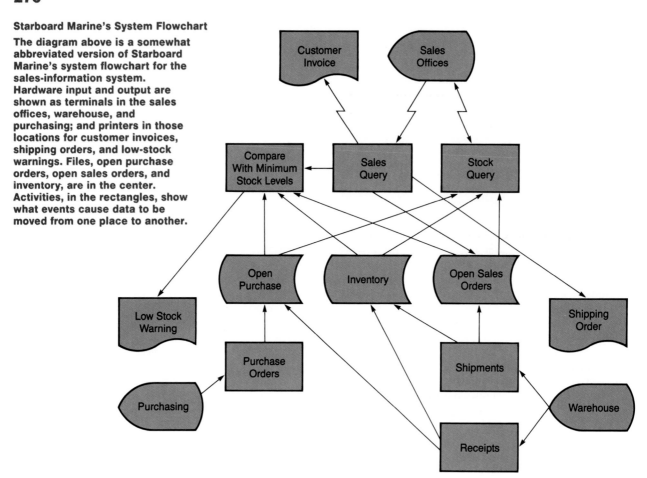

Group Terms:

sale item   stock number + quantity + price

product   stock number + product description + vendor + cost

Individual Terms:

stock number   alpha, 7 chrs, aaannnn. A distinct code assigned to each different item for sale. The first three characters are letters giving the product category and the last four are numbers.

price   numeric, nnnnn.nn. The price that an item sold for.

product   alpha, 25 chrs. The product description that
description   appears on all internal reports and customer invoices.

This is a piece of Starboard Marine's data dictionary. It shows both group and individual terms.

are to be stored. We will add any other data—indices and such—that the system might need to access the users' data. And we will provide for security to keep certain data from unauthorized users and to assure that no data is lost.

We will probably create a **data dictionary,** the main objective of which is to provide precise, standardized names and descriptions of all the data to be used in the system. If everyone working with the system uses exactly the same terms, there will be less confusion. The dictionary contains a description of each data item, including whether it is a number or a set of characters, how many characters are allowed, how many decimal places, ranges of acceptable data, and a narrative description of the item. It should also contain terms for groups of data and which individual items belong to that group.

Our **file layouts,** descriptions of what data are in what files, will differ for different kinds of file-access systems. In a simple system, the layouts will show each file and the position of each data item within that file's records. When we look at database management systems in Chapter 13, we will see that our file descriptions will be more concerned about the individual data items and their relationships to other items than their actual locations within specific files.

If you gave managers a choice of blowing up all their hardware or destroying all their data, they would invariably choose blowing up the hardware. That is replaceable; often the data are not. As part of our data descriptions we will devise **backup** procedures which will provide for copies of all our data, and methods for restoring them to the system if something tragic happens.

System Flowchart

A system flowchart is similar in appearance and concept to a program flowchart. It shows all the parts of the system—people, data files, and hardware—and how they interact. Inputs and outputs are shown typically as either display terminals or printed reports; activities which use or modify data are depicted; and the files which contain the data are usually shown in the center of the flowchart. Lines with arrows show how the data flow between files, activities, and inputs and outputs. The system flowchart will become part of the final documentation.

Hardware Specifications

Systems analysts do not generally design hardware, they integrate existing hardware into their system. The analyst will look at the hardware that is available and decide which components are needed; the hardware specifications will state the components in the system and how they interact.

Software Specifications

The systems analyst will design the software, not as a set of programs in computer language but as a detailed set of software specifications that

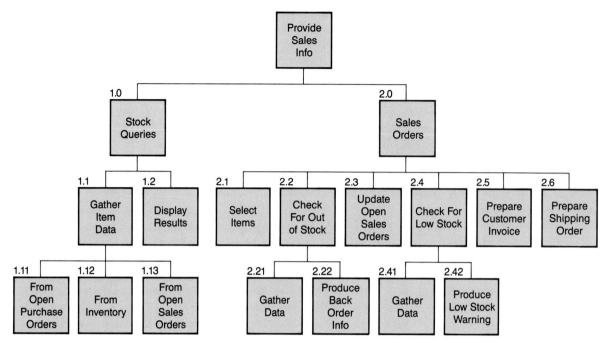

**Starboard Marine's
Visual Table of Contents**

This is an abbreviated visual table of contents for Starboard Marine's new system. It shows only some of the third-level items expanded to the fourth level. The actual VTOC also has more than four levels.

describe what each program is to do. Here, as in so many other computer-oriented tasks, there are a few, commonly used design tools.

One tool, the **visual table of contents (VTOC),** provides a good way to show the software's top-down, modular design. In diagram form, it starts with a general statement of the system's purpose at the top level. The second level divides that overall purpose into several key modules. The third level divides the second-level modules down further, and so on for as many levels as it takes to describe the software fully.

Describing what goes on in any one module is often accomplished by an **input, process, output chart,** or **IPO chart.** Since any data-handling

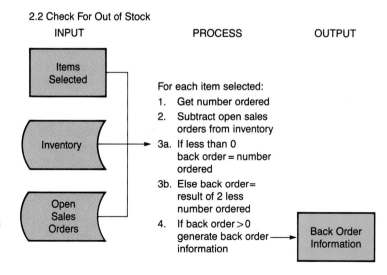

Starboard Marine's IPO Chart

This section of Starboard Marine's IPO chart explains what happens at box 2.2 of the visual table of contents.

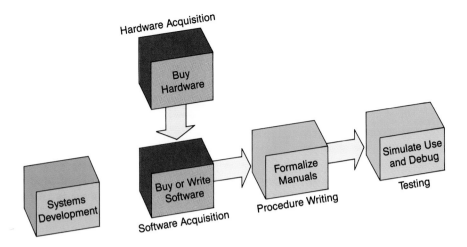

task involves those three elements, it is useful to use them to describe the task. The IPO chart for a task shows all the inputs—files, operator inputs, or whatever—on the right side, the process—how the input data is operated upon—in the middle, and the outputs—changed files, screen displays, or reports—on the left. Since the VTOC is arranged in a hierarchy of operations, the combination of VTOC and IPO chart is often referred to as a **hierarchical input, process, output chart,** or **HIPO chart.**

A number of other design methods are in use, but all the popular ones are ways of describing structured-design methodology, that is, top-down, modular design.

Once the software specifications are completed, many organizations test the design itself (remember, the software has not been written yet) using a **structured walkthrough.** The analyst "walks through," explains in detail, the design to other analysts and the project team. This allows people who are not so intimately associated with the design to analyze it, spot problem areas, and suggest improvements.

Structured walkthroughs allow a number of brains to become involved in the same project and usually produce designs with a minimum of design problems. The walkthroughs can produce human problems, however. Imagine yourself, the analyst, exposing your design, your "baby," so that a group of other people can examine, pick at, and poke holes in it. It requires that both the designing analyst and the others at the walkthrough adopt a philosophy often called **egoless programming,** where the design is not viewed as an extension of the analyst's ego but simply a product to be improved. Easier said than done, but it is a successful technique.

SYSTEMS DEVELOPMENT

During **systems development** the system becomes a real, tangible thing. The people most heavily involved will be systems analysts and programmers. In this phase we must accomplish these things:

1. **Hardware acquisition.** Purchase and assemble the hardware specified for the system.

Systems Development

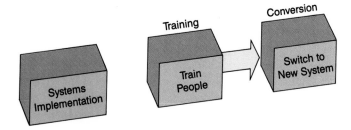

2. **Software acquisition.** Purchase or write the software specified.
3. **Procedure writing.** Write both user and operator procedures in final form.
4. **Test.** Make sure everything works.

Hardware Acquisition

The hardware specification made during the systems design stage determined the necessary hardware acquisitions. Where there are choices in the specification, we must find the vendors with the best prices and service. As we receive the hardware, we configure it (set it up to fit our system), test it, and plug it in to the rest of the system hardware.

Software Acquisition

As with the hardware acquisition, the software acquisition is determined by the software specification. In our system we may have specified **custom software,** to be written specifically for our application; **off-the-shelf software,** to be purchased from a vendor that writes general applications packages that many organizations might use; or **modified software,** purchased software that has to be changed to better fit our application.

Off-the-shelf software is the least expensive, since the same package is sold to perhaps hundreds of companies. It is already written so we do not have to wait for it. And it has probably been used by others before us, so we should not find any bugs (problems) in it.

Off-the-shelf software must please many users, so it ends up not being exactly what any particular user wants. Custom software, on the other hand, is expensive to write, takes a lot of time, and is more bug prone, but it will do exactly what we want it to.

Modified software is between the two. Here we find a software package that is close to what we want, and we either make the changes ourselves or have the vendor make the changes. Software modification is not possible or practical in all cases, however. Often, the vendor is unwilling to make changes because of lack of programmer resources and because changes create the possibilities for new bugs. Our organization may not be able to make the changes for the same reasons. In addition, vendors are often reluctant to release source code (the program in human-readable form rather than machine language). Further, if the program is changed, the vendor may cancel any warranties and may not provide us with any support (offer us help if we have problems).

BOX 11-5

A Document-First Strategy May Cure Specification Indigestion

If you ever visit a software development shop and you want to hear a lot of complaining, just ask anyone about specifications and documentation.

Working on the documentation end, I once saw a situation in which a technical writer had to write part of a manual without a chance to become familiar with the program. When the discrepancy was found, the system analyst who designed the program exclaimed, "I wish it *did* do that!" Then she redesigned the program to fit the manual.

An entry-level coder I know confessed to me once that he really didn't know what the blocks of code he was writing were supposed to do until he read the rough draft of the tutorial.

The above observations make sense if you consider that the level of abstraction is much closer between specification and manual than between specification and program. A programmer, after all, worries primarily about how a program does something; analysts and technical writers worry about what it does.

A tutorial is an intensive walk-through with examples of the main things a program does. A manual is a detailed description of what the program can be expected to do in all circumstances, along with definitions of terms and descriptions of given

procedures that should produce given effects.

At this point, look at the definitions and ask, "Doesn't that sound like an extremely well-done specification?"

What if, on the next program to be developed from scratch, you were to put the system analysts together with the technical writers and have them write the manual and tutorial for the program before any programming was done? And then you used the manual and tutorial as a specification for the programmers?

The idea of a document-first strategy may sound absurd at first, but consider its possible advantages:

- **Clearer specification.** The biggest problem with almost all program documentation is what is taken for granted. Designers assume the programmer can read minds, but writers don't assume a naive user can.
- **Bolder, more advanced designs.** Designers sometimes work too closely with programmers and are subject to "whineback," a low-level, negative feedback that saps the will to push things to the limit. "Couldn't we just . . . ?" "Wouldn't it be better in this version if we limited it to . . . ?" and so forth. A document-first strategy allows the concept to grow as strong as possible without being subordinated to programmer convenience.

- **Keeping designers honest.** Sometimes, when the concept isn't clear, a deliberately vague specification is given to the programmers in the hope that they'll come up with something suitable. A manual, with its do-this-and-get-that approach, eliminates the room to hide.
- **Drawing on programmer strengths in a positive way.** A good manual tells you a lot about the software's design philosophy and about what the designers thought was important. It doesn't burden you with how the technical writer wrote code 10 years ago.
- **More informative manuals.** I do a lot of modeling. Quite often, the fine structure of a model's behavior depends on the exact algorithm that a program uses to approximate a mathematical function. On more than one occasion, that algorithm has been so poorly documented that nobody, even at the shop that wrote the program, has been able to tell exactly what it does.
- **Improved communication with management.** Managers who don't speak computerese—and even those who do—will actually be able to read the specifications comfortably and to solicit comment from a much wider community.

Is anyone trying this document-first strategy?

Source: John Barnes, *Computerworld*, July 25, 1988, p. 17.

Starboard Marine specified both custom and off-the-shelf software for their new system. They purchased a communications package that would allow the sales offices to communicate with the main computer. They had to be sure that these programs were compatible with the hardware and software on either end, and that it worked with their current communications package for the warehouses. As it turned out, Clancy O'Rourke, the analyst, was able to buy a new package from the same vendor as their current warehouse package. This way, the same vendor would support both packages. If there were inconsistencies between them, Starboard Marine would not be faced with two vendors, each blaming the other.

The rest of the software was written by Starboard Marine's own programming staff.

Procedure Writing

Much of the documentation we have produced up until this time deals with the interaction of the user with the system. As part of the logical design, we outlined the users' description and presented it to the users for their comment and approval. Now we will take that groundwork and produce the formal **users' manual** which tells the user how to use and get the benefits of the system.

Now that we know all the actual components of the system, we are prepared to write the **operator's manual.** This outlines the procedures that the operators in the computer information-systems department will follow to run the system, including starting it, distributing outputs, backups, handling problems, and other operations.

Testing

As we said before, nothing is more important in the success of an information system than acceptance by the users. A user will become discouraged very quickly if the new system comes up with the wrong answers. The user should receive the new system as bug free as possible, so we must test, test, and test again.

Systems Implementation

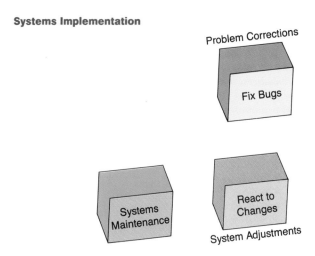

It is important to have a **test plan.** In developing the plan we try to anticipate the kinds of data and usage the system will encounter and put it under similar or even harsher loads. One common technique for early testing is called **module testing;** each module is tested individually to ensure that it performs its part of the whole.

When the module testing is completed, the entire system must be tested. The data we use for test purposes may be either made up by those working on the project or, if possible, real data from actual operations.

Part of the testing should include the users themselves. Here we are not only testing the accuracy of the system but also its practicality, ease of use, effectiveness of the users' manual, and further involving the user in the development of the system.

SYSTEMS IMPLEMENTATION

Now it is time to let the system start earning its keep. During the **systems implementation** we will actually put the system into use. In this phase we will perform these functions:

1. **Training.** Familiarize the people with the system and procedures for using it.
2. **Conversion.** Change from the old system to the new one.

Training

Here again we are working with people, not just ordinary people, but the ones who will make or break our system. We must design a training program that will ease the users into the system, make them comfortable with it, and gain their participation and support.

Conversion

The conversion process starts the use of the new system. In a **plunge** or **crash conversion,** we simply throw out the old system and put the new one in operation. This is probably the cheapest way to go, if everything turns out right. If the system has a problem, though, we have no working system to fall back on; we may have filled our data banks with erroneous data; and we may have done significant harm to the operation of the business.

In a **parallel conversion** we operate the new system side by side with the old. We can compare data, giving us another testing opportunity, and if there is a problem, we can continue to operate the old system while we fix the new one. Parallel conversion is safer, but it requires more manpower to handle the data twice.

We may use either of the above methods in a **pilot conversion,** picking a small section of the system—one department or the Western region, for example—and converting it first. Once it is running smoothly, we can move on to other sections of the system.

Starboard Marine used Wayne Bostrom's Pacific Northwest sales office

Business Focus   BOX 11-6

Learning Systems Integration the Hard Way

When the U.S. Government Patent Office set out to automate its patent system it got more than it bargained for: some lessons from the school of hard knocks. Four years and $460 million later, it learned the hard way that bypassing federal procedures did not provide any shortcuts. The project, originally scheduled to be completed in eight months, is still unfinished, and the original $300 million price tag has ballooned more than 50%.

The original goal was to increase the efficiency of the paper-based system. The Patent Office processes an average of 126,000 patent applications a year. For each patent, examiners have to search through about 1,600 pages out of a total of 27 million paper documents. Combine a little multiplication with the fact that the number of patent applications is steadily growing each year and you can begin to picture the avalanche of paper that threatened to swamp the agency. In 1983, the decision was made to find an external vendor to put all the documents on-line for search and retrieval.

The agency issued a 2,500-page request for proposal outlining the planned system, which was to increase the efficiency of the paper-based system. Despite the complexity of the task, the office obtained a waiver from the Commerce department that exempted it from fulfilling the requirements of Circular A-109, the Office of Management and Budget's directive governing federal procurement of major systems. (The waiver was granted because the Commerce department considered the system to be off-the-shelf and not one-of-a-kind.) Instead, the Patent Office chose a systems integrator based primarily on its own subjective assessment of the proposal and delegated major decisionmaking power to it.

More than a year after the award, the agency changed the scope of the project. Its objective went from increasing efficiency to improving the quality of the patent search—a far more ambitious goal. The integrator and the Patent Office spent the next 18 months trying to agree on what the new system should look like. During this time, the integrator attempted to develop the necessary software for the system—an impossible task given that the system architecture had yet to be defined. The storage devices with the necessary speed and capacity were not available until three years into the project.

The development's expensive disarray provoked strong criticism from the Government Accounting Office and Congress. The Commerce department took steps to right the project and replaced the project director with Thomas P. Giammo, who had been among the most vocal GAO critics of project. A more cautious approach has been adopted, and overly optimistic technology assessments and schedules have been adjusted to more realistic levels. The text search system is now operational, and the image search is scheduled to be complete next year.

The Patent Office's experience offers many lessons. First and foremost, it should have made sure that there was internal agreement on the basic objectives of the project, which would have prevented the catastrophic act of attempting to switch horses in midstream. The lack of full accord also contributed to an environment in which the systems integrator assumed responsiblility that top management should have retained. Further, if the office had not tried to shoot for the moon and had instead established realistic goals from the start, the project would have gotten off the ground sooner. Finally, if the office had not foregone competitive test demonstrations of the proposed solutions and required the integrator to demonstrate key elements of the solution before making the award, it would have understood the limitations of the existing technology and not bet on advancements that didn't materialize on cue. It also would have been able to assess the system's total costs more accurately.

Source: *Datamation*, Nov. 1, 1988, p. 122.

as a pilot project in the implementation. Wayne was to use the new system in parallel with what he was already doing for a period of two months. This caused Wayne and his secretary some extra work during the conversion, but they could both see that the new system would save them time after the conversion was completed.

After the pilot, Clancy O'Rourke and his crew made a few small changes in the programs and the training procedures, and started converting the rest of the offices.

SYSTEMS MAINTENANCE

The perfect information system has not yet been developed, nor has the perfect human being. It is estimated that most systems spend over two thirds of their lives in the maintenance stage. When we speak of **systems maintenance,** we do not refer to the repair of broken hardware. That type of maintenance must also be done, but we are speaking of the following activities:

1. **Problem corrections.** Catching bugs not seen in the testing stage.
2. **System Adjustments.** Making changes to react to changes in the system's environment.

At this stage, the user is heavily involved; it is he or she who will most probably initiate the maintenance. The systems analyst may be involved in large changes, and we may have a separate group, called **maintenance programmers,** who will make software changes.

Ideally, the system is bug free once it gets to the conversion stage. In reality, situations will occur that the designers of the tests never could have anticipated and some of those situations will uncover bugs. **Problem corrections,** or "bug fixes," should be made as quickly as possible.

Neither people nor the systems they use are static things. Situations continually change. Someone finds a better way of doing something, a manager wants more information on a report, or North Dakota secedes from the United States and we don't have a sales office there any more. All these things require system adjustments.

Since, in many organizations, maintenance programmers who have never seen the software before will be making the changes, it is extremely important that the system and programs were well documented as they were written.

What's happened at Starboard Marine? Jock Staud bought a summer cottage on Cape Cod with her bonuses from the increased sales. Clancy O'Rourke has quit the computer field and now writes romance novels under the name of Heather Swann. But, because of his good documentation, his replacement was able to maintain the system.

SUMMARY

New information systems are constantly needed because new information technology is constantly being developed and because the needs of organizations are constantly changing.

An information system exists to satisfy the needs of people, and people are the most important ingredient in the system. The classes of people most involved in developing a system are users, systems analysts, programmers, and management. In order to make a new system successful, it is important to involve all the people who will be affected by it and gain their commitment to it. A project team of users and technical people usually directs the development of a new system.

Most organizations are quite orderly in their systems development efforts, using structured design and many of the common tools of development. The systems-development cycle consists of systems analysis, systems design, systems development, systems implementation, and systems maintenance.

The systems-analysis stage starts with a definition of the problem where the symptoms are examined and the underlying problem identified. When a computer solution to the problem seems likely, the project's objectives and scope are defined. After management approval to proceed, the project team will perform a feasibility study to determine whether the project is technically practical, can be completed in time to do some good, and whether the benefits from the proposed system will exceeds its costs. After management approval, the team will create a logical design of the system—probably including data definitions, data-flow diagrams, input and output layouts, and a preliminary user's manual.

During the systems-design stage, the project team will produce a physical design of the system with data descriptions (including a data dictionary and file layouts), a system flowchart, hardware specifications and software specifications (with such software design tools as visual tables of contents and IPO charts). A software design is not finished until the design itself is tested, often using a structured walkthrough with people not involved in the project asked to contribute.

The system is assembled during the systems-development stage. Here the hardware is purchased and put in place; the software, whether custom, off the shelf, or modified, is written and/or purchased; both user and operator manuals are written; and the system is tested before going to the users.

During the system implementation, the users will be trained and made familiar with the system; and the conversion to the new system will be accomplished. The conversion can be handled in plunge or parallel fashion, with either method possibly being used first in a pilot conversion before the rest of the organization is converted.

Rarely does a system remain as it was when it was "finished." The rest of its life, the system is in maintenance, where stray problems are corrected that were not caught earlier, and where it is modified to suit the changing needs of the organization.

KEY WORDS

(in order of appearance in text)
Project team
Structured design
Systems development cycle
Systems analysis
Problem definition
Project definition
Feasibility study
Logical design
Cost/benefit analysis
System requirements
Data definitions
Data-flow diagram
Input and output layouts
Users' description
Systems design
Physical design
Data descriptions

System flowchart
Hardware specifications
Software specifications
Data dictionary
File layouts
Backup
Visual table of contents (VTOC)
Input, process, output chart (IPO chart)
Hierarchical input, process, output chart (HIPO chart)
Structured walkthrough
Egoless programming
Systems development
Hardware acquisition
Software acquisition
Procedure writing
Test

Custom software
Off-the-shelf software
Modified software
Users' manual
Operator's manual
Test plan
Module testing
Systems implementation
Training
Conversion
Plunge conversion
Crash conversion
Parallel conversion
Pilot conversion
Systems maintenance
Problem corrections
System adjustments
Maintenance programmer

REVIEW QUESTIONS

1. Why do we constantly design new information systems instead of sticking with the current ones?

2. What is the most important class of person involved in the creation of an information system? What other classes of people are involved?

3. What is the function of a project team? Who is on it and who leads it?

4. What is structured design and what are its most important characteristics?

5. Name the five stages of the systems development cycle.

6. What are the objectives of the systems-analysis stage, who are the people most involved, and what are the end products?

7. What four things must be accomplished during systems analysis?

8. Compare a problem with a symptom.

9. What two major concepts comprise a project definition?

10. Name the three types of feasibility that are addressed in a feasibility study.

11. Is a cost/benefit analysis a very accurate study? Why or why not?

12. How does a logical design differ from a physical design?

13. Name five elements usually included in a logical design.

14. What are the objectives of the systems-design stage, who are the people most involved, and what are the end products?

15. What four things are accomplished during systems design?

16. What is the purpose of a data dictionary?

17. What is the purpose of a visual table of contents?

18. What does IPO stand for? What is an IPO chart?

19. Why is egoless programming important to structured walkthroughs?

20. What are the objectives of the systems-development stage, who are the people most involved, and what are the end products?

21. What four things are accomplished during systems development?

22. Name three ways software can be acquired. How do they differ?

23. What are the objectives of the systems-implementation stage, who are the people involved, and what are the end products?

24. What two things are accomplished during systems implementation?

25. Name and compare three different conversion methods.

26. What are the objectives of the systems-maintenance stage, who are the people most involved, and what are the end products?

27. What two activities are carried on during the systems-maintenance stage?

THINK ABOUT IT

1. Why is the user the most important class of people in systems development? How would you react if someone handed you a new method for doing your homework and said "This is great. From now on, do it this way"?

2. Who would you choose to be the leader of a project team—a systems analyst, a user, the manager of a user department, or the manager of the information-systems department? Why?

3. Why is a visual table of contents considered a structured-design tool?

4. If cost was not a factor, would there be reasons to choose off-the-shelf over custom software?

5. In implementing an accounting system, what are the advantages of plunge versus parallel conversion and vice versa.

6. Why might modular testing each individual part of a system before testing the system as a whole reduce testing and correction time over just testing the system as a whole?

7. Why do some companies have a separate crew of maintenance programmers rather than letting the original programmers perform the maintenance?

CHALLENGES

1. Assuming that you do not own or have access to a computer, analyze the costs and benefits of buying a $2000 personal computer to assist you in your school work.

2. Construct a visual table of contents for the process of getting up and going to work or school in the morning.

   Pick a couple of modules in it and draw IPO charts for them.

3. Using a local computer system, identify a problem that might have a computer solution and carry the systems development through the systems design phase.

12

DATA COMMUNI-CATIONS

PREVIEW

Back in the covered-wagon days, trading gossip with your cousin across the state could have taken days. Now it is a matter of seconds. Gossip has been made more efficient. Because of communications, trading information by computers has also become more efficient. Instead of carrying data to the machine and information back from it, we stay where we are and send them back and forth electronically. It takes seconds rather than hours or days. In this chapter we will examine how those data are transmitted. In this chapter you will learn:

■ The criteria we use to judge a communications system.

■ The types of materials and media we use for data communications.

■ The many ways we send data.

■ The kinds of hardware we use to send and receive data.

■ How we set up communications systems to allow access by many different people.

■ What the companies are like that supply data services.

■ What the common applications of communications by businesses and individuals are.

The casual observer would have called it a normal, if somewhat damp, afternoon on Berlin's Kaiserstrasse. The trained eye, however, would have picked out the shadowy man in the dark trench coat walking with a telltale hint of anxiety down the street. His left hand clutched the handle of a black-leather attaché case. It might have looked innocent enough lying on a desk somewhere, but one suspected by the way he held it that it didn't contain contracts or the man's lunch.

After looking quickly over his shoulder, the man ducked into the Kessler hotel. It was one of those places that exist in every old city in the world. Once it was opulent and luxurious, now it was simply faded and forlorn. He picked his way across the lobby to the line of phone booths, entered the second from the left, and closed the door.

Once inside, out of the way of the sea of eyes that seemed to surround him, he went into action. He had done it hundreds of times before, and the movements came easy for him now. He dialed a number and waited. After about four endless seconds, a high-pitched tone came over the telephone. He opened the case and, instead of papers, the dim light in the phone booth revealed the neat and precise, but very efficient-looking, electronic gear. He forced the telephone handset down onto a pair of rubber cups

mounted in the case. There was a slight buzzing sound and some paper appeared with the word "IDENTIFY" printed on it. He tapped in some characters on a keyboard and the buzzing paper answered "GO AHEAD." His pace quickened as he played a kind of frantic fugue on the keyboard. Then he waited. If the answer that came back was not what he wanted—what he had to have—he was sunk. The other side would triumph and he would lose.

He felt his pulse pounding, but it pounded only twice because the answer took less than two seconds to come back. When the buzzing stopped and the paper rose out of its slot he saw the words "Can ship 12 D145-2 immediately." No one in the lobby of the shabby hotel would have understood that cryptic sentence but he knew that he had been saved, the other side had lost. Larry Turgeson, tractor parts salesman from Des Moines, Iowa, could now go back to the buyer and say with confidence that the 12 diesel tractor engines they wanted could be delivered within three weeks, at least a week and a half quicker than the competition.

Larry was using a portable computer terminal with a built-in communications device that allowed it to send and receive data over the normal telephone wires. Larry dialed a local number in Berlin which connected him to a computer network that included his company's computer in Des Moines, Iowa. From his phone booth, he started a computer program that checked the current inventory of D145-2s and reported the figure to him. He had to identify himself with a secret code because his company did not want just anybody to have access to company information.

In order to be useful, data must be delivered to the user. The data must travel as little as from the back of the computer to a printer, or as much as a few million miles through space. This chapter examines some of the means, methods, and criteria for sending and receiving computer data.

COMMUNICATIONS CRITERIA

We would like to get our data from here to there as quickly and as cheaply as possible. Often there is a trade-off between these two criteria—the faster the communication method, the more expensive it is. Within reasonable limits, it usually pays to use the fastest method that you can keep busy. Usually, it does not cost twice as much to send data twice as fast, but if you are spending almost twice as much for a communications method that you keep in use only half the time, you are wasting money.

The top criterion for communications is accuracy. It would be a shame to have the data that we were so careful to input correctly become garbled during communications. Data with errors is not like a car with a rumpled fender; the car can still be driven but flawed data is worthless. Rarely will an organization trade accuracy for either speed or cost.

MEDIA

A communications **channel** (like an I/O channel) is the path the data take getting from here to there. In traversing the channel, the data will travel through some medium or carrier, or perhaps a combination of media. There are several communications media and we can send data by any one or a combination of them.

A **wire** is probably the most obvious medium. The wires coming out of your telephone are a good example. At some time in its travels almost all data go through wires. Wires are best for short-distance communication (perhaps a few feet to a few miles). Wires, or the printed-circuit equivalent, are used inside the computer. At least for short-distance communications (a few feet) outside the computer, using wires as the medium allows the data to stay in the same form.

One of the strongest reasons for using wires for medium- to long-distance communications is that the wires already exist in the form of telephone lines. In these cases, however, the data's form is almost always altered, for reasons which we shall see.

Your favorite television programs are carried by **radio waves. Radio-teletype (RTTY)** is a common data-communication method that utilizes radio waves. Radio waves have an advantage over wires in that the medium is free, wires cost money. Also, in some frequency ranges, radio waves can be reflected off both the upper atmosphere and the earth itself, a phenomenon known as "skip." Hence, it is possible for a signal such as the Voice of America to originate in the United States, bounce around between the earth and upper atmosphere, and be received in central Russia.

Long-distance radio waves are rarely used for data, however, because these same atmospheric effects make it unreliable. Sometimes you get skip,

Wires

Wires for both inside and outside a computer come in all shapes and sizes.

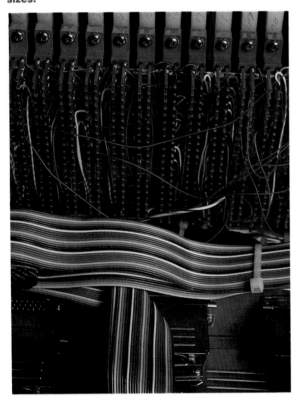

sometimes you don't. Sometimes the signals from other, far-away transmitters that you have never heard before will skip into your receiver, interfering with your signal. Also, the medium may be free, but the ends—receivers and transmitters—are expensive. Wires usually end in a 29¢ plug.

Microwaves are actually radio waves, but in the extremely high frequency ranges (above 300M Hz, for you radio fans). Microwaves, unlike most radio waves, are relatively unaffected by the atmosphere and are absorbed by the earth. That makes them line-of-sight, meaning that the receiver must be in a direct line with the transmitter. This makes their distance considerably less, perhaps 30 to 100 miles, depending on what mountaintops they can be mounted on. But, they are quite consistent because there is little atmospheric interference.

Again, the medium is free, but the transmitters and receivers are even more expensive. The receiver's antenna is usually dish shaped and about a foot to over 20 feet across. You often see them on mountaintops, buildings, and even in backyards facing skyward.

Microwave Relays

To use microwaves, the receiver must be able to "see" the sender; so to get around the curvature of the earth, microwave signals are relayed from high point to high point. Satellites, of course, provide a very high point.

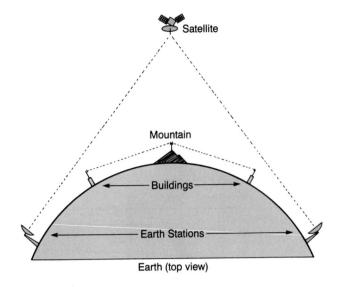

Earth (top view)

Microwave-carried data often travel from Seattle to Miami. But how—since even by standing on top of the Space Needle and squinting hard, no one can see even the top of the Fontainebleau? The signal is **relayed**—that is, received and retransmitted—from one mountaintop to another until it reaches its destination.

That works from Seattle to Miami, but what about Miami to Paris, without a lot of mountains in between? We can still use microwaves, but our relay station will be a **satellite** with a receiver and transmitter instead of a mountaintop. The satellite must be as stable as a mountain, so it is put in **geostationary orbit,** 22,300 miles above the earth's equator, where it rotates exactly with the earth. In relation to transmitters and receivers on the earth, then, it does not move. Many individuals, especially in rural areas with poor television reception, have satellite dishes—receivers that pick up relayed television signals from various satellites.

Microwaves and satellite relays have almost completely replaced the undersea cables that used to connect North America with Europe and countries on the Pacific Ocean.

Light is another medium becoming quite popular for communications. Typically, the light is not sent through the air but carried in **glass fibers** thinner than a human hair. In such **fiber optic** links, an electric signal drives a laser which generates light at one end. The fiber contains the light and directs it. A light sensor at the other end picks it up and changes it back to electric signals.

Fiber optics are replacing wires in many applications. The medium, glass, is cheaper than the copper in the wire, although the ends (receivers and transmitters) are more expensive. Glass fibers are tougher and not subject to corrosion and water damage. Perhaps the greatest advantage is that glass fibers can carry many times the data as can wires. It is estimated the a single glass fiber can carry all the telephone conversations made at any one time in the United States.

Where microwaves have all but made undersea wire cables obsolete, fiber-optic cables are becoming so efficient that they are now being laid to replace microwave signals.

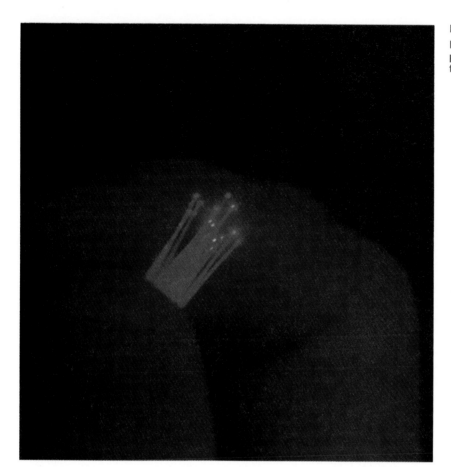

Fiber Optics
Information in the form of light pulses is carried by thin glass fibers.

CHANNEL CHARACTERISTICS

Just as there are many different communications media, there are many different ways of using these media. We will examine some of the choices available, and look at some of their advantages and disadvantages.

Simplex versus Duplex

The least demanding for the communications channel is **simplex,** or one-way communications. Broadcast radio and television stations communicate in the simplex mode—you can receive them but don't bother talking back. There is very little simplex communication of computer data. Even if the data goes only one way, there are usually other signals (typically status signals, like a printer saying to the computer, "Don't send more data, I haven't finished with the last batch.") going the other way.

Duplex communication is two way. Either end can both receive and transmit. Using **half-duplex** communication, the data can go only one way at a time. A two-way radio conversation, where one side speaks, says "over," and the other side speaks, is half duplex.

Full duplex is like two gabby people on the telephone. Both can talk at the same time. A full-duplex channel must be more complex than a

Simplex is one-way communication. Half duplex is two ways, but only one at a time. Full duplex is two ways simultaneously.

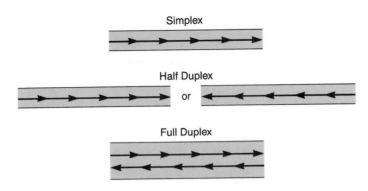

half-duplex channel because it must be capable of carrying two messages in different directions simultaneously. Despite the extra complexity and cost, most computer communications channels are full duplex. The equipment at either end must be more sophisticated than two gabby people because it must be capable of listening while talking.

Baseband versus Broadband

A **baseband** medium is like a standard telephone wire. It can carry only one conversation at a time. Your television set receives a **broadband** signal. By picking out various frequencies in the signal it receives, it can divide the medium into a number of channels. Similarly, broadband data-communications media can carry a number of messages simultaneously. Naturally, broadband media are more complex and expensive than baseband media.

Analog versus Digital

In Chapter 4, we looked at the difference between digital and analog. In communications, digital signals are sent as a series of offs and ons or negative and positive voltages. Analog signals are represented by waves of varying frequency (pitch) or amplitude (loudness). The sound of your voice is an analog signal. It is a series of waves that can vary over continuous

Digital versus Analog Signal

A digital signal is most easily represented by either having power on a line or no power—on or off. An analog signal, such as that in a telephone line, is a continuous wave pattern. We modulate the digital signal onto the analog signal by changing the frequency (the tone) of the continous wave. In this example, low tones (less waves) represent offs and high tones (more waves) represent ons.

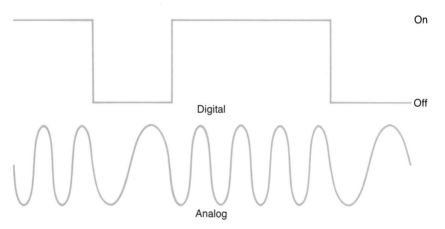

ranges of frequency and amplitude. Both radio and television transmission are analog as well.

If virtually all computers work with digital data, why do we even consider converting our digital data to analog and sending it that way? One major reason is that one of our most popular sets of communications channels, the telephone system, is **voice grade,** designed to carry the human voice. In other words, analog. It works well with different tones but poorly with ons and offs.

Synchronous versus Asynchronous

Data are always transmitted as a series of bits. The sending device takes bytes of information and sends the bits in those bytes out the communications channel. The receiving end must capture these bits and reassemble them into bytes. The order of the bits is no problem. They are always received in the order that they are sent. But what if the receiver somehow lost track of where each byte began? Let us say that, as part of a message, the sending device has sent out the characters "dog". These bits (in ASCII code, even parity) would travel down the channel as:

...10111100100011011111100111101... (and so forth)

d   o   g

If the receiving device were one bit late in its understanding of where the byte started, it would receive

...01111001000110111111001111101... (and so forth)

Which translates to "H—O", not even close to dog. The first and second characters, *H* and underscore, would produce parity errors because each has an odd number of one bits, but the other would be accepted as correct.

Such a situation could not be tolerated. The sending and receiving ends must be synchronized so that the receiving end knows exactly where each byte starts.

If you were singing along with Lawrence Welk, he would give you a chance to get your rhythm in agreement with his by saying "Ah-one, Ah-two, Ah-three, Ah-four," and then launching into the song. This describes **synchronous communication.** The sender transmits a series of bits that the receiver uses to "set the rhythm," so to speak, and then launches into the message.

Typically, synchronous data transmission is accomplished in fixed blocks, each block containing the same number of bytes. After transferring each block, there is usually some error checking, then the two ends will resynchronize and transfer the next block.

Transmission speeds are usually measured in bits per second (BPS) and common synchronous speeds vary from 1,200 BPS to over 4 million BPS. At eight bits per byte or character, that is 150 CPS to 500,000 CPS.

Synchronous transmission depends on having an entire block of data (perhaps a few thousand characters) ready to transmit at one time. It requires nonstop transmission. This is very practical for transferring data from computer to computer but, unless you can type continuously at 150 CPS or more, it does not work well when transferring data from human-oriented devices, such as keyboards and terminals.

Humans, even if they could type that fast, must stop and think, or shuffle papers, answer the phone, or go on a coffee break. We need **asynchronous communication** which allows characters to be sent one at a time with any amount of time in between. Using asynchronous communication, the sender and the receiver must initially be set to the same speed and then each character is individually synchronized as part of the transferring process.

Transmission speeds for asynchronous communication vary from 110 BPS (10 CPS, because this standard uses 11 bits per byte) to 9,600 BPS (960 CPS, 10 bits per byte) over most long-distance communications channels, or up to 57,600 BPS (5,760 CPS) in a terminal plugged directly into a computer. The popular EIA (for Electronics Industries Association) RS-232C is the most common asynchronous standard.

HARDWARE

A simple set of wires is all you need to plug a printer into a socket in the back of a computer. This type of connection is limited to between a few feet to a few thousand feet. Beyond that, the weak signal that is generated by either device would be lost in the wires and would have to be amplified, increased in strength. Also you would have to string a lot of wires and have a lot of amplifiers. Therefore, communications over moderate to long distances usually require some extra hardware to be efficient.

Modems

A Telephone Communications Channel using Modems

The common method of sending data over the normal telephone system is to put modems between the telephone lines and the computer devices on each end.

One of the most common data communications choices is a vast network of already existing channels, the telephone system. These channels are voice grade, designed to carry voice messages: therefore, we must make a conversion from digital to analog and vice versa. The digital signal from the computer device is converted to analog (modulated) and sent into the telephone system. At the other end, this analog signal coming from the

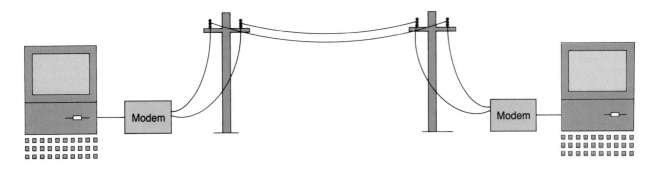

Source: *Business Week*, Nov. 7, 1988, p. 168.

BOX 12-1

*Helping the Deaf Keep In Touch—
From Anywhere*

Advances in telecommunications technology have helped set the stage for the portable executive. But for the nation's 20 million deaf and hearing-impaired, portability hasn't been easily achieved. For instance, to communicate by phone, those who can't speak must first connect a transmission device—about the size of a typewriter—to a phone, and then key in messages to a similar device on the receiving end.

Now, Selective Technologies Inc. in Hampstead, N. H., claims to have a better idea. Its Freedom 415 telecommunications device measures four inches by eight inches and weighs just two pounds. Like its bulkier counterparts, the device plugs into a phone to transmit messages. But unlike the others, it can store up to 20 pages of text and display messages on a seven-line screen. The larger machines have just one line of display and far less memory. At $695, the Freedom 415 is about twice the price of the older devices. But "it's worth the money for deaf professionals who travel a lot," says Virginia Hartling, president of Hartling Communications, a Burlington (Mass.) company that specializes in equipment for the deaf.

telephone is converted back to digital (demodulated) and sent to the other computer device. A modulator-demodulator, commonly called a **modem** performs both conversions. This device converts the on-offs from the computer to beeps and squawks for the phone system and vice versa.

A common addition to a modem is an **acoustic coupler** like the one Larry Turgeson used in the beginning of the chapter. Instead of plugging the modem directly into the telephone plug in the wall, the connection between the modem and the telephone line is made by putting the telephone handset into rubber cups, one with a speaker and the other a microphone. The interface is entirely acoustic, by sound.

Multiplexers

In many cases, the channel is capable of carrying data at a much faster rate than the data is actually sent. For example, if you have a communications channel capable of 9,600 BPS that is connected to a keyboard and you can only type at 50 BPS (5 CPS), most of the capability of that channel will be wasted. Even if the devices are capable of 9,600 BPS but are not used constantly, the line's capability will be wasted.

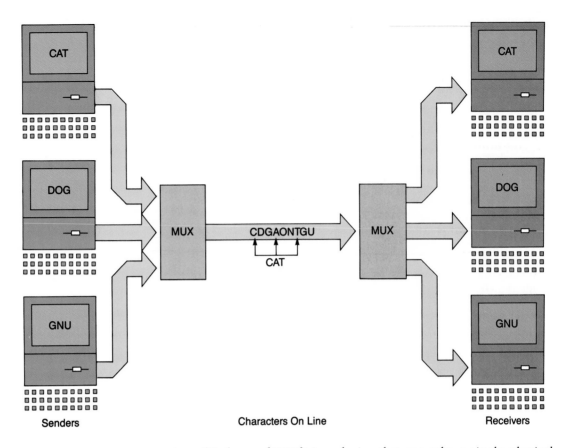

Senders   Characters On Line   Receivers

Time-Division Multiplexing

Time-division multiplexing is accomplished by dividing the time on the communications channel between the various users of the channel. In the example here, the channel can handle three different users, so every third character on the line belongs to a particular user.

A **multiplexer (MUX)** is a device that can take a single physical channel and divide it into a number of logical channels so that many communications can be carried on concurrently. One common multiplexing method is **time division multiplexing (TDM),** where the time on the channel is divided between various users. For example, if there were three users on a channel, it could be divided into three channels by sending one byte from user one, one byte from user two, one byte from user three, a second byte from user one, and so forth.

When it is received at the other end, it must be demultiplexed—the individual bytes must be directed to the correct receiver.

Frequency-division multiplexing (FDM) uses different frequencies on a physical communications channel to separate the logical channels. A broad example of frequency-division multiplexing is the radio-broadcast band, with many different stations or channels using the same medium. Satellite, microwave, and fiber-optic channels, as well as many wire channels, are frequency divided (and may also be time divided).

Concentrators

The objective of using a **concentrator** is the same as that for using a multiplexer—to allow more than one device to use the same physical communications channel at once. Concentrators, however, are more complicated, computer-controlled devices that assign the communications channel to one user at a time. Data from other users are generally buffered (remember, a buffer is a small, temporary memory) until the channel is free and can be assigned to each in turn.

Front-End Processors

Handling communications requires computer time and resources. Often, medium and large computers delegate the communications jobs to specialized **communications processors,** or **front-end processors,** connected to the main processor. The main computer generates the data and passes it to the communications processor, which is often a complete computer system in itself, to be sent to the proper place.

DATA EXCHANGE OPTIONS

The whole idea of communications is to get data from here to there. With all the options available, you must choose the one that will give the most effectiveness for the least cost. Four very important factors will guide your choices.

1. The amount of data that must be exchanged.
2. The number of different people who must use the data.
3. How often data must be exchanged.
4. The time value of the data.

If there is a lot of data to be exchanged between many different people, if it must be exchanged often, and/or if currency of the data is important, your communications will tend to be more complicated and expensive.

If, once a week, you have to give the sales analysis you worked out on your PC to Yolanda in the next office, or if you just need monthly purchasing data from the mainframe, you should consider what is affectionately known as the "sneaker net." Copy the data on a floppy disk, put on your sneakers, and carry it to its destination. Large amounts of data can be put on disks or tape cartridges and mailed overnight to anywhere in the country for ten to twenty dollars.

To get the data there faster and avoid physically handling the media, you might consider **point-to-point communications.** This occurs when one computer device is connected to one other computer device. An intercom between the boss's office and the secretary's is point to point. In Chapter 11, sales offices in various parts of the country were connected to a central computer. Each of those was a point-to-point connection. Point-to-point connections may be simple (your computer plugged into the back of Yolanda's) or complicated (the communication going through the telephone lines to an earth station where it is both time and frequency multiplexed to a satellite, and so forth). If one of the devices is limited to conversations with only one other device, it is point to point.

To allow communications between a number of different devices at reasonable expense, you should consider a **circuit-switched system.**

Here you use appropriate software on both the sending and receiving machines, and nonpermanent connections between them. The connection could be as simple as a wire that you plug and unplug at the back of the machines around the office, or as sophisticated as the entire telephone system. A common application is to equip your computer with a modem ($100 to $600) and a communications-software package ($25 to $200) and dial up a similarly equipped computer on the phone.

Another data-exchange option is simultaneous access to the same data with a multiuser computer system. Unless your application is very small, this will require a minicomputer or a mainframe.

When a number of devices are connected together so that each has the capability of communicating with any of the others, we have a **network.** The telephone system is a network. By dialing a number, you can connect your phone to any of millions of others in the world. Computer networks can consist of many types of computer devices—computers (both large and small), printers, displays, communications devices, and so forth. Any device that originates or is the final destination for data is referred to as a **node.** Computers, printers and displays fall into that category.

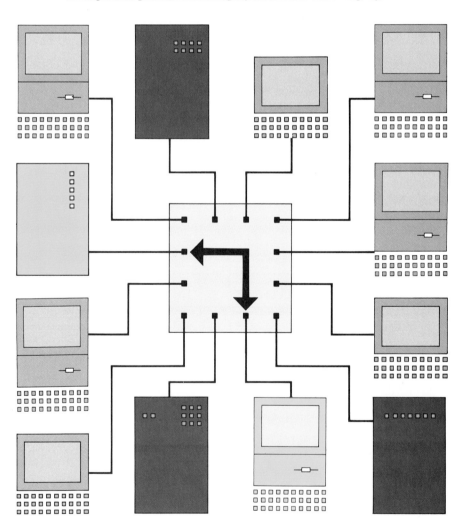

A Circuit-Switched System

Using a circuit-switched system, pairs of computer devices may be connected by a central switching mechanism.

Networking, using dedicated connections between possibly dissimilar computers, can handle almost any situation, but can also be expensive. You might have three PCs tied together with cables and network software (perhaps $150 per PC), to networks including hundreds of PCs, shared printers, a number of mainframes, and satellite links.

NETWORK ARCHITECTURES

The physical layout of a network, what is connected to what, is the network's **architecture** or **topology** (borrowing some terms from the building designers and map makers). As you might imagine, a number of choices are available for network designers. In fact, the choices are almost limitless because the basic architectures can be combined into extremely complicated configurations. Let us look at the basics.

Star Network

A **star network** has all the nodes connected to a central, **host computer.** All communications go through the host, which acts as the controller or traffic director for the network. A bank might use a star network where the computer in the main office acts as the host and all the branch-office computers connect directly to it. If one branch is to communicate to another, it does so through the main office. Star networks are often combined with other star networks where one point on the star is the host computer of another star.

Ring Network

A **ring network** is a circle of point-to-point connections between the various nodes. There is no host computer and no central control of access to the computer. We shall see shortly how access to the network is controlled without a designated traffic director.

The ring has some advantages over the star. It can be more reliable because there are always two possible paths between nodes, clockwise and counterclockwise. If the point-to-point connection between a node and the host in a star network fails, that node is left out of the network. In a ring, the entire network can still communicate with one point-to-point connection out.

Ring networks can be less expensive than stars because connections are made between adjacent nodes rather than all going to the host computer. If the main office was in Chicago with branches in Seattle, Los Angeles, Dallas, Tampa, and New York City, the total length of the connections would be much less going from city to city than all going to Chicago.

Ring communications can be more complicated, however. A star connection involves at most three nodes, including the host. Ring connections must involve each node on the ring between the two communicating nodes. The ones in the middle simply relay the message, but it does require resources from them.

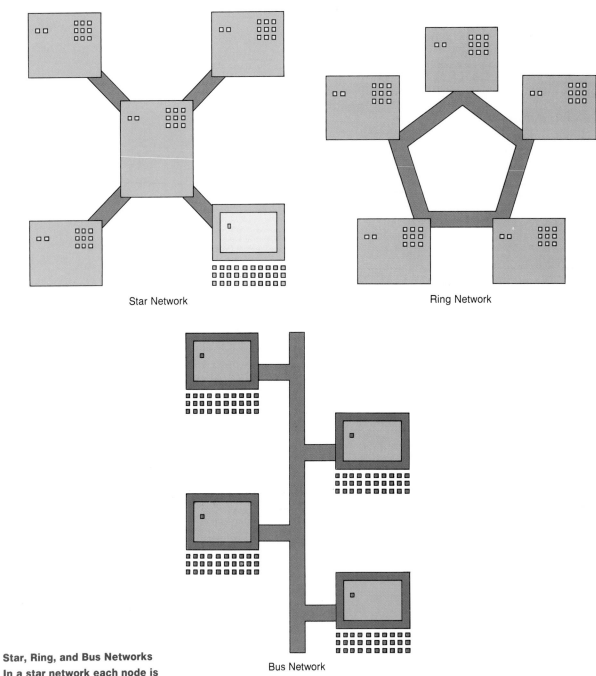

Star Network

Ring Network

Bus Network

Star, Ring, and Bus Networks

In a star network each node is
connected to a central computer,
while in a ring network each node
is connected to two adjacent
nodes, and in a bus network a
number of devices are connected
to the same line.

Source: *Time*, Oct. 24, 1988, p. 80.

BOX 12-2

Quick, What Are the Prime Factors of
9,412,343,607,359,262,946,971,172,136,294,514,357,
528,981,378,983,082,541,347,532,211,942,640,
121,301,590,698,634,089,611,468,911,681?

Don't bother reaching for your calculator. To turn this 100-digit monster into its indivisible primes—as in reducing 15 to the product of 3 and 5—would ordinarily require the undivided attention of a supercomputer for as long as two months. But last week the record-size problem was solved after just 26 days by a group of more than 50 smaller machines scattered across the U.S., Europe and Australia.

Employing a technique called distributed processing, Arjen Lenstra, a Dutch-born computer scientist working as a visiting professor at the University of Chicago, broke the task into smaller pieces and dispatched them over ordinary phone lines to computers at universities and corporations. The results were then compiled by minicomputers at a Digital Equipment lab in Palo Alto, Calif. The success of the adhoc network, one of the largest ever assembled, raises problems for cryptographers and intelligence agenices, whose code solutions are often based on the prime factors of long, hard-to-solve integers. But it certainly demonstrates the enormous power of small computers linked together by electronic mail. Their answer: 86,759,222,313,428,390,812,218, 077,095,850,708,048,977 × 108, 488,104,853,637,470,612,961,399, 842,972,948,409,834,611,525,790, 577,216,753.

Bus Network

In a **bus network,** all the nodes are connected to the same logical channel, usually the same wire or fiber-optic cable. This type of network may or may not have a designated host computer.

It has advantages over the star and the ring because there need be no relaying of messages. One node puts a message on the line, all of the others can receive it, but only the one it is actually destined for responds to it. The others say, "That's not for me" and go on about their business.

NETWORK PROTOCOLS

An announcement for a computer conference came in the mail the other day. On the agenda were a number of lectures and seminars, and a dinner to be followed by informal "networking" in the bar. Networking? That simply meant that the conference participants were going to get together and chat after dinner.

Although the dictionary does not list this particular definition, networking is a good term to describe a group of people informally talking. Each is independent and can talk with any of the others. The conversation is not a free-for-all, however. There are rules of good manners that govern it. Can you imagine if everyone talked all at once in different languages as loudly as they could?

A computer network must also have rules, called **protocols,** that govern the use of the network—the conversation, so to speak. They describe such things as:

- The "language" to be used—ASCII or EBCDIC, number of data bits, number of bits (if asynchronous), how to synchronize (if synchronous), and so forth.
- The speed at which the data are sent.
- The types of codes that identify nodes and data-storage locations on the network.
- The type of line control in use—how an individual node gains control of the line so that it can "talk" without interrupting others or being interrupted.

We will look at some of the protocols that define line control in networks.

Polling

Polling was one of the first methods of line control for network communications. In a **polling** system, one of the nodes (it must be a computer) is designated as the controller and assigns the line to the others by asking each, in a round-robin fashion, if they have anything to transmit.

The controller sends out a code that is responded to by only the first device. If that device has anything to transmit, it will do so. Otherwise it will not respond. After the first device's message, or lack of, the controller will send out the code for the second device, which will either send its message or keep quiet. After the controller has given the opportunity to transmit to the last device on the line, it will start the whole process over with the first.

Contention

Contention is similar to a group of polite people in conversation. When someone is talking, the others will remain silent. When that person finishes, others will start talking, but if they hear someone else also talking, they will politely stop. No one person is controlling the conversation and no time is spent asking those who do not wish to talk if they have anything to say.

A device in a contention network with a message to send will wait until the line is clear and then start sending. While it is sending, it is also listening. If it hears another device sending, it (and the other device) will stop. Once the line is free, the device will try again.

If this was all there was to it, when the line became free, all the devices with messages to send would start transmitting at the same time and, hearing the others, stop. Then start. Then stop. And so forth. Each device, however, delays a random amount of time before retrying, and whichever has the shortest delay at that particular time will capture the line. Since the delay time is random, each device has an equal chance of capturing the line.

Token Passing

The **token-passing** network protocol was originated well over ten thousand years ago. It was the custom for some tribes to have a "talking stone" or "talking stick" that was used in tribal meetings. The item was passed from person to person and only the person holding the talking stone could talk. The others had to shut up.

This Cro-Magnon custom was applied to computer networks. A "token," an agreed-upon set of bytes, is passed from node to node in a network. Before an individual node may transmit data, it first must receive the token.

Information Packets

Data sent over a network is often collected into fixed-size chunks called **packets.** Depending on the protocol, the packet might consist of from about 128 to 5000 bytes each. If your network used packets of 200 bytes each and your message had 500 bytes, your node would send it in three packets, the last being half blank.

chunks of bytes.

Fixed packets allow messages to be sent in synchronous fashion, and also keep one node from dominating the network. After one packet is sent, other nodes are given the opportunity to transmit, and your next packet will have to wait its turn.

Standards and Gateways

With so many protocol options, which one do we all use? Like so many things in the computer field, we all use different ones. There are some standards, but the more standards that are developed, the less standard things become. Each new standard adds another set of initials to the computer vocabulary. One of the current controversies can be summed up as follows:

"For WANs, since the UN's CCITT has endorsed ISO's OSI model, IBM's SNA is being enhanced to conform."

Translating the computerese into English, wide-area networks—those that span cities and continents—often use protocols based on IBM's **Systems Network Architecture (SNA).** IBM initially set the standard in this case because they are big and they developed their standard early in the game.

The **International Standards Organization (ISO)** is exactly as the name implies, an international body created to establish standards. Our ANSI (American National Standards Institute) is an ISO member. If you look on a package of film for your camera, for example, you will see a standard ISO film-speed rating. The ISO developed, and is still in the process of refining, the **OSI (open systems interconnection)** model for network communications. Since the **Comité Consultatif International Télégraphique et Téléphonique (CCITT),** a world-respected, United Nations committee on communications standards, has endorsed the OSI model, IBM has expanded their systems network architecture to allow it to conform.

This does not solve the problem, however, because most networks, especially those involving personal computers, do not follow the standard. Even if they did, the OSI model has many different options and seven different levels of standards which may or may not be included in an individual network. Many manufacturers are getting around this problem by offering **gateways,** software and/or hardware that allow equipment designed for connection to one type of network to work in another type. Entire networks are often connected to other, dissimilar networks using gateways.

LOCAL AREA NETWORKS

A PC Network with a Server

In this network of personal computers, the server provides the PCs with a selection of common software, access to data that all the users typically need, and the choice of two printers.

In the beginning, there were computers in back rooms. Nobody actually saw them, but they assumed they were there because they had to fill in various data forms and they got printed reports back. Then came terminals. People could actually "talk" to the computer and get responses back. It came to pass, however, that the information-systems world was torn asunder—the personal computer evolved. Now everyone went out and got their own computers and put them on their desks.

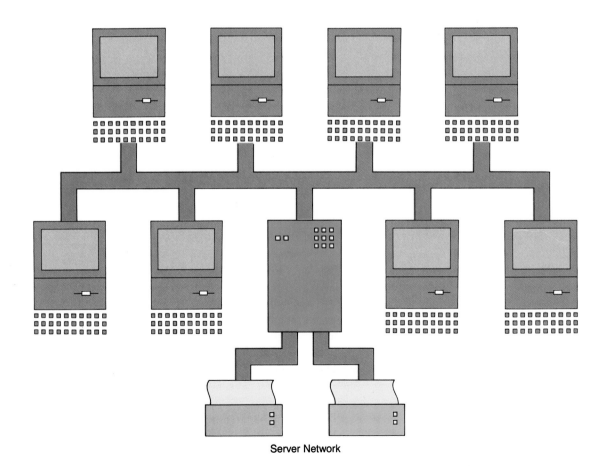

Server Network

Where did these people get the data for their computers? At first, it was all typed in at the individual keyboards. People actually took printout from the main computer and keyed those data into their personal computers. To transfer data from one PC to another, they traded floppy disks—if they were compatible, and many were not. Everyone said, "Why don't these computers talk to each other?"

The whole idea of a network is to allow computers to talk to each other. Most networks, however, were complicated things carrying large blocks of data from city to city. Such a network is commonly referred to as a **wide-area network (WAN).** Since WANs could not be used to tie Marvin's computer to Elfreda's down the hall, **local-area networks (LANs)**—networks that tie the nodes within a building or two—were developed.

Again, there is no one standard but a variety of choices. Media vary. Some use the existing telephone wiring, others use special cables, and still others, fiber optics. Protocols and architectures vary. One popular LAN, Ethernet, uses a bus network controlled by contention. IBM's token–ring network is a ring network controlled by token passing.

A popular configuration for a microcomputer network is to have a number of individual PCs networked together with a central box called a **server.** The purpose of the server is to provide common services to each of the PCs on the network. Typical of these services is shared secondary storage so that all the PCs can access the same programs and files. Another typical service is access to one or more common printers. Others may include communications gateways to other networks, special output devices such as plotters or laser printers, and so forth.

CHANNEL PROVIDERS

Setting up a network of communications channels over a vast geographical area is an expensive proposition that only a large company could undertake by itself. Some organizations—like Lockheed, IBM, and the United States government—have extensive communications lines dedicated to their exclusive use. Most, however, rely on facilities made available for a price from companies whose business it is to sell communications services to others.

Common Carriers

A **common carrier** is in the communications business. Most, like AT&T, General Telephone and Electronics, Western Union, and MCI, started out in the telephone and/or telegraph business. Others, like Satellite Business Systems, RCA Americom (SATCOM satellites), and American Satellite Company, were set up with the idea of data transmission as their principal service. Most of these latter companies' data networks center around high-speed, satellite transmission of data with voice being only an incidental or nonexistent part of their business.

Communications through a common carrier can either be over **switched lines** like a normal telephone call, where you call the local

BOX 12-3

"Wingnet"—It's Definitely for the Birds

Sunnyvale, Calif.—Some companies use local-area networks and leased lines. Others swear by microwave dishes and satellites.

But here in the center of high technology and computer innovation, the Lockheed Missiles and Space Co. has found an older, faster and less expensive way of getting information from here to there—by Columbidae, more commonly known as pigeons.

Lockheed uses its feathered fleet—which numbers about 15—to shuttle microfilmed data from its headquarters here to its isolated research and design facility located about 30 miles away on a mountaintop just outside Santa Cruz. The firm can transmit the data over telephone lines from Sunnyvale's IBM computers to a Versatec, Inc., electrostatic printer at its other facility, but using the pigeons instead costs about 10 times less than using the machines, explained Will Hilbrink, a spokesman for the firm.

The data in question is actually a product of the mountaintop research site, but is transmitted to and printed in Sunnyvale. Lockheed's headquarters sends the microfilmed material back via carrier pigeon so that the

firm's engineers there can review what they have produced, Hilbrink said.

Like all carriers of the winged persuasion, the pigeons are trained to fly just one way—from Point A to home. So before the pigeon-toed network can become operative, a bird must be transported along winding roads down the mountainside from the isolated site to the Sunnyvale headquarters. This is done on a daily basis as part of the regular mail run.

When shipment time arrives, a capsule containing the microfilm is attached to the pigeon's leg, and the bird is released to begin its journey home. "We fly about one bird a day," Hilbrink said. "This gives them a lot of rest."

Lockheed launched "Wingnet" after one of the firm's scientists saw a television show depicting a hospital that used pigeons to transport blood samples to a nearby testing laboratory. Since shipping the needed Lockheed data manually involved driving over 50 miles of rugged mountain roads—a full day's work—the firm decided to adopt the hospital's transportation means-of-another-feather, so to speak.

Lockheed has been

contacted by other firms that have expressed interest in augmenting their computer-based information retrieval systems with pigeons.

Lockheed, which has been using pigeon power to transmit data on a full-time basis since the beginning of this year, bought its first birds from a local pigeon racing club. The firm recently began breeding its own carrier pigeons.

A Few Glitches

However, even the best systems have a few glitches.

During its trial run, Lockheed's feathered fleet logged two casualties: one bird flew into a high-powered electrical wire and the other just kept on flying. Fortunately, only test data was lost.

Also, unlike the U.S. Postal Service, Lockheed's pigeons think rain, sleet and gloom of night are not for the birds.

"If it's too stormy, they won't fly," Hilbrink said. "They'll just roost and sit out the storm."

When this happens, the' computer understudies are used to transport data instead of the grounded birds.

Source: Tim Scannell, *Computerworld,* Sept. 6, 1982.

switching facility and your transmission is routed through available lines to its destinations, or private, **leased lines,** where a company leases a specific set of lines from one point to another. Switched lines have the advantage of allowing your communications to go to anywhere there is a telephone. Leased lines are more reliable (all of us have made long-distance calls where there was so much noise on the line that we could hardly hear the other party), always instantly available, and usually allow higher-speed transmission because they are often either specially "conditioned" by the common carrier or they are designed to carry high-speed data.

Common carriers, especially AT&T and the regional telephone companies, are setting up **integrated services digital networks (ISDN).** The standard telephone system, at least at the local level, is analog. Digital data must be converted to analog to make use of it, but analog transmission of data is inefficient and slow. The ISDN is a digital system which carries data quite efficiently. It also carries voice communications by converting the analog voices to digital signals at the telephone itself, so that everything carried on the network is digital. ISDNs are being used in telephone voice/data systems within companies as well as allowing connections to world-wide data networks.

Value-Added Carriers

A **value-added carrier** leases lines from a common carrier and adds value to those lines, namely setting them up as high-speed communications channels. Two such companies are Tymnet and Telenet (a subsidiary of GTE). Both of these are referred to as **packet-switching networks** because, when you send messages through either network, your messages are assembled into packets, specific-sized blocks of information, and these packets are individually sent to their destinations in the best possible, available route. It is conceivable that your message might be divided into five packets and each of them, because of channel use and availability at the moment, could reach the destination by a different route. You would never know it, though, because the message is reassembled at the destination.

APPLICATIONS

Being able to electronically communicate data means that the user and the computer do not have to be physically close. The user may be miles, thousands of miles, or even millions of miles away. The data available to you, the user, are not just the stuff down the hall, but stuff all over the world. Not only that, data does not have to be transported slowly by hand, they can be sent instantly electronically. A number of organizations are taking advantage of these capabilities.

Time-Sharing and Remote Computing Services

If you need access to a sophisticated computer but do not have enough usage to justify buying your own, you can take advantage of one of the commercial time-sharing services. You can have a terminal and a modem in your office and be connected to their computer across town (or across the country). It will be just like having your own computer except that the cost will be less because the computer is actually being shared by a number of customers.

Personal Computer Focus   BOX 12-4

Linked PCs Deliver Newspaper

Distributed LAN brings expandability, sanity to beleaguered daily

Insufficient memory and a system that crashed eight to 10 times a day were unbearable, but *The Middlesex News* managed to plug along and get the paper published daily.

As time went by, however, meeting news deadlines became a nightmare as reporters competed for open terminals and new terminals, since the aging computer system could no longer be updated. The 45,000-circulation daily newspaper either had to stop growing or adopt an alternative system.

In response to this problem, the newspaper's management formed a team that began a months-long

search to replace the more than 10-year-old ECRM, Inc. publishing system. The patched and repatched system boasted a Digital Equipment Corp. mainframe at its heart that was replaced with a distributed network of personal computers, according to Eric D. Bauer, director of editorial operations.

Bauer said many minicomputer-based alternatives were explored, but the project team was leery of any system that could crash, bringing down all of the reporters and editors as well as the advertising department, while also cutting off access to news wire capture services like The Associated Press and United Press International.

With a distributed PC network, "There's no CPU to

crash across the network," Bauer said. "Individual terminals could crash, but as a system it wouldn't crash, so it's more reliable."

The chosen system was pieced together by Information International, Inc. in Culver City, Calif., a supplier of newspaper and magazine publishing systems that features Tecs/2 publishing software developed by Morris Publishing Co. in Atlanta, Ga.

The main CPU on each desk is a generic 8-MHz, 40M-byte hard-disk system based on Intel Corp.'s 80286 chip. The distributed system, which also features an IBM Enhanced Graphics Adapter-compatible Amdek Corp. color monitor for each user and a 1.2M-byte, 5 1/4-in. floppy drive, is networked

Remote computing services are similar in that the input and output facilities can be in your office, but they will handle all the computer software chores like writing and maintaining programs for you. Again, the computer that your data is processed on is probably shared among a number of customers.

Banking

Banks have used data-communications methods for **electronic funds transfers (EFT)** from one bank to another for years, but now they are offering the consumer special bank-at-home services. Using a personal computer or sometimes just a touch-tone telephone, customers can find out account statuses, apply for loans, or pay bills while sitting at home.

Remote Data Banks

If you want current information on the stock market, you can access data from Dow Jones, you can get news from NEXIS or the New York Times

using Proteon, Inc.'s Pronet 10 10M-bit token-ring network.

Bauer said the system is readily expandable. With the ECRM system, the terminals were proprietary. Once the company went out of business, the terminals become harder and harder to find.

The Information International system allows the editors to converse more easily with bureau locations. Reporters had previously been using Tandy Corp. Radio Shack Model 100 portables. The new system provides the bureaus with two-way communications access to the home office.

"This is the first piece of what will be a multiyear effort, called the integrated text processing system project," Bauer said. "We want a totally integrated, totally electronic prepress operation." The company also plans to install a classified advertisement system, an advertising make-up system and an editorial pagination system.

The system has no central data base, but there is a designated master station to which only editors have access and which allows them to work on stories for the next day's paper.

From the user perspective, there were drawbacks to the PC-based system, Bauer said. Because there is no distributed data base, reporters do not have access to other queues as they did previously. And, although the system offers many benefits, the additional features have made it more complex.

In order to ease the transition from the "elegantly simple" old system, the company held a series of classes followed by a one-month period in which users could tinker with the new system while still relying on the old.

Still, when the day arrived to complete the transition, problems arose. Fortunately, it took place on a Sunday evening, the paper's easiest night. "We had a pretty tough night," Bauer admitted, "but there were no problems with the system. Some people were slow, but on the second day we saw a dramatic improvement." After several weeks in place, the paper is back to full speed, Bauer said. This time though there are no crashes waiting in the wings.

Source: Alan Ryan, *Computerworld,* April 18, 1988, p. 69.

Information Service, legal information from WestLaw or LEXIS, or almost anything from Lockheed's DIALOG system. These are **remote data banks.** They supply data in various categories to their subscribers. Typically, these services cost a few hundred to a few thousand dollars to join and charge a fee for "connect time," the time that your remote terminal is connected to their equipment.

Electronic Mail

A computer can be used as a kind of **electronic mail** box. If it is left on and available for contact by other computers, someone in another office or another city can leave a message on it. When you return, you can not only check your "box" to see if there are messages but with most "E-mail" systems you can also see who left messages and when, and perhaps what the message was about. You can look at these mail summaries and decide to answer your boss right away (perhaps by return E-mail), but leave the aluminum siding salesman for later (or never).

Information Utilities

A number of companies provide a wide range of computer services, all based around communications. Such **information utilities** exist for both the general public and for specific kinds of organizations. Anyone with a computer, a telephone, and a modem can subscribe to Compuserve or The Source. There is a small initial fee, less than $30, and a charge for connect time plus occasional premium charges for certain services. These services offer access to news and financial data bases, electronic mail, software exchanges, home shopping, travel reservations, computer games, and a host of other things. There is even a "CB" (as in citizen's band radio) service that allows anyone who dials up to "chew the rag" with everyone else connected at the time.

Other information utilities serve specific businesses. For example, Official Airline Guide is for the travel industry, E. F. Huttonline for the financial community, and NewsNet for news.

In addition to these nationwide services, there are any number of **bulletin boards,** computers to dial up that may provide software sharing, simple electronic mail, computers for sale, or whatever. These bulletin boards are often sponsored by a local computer dealer, club, or special interest group and are free to the users.

The Office at Home

Many gainfully employed people rarely see their places of business. They are either stuck on the freeway for interminable hours or they are **telecommuters**—they stay at home and keep in contact with the office through telephones and their computers.

SUMMARY

The three main criteria by which we measure communications systems are accuracy, speed, and cost. The faster and more accurate the system, the more it will cost.

The data can travel by means of any number of media. Wire is the most common, but glass fibers are replacing wire in many applications. Data are sometimes transmitted by relatively low-frequency radio waves, but reliability and interference problems make super-high-frequency microwaves more popular. Unlike radio waves, microwaves can only transmit line of sight, but they are often relayed from one place to another by receiving and transmitting stations on the tops of buildings or mountains, or by satellites.

Data are sent in many forms and fashions over communications channels. It can be either simplex, one way; half duplex, two ways but only one at a time; or full duplex, two ways simultaneously. Channels may be either baseband, capable of handling one message at a time; or broadband, capable of many simultaneous messages. Transmissions may be either synchronous, if blocks of continuous data are to be sent; or asynchronous, if the data must be interrupted frequently.

Data communications often require their own kinds of unique hardware. Modems convert the computer's digital signals into the analog signals needed for the telephone system and vice versa. Multiplexers and concentrators allow the same communications channel to be used for many communications concurrently. Front-end communications processors are often used on large computer systems to handle the communications chores while the normal CPU goes about its other business.

In the exchange of data between computer devices, one has a number of options. Hand carrying the data on disks or tape is the simplest. Point-to-point connections allow two computers to talk to each other. Circuit-switched systems allow any number of individual devices to be temporarily connected to others. The same data may be shared by connecting terminals to a multiuser computer. Networks allow possibly dissimilar computer devices to share data directly between them.

A network's physical connection scheme is known as its architecture. The basic types are the star, the ring, and the bus. Actual networks may contain combinations of all three.

Protocols are the rules governing the use of the network. One important body of protocol is that controlling which device is allowed access to the network at any one time. The common line-control protocols are contention, polling, and token passing. Common to many protocols is the idea of sending data in fixed-length packets. Many standard protocols exist, making it difficult for a device or network using one standard to communicate with one using another standard. Gateways allow dissimilar hardware and protocols to communicate.

A number of companies are in the business of providing communications facilities to others. These can be categorized as common carriers and value-added carriers. Many other services depend upon computer communications to function. Among them are time sharing and remote computing, electronic banking, remote data banks, electronic mail, various information utilities, and telecommuting.

KEY WORDS

(in order of appearance in text)
Channel
Medium
Wire
Radio wave
Radioteletype (RTTY)
Microwave
Relay
Satellite
Geostationary orbit
Light
Glass fiber
Fiber optics
Simplex
Duplex
Half duplex
Full duplex
Baseband
Broadband
Voice grade
Synchronous communication
Asynchronous communication
Modem
Acoustic coupler
Multiplexer (MUX)

Time-division multiplexing (TDM)
Frequency-division multiplexing (FDM)
Concentrator
Communications processor
Front-end processor
Point-to-point communication
Circuit-switched system
Network
Node
Architecture
Topology
Star network
Host computer
Ring network
Bus network
Protocol
Polling
Contention
Token passing
Packet
Systems Network Architecture (SNA)
International Standards Organization (ISO)

Open systems interconnection (OSI)
Comité Consultatif International Télégraphique et Téléphonique (CCITT)
Gateway
Wide-area network (WAN)
Local-area network (LAN)
Server
Common carrier
Switched line
Leased line
Integrated services digital network (ISDN)
Value-added carrier
Packet-switching network
Remote computing service
Electronic funds transfer (EFT)
Remote data bank
Electronic mail
Information utility
Bulletin board
Telecommuter

REVIEW QUESTIONS

1. Name the three important criteria by which most communications systems are judged.

2. What is a communications channel?

3. Which was the first and still most popular communications medium?

4. What are the advantages of microwaves over the lower-frequency radio waves?

5. What are satellites used for in data communications?

6. What is a geostationary orbit?

7. Name some advantages of glass fibers over wires as a communications medium.

8. How does simplex communication differ from duplex? Half duplex from full duplex?

9. Compare a baseband channel to a broad band channel.

10. Is a voice-grade channel analog or digital?

11. Why is synchronizing the receiver and transmitter important?

12. What does a modem do?

13. What do multiplexers and concentrators do?

14. Explain the difference between frequency and time-division multiplexing.

15. How do the terms architecture and protocol differ?

16. Name three basic types of network architecture and explain how they differ?

17. Name three basic types of line-control protocols and explain how they differ.

18. How do gateways help to overcome lack of network standards?

19. What is a local-area network?

20. What value does a value-added carrier add to the services of a common carrier?

21. Name some of the services offered by information utilities.

THINK ABOUT IT

1. If you could get a communications system with a 98 percent accuracy rate at one quarter the cost of one with virtually 100 percent accuracy, could you make it work for you? If so, how?

2. You must send large amounts of data between your head office and your factory five miles away. Assuming no physical restrictions, which medium would you choose and why?

3. In a time-division multiplexing scheme, what happens when one of the logical channels has no data to send?

4. What advantages would a local-area network have over a time-sharing scheme?

5. Which would require less cable, a star, bus, or ring network?

6. Could token passing work in a star network? If so, how?

CHALLENGES

1. You are setting up a local-area network for your company's headquarters in the top eight floors of a downtown building. The network should include the company's mainframe computer and 100 PCs in various offices. The average PC makes only intermittent use of the network, being "on the air" about 5 percent of the time. What medium, architecture, and line-control protocol would you use? Justify your answers.

2. Look at your school or where you work. If they have an adequate data-communications network, find out how it is designed. If not, design one for them. Diagram the architecture, identify the media in use, and describe the protocols.

13
ACCESS TO STORED DATA

PREVIEW
The objective of a computer information system is to provide information. This requires accessing, that is, storing and retrieving, data. In this chapter we will look at various ways of accessing data. At its conclusion, you should understand:

■ The basics of traditional file-processing methods.

■ Differences in how we as humans view data and how they are often arranged for the benefit of the computer.

■ How database management systems differ from earlier file-access methods.

■ The important features of database management systems.

■ The three basic types of physical database models.

■ Some of the criteria for choosing either a file-processing system or a database system.

File-processing systems were based on manual filing methods.

The phone book is a good example of a sequential file. The key field is the name.

Much of the work of an information-processing system is storing and retrieving data. While storing the data is important, even more important is retrieving and modifying them. We shall see that how we organize the data when we store them depends upon how we wish to work with them, that is, retrieve and modify them.

FILE-PROCESSING SYSTEMS

The idea of storing data in files certainly is not new. We have been using manual filing systems for centuries. As with most computer applications, the first file-storage schemes were based on the filing methods we had been using before the computer was invented. **File-processing systems** are based on these manual data-storage methods. In Chapter 3, we introduced the concepts of fields, records, and files. These are the basic building blocks of a file-processing system.

A **file** is a collection of related data. A phone book could be thought of as a file. To use a manual filing-system analogy, the file might be file drawer two, where all of our customer data are kept. A **record** is all the data relating to a particular entity, a single listing in the phone book. The file folder with all the data for the customer "Menschle, Marvin" would be a record. A **field** is a particular characteristic of an entity; a name, address, or phone number in the phone book listing. Our file folder would contain data such as Marvin Menschle's address, current balance, credit limit, last items ordered, and so forth. As in the phone book listings or our file folders, each record consists of the same fields so that we store the same characteristics for each entity.

A **key** is a field in the record that uniquely identifies the record. For example, the name in the phone book. In our customer file, the key might be the customer's name or a customer number. We would refer to the "Menschle" record or customer 42709. Typically, files are organized so that referring to the key is the fastest way to find a record. We shall see that more sophisticated file systems allow more than one key to identify a record.

File Organization

Since file-processing systems are based on manual filing systems, the organizational methods of the computer files resemble those used in manual systems. One typical method is **sequential file** organization where the file is ordered by the key. A phone book is a sequentially organized file. This is perhaps the most straightforward organizational method, but it has its drawbacks, especially in making modifications. One cannot simply insert a name in the phone book; the entire book must be reprinted. In a sequential computer file, the file must be substantially, if not totally, rewritten to insert a record in the proper place.

An **indexed file** overcomes some of these problems. With such a scheme, the organization of the records is not important, only that we be able to identify where a record resides. A phone book is an index to residences and places of business. We look up a name in the phone book and it tells us the address. A library card catalog is another good example of

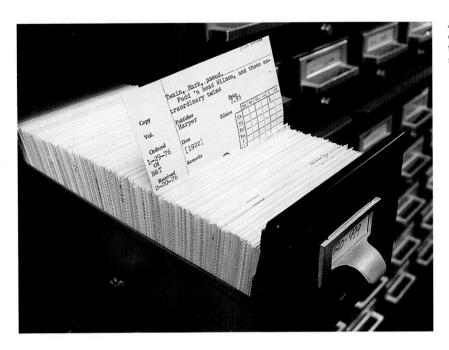

A library card catalog is an example of an index. In fact, it is three indices—author, title, and subject.

an index. We can look up an author in the catalog and the card will tell us where to find the book on the shelves.

Additions and modifications are easier using an indexed file. The data record can go anywhere in the file, and its location added to the index. It is true that the index itself must be kept in order, but the index is much smaller than the data file itself. Resorting a card catalog is a much simpler task than reshuffling all the books on the shelves. As in the example of the card catalog, a computer file may have many indices. Library books we can access by author, title, or subject. We might access our customer file by customer name, number, or geographical area.

On the negative side, indexed files require more storage space than simple sequential files. We must not only store the data but also the indices.

TABLE 13-1 An Indexed File

Index		Data File	
Key	Pointer	Record	Key and Data
Able	3	1	Dumpke 123 Oak . . . . .
Baker	7	2	Grinch 27 Elm . . . . .
Charles	6	3	Able 42A Maple . . . . .
Dumpke	1	4	Effron 7 Eucalyptus . . . . .
Effron	4	5	Flakey 36-2 Pine . . . . .
Flakey	5	6	Charles 4926 Mulberry . . . . .
Grinch	2	7	Baker 79 Birch . . . . .

An indexed file allows easier updates because only the relatively small index must be reorganized rather than the larger data file.

An indexed file allows easier updates because only the relatively small index must be reorganized rather than the larger data file.

Another popular file organization is the **hashed file.** (This is often called a direct-access file, but that term is too easily confused with direct-access storage methods as discussed in Chapter 5.) Using this method, the key leads us directly to the record's location in the file. A simple example would be to assign each customer a number that is the same as the record location in the customer file. Customer number 649 would be found in record 649 in the file.

If we wished to refer to our customers by name instead of number, we could still use a hashed file. We could convert the name to a record number by applying a **hashing algorithm** to it. The algorithm might convert the name to a number by using the ASCII codes for the letters in the name, and then put that number through some formula that would result in another number that was within the range of records in the file.

The hashed file allows faster access because the computer does not have to refer to an index and then to a data file. However, the hashed file can use only one key. Designing hashing algorithms that would take two dissimilar keys, such as name and address, and result in the same record number would be impossible.

PROBLEMS OF FILE-PROCESSING SYSTEMS

File processing utilized the power of the computer to manage our data much faster and more accurately than we could by hand. Retrieving data was a comparative breeze. We had all kinds of data at our finger tips and could print out miles of meaningful reports. Like normal human beings, though, once we got a taste of the good life, we wanted more. File-processing systems had taken us about as far as we could go by imitating manual methods. But file-processing systems require that we fit our **logical views** of the data—how we humans see the data and their relationships—with the **physical views** of the data—how the data are actually organized in the hardware.

For questions such as "What products did the Jones Company order last?" a file-processing system is quite adequate. We simply have the computer search the order file for the most recent record with "Jones" in the name field.

But "Show me all the customers' names and addresses with yearly purchases greater than $100,000 who have backordered items provided to us by Smith Manufacturing" stretches the limits of a file-processing system. We must have our computer search through our vendor files for all the products provided by Smith; look for those products in our purchase order and inventory files; for those that we are out of stock on, search our order file for any order for them; and go to our customer file and print out the names and addresses of the customers for those orders with the appropriate total sales.

A major difficulty is that file-processing systems are designed to use data from one file at a time. This does not mean that a program in such a system might not use more than one file. For example, to build our sales-order file, we might use our customer file to fill in the name and address of the customer, and the sales-tax file to provide the proper sales-tax rates. But each file contains data that is not related to the others.

File-processing systems become inefficient when we try to relate data in one file to that in another. If our order file contains a customer number and we want to print out the name and address of the customer for that order, we must have a program that searches the customer file for that customer number. We could, and often do, save the cost of the search program and the execution time for the search by repeating the customer name and address in the order file.

This often necessary shortcut creates one of the biggest problems of file-processing systems—**data redundancy,** having the same data more than once in various files. Besides wasting storage space, redundancy makes **data updates,** changing the data in the files, much more difficult. If, for example, the Jones Company were taken over by Amalgamated Octopus, Inc., that name change would have to be made in perhaps dozens of different places in many different files.

Typically, the files in file-processing systems are physically arranged to work with specific programs. A **program–data dependence** exists. Integrating the data into other programs not specifically designed with those files in mind is difficult. Not only that, but major changes in either hardware or software are also difficult. Changing to a new order-processing software package might require rearranging all the files. Changing the storage hardware might require rewriting the programs that access the files.

LOGICAL VIEWS OF DATA

In traditional file-processing terms, a customer's address is a field in a record in the customer file which the computer can translate to a surface, track, and sector on a disk. But for the rest of the chapter, let us free ourselves from the traditional terms—field, record, and file—and examine some of the ways we logically view data. We will see some of the difficulties we encounter in applying file processing systems, and then we will look at how we address these problems using other data-access methods.

Data Objects

From the user's perspective, a collection of data may be viewed as consisting of a number of **objects,** specific things that can be unambiguously described by the user. For clarity and so that these objects can be discussed with other users, they are given names. As a case in point, let us look at some of the various objects involved in the data for a university.

There is the student, Agatha Prindle; the professor, Elvin Cornthwaite, Ph.D.; the course, CIS 301 or BUS 286; and the grade, A, B, C, or whatever. We can use a file-processing system to store and retrieve objects such as these; each of them could be fields in various files in the system. Looking up data concerning these objects would be relatively easy using any of the file-processing methods we have discussed.

Complex Objects

In the real world, we rarely view data as single items. More often we must look at **relationships,** associations between different kinds of data. For example, a student's transcript is not a single piece of data. It consists of the student's name, each course the student has completed, and the grade in each course.

The transcript created by the relationship between these three objects forms a **complex object,** one consisting of more than a single piece of data. Traditional file-processing systems fall short when trying to work with complex objects. To assemble a transcript, for example, we might have to get the student's name from the student file, search each class in the class file for that name, look up the grade for that student in the class file, and credit the grade in that class to the proper course in the transcript. This requires a lot of programming and a lot of execution time in searching.

The number of searches could be reduced by keeping redundant data in the file-processing system, but, as we have already seen, redundancy carries its own problems.

Variable-Length Objects

File-processing systems thrive on consistency. Typically, a fixed amount of space is allocated for each kind of data. Transcripts, however, are not all the same size. Some students have taken many courses, others just a few. The transcript is an example of a **variable-length object** and as such is difficult to assemble, store, and access using a file-processing system.

Overlapping Objects

Complex objects often overlap other complex objects. In other words, two or more complex objects may share some of the same data. In our university example, we used four simple objects—student, professor, course, and grade. We saw that the complex object, transcript, combined the student, course, and grade. We could make a number of other complex objects out of the basic four.

TABLE 13-2   Descriptions of Objects in a University

Object Name	Object Description
Simple Objects	
Student	Name, social security number, address, phone
Professor	Name, social security number, address, phone, degree, rank
Class	Course, days, times
Grade	A, B, C, D, or F
Complex Objects	
Transcript	Student, class, grade
Schedule	Student, class
Class load	Professor, class
Student load	Professor, student
Class roster	Professor, class, student
Grade book	Professor, class, student, grade

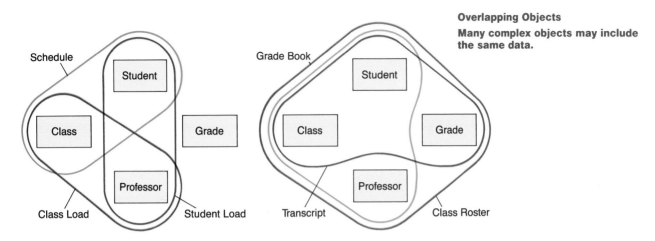

Overlapping Objects
Many complex objects may include the same data.

A professor's class load combines the professor and the class. A student schedule combines the student and the class. Some of the possible objects in a university are described in the figure here. A diagram of the complex objects and how they overlap is also shown.

DATABASE MANAGEMENT SYSTEMS

A **database management system (DBMS)** is a software package that frees us from concern about the physical (computer) particulars of data storage and allows us to think about them in logical (human) terms. Using a database management system, we can work with objects and complex object relationships without having to relate them to physical storage in the computer.

We saw in Chapter 8 that the operating system is a software package that goes between us (or our applications programs) and the hardware and translates our requests into hardware-specific instructions. The concept of the database management system is similar. The DBMS takes our data requests stated in logical terms, translates them into more detailed computer terms, and passes them on to the rest of the system. Physically, the DBMS sits between the applications programs (or user) and the operating system.

In order for the operating system to find specific data—the address of Falkmeier, Inc., for example—the applications program would have to tell it to look in the customer file at record 1014. With a database management system in place, the applications program would ask the DBMS for the

The Database Management System

The DBMS allows us to make very simple, logical data requests. It translates these to the detailed physical requests needed by the operating system, which further translates them to the specific instructions needed by the hardware.

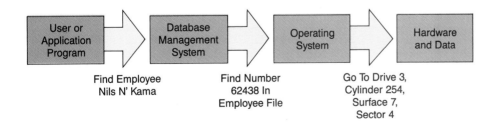

address of customer Falkmeier, Inc. The DBMS would tell the operating system where to look for it.

The DBMS, like the operating system, is another assistant in the computer system. Where data are concerned, however, the DBMS is more helpful and can tell the operating system what to do. Using a DBMS, we do not have to tell the operating system exactly in which file and record our data resides, or write elaborate search procedures to find them; we can ask for objects by name and the DBMS will find them. We can also work with complex objects with little regard for the physical organization of the data. The DBMS will find the component parts and combine them into the complex object for us.

DATABASE FEATURES

Many types and brands of database management systems offer many different capabilities and capacities. Generally speaking, the larger the computer system, the more sophisticated and expensive the DBMS. Prices range from $400 to $800 for microcomputer DBMSs such as dBase IV and R:BASE, to $100,000 to $600,000 for mainframe DBMSs such as IDMS and ADABAS. We will examine some of the general features of DBMSs and indicate how and whether these features are implemented in low- and high-end DBMSs.

Program–Data Independence

As we noted, in a database environment the programmer need not be concerned with the physical particulars of data storage. The database management system is **self-descriptive,** meaning that the DBMS itself determines where the data are to be stored and maintains records of where and how to access these data. In file-processing systems, the computer doesn't know where anything is. It is up to the programmer to determine and maintain the description of the data formats.

The description of the database is maintained in a **data dictionary.** This includes things that the user needs to know about the data such as the data terms used, record formats, lengths of fields, and the relationships between records and fields. It also contains the things that the DBMS needs to know, such as how to effect the relationships described, and how to store and retrieve data. The choice of the term, data dictionary, is somewhat unfortunate. The industry also uses the term to describe the system-design tool we introduced in Chapter 11. The design tool, however, does provide the basis for the user part of the DBMS data dictionary.

This self-descriptive nature provides for **program–data independence.** Since the database carries its description with it, the format, or physical organization of the data, or even the hardware on which they are stored, can be changed without having to change the applications programs. Remember, the programs just know what data they want, not where the data are stored. This makes upgrading or changing computer systems much less expensive.

Self-description is a feature of all databases from the inexpensive microcomputer DBMSs to the expensive mainframe packages. Program–

data independence has its limits, however. You cannot make radical changes, like going from a micro to a mini, without applications-program changes because you will also probably have to change database management systems, which in turn will necessitate a change in the data dictionary.

Query Facilities

Since retrieving data from a database does not require intimate knowledge of the structure of the data, something only a specialized database programmer would have, it would seem reasonable that access to the data might be opened up to nonprogrammers. All modern database systems do just that through **query languages,** languages developed for nonprogrammers to allow them to ask direct questions of the DBMS.

There are a number of query languages, almost every DBMS has a different one, but they all share some common traits. The most important is ease of use—trying to make database query as easy as asking questions of a person. A few of them, such as the Intellect query language allow you to use almost everyday English. For example, you might say, "List all students who earned B or better in Professor Prabatnik's classes in the current year." If the system did not understand one of your words, it would prompt you for an explanation and file your answer away so that it would understand the next time.

Standards are too few in the computer industry, but the **Structured Query Language (SQL),** formalized by ANSI (the American National Standards Institute) in 1985, is gaining acceptance. It is being used by some established database management systems such as ORACLE and will soon be available for popular microcomputer DBMSs such as dBase IV and IBM's database facility for the OS/2 operating system. An SQL query for the example above would take this form:

```
SELECT Student name, Grade
  FROM  Student, Class
 WHERE Grade >= B
 AND    Professor = Prabatnik
 AND    Year = 1989
```

Host-Language Interface

To use the database management system in an application program, the **host language,** that in which the application program was written, must be able to communicate with the DBMS. Programming languages, however, are not written with specific database management systems in mind and do not have the proper statements to direct them. To overcome this limitation, DBMS suppliers sell their packages with extra statements to add to your host language and **precompilers** to find and translate those extra statements before the actual compilation step.

Until now, most microcomputer database management packages do not have host-language interfaces. Instead, they rely on their own applications languages to store and retrieve data and to format reports. These applications languages are mainly extensions of their on-line data entry and query languages. They are good at storage and retrieval but often fall short in other processing tasks. As microcomputer power and capacity increases, we are beginning to see effective host-language interfaces for languages such as C and BASIC for micros.

Security

A feature of a database is that it allows easy access by nonskilled people. This can also be one of its drawbacks. Now that almost everyone is capable of using the database, how do we keep the data secure? Multiuser database management systems, those principally used on minis and mainframes, provide for **data security,** allowing access for those who should have it but keeping others away.

Security is controlled by either passwords or station identification, or possibly both. A **password** is a secret code that identifies a particular user. Before a user can use a work station (a terminal or computer connected to the database) he or she must **log on** by typing in the password, and allow

---

BOX 13-1

Security Blankets: Diskless PCs

One of the easiest ways to guard information on a computer is to remove the disk drive. Working on a diskless PC—a computer connected to a network but with no internal memory—leaves a user no way to upload information into a database or download programs or data and head out of the building with them.

Diskless PCs are cost efficient, easy to use, and compact. Because they have no moving parts, they're exceptionally quiet desktop units. Best of all, they provide a safeguard for corporate software and hardware investments and a secure way to protect data.

Companies that spend large amounts of money to upgrade their software and hardware aren't anxious to

subsidize their employees' extracurricular projects. And with more personal computers installed in homes, many people are "just a few thousand dollars away from duplicating the environment they have at work," says Ernest Wassmann, products marketing director for Esprit Systems, a maker of diskless workstations in Melville, New York.

Before NCNB Texas bought 200 diskless workstations from 3Com, the commerical bank had been ordering Compaq computers with the disk drives removed. "We wanted as little data as possible stored locally," say Tim Crowell, NCNB Texas's vice president in charge of local-area-network support. The low cost of 3Com's 3Station attracted the bank initially, says Crowell, but the product's

security features made it especially appealing for the network expansion Crowell had in mind. "We had to put in many of the stations at the clerical level, and we didn't want them [the workers] to have the capability to copy the software or company data and walk off with it," he says.

New federal regulations covering the banking industry will make diskless PCs even more attractive for system administrators like Crowell. While auditors have always carefully scrutinized mainframe security procedures, they'll soon be applying the same stringent checks to standalone PC systems. A network with 100 diskless PCs tied into it will eliminate the annual auditing headaches that 100 standalone the computer to compare it with valid passwords. The database will grant only certain types of access to certain user passwords.

Station identification grants access to specific work stations, no matter who is at the keyboard. For example, the work stations in the warehouse may have access to shipping data but not accounting data.

The database security system manages various types of **access rights,** specific types of access. Depending on the system, these access rights can be controlled for specific users, specific stations, and/or specific data. There are five types of access rights:

Select.   The user may see the data but not make any changes.

Update.   The user may read and change existing data.

Insert.   The user may read and modify existing data as well as add new data.

Delete.   The user may read, modify, and insert data as well as delete existing data.

---

systems would create.

Heavy network users such as banks and insurance companies are the main customers of diskless PCs, but the terminals are also a big hit with the U.S. government. George Gazurian, president of Consolidated Professional Systems, a consulting firm in Cherry Hill, New Jersey, specializing in mainframe-to-PC integration, counts federal agencies among his best customers. The company's recent clients include the Federal Aviation Administration. "They're setting up networks throughout the country, and they're looking to control their software," says Gazurian. "They don't want any software inserted into or extracted from the system."

The computer-virus scare has also made companies more security-conscious. Gazurian says that although he's been selling the Earth-station-Ie diskless workstation for nearly a year, he's seen a sharp rise in interest during the past six months due to the threat of viruses. "Whenever we mention security, it has more of an impact now," he says. "More than anything else, computer viruses have made organizations interested in diskless PCs."

Crowell has discovered an unexpected benefit of the added security of a diskless PC—it's helped him coax computer-wary executives into using their desktop machines. The knowledge that information can be neither uploaded nor downloaded has

given many executives the confidence to take advantage of all the system's capabilites.

Market forecasters expect the diskless-PC business to explode over the next few years. Dataquest predicts shipments will leap from 25,000 in 1987 to 1 million in 1992. TeleVideo and 3Com hold the largest market shares, but the potential is attracting new entrants, including some of the computer industry's major players. Both NCR and Unisys have introduced diskless PCs, and last year IBM shipped thousands of PS/2s with the drives removed. While IBM has no official diskless product, it hints that it might jump into the market in the future.

Source: Deborah Asbrand, *PC Computing,* Nov. 1988, p. 220.

> **Grant.** The user may grant any of the four preceding access rights to other users in a specific group. For example, the chief accountant may have the granting right for the people in the accounting department.

Microcomputer database management systems rarely offer much security because they are typically designed for a single user. Security is locking the door to the office that contains the computer.

Recovery

As machines go, computers are quite reliable. They work for thousands and thousands of hours without failure. However, one failure is all you need to lose your data. The database system must provide for not only backup of data but also **recovery,** reconstruction of the database after the problem is fixed.

Physically, a database is a complicated thing. A high percentage of the total bytes stored is not user data but internal overhead data, those needed by the database management system to keep track of the user data. These include the data dictionary, and the millions of bytes that tell the DBMS where to find things and how to put them together.

When the system fails, these data, both overhead and user, must be reconstructed. Much of the data can be **restored,** copied back onto the disks from the last backup. The activity between the last backup and the actual failure can be a problem. The most straightforward reconstruction strategy is to repeat all the activity that occurred after the backup. This is always time consuming and often impossible.

Another solution is the **rollback** strategy. The data are not restored from the backup. Instead, the system looks for incomplete transactions (usually those occurring during the time of the failure), lists them, eliminates them, and then the users must reenter them. Rollback is not efficient, however, if large amounts of data, especially old data, are lost.

Sophisticated recovery facilities are common on large database management systems but not on microcomputer systems.

DATABASE MODELS

One of the major advantages of database over file-processing systems is that the programmers and users need not concern themselves with the physical storage of the data. Here, we will introduce just enough about the three most popular physical database designs so that you will have some appreciation of their differences.

Hierarchical

The **hierarchical database** or **tree** model was the first of the three developed. Systems using it appeared in the late 1960s. In this model, data are grouped into major classifications, which are divided into subclassifications, which are then divided into sub-subclassifications and so forth. A

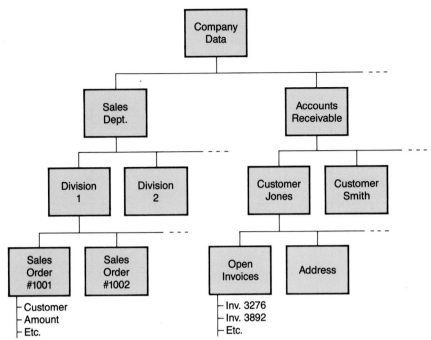

relationship between data in this model is often complicated to establish because the paths up and down the tree from one data object to another must be strictly followed.

Part of a company's hierarchical database is shown in the figure. Before a product is shipped, the shipping department must be sure that a customer's account is not delinquent. They will, of course, query their computer. But to establish the relationship between the sales order and the customer's current open invoices, the computer must follow a path through the division data, the sales department, over to accounts receivable, down to the customer, and finally to the open invoices. The process consumes time and computer resources.

Few strictly hierarchical databases are in existence today. IBM's IMS database package was one of the first on the market and still exists in a few installations.

Network

A **network database** is principally a modification and improvement over the hierarchical database. It allows more than one path between objects and these paths can go across the tree rather than just following the up and down pattern of the purely hierarchical database. For example, in our previous illustration, a network database may make a direct path between the customer and the sales order. The path will require that more overhead data be stored but the access time for information relating customer and sales order will be sharply reduced.

The following figure shows the kinds of paths that may exist between customer and product in a hierarchy and a network. The paths in the network are established as a particular customer buys a particular product.

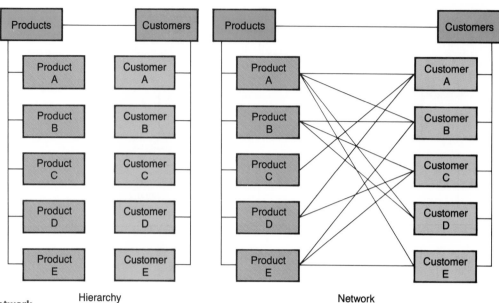

Hierarchical versus Network Database Paths

Many network databases are on the market today, including one of the largest and most expensive—Cullinet's IDMS for mainframe computers.

Relational

Both the hierarchical and network databases require that the logical structure of the database—that is, the paths and path possibilities—be determined at the outset. Changing structures later, adding new paths for example, would require a redesign and reformatting of the database.

The **relational database** model is based on tables of objects rather than specific paths between objects. It is more flexible than either of the other two and further removes the user from the actual structure of the database.

Each **table** in a relational database (or **relation** as it is called in relational jargon) is analogous to a file in a file-processing system. It is a collection of similar entities—customers, for example. The table is composed of rows and columns. The rows (or **tuples**) are analogous to records, a single entity—the customer Jones, for example. Columns (or **attributes**) are like fields, characteristics of the record—the customer's name or address, for example.

Relationships, associations between objects, can be established between tables which have overlapping columns. For example, if the customer table has a customer-number column, the sales-order table has a customer-number column and a product-ID column, and the product table also has a product-ID column, then the system can establish a relationship between customer name and product name. The determination of which columns go in which tables is made to ensure overlap so that relationships can be established, but with as little overlap as possible to reduce ambiguity.

CUSTOMER			
Name	Number	Address	Phone
Smith	1042	124 Oak	123-4567
Albert	3129	32 Elm	555-1212
Brown	7114	652 Fig	767-2676
Jones	4499	12 Palm	543-6789

SALES ORDER			
Quant	Product I.D.	Price	Customer Number
124	307X	6.24	7114
300	112R	0.48	3129
100	307X	6.32	3129
650	772A	15.44	7114
50	311F	8.92	4499

PRODUCT			
Name	I.D.	Cost	On Hand
Widget	112R	0.36	4266
Frammel	307X	5.88	3389
Dreep	772A	13.26	10425
Plinc	311F	8.03	342

Establishing Relationships in a Relational Database

The relationship between the customer name, Albert, and the product purchased, Widget, is established by the overlapping (shaded) items in the tables.

The relational model has some advantages over the other two:

- Relationships may be expressed easily in human terms because the relationships are explicit in the data themselves.
- Relationships do not have to be predefined so new objects and relationships can be added or deleted without restructuring the database.

These advantages are not without offsetting costs. Relational databases are more physically complicated and have more overhead data. Therefore, they require more computer-system resources and longer processing times.

Almost all database products introduced in the last few years are relational. This includes packages for larger machines such as ORACLE and microcomputer packages such as dBase and R:BASE.

THE DATABASE ADMINISTRATOR

Database systems have increased the access to and use of data to such a degree that companies find it necessary to facilitate and control data access just as they would any other resource of the company. To this end many organizations have established the position of **database administrator (DBA),** whose responsibility it is to see that access to the data is efficient and correct.

The DBA manages the structure of the database. He or she maintains and documents the views of the data, the trees or tables; responds to requests for changes in the structure; ensures that changes will not negatively affect the database; and communicates changes to the users.

The DBA also manages database activity. This includes being the arbiter of access rights to the data, checking to see that proper data is going into the system, and monitoring the backup and recovery procedures.

This person is also expected to evaluate the effectiveness of the database system. Are there areas where access is slow? Are there users that cannot get the required data? Is the cost of the system remaining within

---

BOX 13-2

Database Machine Watches the Options

Surveillance helps Options Exchange catch "insiders"

Technically it's called "open outcry" but in reality, it's yelling very loudly.

On March 10, the traders in the "OEX" pit at the Chicago Board Options Exchange were yelling loudly indeed. These OEX options represent an index of 100 stocks, and the market in New York that day was going steadily down.

By the end of the day, the Dow Jones Industrial Index had dropped over 48 points. It was the busiest day at CBOE since Oct. 19, which has come to be known as "Black Monday," the day of the 1987 Wall Street crash.

This seemingly chaotic scene—loud yelling, furious signalling, traders jumping up and down, runners scrambling all over the floor, papers strewn everywhere underfoot, screens reading out constant price changes—is actually a finely-developed system for setting fair market prices.

Rolfe Jaremus is partly responsible for making sure this system is indeed fair. As manager of general business systems for the systems division of the Options Exchange, Jaremus manages the Market Surveillance System. The MSS is used to help the exchange fulfill its obligation to the Securities and Exchange Commission to regulate—and catch insider—trading.

MSS runs on a Teradata DBC/1012 database machine, which some in the industry call "Boesky machines," after the infamous Wall Street trader convicted of illegally using inside information.

Jaremus said, "With the surveillance system, we try to recreate with data what is happening on the floor. It's a difficult thing to do, because many factors are at work. Who's trading with whom at a certain time, and how the trades relate to the Dow Jones and news announcements of the day, are all important in the business of surveillance."

The program was

developed to watch for violations, based on requirements specified by the users. Mark King, the user liaison for system development from the Surveillance Department, said "Insider trading is still the biggest issue and is the main concern of the SEC."

King, who started out as a runner at the Options Exchange six years ago, said, "I know the information and how it relates; I communicate that to Rolfe's area to help him design the database."

MSS can examine the option trading activity before or after the announcement, identify who is doing the trading, and relate basically anything to anything else in the database.

Because of the changing volumes and types of financial instruments traded at the exchange, "We have to be very flexible to manage change," King said. "And the database machine is "a key part of helping us to manage that change."

Source: John Desmond, *Software Magazine*, April 1988.

---

proper guidelines? The database administrator should identify problems and develop solutions for them.

FILE PROCESSING OR DATABASE MANAGEMENT SYSTEM?

All the features of a database management system would seem to make it the file-access method of choice and in more and more cases it is becoming so. However, file-processing systems are not dead yet, nor should they be. Each system has its own advantages and disadvantages.

The database administrator is responsible for keeping the database systems running smoothly for the users.

Database Management System Advantages

- *Logical access.* This is the principal advantage of the DBMS, and the one on which many of the others are based. Programmers and/or users do not have to be concerned with the physical structure of the files, the DBMS will take a logical request for data and translate it into the physical operations needed to access the data.
- *Query access.* Because the DBMS makes it unnecessary to understand the technical aspects of data storage, nontechnical people can access the data through query languages.
- *Relationship facility.* In order to establish a relationship between two data objects in a file-processing system, the programmer must understand and navigate through the physical data structure. A DBMS handles that chore.
- *Program–data independence.* Database systems are self-descriptive, so even when the physical structure of the data changes, the programs that access those data need not.
- *No redundant data.* Even though it may appear on a number of tables, each piece of data is stored only once in a database management system. It might be repeated many times in a file-processing system.

File-Processing System Advantages

- *Software cost.* The database management system is a completely separate and extra software package costing up to $600,000. A comparable package is simply not necessary for a file-processing system, although there will certainly be some offsetting programming costs.

Business Focus   BOX 13-3

Relational Data Base System Provides Speedy Information Services

At the New York branch of Credit Lyonnais, where hundreds of banking decisions are made daily, quick access to current customer information is more than just a convenience; it is a necessity.

So when bank officers found themselves paging through stacks of paper reports to locate information on loan rates, credit histories, foreign exchange rates, and other vital information, the bank's management decided to act. What was needed, it was agreed, was a system that could put customer data at the fingertips of bank officers and deliver detailed information in a matter of seconds.

Until late 1984, the branch had a typical batch-oriented data processing system, characterized by its dependence upon voluminous printed reports, according to Donald Wyner, vice president in charge of the central systems department, the group responsible for data base systems development. "The user community was information starved when we found them," says Wyner, who was recruited from a Big Eight accounting firm by Credit Lyonnais to head the information system development effort along with Frederic Melul, senior vice president of the management information department, and Irv Pollack, vice president of data processing and organization. "They had just a

few paper reports that were delivered to them each morning. There were also a few computers or terminals in use by the commercial officers."

Headquarted in Paris, Credit Lyonnais is a big player in the multinational banking world, with various financial interests located on six continents. In the United States the bank has nine offices in major cities across the country. Credit Lyonnais' New York branch, also known as Credit Lyonnais USA (CLUSA) is the hub of the bank's U.S. activities. These activities include cash management, correspondent banking, euro/local currency financing, export financing, foreign exchange and government securities trading, interest rate and currency swaps, letters of credit, mergers and acquisitions, and international banking. It is here that a major part of the bank's decisions concerning U.S. accounts are made.

To Wyner, the challenge of developing a new system for quick access to customer information, was twofold. Not only would it need to address the numerous information needs of the branch office, but it would also have to do so in a manner easily embraced by bank officers with little or no computer experience. "Our initial rough sketch said that the officers were going to need access to data concerning clients, their accounts, and

Source: Scott Humphrey, *Computers in Banking,* Jan. 1988.

their accounting transactions," Wyner explains. "They would also need the greatest level of detail information we could give concerning loan, deposit, foreign exchange, and other specialized banking contracts." In addition, Wyner saw the need to add support for credit authorization and credit-line information into the system.

Wyner's job was to find a combination of computer hardware and software to fit these needs. Since no on-line system was in place to serve this function prior to his arrival, the options available to him were numerous. Yet from the outset, several factors influenced the decision on the final system configuration. Foremost among these factors was the decision that the cornerstone of the new system would be a relational data base management model.

By using the tools unique to relational models—namely fourth generation languages and the industry standard Structured Query Language (SQL)—Wyner reasoned that system development efforts to provide the commerical officers with the power and flexibility they would need to navigate the complex data would be minimal. But with the relational model's promise of flexibility and ease of use also came its problems—slow processing time and heavy CPU consumption. Wyner relates that he was concerned by past experiences he had had with

software-based data base systems and "horror stories" he had heard about companies running IDMS or IMS on even larger mainframes.

Wyner wanted the power and ease-of-use offered by a relational data base but he didn't want to compromise system performance. After exploring several alternatives, he came across a hardware-based relational data base management system manufactured by Britton Lee Inc. of Los Gatos, Calif.

The Britton Lee Shared Data Base System is a combination of hardware and software that optimizes the execution of relational data base functions as well as offering the ability to share data between multiple computers from different vendors. With the proliferation during the past few years of IBM PCs and compatibles, Apple Macintoshes, and Digital Equipment Corp. (DEC) VAXs in branch offices, this latter feature proved to be vital.

"The initial Britton Lee decision was, at the time, as much an emotional decision as a business one," Wyner admits, "because hardware-based data base systems were largely an unknown. We were somewhat influenced by a benchmark study that documented what a lot of us already believed—that a software solution was likely to saturate the machine a lot faster than [adding] a hardware

(Continued)

BOX 13-3 Continued

solution. Today, we are much more comfortable with the choice of the machine as a tool for information retrieval." According to Wyner, other issues considered included application availability, upward compatibility, ease-of-use, and networking capabilities.

The Shared Data Base System is dedicated to the task of data base management. By offloading the host computer of its CPU-intensive data base functions, the system is able to process relational data base queries at speeds unrelated to the host computer. CLUSA purchased the Britton Lee system in late 1985.

Within CLUSA, the system is referred to as the information processing facility (IPF). Designed and built in-house, the IPF resides on a DEC VAX 8500 system. The IPF takes advantage of both the third- and fourth-generation language capabilities available with Omnibase—a VAX/VMS software package distributed by Signal Technology Inc. of Goleta, Calif.—and the advantages of a relational data base management system.

Each floor of the branch has a number of DEC terminal servers that permit connection of asynchronous terminals, IBM PCs and compatibles, and Apple Macintosh microcomputers to Ethernet through DECnet. Also residing within the computer room are two DEC VAX 11/70 systems, one for funds transfer operations and the other for applications development and backup purposes.

Approximately 70 users within the branch office use the IPF on a continual basis, accessing its 250 megabyte data base each day. Now customer information, which previously took hours to locate, is at the fingertips of bank officers.

Bankers who previously had to sort through pages of paper reports now have the ability to call up only the information pertinent to the job at hand. For instance, if a loan officer wants information about a customer's credit history with the bank, he can access that data via a series of menu choices and/or keystroke commands to the IPF. A response containing only the information requested will be returned to that officer in a matter of seconds.

"It's an order of magnitude of difference in ease of use," Wyner explains. "Mainly it's the sort of environment to have when you need to make changes or you want to do your design development interactively." The ability to share information in a real-time environment is a vital aspect in the multinational banking world, he adds. "The IPF gives us this ability."

CLUSA now plans to extend access to Britton Lee's shared data systems to its other offices in the U.S. "We have installed several high-speed lines to the larger offices with statistical multiplexors and plan to put them on-line to the IPF this year," Wyner concludes.

- *Processing costs.* Many things that a programmer specifies to a file-processing system, the database management system must figure out by itself. This requires much more processing time and more powerful processors, as well as larger main memories for the DBMS.
- *Storage costs.* A DBMS must keep track of and maintain numerous data relationships, the file-processing system does not. This means that a DBMS will have much more overhead data. It is common for a DBMS to have two to three times as much overhead data as user data.
- *Access speed.* Certain types of data relationships are impractical to access in a file-processing system. But for routine access the file-processing system will find the data much quicker because the program tells it where to look; it does not have to figure it all out by itself.

The real comparison is between the ease of access of the database management system and the lower cost of the file-processing system. If the access is necessary, then the money is well spent. If not, you can be sure that the organization will find other uses for the money.

SUMMARY

Our earlier methods of file access closely approximated the techniques we used with manual filing systems. We used separate files which consisted of records made up of fields. One or more of these fields was a key used to identify the record.

Files are organized in a number of different ways depending on how we want to use the data. A sequential file is ordered by the key field. It is the most straightforward, but is difficult to update. The order of the records in an indexed file is not critical since a separate, and much smaller, ordered index is maintained. Updates to such files are easier and multiple keys can be referenced by using multiple indices, but the indices themselves are overhead data and so indexed files require more storage.

Using a hashed file we determine the storage location of a record by applying a hashing algorithm to the key. This allows fast access because there is no searching involved, but we are limited to one key.

File-processing systems allowed us to manage data faster and more accurately than we could by hand, but we still encountered many limitations. Using file-processing methods we were forced to think about data in the computer's physical terms instead of our own logical terms. Because of this, our files were designed to work with only specific programs, and these programs used files one at a time without recognizing relationships between the data in different files. Relationships could be established only by programming in complicated searches going from one file to another.

Some searching was eliminated by repeating data in various files, but this data redundancy created other problems such as wasting storage space and making updates difficult.

To progress in our ability to handle large amounts of data we had to free ourselves from concern for the physical storage of the data and concentrate on our logical requirements. In examining simple, complex, and variable-length data objects we found many cases where the relationships formed by overlapping objects were the ones that we really needed. Overlapping data in a traditional file-processing system was difficult.

Database management systems freed us from concern for the physical structure of data. We could now concentrate on data as we wished to see it, not as it was stored in the computer. The DBMS was self-descriptive, meaning that it, rather than us, kept track of the physical details of the data storage.

Large-machine database management systems provide us with program–data independence, query facilities, host-language interfaces, data-recovery facilities, and data security. Users have certain access rights to the data which allow them to read, modify, insert, or delete data, or grant those rights to others.

Almost all databases follow one of three physical models. The hierarchy, where relationships must follow a strict vertical path between layers, was first but is being overshadowed by the other two. Network databases provide many paths between data objects, but the overall structure is still hierarchical. Relational databases are based on logical tables. An overlap in columns in two tables provides a path for the establishment of relationships.

Database administrators have been hired in many organizations that use databases. The DBA is responsible for the effective utilization of the database and manages its structure, activity, and evaluation.

Both file-processing and database management systems have their advantages. Database management systems allow logical (as opposed to physical) views of the database, query access, ease of forming relationships, program–data independence, and freedom from redundant data. File-processing systems are cheaper in practically all areas—including software, processing, and storage—and can access specific data items faster.

KEY WORDS

(in order of appearance in text)

File-processing system	Complex object	Update
File	Variable-length object	Insert
Record	Database management system	Delete
Field	(DBMS)	Grant
Key	Self-descriptive	Recovery
Sequential file	Data dictionary	Restore
Indexed file	Program–data independence	Rollback
Hashed file	Query language	Hierarchical database
Hashing algorithm	Structured Query Language (SQL)	Tree database
Logical view	Host language	Network database
Physical view	Precompiler	Relational database
Data redundancy	Data security	Table
Data update	Password	Relation
Program–data dependence	Log on	Tuple
Object	Access rights	Attribute
Relationship	Select	Database administrator (DBA)

REVIEW QUESTIONS

1. What are fields, records, and files in a file-processing system?

2. What is a key?

3. How do sequential files differ from indexed and hashed files?

4. What advantages do indexed files have over sequential files? Over hashed files?

5. What advantages do hashed files have over indexed files? Over sequential files?

6. What are the main drawbacks to traditional file-processing methods?

7. Define and give an example of a complex data object.

8. Define and give an example of a variable-length data object.

9. Define and give an example of overlapping data objects.

10. Where does the database management system fall in relation to applications programs and the operating system?

11. Why do we say that a database is self-descriptive?

12. Why is program–data independence important?

13. What do we call the language a nonprogrammer uses to access a database?

14. Why is a host-language interface important?

15. Describe the five types of database access rights.

16. What are two types of security controls used by database management systems?

17. How does the rollback method of data recovery work?

18. What are the advantages of a network over a hierarchy database?

19. How is a relationship established in a relational database?

20. Describe the advantages and disadvantages of a relational database over hierarchies and networks.

21. What are the functions of a database administrator?

22. What are the advantages of a database over a file-processing system?

23. What are the advantages of a file processing over a database system?

THINK ABOUT IT

1. The phone book is an example of a sequential file. How would you find a specific address in the phone book?

2. Would storing the phone book in a sequential file be practical if you were required to make frequent accesses by address? If not, what other type of organization would you suggest?

3. You want to keep track of all your record albums by both title and artist. Would you use a hashed or an indexed file? Why?

4. Would it be possible to construct complex data objects using a file-processing system? If not, why not? If so, what types of difficulties would you encounter?

5. Why are data-security features of a DBMS less important on a microcomputer?

6. Do tables in a relational database describe the logical or physical structure of the database?

7. There is much discussion in the industry as to whether the database administrator should or should not be a computer expert. Your opinion?

CHALLENGES

1. Your company sells five different products in three sales regions. Among other things, they want to be able to mail letters to customers in any combination of regions who have ordered any combination of products. To accommodate this, design a set of files using traditional file-processing methods and then a set of tables using relational database methods. Compare the two.

2. Examine a microcomputer database management system. Evaluate its query language for ease of use and see how or whether you can write programs that will access the database.

3. Look at the computer system at your school or a local company. What kinds of file-access methods do they use? Are they adequate for the job? Are they too expensive?

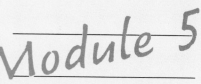

Module 5

COMPUTERS IN BUSINESS

Most of the information produced for business in a computer information system goes to management. Chapter Fourteen considers the functions of management in planning, organizing, directing, and controlling that require information in various forms of reports. Decision support systems, which make use of personal computers, are also becoming increasingly important to managers in areas such as modeling and simulation, spreadsheet software, and graphics.

Chapter Fifteen looks at the computer's increasing role in business and suggests some ways that computers may be important to business in the future.

14

MANAGEMENT INFORMATION SYSTEMS

PREVIEW
Much of the information produced goes directly to managers for their decision making. In this chapter we will look at how and in what forms that information is provided. You will gain an understanding of:

■ Different forms of information reporting.

■ The types of information systems that comprise the organization's information-producing efforts.

■ What managers do and how they make decisions.

■ How information relates to the various functions of management.

■ The levels of management and their different information requirements.

■ How personal computing has affected management information systems.

Harry was "one of the guys." He had worked in the factory for the last seven years, had the respect and friendship of his coworkers, and was proud of the work he performed. When he and his friends got together in the lunch room, he used to say, "There are two kinds of people in business, us guys who get the job done—and managers." His English wasn't great, but he'd get a chuckle out of his buddies. "What do those guys get paid for?" he would muse aloud, "All they do is sit around in their offices or go out to lunch!"

Then he got himself promoted.

He got an office. He went out for lunch occasionally. He also found out what managers are paid for. They make decisions. Some decisions caused him a few sleepless nights, but he found he was good at it and he enjoyed it.

Harry also found that to make good decisions you need good information and that is what this chapter is all about. We will first look at the types of information available; then at the nature, functions, and needs of management; and finally, how we can use the information to satisfy management's differing needs.

FORMS OF INFORMATION REPORTING

Information comes in many forms, from numbers on seemingly miles of detailed computer printout, to a response to a question of the person in the next office. When we think of computer information systems, we tend to think of information in more formalized fashion, usually reports of some kind. It is useful to look at the various forms in which information can be delivered to us.

Periodic Versus Demand Reporting

Periodic reports are recurring ones produced at the end of a designated period—a day, week, month, or whatever. These are typically printed rather than displayed, and include such things as weekly sales in product categories, payroll expenses by department, and profit-and-loss statements.

Neither the distribution nor the format of a periodic report varies from period to period—the same people get the same information each week. Generally, more information must be put on the report than is actually used by any one person. Since the report usually goes to many people and those people may have slightly different information needs, the one report must satisfy all those needs. In addition, this report may be the only source for a particular kind of information. Each piece of that information may not be needed this week, but if there is a chance that it might be, it must be included on the report.

Periodic reports are easily produced by batch processing and so are relatively inexpensive per piece of information. However, if much of the information is not used, periodic reports could actually be quite expensive.

A **demand reporting** system produces information only when it is asked for. This type of information is usually requested by entering the request on a terminal keyboard, and the response is typically displayed

Periodic Reports

Most periodic reports are in the form of the typical computer "printout" we see here.

rather than <u>printed</u>. A periodic system might provide pages upon pages of sales orders for the week. Using a demand system, you could ask for the details of the order that Jones placed yesterday.

A good demand-reporting system allows much more flexibility in the information provided. It is not usually limited to the fixed pieces of information provided by a periodic-reporting system. For example, using a database management system's query language, you might type into your keyboard, "Show sales over $100,000 in the northeast for the month." The computer would assemble that information and display it on your screen.

Such a demand reporting system requires interactive processing, all the relevant data stored on line, and terminals accessible to the users. Because of this, it is more expensive per piece of information produced, but often is cheaper in the long run because only the information needed is actually provided. It is certainly more convenient.

Detail Versus Summary Reports

Detail reports contain data from each transaction—perhaps not all the data of each transaction but at least some of it. For example, we may produce a "Sales by Customer" report which shows all of our sales sorted by customer. The report may not include the salesperson's name or the terms of payment, but each sale is represented. Although it is a detail report, it might be, and probably is, totaled by each customer. These totals are technically summaries but are often included in detail reports.

A **summary report,** as the name implies, shows only summaries by categories, not the individual transactions. We might have a "Sales by Customer Summary" report which shows just the total sales for each customer. Our "Sales by Region Summary" may be only ten lines long— one for each of the nine sales regions and the tenth for the totals.

Most financial statements—such as income statements and balance sheets—are examples of summary reports.

Detail and summary reports can be provided either periodically or on demand. For example, financial statements are typically periodic summary reports, but a user might demand a listing of the detail of travel expenses for the month.

Exception Reporting

"I'm too busy to pour over all the numbers in those reports. All I want to see are the items that I have to do something about." This person's information-systems department should provide him with **exception reports** which show only the data that are out of a specified range, not the data that is within normal ranges. We might have a report showing department expenditures that are 10 percent over or under budget. The expenditures within 10 percent of budget will not show up.

Our "Sales by Customer Summary" exception report may show only customers with purchases greater than $100,000, or those with more than a 20 percent variance between this year and last. A report for a school class may print out those with five or more absences, or more than two homework assignments behind.

```
SALES ORDER BY CUSTOMER DETAIL REPORT

FARFEL CORPORATION
    #4125   4/26/90
        140     6642A       OP AMPS                      7.25    1015.00
        500     1286P       6-BIT D TO A CNVTRS         12.42    6201.00
        250     7110D       FLIP FLOPS                   1.31     327.50
                                                                 7543.50


    #4288   4/29/90
        125     4151W       256K MEMORY                  1.37     171.25
                                                                  171.25


FASBINDER INC.
    #4066   4/25/90
        375     8335G       GATE ARRAYS                 15.23    5711.25
```

```
CUSTOMER ORDER SUMMARY FOR WEEK ENDING 4/30/90

FAMOUS PRODUCTS CO.                                              24622.58
FARFEL CORPORATION                                                7741.75
FASBINDER INC.                                                   12105.40
FATAL ERROR SOFTWARE                                               482.00
```

Exception reports were developed because most people scan detail or summary reports only for the unusual, something that requires their action. The computer, by itself, would have a hard time deciding what constitutes "unusual." However, as long as we give it our criteria for unusual, the computer is much more efficient than we are at picking these things out.

Detail and Summary Reports

Parts of detail and summary reports are shown above. The detail report shows data from each transaction, while the summary report groups transactions together and shows totals.

TYPES OF MANAGEMENT INFORMATION SYSTEMS

Different parts of an organization have differing information needs. The information services that provide for these needs must be flexible enough to accommodate them. Therefore, we have many information subsystems, which we can divide into three categories—transaction-processing systems, management information systems, and decision-support systems. Notice that the term "management information system" is being used in two contexts: it describes the overall system and also one of the subsystems. This is unfortunate, but as we stated before, terminology in this field is often not precise, and this double use seems to be the most prevalent. We could make up our own precise terms, but then no one else would know what we were talking about.

Transaction-Processing Systems

The title, **transaction-processing systems,** almost says it all. These are the sets of information systems which handle the day-to-day transactions that are part of any business. Sales, purchases, cash payments and receipts, employee paychecks, and taxes withheld are all examples of business transactions and inputs to the system. The outputs are principally the organized detail and summations of these transactions that have occurred over a certain time period. Most of an organization's information-processing efforts go toward their transaction-processing system. It is this system that provides practically all the company's **internal data,** that is, data about the company itself.

The transaction-processing system is a standardized system. Data are entered into the system the same way each time. In fact, the required amount of data must be entered into the system, and at the proper time, for the system to be effective. The information produced by the system is also standard and principally in the form of periodic reports. The same reports come out of the system each cycle—day, week, or whatever. The reports may be in detail, such as a payroll journal showing each paycheck written; summaries, such as sales by department; or exceptions, such as stock below minimum inventory levels.

It sounds dull, but the transaction processing system is the basis for all the company's information-systems efforts. If it fails or is delayed, the rest of the company's information output comes to a halt. Therefore, all its parts must be carefully fed, maintained, and nurtured.

For example, the company's monthly profit-and-loss statements are products of the transaction-processing system. These reports are a summation of almost all of the transactions that have occurred during the month. If the sales entry (or payroll or whatever) parts of the system were to stop functioning, or their data lost, the profit-and-loss statements could not be produced. A high-level manager deprived of the P and Ls is not a pretty sight.

Transaction processing could be accomplished in either batch or on-line modes but, as we have seen earlier, the trend is toward on line. In fact, the trend has become so strong lately, that a new acronym has become commonplace in the jargon. It is **OLTP, on-line transaction-processing** systems. These are multiuser, multistation hardware and software systems specifically suited for handling transactions as they occur from many different sources.

Management Information Systems

The **management information system (MIS)** provides regular and recurring information, the objective of which is to specifically support decision making. Practically all of the internal data come from the transaction-reporting system. To this is added **external data,** from sources outside the organization.

There are many possible sources of external data. The United States government, through the Department of Commerce and other agencies, provides a wealth of economic data, demographic data on the social and economic make-up of various sections of the country, and information on past and present performance in various key industries. They also provide specific reports on various domestic and international markets. State governments provide many of the same things in more detail within the particular state.

Industry associations such as the Electronic Industries Association (EIA) and the National Association of Manufacturers (NAM) are sources for sales and performance in product areas in the industries they serve. Trade publications such as *Datamation, Variety,* and *Women's Wear Daily* are also sources for the same types of information.

The management information reports tend to be summaries or exceptions. Some examples might be "Sales by Product Line vs. Industry Average" or "Analysis of Economic Indicators in Electronics" or "Profit Margins by Sales Region." MIS reporting is typically periodic, but often MISs allow demand access to specific information.

Decision-Support Systems

Decision-support systems provide generalized tools, typically software packages, for use by managers in making decisions. The key element here is not that a decision-support system produces information, ultimately it does, but that it provides various ways for the users themselves to access, organize, and assemble data into information to apply to a specific decision.

Both transaction-processing and management information systems turn out the same information in the same form all the time. What if we want to see it presented differently, assembled in a different manner, or compared to some other data in the system? Without decision-support systems, we would have to prevail upon the information-systems department to write new programs to present us with what we wanted. For a one-time project, this would probably not be cost effective.

Decision-support systems can provide us with a number of different information-producing tools. Among the more common ones are:

- Database management and access.
- Modeling and simulation.
- Spreadsheet software.
- Graphics and presentation software.
- Report-writing software.

Database Management Systems

As we saw in Chapter 13, **database management systems,** through their query facilities, allow us to access and assemble data in ways other than those specifically written in some applications program. Through a DBMS, we can get the data we need organized in the way we want to see it to deal with a specific decision.

For example, Starboard Marine Products has decided to combine two sales regions into one. Jock Staud, the National Sales Manager, wanted to classify the customers in the new region as "frequent call," those that should be visited often, and "infrequent call," those that will be contacted principally by telephone. Using the DBMS query language, she generated a report combining the two old regions together showing the customer name, yearly sales in thousands, and average dollars per order. She had this sorted by average dollars per order and printed out. She considered the top 50 customers on the list as "frequent call."

We will look at database productivity packages more fully in the Appendix.

Modeling and Simulation

To make decisions for the future, we would like to know what will happen in the future. Crystal balls were invented long before computers, but they have not proven very effective, especially in business situations. Computers cannot tell us the future either, but they can help us to predict it.

Before a new aircraft is built, a small model is constructed and tested in a wind tunnel. The model and its environment, the wind tunnel, simulate the performance of the real aircraft in actual conditions. We can use a similar concept with a business. Using past data and perhaps some assumptions about the future, we can build a model of a business or some aspect of the business. This is not something you can hold in your hand, the **model** is a set of formulas that shows the effect on the business of the various factors affecting the business. For example, what has happened to sales or profit with changes in the product's price, appearance, competitor's prices, economic inflation, state of the economy, or whatever.

Using the model, we can **simulate** what will happen to the business in the future. For example, if we assume that the price of our product will be stable but the competitor's will rise by 3 percent, we put the product in a fresh, new package, inflation will be about 5 percent, the gross national product will rise by 3 percent, and other factors will remain constant, what will our profits be?

Using the model in simulations we can also play "what-if" games. What if we stayed with the old package? What if we raised our price but the economy started a mild recession? What if inflation were to rise and drive up the cost of our raw materials but we held firm on prices? Our decisions would still be based on assumptions and a bit of stargazing, but we would have a more accurate picture of how the business would react to those assumptions.

Spreadsheet Software

A **spreadsheet** is a document with headings and labels, columns of numbers, and totals, cross totals, ratios, percentages, and various other calculated figures. Spreadsheet software can help us generate such a document. A typical computer spreadsheet is shown in rows and columns. The intersection of a column and row, column C row 6, for example, is known as a **cell.** Into each cell you may put one of three things:

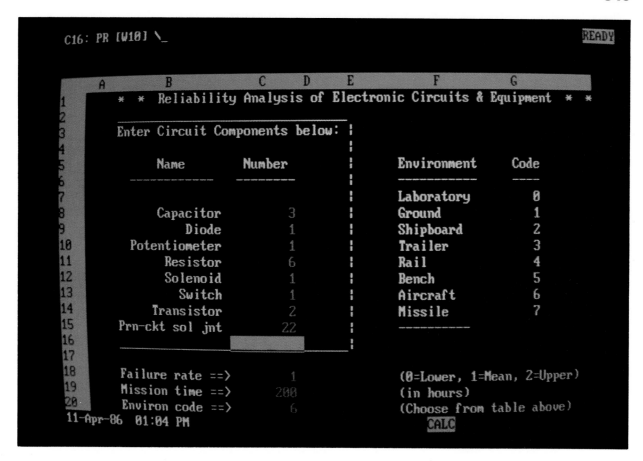

```
C16: PR [W10] \_                                                    READY

     A      B           C        D      E          F            G
1            * * Reliability Analysis of Electronic Circuits & Equipment * *
2
3            Enter Circuit Components below: |
4                                            |
5                  Name        Number        |     Environment      Code
6            ------------     --------       |     -----------      ----
7                                            |     Laboratory        0
8              Capacitor         3           |     Ground            1
9                  Diode         1           |     Shipboard         2
10          Potentiometer        1           |     Trailer           3
11             Resistor          6           |     Rail              4
12             Solenoid          1           |     Bench             5
13               Switch          1           |     Aircraft          6
14           Transistor          2           |     Missile           7
15       Prn-ckt sol jnt        22           |     ----------
16                                           |
17          ------------------------         |
18          Failure rate ==>       1         (0=Lower, 1=Mean, 2=Upper)
19          Mission time ==>     200         (in hours)
20          Environ code ==>       6         (Choose from table above)
    11-Apr-86  01:04 PM                          CALC
```

1. A label such as "Gross Margin", the salesperson "JONES", or perhaps "= = = = = =" to use as a double underscore between figures.
2. A number such as 150, −0.234, or whatever.
3. A formula using a combination of numbers and references to other cells. For example, A9/C12*100 is the value in column A, row 9 divided by the value in C12, and the result multiplied by 100.

Spreadsheets

Spreadsheet packages can reduce the time it takes to prepare reports.

Rows and columns may be formatted by changing the column width or the appearance of the data in the columns. Titles may be left justified, right justified, or centered. Numbers may be expressed with any amount of decimal places. Entire rows or columns may be replicated, moved, inserted, or deleted.

One of the major advantages of spreadsheet software is that if you change any of the numbers, the computer will recalculate the rest of the spreadsheet based on your new numbers. Using this feature, you can build a template of formulas and titles, and put in different sets of numbers to get out different reports.

For example, you might build a template for an income statement. Each month you could put in the relevant numbers and have the computer produce that month's statement. You could play what-if games. What if we reduced inventories? What if labor expenses went up by 5 percent? Each time, the computer would recalculate the report based upon the new numbers.

We will discuss spreadsheet software in more detail in the Appendix.

Graphics and Presentation Software

Decisions usually involve more than a single person. One person may make a decision, but then must present it to others for approval. After a decision is made and approved, the people who are to implement the decision must have it clearly communicated to them and must be convinced of the decision's merit. All this involves communicating ideas between people.

They say a picture is worth a thousand words, give or take a few. The pertinent facts of the thinking behind the decision and its future effects may be presented in straight text, but numbers and the relationships between them are more readily understood if they are given some visual presentation. A couple of columns of numbers showing monthly sales this year versus last year does not have the same impact as a graph with both sales levels shown on one set of axes. The share of the sales dollar going toward research and development becomes more alive when it is shown in a pie chart with that slice pulled out.

All of these graphics could be produced by pen and ink, or brush, or crayons, for that matter, but there are a number of software packages that will produce them almost automatically. Using a **graphics-presentation package,** you give the computer the numbers and the type of graph (line, bar, pie, or whatever) you want produced, and the computer takes it from there. It will apply the proper scale to the graph, put the titles on the axes,

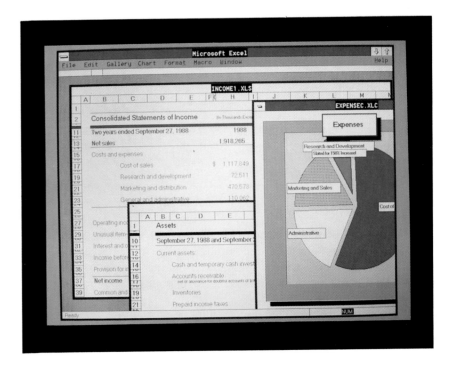

Integrated Spreadsheet Package

Using software that integrates spreadsheets and graphics, the user can add extra impact to the figures with output such as this.

pick colors or line patterns for the various elements of the graph, and print it out. Possibly hours of work that would have been done by hand is reduced to minutes.

Most of these graphics packages will accept numbers in various forms, including those produced by other software packages. In most cases, your graphics package can directly use the files produced by your spreadsheet or database management software. Some software vendors sell **integrated packages** that combine spreadsheet and graphics software as well as some database management capability. Using such a package, while you are working on your spreadsheet, you can direct the computer to show you the figures in graphic form, then go back to the spreadsheet, back to graphics, and so forth.

Report-Writing Software

Even with good graphics, if the text of the report looks like it was scribbled on the back of a cocktail napkin, no one will want to read it. Fortunately, a number of good word-processing packages exist. A few of these will even allow you to combine text and graphics in the same document. We will discuss word processing in more detail in the Appendix.

FUNCTIONS OF MANAGEMENT

Let us examine how these various computer tools aid management. Classical management theory holds that the functions of management can be divided into four major categories—planning, organizing, directing, and controlling.

(1) Planning activities are those involved in setting goals and directions for the future of the organization. The organization referred to here may be an entire nation, a single business, or a small department within the business. To make such plans, we would have to know a number of things. How did the organization fare in the past; what were its strong points and shortcomings? What are its parent organization's objectives; are we expecting growth or a change in direction? What is the climate for the future; is financing available or are new markets emerging?

(2) Organizing means drawing together resources to implement the plan. We might need more factory floor space or extra machinery, or we might have to hire new employees or terminate some others. To do these things we must know what is available, how it will suit our needs, how much it will cost, and how much it will benefit us.

(3) A manager achieves his goals with the help of other people and so must direct them in the performance of their jobs. There is more here than just shouting orders. It requires giving them information on what must be accomplished, how to accomplish it, and what is expected of them.

(4) Controlling is evaluating performance against the plans that were set. The manager must know exactly how much was accomplished, what it cost, whether it met the plan, and many other details about the accomplishments of the organization.

These four functions encompass many different management activities but they all have one thing in common—the need for information. If

① Planning
② Organizing
③ Directing
④ Controlling

Management Functions

Managers perform the four functions of management in a constant cycle.

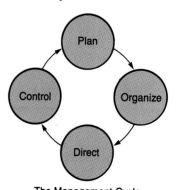

The Management Cycle

you asked a high-level manager what the organization's most important asset is, that manager might just say information. It is the constant flow of information that allows the manager to do the job, and effective management is the key to any organization's success.

THE DECISION-MAKING PROCESS

Managers all have their own styles of making decisions, but if we examined these different styles we would likely find a common, overall pattern. We can outline this pattern in five steps:

1. **Problem Identification** To begin the process, the manager must recognize that a problem exists and, as we saw in information systems development in Chapter 11, isolate the actual problem.
2. **Alternative Development** There are many ways to solve almost any problem. A good manager will identify a number of alternatives and investigate each.
3. **Alternative Selection** After comparing the alternatives, the manager will select the best one.
4. **Implementation** Once the decision is made, it must be implemented, put in practice.
5. **Follow Up** A decision cannot be implemented and then forgotten. It must be constantly monitored and evaluated. Was the decision correct in the first place? Have conditions changed so as to make another alternative preferable? Do the underlying factors creating the problem still exist?

Each step of the process will require information and evaluation of that information. And at each step, it is possible that the manager will realize that the chosen direction is wrong and the process will have to revert to some previous step.

Types of Management Decisions

No two decisions are alike, but we can look at two extremes in decision types, understanding that actual decisions fall somewhere between. A **structured decision** is one where specific rules, procedures, and guidelines direct the decision. The selection structure in programming is a good

The Decision-Making Process

Most decision making follows these five steps. At each step a subdecision must be made to either go on to the next step or revert to some previous step.

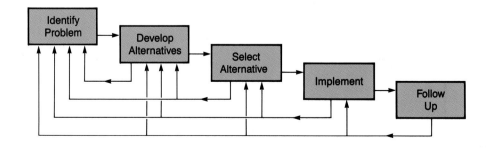

example of a completely structured decision. IF certain conditions exist THEN do this ELSE do that. Such a decision in pure form is not really a decision but simply a reaction to conditions. A salesperson might make a structured decision such as "If the credit card purchase is for more than $75, then I will have to call for authorization."

An **unstructured decision** is just the opposite. There are no rules. In actuality it would be difficult to think of an example of an unstructured decision in its purist form—there are always some rules—but certain decisions come close. A salesperson must make an unstructured decision when determining which customer to spend time with. An executive trying to decide whether to spend the millions of dollars required to enter a new market will have very few set rules and guidelines to fall back on.

LEVELS OF MANAGEMENT

A management position is defined by its responsibility and authority. Responsibility is the accountability for the successful operation of the organization or that manager's section of it, and authority is the power to direct resources and people toward fulfilling that responsibility. People at different positions in the management hierarchy have different responsibilities and require different types of information.

For our discussion we will divide management into three levels and examine the differing information needs of each level. Top managers—directors on the board, presidents, and vice presidents—have the broadest responsibilities. Middle managers—department heads and such—are responsible for their own departments. Operating managers—supervisors and foremen—are directly responsible for those producing the output for that group.

Top Management

Top management people set overall goals and long-range plans for their organizations, and are responsible for the successful execution of those

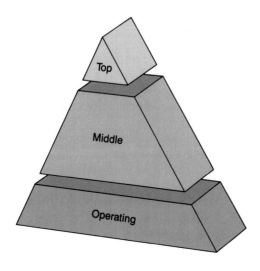

There are few top managers but they have wide ranges of responsibilities. There are many operating managers but each is responsible for only a narrow portion of the whole organization.

goals and plans. In regard to the four management functions, most of their time is spent planning and organizing—shaping things for the future and providing for the allocation of resources for those future plans.

Less of their time is spent directing. They are immediately responsible for other top and middle managers reporting to them, but those people, being managers themselves, should require little direction. Controlling is important at every level and top managers must have feedback on whether the plans are working or not.

The top manager has the broadest range of responsibility, being accountable for the entire organization under him. It would be impossible to direct all the activities of that organization, so the top manager delegates parts of the job to others below. The responsibility is always shared with a lower-level manager. It can never be totally turned over to the person below because the top person still must remain accountable. The authority to fulfill that responsibility, however, is passed to the lower-level manager.

Most of a top manager's decisions are relatively unstructured. It is at this level that the rules and guidelines are set. They do not exist beforehand.

Although the top manager is responsible for the entire organization, it would also be impossible to monitor all the information that concerns the organization. Therefore, the top manager looks at summaries of the information, and delegates the detail to those below. The higher the manager, the broader the responsibility and the more summarized the information. A top manager rarely, if ever, looks at a detail report.

A top manager's typical mix of information will consist of outputs from all three types of information systems. From the transaction reporting system will come income statements and overall sales and expense summaries. Management information systems will provide performance against budget reports for the major sections of the organizations, comparisons to total industry figures, and general economic and financial reports.

The decision-support systems will provide for the specific, short-term information needs not addressed by the other systems. Examples might be an analysis of the effect of an impending recession on the price of the company's stock, a model of future company performance if a certain acquisition were made, or the effect on profitability of closing two regional warehouses.

Middle Management

Middle management people are responsible for carrying out the plans of top management. They still do a lot of planning but the plans are usually short rather than long range, and tactical rather than strategic. The question is not "What should we accomplish?" but "I know what we are to accomplish, how do we do it?"

A person at this level does less organizing. Resources and people are for the most part allocated, it is this person's job to use them properly. More time is spent directing, working with operating managers to carry out the tactics. Controlling, again, is an important aspect at any level, and a greater percentage of a middle manager's information is directed toward control feedback.

Decisions still tend to be unstructured. Part of the process of developing tactics is laying out guidelines and procedures so that decisions at lower levels can be more structured.

As we go down in management levels, responsibilities and the information required to fulfill them become narrower. Therefore, the reports will be in more detail. The bulk of middle management reports will still be summaries, but at a lower level. The top-level division vice president might get a report on sales by product line. The middle-level product manager would get a report on the individual products in his or her line.

More of the middle-level manager's information will come from the transaction-reporting system. The report mentioned above would be one example. Departmental expense reports and sales by salesperson might be others. Management information systems might offer actual versus planned output, changes in product sales between this year and last, or an accounts-receivable report which shows how long individual customer's payments are overdue.

Decision-support systems might be used to study seasonality of sales by making a spreadsheet showing sales in various product categories by month and graphing the result, or examining productivity by comparing dollar output of product to the man-hours spent in producing it.

Operating Management

Being at the end of the responsibility—authority chain, **operating managers** are responsible for carrying out the tactics of middle management. Planning is required, but it is principally day to day. Organizing is not as important as it is at the upper levels. Most of the operating manager's time is spent directing—supervising the people who are producing the output. Controlling is, of course, important and most of the information that comes to this manager is direct operational feedback.

Decisions at this level tend to be highly structured. Operating managers are charged with implementing the guidelines given them from higher-level managers.

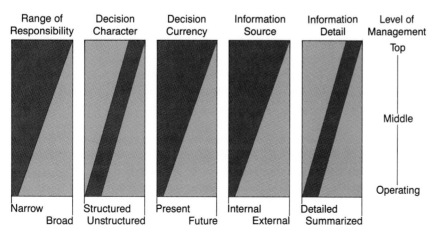

Information and Decision-Making at Various Levels

Operating management is responsible for the detail and so receives detail reports, much of it direct output from the transaction-reporting system. Examples might be individual sales to customers, number of each product produced, listings of expenses and raw materials used.

THE EFFECT OF PERSONAL COMPUTING

Back in the old days, when computers were big, ungainly monsters and only designated wizards were allowed to touch them, all computer-generated data came from one department, usually referred to as DP—data processing. Reports of various ilk spewed forth from this mythical department and the people were happy . . . sometimes. If they weren't, they were faced with few choices, all of them unhappy. They could smile, pretend to be happy, and not rock the boat. They could take the data from the reports and assemble them by hand so that the information was more to their liking. Or they could perform a ritual consisting of begging, pleading, cajoling, paying through the nose, and waiting to get reports in more suitable formats.

Along came the personal computer. Now a manager could have a computer on the desk top and assemble whatever information was required. It sounds like heaven, but the transition was not so easy and, in fact, is still going on. The problems to be overcome fall in three main categories:

1. Getting data to the personal computer.
2. Maintaining some standards in personal computers and their use.
3. Providing the assistance and training to make the personal computer useful.

PC Data

The original method of getting data for personal computers was to take the printed reports from the information-systems department and type the pertinent data into the PC. This required a great deal of manual keying and led to frequent errors being introduced into the data. More efficient methods of transferring data were thwarted for a number of reasons. Often, they did not exist. Just as often they were discouraged by the information-systems people who had too much other work to do to implement them, worried about security for data that might be spread all over the company and beyond, and felt threatened by the new trend.

Gradually, the reluctance to share data in machine-readable form melted away as information-systems people realized that personal computing could ease their workload by moving short-term projects to the user, and that the phenomenon was not going to go away. Better transfer methods with accompanying security measures were instituted.

One method was to put the data on some transportable medium such as floppy disk and hand-carry it to the PC. This was a major improvement over rekeying the data.

The trend now is to have the PCs connected in a network that includes the mainframe in the information-systems department. Assuming that the PC user has the right security access, he or she can **download** the data—copy the data directly from the mainframe to the PC. In a like manner, data may be **uploaded**—copied from the PC to the mainframe. This is done less often because the information-systems department is responsible for the overall data integrity and uploading data from individual PCs reduces their control over those data.

Maintaining PC Standards

When PCs first began to be used in offices, users went out and bought whichever models they liked. They might have been Apples, IBMs, Kaypros, Compaqs, or any of a variety of other incompatible machines. Software, also, was a hodgepodge. Operating systems might be CPM, AppleDos, MS-DOS, or any of a hundred others. Applications packages such as spreadsheets might be chosen from a smorgasbord including Visicalc, SuperCalc, CalcStar, or Lotus.

Different equipment and different software requires data in different forms. Data written on a floppy disk on an Apple cannot be read by an IBM PC, even though, in many cases, the disks look exactly the same. Connections to a network, operating systems, and software are also different. Even if the equipment is the same, different software packages cannot work with the same data. The Lotus spreadsheet package, for example, cannot work directly with data produced by SuperCalc. It is similar to trying to operate a company in which everyone speaks a different language. Communication is difficult.

Many companies, after experiencing such problems, have set up certain standards for both hardware and software. The firm will only fund particular brands and types of equipment, and only specific software packages. This ensures that data sharing will be possible and that employees will not be buying inappropriate items. As in most situations, trade-offs are involved. The individual may feel that better things are available, especially for a specific application, but the needs of the organization as a whole are better served by maintaining consistency.

Providing Assistance and Training

At first, only dedicated hackers (people who enjoy the computer for its own sake) used personal computers. Management realized, however, that the productivity of those hackers (when they weren't just hacking) was quite high, so they encouraged the use of PCs among the rest of the employees.

Hackers enjoy learning about new equipment and software tools. They are willing to go through the agonies of reading some nearly indecipherable manuals and a lot of experimentation to get these systems going. Most people aren't. If the majority are to become productive PC users they need help—someone to show them how to set up the system and someone to fall back on when they get into trouble.

Many companies have attacked the problem by setting up PC **information centers,** a group which exists to help others in the

Information centers in a company help people become productive users of personal computers.

Business Focus   BOX 14-1
Runaway Computer Projects Trample Companies

Computer project gone wild threatens to turn the Blues' black ink into red.

For a while, None, Wisconsin, had the highest per capita income of any city in the world. Hundreds of insurance checks were mailed there, but the city doesn't exist. How did it happen? An entry error that was multiplied hundredfold by a poorly performing computer system.

In 1983, Blue Cross and Blue Shield United of Wisconsin hired Electronic Data Systems Corporation to pull together the functions of five computer systems into one big integrated system. The $200 million cost and the 18-month completion time were reasonable—if the system had worked. In its first year of operation, however, the system had invented the town of None, sent out another $60 million in overpayments and duplicate checks, and cost the insurer an estimated 35,000 members. EDS contends that bugs were inevitable because of the size of the system and the massive amounts of data that had to be converted from the old system. The Blues will concede some bugs, but not a wholesale disaster. They want EDS to reimburse them for some of their lost revenue. At last report, the dispute was still in arbitration.

It would be nice to think that this was just an isolated case, but it wasn't. New examples of runaway computer projects are appearing all the time.

The City of Richmond, Virginia, hired Arthur Young to develop a $1.2 million billing and information system for its gas and water utilities. Richmond paid out almost $1 million and was prepared to pay the rest, but two years after the contracted completion date, the system still had not been delivered, so they cancelled the contract. Arthur Young has filed suit against the city.

The State of Oklahoma hired one of the nation's largest accounting firms to design a $500,000 system to handle worker's compensation claims. It was completed just recently, five years and $4 million later.

The good hands of Allstate Insurance felt it had put itself in some bad hands when it hired EDS to develop a system to integrate its office operations and shorten the introduction time of new types of policies from three years to one month. The estimated cost was $8 million. Almost a year after the target date and after spending $15 million, Allstate hired a new consultant, Peat Marwick Mitchell & Co., set a new completion date, and made a new cost estimate—$100 million.

How can these things happen to big, well-run organizations working in conjunction with highly respected information-systems consulting firms? There seem to be some fundamental and disturbing common threads in most of these disasters. Many professionals on both the buyers' and the builders' sides have not adjusted to the increased complexity of today's information systems. A few years ago the typical large company had a number of separate systems doing separate jobs, each rather simple by today's standards. The word now is "connectivity." One system connects all the various functions and information needs of the company. To connect five systems together requires far more than five times the complexity because not only must the individual jobs be done but also all the data must be connected together.

Many systems go through the development process without adequate monitoring by the buyer. Industry experts agree that a system development process should have built-in checkpoints against which to measure progress and that representatives of the buyer should take a more active role in the development. Often systems go through a preliminary design and then the developer goes back to the shop and works almost in isolation until the system is completed.

Another common buyer's complaint is that the experienced technical people that they talk to in the initial stages of the system's development are replaced with relatively inexperienced people. The old hands are out bringing in new business.

The problems have become so prevalent that they have spawned a new industry—catching runaways. Peat Marwick, for example, set up a group for just that purpose. So far, it has taken in over $20 million in revenues.

Is there hope? Yes. People on both sides of the fence are becoming increasingly aware of the problems and are exercising greater diligence in preventing them. More disasters are bound to happen, but hopefully they will be less frequent.

organization get the most out of their PCs. Most information centers provide these services:

- Help in purchasing hardware and software.
- Assistance in setting up new systems.
- Training in standard software packages such as spreadsheets, word processing, and databases.
- Consulting on specific applications of the standard software.
- Help when you have a problem.

The information center would not be practical if the company PC standards we referred to did not exist.

SUMMARY

Information output can come in many forms. Periodic reports are relatively constant reports, usually printed, that appear at the end of the week, month, or whatever. In a demand reporting system, information is produced only by request. Periodic reporting produced more information at a lower cost per piece, but much of it is never looked at.

A detail report shows data from each transaction, while summary reports gather data together and show only the totals. Exception reports can be based on either detail or summary information, but they show only the items that are out of some "normal" range.

Most of the data that enters a computer-information system and the information that comes out goes through the transaction-processing system. This handles most of the standardized internal data and produces most of the periodic reports, as well as supplying the bulk of the data for the other systems.

Management information systems also supply recurring information, but the objective is specifically to support management decision making. External data is often added to that provided by the transaction-reporting system to allow evaluation of the company in its industry environment.

Decision-support systems exist to provide for nonre-

curring information needs. Through software packages such as database management, modeling and simulation, spreadsheet, graphics and presentation, and report writing, users can retrieve and organize data without the aid of the information-systems specialists.

Information is an important factor in all four of the traditional management functions—planning, organizing, directing, and controlling. As the level of management gets higher, responsibilities become broader and data more plentiful, so higher-level managers must rely on summary information. There would be no time to analyze information in detail. This task is delegated to the lower levels.

Personal computers have had a significant effect on the character of management information and decision-support systems. More processing, especially decision-support effort, is being done by the user on a PC. This trend increases the efficient use of the data and shifts some of the load away from the computer-information systems department to the users. CIS departments have had to adjust by making the data available in electronic form, principally through networking; providing standards for compatibility in PC hardware and software; and giving assistance and training to the users.

KEY WORDS

(in order of appearance in text)
Periodic reporting
Demand reporting
Detail report
Summary report
Exception report
Transaction-processing system
Internal data
On-line transaction processing
  (OLTP)
Management information system
  (MIS)

External data
Decision-support system
Database management system
Model
Simulation
Spreadsheet
Cell
Graphics-presentation package
Integrated package
Problem Identification
Alternative Development

Alternative Selection
Implementation
Follow Up
Structured decision
Unstructured decision
Top management
Middle management
Operating management
Download
Upload
Information center

REVIEW QUESTIONS

1. What is the difference between periodic and demand reporting?
2. Can periodic reports be produced by a batch system? Demand reports?
3. What is the difference between detail and summary reports?
4. What is an exception report?
5. What kinds of reports are produced by a transaction-reporting system?
6. Does a transaction-reporting system use primarily internal or external data?
7. How do management information systems differ from transaction-reporting systems?
8. How do decision-support systems differ from the other two?
9. What are the common types of software packages used in decision support packages?
10. Describe a model of a business.

11. What are spreadsheets used for?
12. What three things may be entered into a spreadsheet cell?
13. How does using a graphics-presentation package save time?
14. What are the four functions of management?
15. What characteristics differentiate the three levels of management?
16. Which management level requires information in greatest detail? Least detail?
17. How do personal computers usually get their data in a typical organizational setting?
18. What kinds of standards might be set for PC use in a company?
19. What services do information centers provide to personal computer users in a company?

THINK ABOUT IT

1. Describe a situation in which periodic reporting would be cheaper overall then demand reporting. Describe the opposite situation.
2. Could you run a management information system without a transaction-reporting system? How or why not?
3. How have decision-support systems relieved some of the burden from the computer information-systems department while increasing the information available to the user?
4. How can an upper-level manager afford to ignore detail reports and only look at summaries?
5. Can a manager delegate information responsibilities as is done with other responsibilities?

6. How have personal computers helped the overall information-systems activity in most organizations? How have they caused problems?
7. Describe the role of the computer information-systems department in the use of personal computers in a company.
8. Why are strict PC hardware and software standards important to a company? Why are they sometimes objected to?
9. What have many computer information-systems departments done to reduce the problems caused by the use of personal computers in business?

CHALLENGES

1. Investigate the computer information system at a local company or your school. What kinds of output are produced by the transaction reporting and management information systems. Do they provide decision support from the main computer system or through PCs or both?

2. Are personal computers used in your school or company? How are standards maintained? If they are not, what types of problems does this cause and what standards would you recommend?

Microcomputers

1. The Kodak Diconix is a small portable ink-jet printer that prints on regular 8½″ paper.

2. The Ultralite microcomputer from NEC Home Electronics (U.S.A.), Inc., is half the size of the smallest laptop currently available, and is designed to fit into the slimmest briefcase.

3. The ProSpeed (also from NEC) is the first personal computer to offer the portability of a laptop computer and the power of a desktop computer.

4. This is a hardcard without its cover so that the plug-in board and hard disk can be viewed.

5. This Seiko wristwatch computer is obviously one of the smallest computers made.

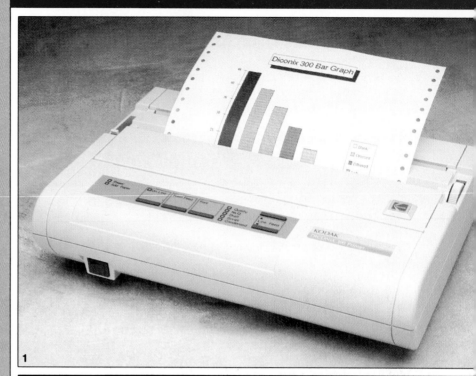

1

4

3

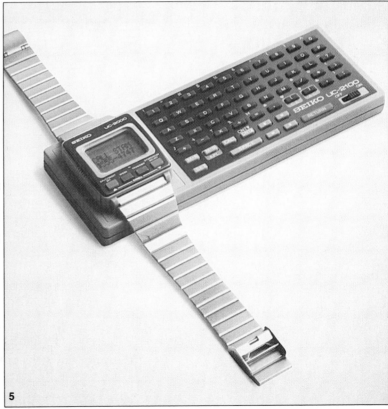

5

6. Computers that use a voice-activated microphone instead of a keyboard for input can be accessed by all ages.

7. Dr. Stephen Hawking (British astrophysicist) who suffers from MLS is shown with his special microcomputer.

8. A new computer system from Matsushita Electric Industrial Co., Ltd., parent company of Panasonic, uses animated graphics to help hearing-impaired students acquire speech.

9. Personal computer pioneer, Steve Jobs, who cofounded Apple Computer, is shown with a NeXT computer.

10. This brain-state analyzer is used to determine mental disorders, as well as to monitor progress of vital blood, by analyzing the flow of blood in the brain.

6

8

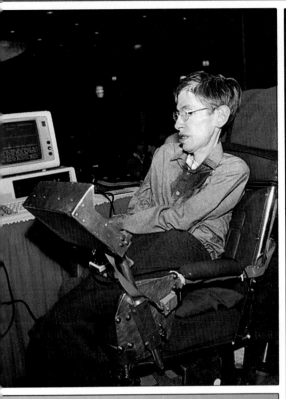

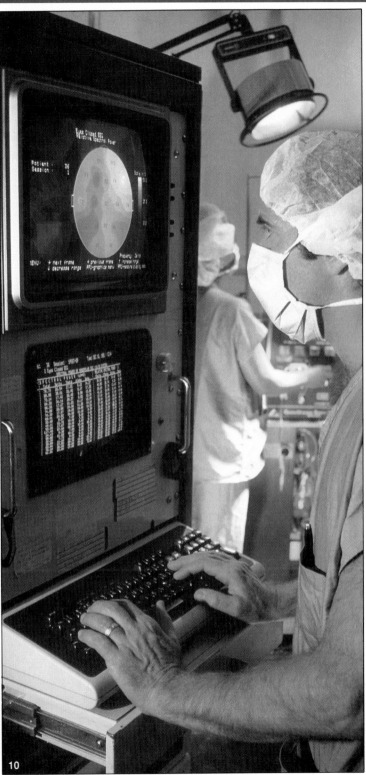

10

15

THE COMPUTER'S INCREASING ROLE

PREVIEW
In the preceding chapters, we have seen what computers are, what functional parts they consist of, how we communicate with them, how we control them, how we integrate them into information systems, ways in which they are used in decision making, and many of the ways in which we take advantage of their capabilities. In this last chapter, we will look at some of the places where computers have become an integral part of the business process and the increasing role they will play in the future.

After reading this chapter you should be familiar with:

■ How and why we automate the office.

■ How computers are helping in design and engineering tasks.

■ Ways in which computers are being used in the factory.

■ The types of hardware and software businesses will be using in the future.

A s we said before, the computer is just a tool. But it is one of the most useful tools that man has created. The computer is no longer an esoteric gadget that only a select few use. It is more like the screwdriver or the typewriter, or perhaps even a combination of the two. A good percentage of us are using computers on the job, or will be in the not-too-distant future. Let us examine some of the areas where the computer has or soon will become so much a part of the environment that it is regarded not as something special but just as a part of the job scene.

IN THE OFFICE

Is there an office without a computer any more? Yes, there undoubtedly is but this is the exception rather than the rule. A very few years ago there was a lot of talk about "The Office of the Future" with computers involved in many of the office's functions. The office of the future is now the office of the present and almost of the past. We find computers either aiding in or taking over many of the clerical tasks of the office. Let us look first at why we are automating the office and then how.

Why Automate the Office?

We automate the office for the same reason we automate almost anything else—for more productivity. If an individual produces more in the same amount of time, then labor costs per unit of output decrease. Since much of that productivity increase is due to new machinery, the capital cost of the machinery will offset some of the decrease in the cost of producing a product or service. But, assuming additional capital costs are less than the decreased labor costs, total expenses will decrease, and profits will increase and/or goods and services will become less expensive.

Office with computer workstations in it.

BOX 15-1

Computer Angst

When Jan L. Guynes, a researcher at the University of Texas at Arlington, began to look at how different people react to a slow computer, she figured the greatest frustration would show up in type A personalities—"You can tell them by the way they bang on their keyboards," she says.

She was wrong. *Everyone's* anxiety jumped to statistically high levels when confronted by slow or inconsistent system response times. "Even some of the more laid-back Type B personalities became quite hostile," she recalls. "I heard quite a few of them swearing mystical oaths."

In her research Guynes classified 86 volunteers as either Type A (competitive, driven, impatient) or Type B (calmer, more patient), then gave them 20 minutes to edit a short text on a terminal. While they worked, she manipulated the computer's response time at random, so that the volunteers faced unpredictable delays of up to ten seconds at a time. Although the Type A personalities began the experiment with the highest anxiety, by the end both groups had reached the same level of agitation.

For employees who spend most of their workday at a PC or terminal with a sluggish response, these results don't come as a surprise. After looking at other studies on the effects of anxiety, Guynes concluded that over time such employees could experience not only emotional tension, apprehension, and erratic short-term memory but also physical effects such as increased heart rate, elevated blood pressure, and muscle tension. The net result: a decline in productivity.

Although the experiment was conducted on terminals, Guynes emphasizes that its outcome is just as valid for workers using personal computers. "This should affect the way software is written," she suggests. "Some of the database software in particular is still too slow."

Source: Norman Boucher, *PC Computing,* Oct. 1988, p. 42.

In the last 25 years, manufacturing productivity (as measured by output per hour) has nearly doubled. This has been due to new machines, better methods, and, of course, to computers. Office output has been much harder to improve. Offices have always resisted increases in productivity because clerical tasks are labor intensive, they require people, and for the foreseeable future they will remain that way.

The percentage of effort being spent on clerical tasks is increasing. First, because the increased productivity of the manufacturing sector requires proportionally less people. Second, because our economy has been shifting from producing goods to offering services. This means that our least productive area is also our fastest growing. Fortunately, computers have been able to help us out. Following are some of the ways we use computers to increase office productivity.

Word Processing

Word processing is all those activities that result in printed text output—memos, reports, letters, manuals, books, and so forth. Dedicated word-processing machines such as those produced by Wang, NBI, and others, as well as word processing software for personal computers such as Word, WordStar, Word Perfect, and a dozen other packages with the word "word" in them have increased the efficiency of our clerical personnel. Following are some of the functions provided by a typical, sophisticated word-processing system.

The capabilities of word processors are examined in more detail in the Appendix.

Desktop Publishing

Desktop publishing is really an outgrowth of word processing. The difference is principally in the quality of the output. **Desktop-publishing** software produces documents that imitate the final product of typesetting and page-layout operations. Typical of the features of documents produced by desktop-publishing software packages (such as PageMaker and Ventura Publisher) are:

- *Multiple fonts.* Various type styles (fonts) are available in sizes ranging from fine print to large headline size.

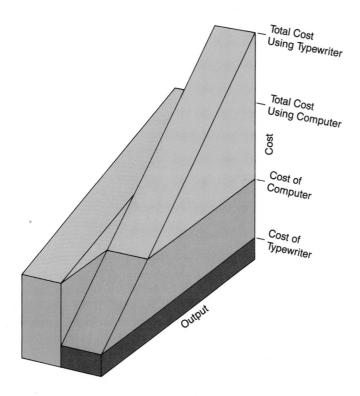

Clerical Productivity

Producing typed documents with the aid of the computer is easier than with just a typewriter. True, the computer costs more than the typewriter, but even adding the cost of the machine to the labor cost of the output shows that for higher levels of output, using the computer costs less.

BOX 15-2

Word Processing versus Desktop Publishing

Two questions have been of paramount interest to users ever since desktop publishing came on the scene in 1986.

■ What is the difference between desktop publishing and word processing?
■ Will word processing and desktop publishing merge?

Approach to Text

There is a fundamental difference between word processors and desktop publishers. The difference? Their approach to the basic office task of recording information on paper. Word processors approach the problem from the viewpoint of the writer, someone who is primarily interested in creating a memo or a document. Word processors are concerned first with the contents of a document and second with the composition of that document. DTP programs approach the problem from the viewpoint of the typesetter; they are concerned first with the composition and second with the contents.

Well, you might ask, "Since DTP programs allow someone to enter text, don't both paths lead to the same result?" Most assuredly, the answer can be yes. If you are an office worker or a writer, however, you are primarily interested in highly productive and easy-to-use tools and commands that will produce a two-page memo, for example. You don't want the burden of worrying about sophisticated layout commands when the boss is breathing down your neck, urging you to meet a deadline. Even though word processing and desktop publishing can lead to the same ultimate result, the paths to that result are completely different. What is productive for a typesetter is not necessarily productive for a writer.

Merge Ahead

The next question is "Will word processing and desktop publishing merge?" The answer is *yes*—word processors are

beginning to incorporate more and more sophisticated document layout capabilities—and, to some extent, *no*—DTP programs are continuing to incorporate more and more sophisticated typesetting and composition capabilities. What we know today as DTP programs will continue to migrate away from general office use into the much narrower market of truly professional publishing.

How Does Word Publishing Fit In?

So far, we've talked of just word processing and desktop publishing. But a third category—word publishing—is developing as a result of the overlap in our expectations of word processing and desktop publishing. In fact, we divide today's market into three segments:

■ *Word Processing.* The traditional market for producing efficient high-quality memos, letters, and documents.

■ *Multiple columns.* The user can form text in two, three, four, or more column pages with lines between or perhaps borders around columns.
■ *Graphics insets.* Images can be placed anywhere on the page with text flowing around or even superimposed over them.
■ *High-resolution graphics.* Drawings or photographs can be scanned at high resolutions (such as 300 by 300 dots per inch, better than newspaper quality) and included in the document.
■ *Page previews.* Most visual display screens are not large enough to view an entire page, so the desktop-publishing software will

■ *Word Publishing.* The new market, brought about by the advent of laser printers and dot matrix printers capable of supporting multiple fonts. Word publishing users demand all the capabilities of traditional word processing plus the ability to mix multiple fonts and graphics. Word publishing is the most rapidly growing market segment and will eventually replace traditional word processing as the product of choice for most home and office use.

■ *Desktop Publishing.* The newest and smallest market, which focuses on page layout capabilities with minimal word processing and word publishing capabilities.

Word processors of the future, like those being developed for the Macintosh and OS/2 Presentation Manager, will incorporate sophisticated layout and graphics capabilities to rival any of the existing DTP programs. These next generation word processors—or word publishers—will share the fundamental emphasis on contents first, layout second. On the surface, they will seem like today's word processors (highly productive tools for writing everything from simple memos to complex documents). On a less obvious level, they will be able to support very sophisticated layout and composition functions. The layout capability, however, must not make the program difficult to use. A new system must pass this acid test before we accept it: Will someone be able to use the software to produce a simple office memo—without having to wrestle with layout problems?

Yes, the disciplines of word processing and desktop publishing are merging. Fortunately, this merging will benefit the millions of office workers whose primary office task is producing memos and documents under tight deadlines.

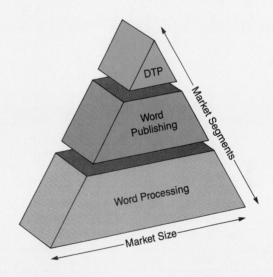

Source: Ray Mussato, *WordStar News,* Fall 1988, p. 4

reduce the page to fit on a normal screen. By doing so, the user can see the overall page layout without flipping back and forth between screens.

The dividing line between the high-end word processors and low-end desktop publishers is often not clear. Many of the features above also exist to some degree in some word-processing packages. Two things set the two types of packages apart, however. First, desktop-publishing software is **page oriented.** Each page is considered and made up individually. Although you can enter text and/or graphics using the desktop publishers, they are typically entered using word processors and/or graphics packages and imported to the desktop-published page. At that point the fonts are changed, columns are determined, graphics are inserted, and each page is made up.

Word processors are **document oriented.** <u>You just keep typing and the word processor separates the pages.</u> Inserting lines in a word-processed document will change the locations of the page breaks. The same action in a desktop-published document usually requires that you reexamine and reset each page.

Second, the output quality of a desktop-published document is better because, although it takes more work to produce it, you have more control over its appearance. Realistic utilization of a desktop-publishing package requires a very high-quality, high-resolution printer such as a laser printer. The complication of the page layout usually requires a far longer output time for a desktop-published page. A laser printer may be capable of producing eight pages per minute of simple word-processed text, while a single desktop-published page may take the same printer up to five minutes to produce.

As an example, the drafts of this book were produced on a high-end word processor with graphics capabilities (WordStar 2000 Plus). It would have looked better to the reviewers and the students that used it during the class-testing phase had it been desktop published, but both the printing time and correction time would have been prohibitive. The final version was typeset and pages made up by hand because, although desktop-published output looks good, traditional typesetting still produces the best quality.

Office Communications

Chatting over the water cooler, typed memos, and telephone calls are still accepted methods of office communications, but the computer has introduced a few others. Consider "telephone tag," a common office game. Ortiz calls Hakimi, who "isn't in," so Ortiz leaves a message for Hakimi to call back. Hakimi calls Ortiz back, but now Ortiz is "in conference" so Hakimi leaves a message for Ortiz. Ortiz calls back Hakimi, who is "presently unavailable" and so on and so forth.

Electronic mail has alleviated the telephone-tag problem. **Electronic mail** is meant to imitate a normal mail system, but uses computers to make it faster and more efficient. Using electronic mail, one person types a message addressed to someone else into a computer. This message is sent

Electronic Mail

This shows an electronic mail transaction on a typical network. One user sends a message to a central computer addressed to another user. The other user requests messages from the central computer and retrieves the message.

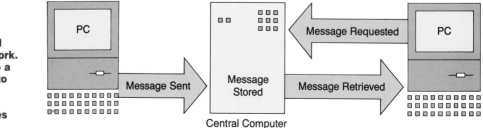

PC

Message Sent

Message Stored

Message Requested

Message Retrieved

PC

Central Computer

over some kind of network, perhaps a local area network or the telephone system, to a holding area for the addressee. Depending on the setup, this holding area might be the addressees' own computer or some other computer to which the addressee has access. The addressee may, at any time, check this holding area for messages.

With most electronic-mail systems, the addressee can tell how many messages are being held, when they were received, and who they are from. Using this information, the addressee can selectively answer the messages. The boss will get a message returned immediately, while the aluminum-siding salesman will simply have his message erased.

The advantage of electronic mail over phone calls is that the message is sent even if there is no one presently there to receive it. The advantage over standard mail is speed. It takes only a second or two, rather than days, for a message to reach its destination.

Office computer communications do not have to be limited to characters and words. If the computers on both ends are capable of graphics, and most office computers are, images such as diagrams, drawings, charts, and graphs can also be sent. More and more electronic-mail systems will also work with "voice mail"; the sender's voice will be digitized and stored.

BOX 15-3

Selling to the Hordes Who Are Working at Home

Be it ever so humble, more people are working at home. Link Resources, a New York-based research firm specializing in electronic information, says that more than 25 million people will do so this year—7.5% more than in 1987. Of those, 22 million or so will work primarily at home. And 4.3 million of those will earn all of their income there—up 27.3% from last year.

This is producing a boom in sales of computer products to home workers. Their expenditures should swell 29% this year, to $8.7 billion, Link says, noting that home workers buy expensive equipment. It estimates that in 1987, for instance, home workers spent an average $2,120 per personal computer vs. $1,167 for the average U.S. household, and $810 for peripherals vs. $312 for home hobbyists. To cash in, Sharp Electronics Corp. has set up a Personal Home Office Equipment Div. to market low-priced facsimile machines and personal computers that are much lighter and cheaper than most office models. Epson America, Apple Computer, and even IBM have their eyes on this booming market as well, since experts say that about half of home workers still don't own a computer.

Source: *Business Week,* Feb. 8, 1988, p. 88.

Many office computers are equipped for **facsimile** (or **fax,** for short) communications—sending a reproduction of some hard copy, such as a sales invoice or a signed contract, to another location. This requires a scanner to digitize an image to be sent, a high-resolution printer such as a laser printer to make hard copy of images received, and some hardware and software in the computers on both ends to make it work.

A network with enough sophistication can allow many forms of **teleconferencing**—having a number of people and devices connected at the same time. This might be as simple as a conference telephone call or as complicated as having voice as well as computer and video communication occurring on the same network.

Desktop Organizers

You can buy a plaque for your office that says, "A messy desk is a sign of genius." Perhaps, but in any case people must keep a number of things readily available for their use, typically on the desktop. These include an appointment calendar, address and telephone listings, a calculator, papers relating to at least three projects in process, a personal computer, and an egg salad sandwich on rye.

Since the personal computer is already on the desk, software companies have developed a number of **desktop organizer** packages (such as Sidekick and DESQview) to clear off the desk, and store the mess in the computer in a form that is easy to use. They have not been able to do anything about the egg salad sandwich but here are some of the other features offered by typical packages:

- *Program switching.* The principal factor that makes desktop organizers practical is the ability to interrupt a program, switch to another, and then come back to the original one where you left off. This feature allows you to be working on something, have your boss call with a question on something else, and set aside your current project without losing your place. The program-switching feature is also a prerequisite for all the following features.
- *Calculator.* Type a couple of keys on the keyboard and a calculator face appears in a window in the middle of your screen. Make whatever calculations you have to, hit another key, the calculator disappears, and you continue with what you were doing before.
- *Note pad.* Had a thought? Need to jot it down? Another couple of keys will make a note pad window appear for you. In many cases, the notes are automatically "date and time stamped"—the computer automatically records the date and time you wrote the note. The text of the note can usually be imported into documents used in other programs, such as word processors. Many desktop organizers allow you to selectively retrieve your notes based on date, time, or other subject keys.
- *Appointment calendar.* The calendar window allows you to enter appointments, or view or print your calendar for a time period.

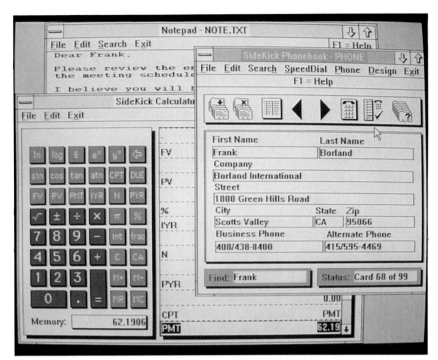

Desktop Organizers

Desktop organizers allow operations to be suspended while other tasks interrupt. The top window in the screen above is active. All the ones behind are suspended. When the top window is closed, the operations in the one directly below will be resumed.

■ *Phone book*. This window keeps track of names, addresses, and phone numbers of the people with whom you do business. It is the computer version of the Rolodex. Computer phone books often have the capability of printing specialized lists based on keys that you include in the listings. For example, you may be able to create a listing of customers in Maryland, vendors of machine tools, or good restaurants in town.

■ *Auto Dialer*. To call someone, you must first look up the name and then dial the number. With some desktop organizers, you have the computer search for the name in the phone book, and, if your computer has the right kind of modem, it will automatically dial the number for you.

■ *Clipboard*. Many organizers can copy a section of a screen being used with one program, put it in memory (the memory space is often referred to as a **clipboard**), and put the clipboard contents into a screen being used with another program. For example, you may electronically **cut** a section of a spreadsheet, put it in your clipboard, call up your word processor, and **paste** that section in your word-processed document.

IN DESIGN AND ENGINEERING

As we have moved toward the present, more and more attention has been given to the design of a product as opposed to its manufacture. This trend shows every indication of continuing into the future. There are many reasons for the phenomenon.

1. Products are becoming more complicated. A horse-drawn carriage could be described in a couple of drawings. An automobile requires a stack of drawings over two feet high.
2. Competition has forced lower-cost production. The expense of the "hand work" that went into products years ago would not be tolerated, or paid for, by today's consumer. Much of the reason for the hand work was that components were not designed or manufactured accurately enough to eliminate manual fitting in final assembly.
3. Manufacturing has become more sophisticated. Poorly or incompletely designed products cannot be made without circumventing and defeating today's automated manufacturing processes. If things don't fit together automatically, our modern factories can't make them.
4. Design is becoming less expensive. Design was, and still is, very labor intensive. There is no substitute for human creativity, but creative people must commit their ideas to paper (or video screen) and that takes time. Computers have significantly reduced the time it takes to put an idea into presentable form.

Computer-Aided Design

Computer-aided design (CAD) is the catch-all term for those facilities that have reduced the time it takes to commit an idea to paper. A typical CAD system consists of a computer, graphics-input devices, a graphics-display system, a plotter for hard copy, and some sophisticated software.

Computer-Aided Design

Using CAD software, the time it takes to commit a design to paper is sharply reduced.

This keyboard, monitor, digitizing tablet, and plotter—along with a computer and CAD software—have all but replaced the drawing board and T square.

The type of computer needed depends on the size and number of projects. Many projects, or larger projects requiring more memory and faster processing speed, will require the use of a mini or mainframe computer. However, a great deal of computer-aided design takes place on personal computers.

Almost all types of graphics-input devices, from mice to video cameras, are used for CAD. The most popular, though, are absolute devices such as graphics tablets, and scanners for inputting images that have been produced elsewhere.

Displays are typically color CRTs. Sizes range from the 7-inch monitors found on some portable PCs to 35-inch giants. High-resolution screens are quite popular because the higher the resolution, the more detail the designer can see, making it easier to use. Hard-copy output is typically from plotters, although many CAD devices can use matrix or laser printers.

CAD software comes in all prices, sizes, and capabilities. For a PC, you can buy Generic CAD starting at about $99, to AutoCAD with prices starting at about $2,500. There are a number of software packages for larger computers with prices ranging into the hundreds of thousands.

Following are some of the typical features of most CAD software:

- *Editing.* Anything may be changed. Objects may be deleted, moved, resized, reproportioned, or rotated.
- *Shapes.* The ability to draw many different shapes is important. The designer must not only be able to draw straight lines but also rectangles, closed polygons, circles, arcs, curves, and so forth. With a typical CAD package, the designer specifies a few points and the computer fills in the rest.
- *Text.* The designer must be able to include descriptions, notations, explanations, and dimensions on the drawing. Most packages offer choices between different type fonts and sizes.
- *Scaling.* The designer must be able to position objects at the correct points on the drawing and make them the correct size. CAD packages show the pointer's exact location (3.75 inches to the right and 5.45 inches down from the upper left corner), and allow the designer to draw objects in any position on the drawing. Many packages will allow you to draw a line from here to there and the package will automatically label it with the correct dimension.
- *Zooming.* It is impossible to show all the detail in a large drawing on a small screen, so a CAD package allows the designer to look at the whole drawing on the screen and then selectively zoom in on individual sections. The zooming process makes that section 2, 3, 5, 10, or however many times as big so that it can be worked on in detail.
- *Layers.* Most CAD packages can work on many layers or aspects of a drawing separately. In a drawing of a car, for example, the body can be in one layer, the interior in another, and the engine and drive train in a third. These are each separate drawings but are on the same scale and can be superimposed on each other and displayed together.
- *Three Dimensions.* More sophisticated CAD packages allow design in three dimensions. Using such a package, you could design a car body as it would appear visually and then work on individual two-dimensional cross sections.

Computer-Aided Engineering

What do you get when you take a CAD system and add to it some capabilities for engineering decision making? **Computer-aided engineering (CAE).** For example, there are structural design and architectural programs that will calculate the breaking strength on design members. The engineer can look at these computer-generated figures and either strengthen or lighten certain parts.

The semiconductor industry uses CAE programs to design integrated circuits. Instead of manually drawing all of the integrated layers of the chip design, the designer tells the computer what types of components are to be used and how they will be interconnected, and the computer lays out the chip in the most efficient manner.

IN THE FACTORY

In the 1820s, Joseph Marie Jacquard revolutionized the weaving industry by inventing a loom controlled by punched cards. Intricate patterns could be stored on the cards and reproduced faithfully and easily on the loom. We would certainly not call this a computer, but it was a device that used a stored program to control a manufacturing process. Now we have many manufacturing processes controlled by stored programs directing computers which, in turn, direct machines. Planning, managing, and controlling manufacturing with the aid of computers is known as **computer-aided manufacturing (CAM).**

Often, products designed with the aid of computers are also manufactured with computer aid. In these cases, many of the data developed in the design stage can be used in the manufacture. These include everything from materials lists to the layout of holes to be drilled in a metal plate. Using CAD data in a CAM process is referred to by the combined term **CAD/CAM.**

Manufacturing Planning and Management

Many of the functions of a computer information system aid in the planning and management of the factory operations. For example, **materials-requirements-planning (MRP)** systems are dedicated to providing the correct raw materials and parts to the manufacturing process at the lowest cost. The inputs to the system are production schedules, parts and materials lists for each product, and current inventory and receiving schedules for these materials. The system produces orders for materials, warnings for materials with dangerously low inventories, and a number of performance analyses.

The information from a correctly used MRP system should allow the factory to reduce inventories to a minimum while providing the proper parts and materials, keeping production on schedule.

The MRP system is often part of a larger **manufacturing-resource-planning (MRP II)** system. (The computer industry seems to be running short of initials for acronyms.) MRP II systems aid in the planning and evaluation of all the manufacturing resources—inventories, machines, labor, and capital. Given estimates of demand, the MRP II system will develop production and inventory schedules to organize the factory's resources in the most efficient manner.

MRP II systems also include evaluation tools that provide information on how well the factory is working to plan, and where adjustments should be made. Many also include simulation programs to help managers decide on alternative courses for the future.

Manufacturing Process Controls

For decades, many of our manufacturing processes have been automated. For years, many of them have been computer controlled. Some of the first applications of computers were replacements of what were called "NC," numerical controlled, machine tools—lathes, drilling machines, and so

BOX 15-4

Art-to-Part Gizmo Makes Plastic Models from CAD Data

Though still experimental, StereoLithography could become a hot item for serious CAD users.

Computer-aided-design (CAD) users should add a new word to their vocabularies: StereoLithography. This new "art-to-part" process produces plastic models from solid-model data prepared by a CAD system. It means that prototypes, which take weeks or months to build, can be turned out in minutes or hours.

"This has the potential to revolutionize the way we do business," says Al DeWitt, an advanced manufacturing engineer at GM's Fisher Guide Division. Fisher has been testing a StereoLithography Apparatus (SLA) from 3D Systems, Sylmar, Calif., for the past year. Experts in fields from aerospace to the toy industry agree that SLA has an exciting future. One current user is Apple Computer, IBM is another.

The 3d Systems machine forms parts from liquid photopolymer plastic, normally used for bathroom tiles that don't need waxing or gloss-coated paper products. It uses an ultraviolet laser beam that "draws" on the surface of the liquid plastic. The liquid plastic cures at the point where the laser beam hits it, forming a solid layer of the part. It begins at the bottom cross-section of the part; an elevator in the SLA (see diagram) gradually lowers the parts a fraction of an inch at a time so the next cross-section can be formed.

By repeating this process thousands of times, the SLA produces a solid copy from CAD data. Copies formed are accurate to within five-thousandths of an inch and at present can be up to one foot square, with larger systems in development.

StereoLithography is far from ready for mass use, but it's not just a pipe-dream. 3D Systems has shipped production SLAs to companies such as Apply, IBM, Ford Motor Company, and Precision Castparts Corp. and at least nine CAD/CAM systems now interface with the SLA.

Most observers agree that development of interfaces for CAD systems like AutoCAD and VersaCAD should boost sales potential and lower prices, now over $175,000, to more affordable levels.

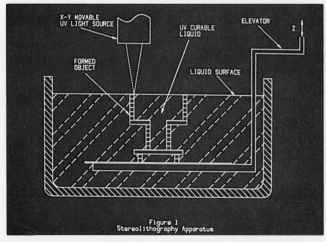

Figure 1
Stereolithography Apparatus

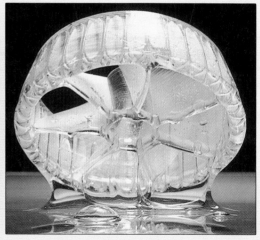

Source: Ken Fermoyle, *Computer Dealer*, Sept. 1988, p. 10.

forth. These NC machines allowed the operator to type in the locations of a set of holes, for example, and then the drilling machine would put the holes in those locations. Some NC machines used punched cards to store machining specifications—essentially programs.

Controlling these machines with computers was a very logical step. Current computer-controlled machine shops can input what amounts to a design for a part, and the tools, under the control of the computer, will make the part.

Robots

C3PO, of Star Wars fame, was a lovable, if somewhat petulant machine. He, or it, or whatever, looked vaguely human—two arms, two legs, a head—and could walk and talk. In reality, C3PO was not a robot, he was a costume with a man inside. R2D2, the squat, dome-topped can that rolled around on wheels, was closer to a real robot. Such a robot today, however, would be more of a curiosity or a toy. The vast majority of today's robots are used in manufacturing processes, are not at all lovable, and bear very little resemblance to anything human.

A **robot** is a programmable, multipurpose manipulator. <u>Mechanically, most of them consist of an arm with some kind of grasping "fingers" and motors to move both the arm and the fingers.</u> A robot is a multipurpose machine, meaning that it can be programmed to do different tasks. For example, the same robot that picks up parts and inserts them in a frame might have a spray gun attached to its arm and be programmed to spray paint a car body.

Early programming of robots used to be done in the same manner as for other computers—someone types in the specific directions on a keyboard. Many robots are now able to "learn." They are manually led through an operation, remember the motions they have made, and can then repeat these motions over and over again. Still others can take a combination of directions—the best of both worlds.

Robotics
Robots do dull, repetitive jobs accurately, tirelessly, and cheaply.

The field of robotics is advancing at least as fast as computers. Its development, of course, is quite dependent on computers because computers are the "brains" behind the robots. Many robots now have one or more "senses"—typically sight and touch. Using these senses, a robot might pick the proper part out of a parts bin, orient it in the proper direction, and insert it into an assembly.

Such capabilities always lead to comparisons of robots and human beings. And in production settings, where the relative advantages of one over the other may mean cheaper, better products and/or loss of jobs to machines, the comparisons should be made. Robots are not nearly as versatile as humans. Their capabilities of sight and touch are extremely crude compared to a human's and they have no capacity for independent judgment. For example, when someone put a grape in with a set of steel balls, one robot happily assembled it into a set of ball bearings. The fact that the robot crushed the grape into a soggy mess of juice and pulp in the process did not seem to bother the robot at all.

The grape, however, was inserted perfectly. Robots are accurate and tireless. When it comes to dull, repetitive tasks (the duller the better) robots are usually cost effective. In a typical robot installation, the machine pays for itself within a year or two in decreased labor costs and improved product quality.

Flexible Manufacturing Systems

Rarely does a factory make the same product all the time. A furniture manufacturer makes a few hundred French Provincial chairs, and then switches to the Early American style. An assembler of printed circuit boards will finish an order for 5,000 modem boards and then start on the order for color display boards. Shifting from one product to another is expensive. It requires that some attention be given to changing the materials going to the machines, adjusting the settings or programming of the machines, and handling the output in a different way. In addition, while these activities are going on, production is interrupted—nothing is being manufactured.

The object of a **flexible manufacturing system (FMS)** is to automate the entire factory so that changeovers from one product to another can be done automatically. In a typical FMS setup, a central computer controls all the machines in the factory—raw material feeds, drilling machines, stamping machines, assembly robots, and so forth. When a product changeover is required, the central computer directs each machine to make the appropriate adjustments.

In an ideal FMS environment, the entire changeover could be accomplished with no human involvement or loss of manufacturing time. In the real world, this goal is rarely achieved. Often a number of things still require human intervention.

Computer-Integrated Manufacturing

Computer-integrated manufacturing (CIM) is the catchall term used for a system that aids, directs, and controls all phases of product-oriented activities—from design to distribution. It includes most of the things

The Computerized Factory
Many manufacturing facilities are using computers to perform a number of tasks from controlling machines to managing the factory.

discussed above. As an example, let us take a typical product, a printed circuit board to be sold to a telephone manufacturer, and trace its progression through a CIM process.

A designer uses a computer-aided design system to specify the functions to be performed by this PC board and the components needed for the board. The CAE system lays out the components on the board and draws the interconnections for the most efficient use of the space on the board. The designer checks these over, makes whatever changes are deemed necessary, and sends the designs to production.

The preproduction people use the designs to make the photographic "masks" used in the etching process for the interconnection layout on the PC board. Purchasing takes care of the orders for components and parts that have been generated in the CIM process.

Once in production the CAE designs are used to control the circuit-board cutting, photoetching, and drilling machinery that makes the boards. Other machines that insert components onto the board and wave solder the connections are also controlled by the CIM system.

When items are shipped to customers, the CIM system generates work orders for their replacements as well as purchase orders for the materials and components needed to make them. From there the manufacturing, shipping, and reordering cycle continues.

THE COMPUTER'S FUTURE IN BUSINESS

One thing is certain, computers are not going to go away. Businesses will continue to rely on them and use them in more and more aspects of business functions. Computers will continue to replace people in some areas, but the computer industry will continue to provide new jobs in other areas. The idea of computers replacing people is both exciting and unsettling. We humans have always felt smugly secure in our ability to think and utilize judgment, but computers are starting to make inroads into those areas, too.

BOX 15-5

If Computers Can Go Anywhere, Why Can't They Reach The Poor?

When he was 13, Ivan began visiting Playing to Win, a nonprofit center that teaches computer technology to East Harlem residents. Fascinated, the shy teenager volunteered for odd jobs at the center in exchange for computer time. "Not a week went by that Ivan didn't show up," says Antonia B. Stone, the center's executive director. Now 18, he's a freshman at the University of Maine, studying computer science.

Ivan's is a heartwarming tale that underscores the value of teaching computer skills to underprivileged youths. Unfortunately, it's also an exception. Few poor kids ever see a computer screen. And as the U.S. is transformed into an electronic society, their computer illiteracy will lessen their already slim chances to win good jobs. Says Stone: "They're being denied the opportunity to become leaders in a technological society."

School isn't helping much. A September report from the federal Office of Technology Assessment says there are about 1.5 million computers in public schools, one for every 30 students. But minority students in urban schools generally have less access than whites to computers. With low tax bases, poor school districts often can't spend as much as suburbs

do. One solution is to teach computers outside school, as Stone does. But she's thwarted by many forces, including the lifestyle of older ghetto kids: "If they're not in school, they're trying to pick up money," she says. "And the girls are home taking care of babies."

Stone's eight-year-old program is one of a few modest efforts to overcome such obstacles. On a $312,000 annual budget raised from foundations, Playing to Win reaches about 1,000 people of all ages a year. Similar programs exist in Richmond, Va., San Francisco, Milwaukee, and Houston. Companies including IBM, Apple, Tandy, and Commodore help, mostly by giving computers to schools. The 115,000 public libraries nationwide help, too, though they have only 25,000 computers. Combined, these efforts are about as effective as Playing to Win is in reaching all 112,000 residents of East Harlem. "It's a drop in the ocean," Stone says.

The problem is becoming more serious as entry-level jobs get more sophisticated: Already, many temporary clerical employees must know basic word processing and spreadsheet programs. If the poor don't adjust, one of the few paths they've recently taken up the economic ladder

could be blocked. From 1960 to 1980, according to the OTA, the share of employed black women with clerical jobs jumped to 29% from 9%, while the share in domestic work fell. During roughly the same period, pay for black women rose from 70% of white women's pay to 94%.

Employers can retrain clericals, but activists want more. "Whether poor kids get computers depends on whether we'll make a public investment," declares Anne W. Branscomb, a Harvard University researcher. Britain's Project Frontline, sponsored by the government and 14 companies, plans to train youths in the high-unemployment North to do keypunching, process insurance claims, and even write software for employers in the labor-short South—all electronically. Minnesota soon will assign a few state jobs to be done remotely by unemployed workers on the Iron Range.

Stone, who once ran a math department at a Manhattan prep school, says that "it isn't a secret to people in East Harlem that this is a technological world. Computers symbolize the society that the parents aren't part of. And they want the best for their kids." But for now, the best is a long way off.

Source: Katherine M. Hafner, *Business Week*, October 10, 1988, p. 106.

As new generations of people who have grown up with the computer and treat it as their ancestors treated the calculator enter the work force, computers will become even more commonplace. They will not be considered anything special, just another work tool.

HARDWARE TRENDS

Computer components will continue to get smaller, faster, less expensive, and more reliable. The trend has been, and will continue to be, putting more capability in a smaller package. The capability of the 1960s IBM mainframe 360, which filled a room and cost about a million of today's dollars can now be duplicated by an IBM PS/2 microcomputer costing less than $10,000 and fitting on a desk top.

Faster Processing

Increases in processing speed will come from three main areas: Improvements in semiconductor manufacturing technology, use of parallel processors to divide the processing down among multiple CPUs, and superconducting computer circuitry.

"They don't make them like they used to." Thank heaven! One of the principal factors increasing processing speed (and reducing the cost of processors) is better manufacturing. Our manufacturing is getting more accurate, allowing IC components to be smaller and closer. Where the first semiconductors put one transistor on a chip, we now routinely put over 4 million on a single chip. The smaller the components, the faster they operate. The closer together they are, the less time it takes for a signal to travel from one to the other.

New semiconductor materials are currently under development. Most semiconductors are now made on chips of silicon, but equivalent components can be made on gallium arsenide (GAs) that work about three times as fast. While GAs is more expensive than silicon, the cost of the material is a low percentage of the total cost of the completed IC, and the increase in performance should prove to be well worth it.

From the first computers to most of those of the present day, processors could do only one thing at a time. Each instruction would have to be fully completed before the next could start. If we were loading a railroad car with boxes and wanted to speed up the process, we could use more people working side by side. In many cases, we can do the same with a computer using **parallel processing**—having more than one processor working on the same task simultaneously. Performing a computer task is usually more complicated than loading a railroad car, so there are some limitations. For example, one operation may require the results of another, so these could not be done simultaneously.

Parallel processing is finding the greatest applications among the specialized, number-crunching supercomputers. The Connection Machine, for example, uses a matrix of 64,000 processors and operates at about 2.5 billion instructions per second. To a small extent, some personal-computer processors utilize parallelism. The Intel 80386 processor, for

The integrated circuits of tomorrow will pack more and more components into a smaller space, allowing faster processing, more capacity, and lower cost.

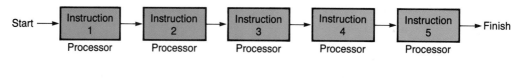

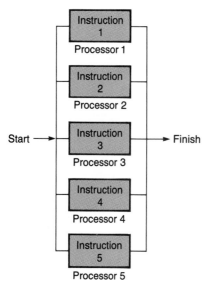

Parallel Processing

Traditional, serial processing uses one processor to process each instruction in turn. Parallel processing uses several processors and allocates instructions to them so that a number of instructions execute simultaneously.

example, is capable of processing one instruction while decoding the next and fetching a third.

Speed of computer processes are limited by the resistance to electrical transfer in the circuit and the distance between components. Scientists have long been aware of **superconductors**—materials that allow electrical currents to pass with virtually no resistance and generating almost no heat. Until about 1987, superconductors only worked at temperatures of almost absolute zero, not an impossible environment but certainly not economically practical. In the last few years, superconductors were developed that would work at much higher temperatures—about that of liquid nitrogen. This is not equivalent to basking in the Florida sunshine, but the liquid nitrogen coolant is relatively inexpensive. Using superconductors, components could be placed closer together without burning up, and currents in them would travel faster, thus speeding up processing.

Storage

The story is familiar here—smaller size, lower cost, greater capacity. The old 14-inch hard disk platters have given way to 8-, 5 1/4-, and even 3 1/2-inch platters, with some of the multiplatter 5 1/4-inch disks holding over 1G byte (one billion characters). From the personal computer viewpoint, we have seen floppy disks go from 8-inch, 128K byte, $10 models to 3 1/2-inch, 1.44M byte, $2 ones. Hard disks, which were unheard of on PCs just a few years ago, are now commonplace.

Erasable optical disks, just a dream a few years ago, have made the optical disk a contender in the storage arena. Access times on these disks

BOX 15-6

Put Enough PCs Together, And You Get a Supercomputer

Who says those little computers-on-a-chip that power desktop PCs can't take on giant mainframes? Ganged together, those tiny Davids can match the big "brains" of Goliath computers—and for so much less money that the new technology just wipes out the old. "It will cause a revolution," declares Casey Powell, president of Sequent Computer Systems Inc. In Beaverton, Ore.

Sequent is one of the small band of pioneers in the burgeoning field known as parallel processing. Using gangs of microprocessors, they build computers that deliver the performance of a main-frame for roughly 10% of the cost. Sequent has sold 450 of its systems directly, and Siemens of West Germany has sold 1,500 others based on Sequent's technology. Co-founder C. Scott Gibson is particularly proud of a recent order from Coca-Cola Enterprises Inc., heretofore an IBM bastion. That makes Gibson more confident than ever that microprocessors will be the brains in computers of every size—"whether it takes 3 or 5 or 10 years" to generate sufficient software and overcome lingering skepticism.

The economics are telling indeed: Sequent's heftiest Symmetry system can deliver 120 mips (millions of instructions per second) and support hundreds of people sitting at terminals and running programs, all at the same time. That puts it "in the range of IBM's largest 3090 mainframe," according to an analysis by William F. Zachmann, executive vice-president of market researcher International Data Corp. But the per-mips cost with Symmetry is about $5,000 vs. roughly $120,000 for a comparable 3090.

The Symmetry system is a cluster of 30 of Intel's latest 80386 chips. Other micro-based parallel-processing machines with more chips can even surpass the blinding speed of supercomputers. For example, Intel's new Scientific Computers division puts 128 of the chips in its top-of-the-line system, and it spews out 512 mips, more than any commercial mainframe.

Running a widely used scientific program, an Intel IPSC machine with only 32 microprocessors outraces a Cray Research Inc. X-MP/12 by 40%. It turns in 100 megaflops (millions of floating-point operations per second, the customary way to measure scientific computers), against 70 megaflops for the supercomputer. Cost per megaflop: less than $10,000 for Intel, more than $100,000 for Cray. That low cost, says Leslie L. Vadasz, an Intel executive vice-president, spells "the end of one era and the start of another."

Other newcomers—Bolt Beranek & Newman, Encore, Ncube, and Teradata—are building systems by patching together chips from Motorola, Inmos, National Semi-conductor or Intel. By the end of last year, Boston's Stratus Computer Inc., which bases its system on Motorola chips, had installed 1,444 computers at places such as Gillette, Visa International, and the National Association of Securities Dealers. Stratus' sales, compounding at roughly 50% a year, hit $184 million in 1987.

Sequent is betting that its Intel-based computers will score big in the market for all classes of office computers. But in engineering markets, where Motorola's chips are dug in and various so-called RISC processors may provide even more muscle, it could be a different story. There, says Sequent's Gibson, "it'll be a huge dogfight."

Source: Port, Levin, Hammonds, *Business Week*, Sept. 26, 1988, p. 80.

are a little slower but their capacities are enormous. In fact, Steven Jobs (one of the founders of Apple Computer, Inc.) chose a 5 1/4-inch 256M byte optical disk as the *only* secondary storage option on his Next computer. Nonerasable optical disk systems with capacities in excess of 1 trillion bytes are available for mainframes, and erasable optical disks are not far behind.

Input and Output

In the future we will rely less on the keyboard and the printer for input and output. More computers will be able to take voice commands and even data by voice, and more output will be on display screens or even spoken. Instead of sending a printed memo or report, more people will rely on things such as electronic and voice mail.

We are already seeing a trend toward higher-resolution and flatter output screens. Higher resolution is a result of smaller, more closely packed dots on the screen and more memory available to hold the data that tells which dots are on or off. The flatter screen is due principally to the use of liquid crystal displays (LCDs). At first, you had your choice of either high-resolution or flat screen. Now LCD technology is at a point where some laptop computers are being equipped with high-resolution, color screens. Picture-frame television screens will not be far behind.

Fast, quiet, high-quality printers like this LED model are taking over the hardcopy output tasks.

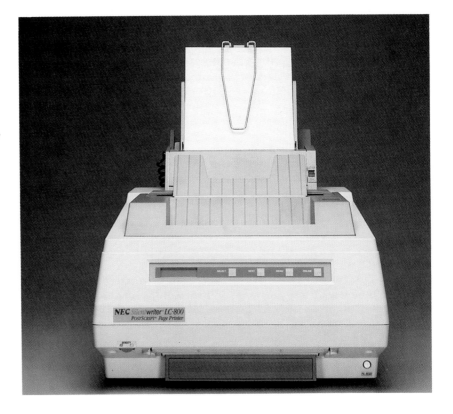

Printers are getting quieter, especially in the office. Impact printers are being used less, replaced by ink-jet, and even more by laser (and LED, a related process) printers. These printers print not only faster than impact models but also with higher resolution, cleaner characters, and better graphics.

SOFTWARE TRENDS

As the computer becomes more of a common fixture and a universal work tool, the software will change to accommodate. We have seen the foundations for future trends being set down in the last few years. Principally because of software, computers will become easier to use, for both the expert and the casual user.

System Software

Operating systems are becoming larger and larger. There are two main reasons for this. First, more memory is available, making larger system programs possible. Second, the operating systems are offering more and more services to both the user and the programmer.

On larger machines, operating systems are implementing parallel processing, fault tolerance (being able to continue running even though a part of the system has failed), automatic backup of data, and a host of other services valuable to the system manager and programmer.

On both large and small systems, operating systems are being enhanced to take over and standardize some of the functions that were being performed by application software. For example, many operating systems, including IBM's PS/2 for micros and UNIX for micros and minis are, or soon will be, taking over many of the communications functions for networks. Other enhancements will include presentation managers that will allow easy control of screen displays, including graphics and windowing.

On personal computers we have already seen early efforts at multi-tasking and suspended processing through windows. Operating environments such as Macintosh, Microsoft Windows, and DESQView were in the forefront of that trend. Now, with PC-hardware speed and capacity increasing, true multitasking becomes much more viable—the computer doesn't slow to a crawl when more than one job is running concurrently. Newer operating systems such as OS/2 and Next include multitasking as part of the basic package.

A lot of people have been doing a lot of talking about portability—being able to take a program from this machine and run it on that one. Portability can only be achieved with compatible operating systems. There has been some movement in this direction; for example, you can add a DOS (for PC-DOS or MS-DOS) "shell" to some UNIX systems that will allow your IBM PC programs to run under UNIX. However, there are too many different machines with too many operating systems (and more coming all the time) to count on extensive portability in the near future.

Application Software

The use of computers is edging beyond just providing information, toward actively participating in the decision-making process. Since the computer itself, rather than just the information it provides, will be used directly by nontechnical people, user-friendliness will be a prime concern. People must be able to access the benefits of the computer without being burdened with inefficiencies in using the computer. Part of this object will be achieved as people change. More people are becoming "computer-friendly" and see the computer as a normal, nonthreatening work tool—something that they use in the usual course of their activities.

Computer-to-human interface software, though, is also changing. In application packages, we are starting to see heavier reliance on visual-input systems and less use of keyboards. This includes graphic aids on screens, easy to use menus of commands, on-screen help facilities (where you can touch a button and the system will give you advice on using the package), and pointing devices (such as mice) for input. We are also seeing the computer interface becoming less visible and more automatic. A prime example is a point-of-sale system where price tags and credit cards are read automatically, and sales slips come out the other end without anyone ever touching a button or keyboard.

People usually talk better than they type, so we will see a greater reliance on the spoken interface. We keep hearing that in the next few years secretaries will be obsolete because people will be able to dictate text directly to the computer. Eventually, that will happen, but firing your secretary today in anticipation would be a mistake. The clerical jobs will shift, however, to areas requiring more thought, judgment, and creativity as computers take over more of the routine tasks.

There will be a number of approaches to the improvements in application software. One will be to make the application package do more so that the user need do less. We have already seen evidence of this—word processing packages that check spelling and grammar, spreadsheets that output in both numbers and graphs. Another approach will be to make application software easier for the nonexpert to write. We have seen this in specialized areas such as the "languages" that are packaged with spreadsheets and database management packages. Apple is marketing a more

On-Screen Help

Pressing one key while working with this word-processing package produces the window on the right. The user may request on-screen help on any of the topics listed by pointing to that topic (with a mouse or the cursor). The system will put the requested information in the window. Other actions will produce more specific help on whatever the user is doing in the text.

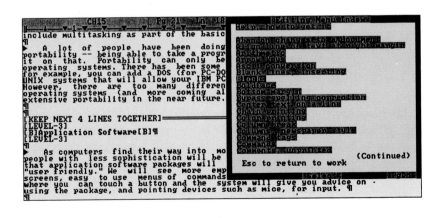

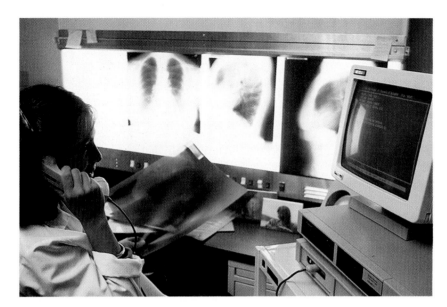

Dictating directly into the computer and receiving printed text in return is not too far off.

complete approach called HyperCard which treats all data like a set of "file folders," and its "language" manipulates these as you might do it manually.

Software Development

Software is getting more complicated all the time. But developing the software is getting easier. Structured programming was at the forefront of this trend, and structured-programming concepts have been integrated into a number of languages such as Pascal, C, Cobol 85, and some BASICs. Other notable trends include the use of standard interface tools for various functions which most programs must perform. OS/2's Presentation Manager allows the programmer to access the screen using relatively simple commands and concepts. SQL (structured query language) provides a common set of programming tools for database access.

One set of software development tools that experts predict will catch on through the 1990s is **computer-aided software engineering (CASE).** CASE techniques include using **application-generator** software; instead of writing the program instructions, the programmer gives task specifications to the application generator which, in turn, generates the program instructions. Cullinet's ADS, Software AG's NATURAL, and Mathematica's RAMIS II are current examples of such software. Also part of CASE methodology is the use of repositories, an idea borrowed from the DBMS data dictionaries of the 1980s. These repositories contain much more than data descriptions, however. They also include information on screen formats and access, reports, and previously used processing techniques. Programming using CASE methods is less a process of writing a procedure for the computer to follow than the assembly of tested procedures into an operating whole.

The languages which we discussed in Chapter 10 are all **procedural languages**—the programmer describes the steps or procedures which the computer must follow to perform a task. A different set of languages, often referred to as **fourth-generation languages (4GLs)** break away from this procedural orientation. Instead of telling the computer *how* to do something, 4GLs allow the programmer to tell the computer *what* it is to accomplish and let the computer figure out how to do it. This approach requires fewer instructions from the programmer, but much more sophisticated language translation programs and more capacity and processing from the computer.

Many of these 4GLs—such as LISP, Smalltalk, and Prolog—have been around for some time. It has only been recently that computer-processing power and capacity have been available to take advantage of them. When they are finally used to their full advantage, many industry experts predict that programming productivity will increase by 10 to 200 times. In other words, a programmer may be able to write a particular program up to 200 times faster.

We have seen the beginnings of fourth-generation language principles in use in some current applications. For example, advanced database query languages, such as SQL or INTELLECT, tell the computer what to extract from a database but not how to do it. Report-generator packages, such as GIS and NOMAD, allow the user to tell the computer what a report should look like, and the computer will assemble it. The application generators, mentioned as part of CASE tools, are also fourth-generation language concepts.

The fourth generation will inevitably lead us into the fifth generation. No one is quite sure what that is yet, but in terms of programming languages, it seems to revolve around the use of **natural language,** human instead of computer language. Fourth-generation application development allows us to communicate with the computer in terms of objectives versus processes. Fifth-generation application development should allow us to communicate in almost purely human terms—perhaps even spoken.

ARTIFICIAL INTELLIGENCE

Can a computer think? Not really. The human thinking process is too complicated for the computer to "understand." In fact, we humans do not fully understand it. However, computers have been programmed to mimic some aspects of human thinking. This is referred to as **artificial intelligence (AI).**

The usual approach to artificial intelligence is to reduce certain human thinking processes to quantifiable terms—concepts that a computer can handle. This type of thinking is reduced to applying logical rules to a base of knowledge. For example, we know that Jack is Harriet's child, Fred is Albert's child, and Harriet and Albert are siblings (brother and sister). According to the rules, children of siblings are first cousins. Therefore, Jack and Fred are first cousins.

This is a relatively straightforward application of knowledge and rules. But what if we wanted to know the relationship, family or social, between Agnes and Bernard? We would have to find appropriate rules to apply to our knowledge base and perhaps even request more data to increase that knowledge. Who were their parents, their parent's parents, where do they

> **BOX 15-7**
>
> ## Computer vs. Grand Master: Still No Contest
>
> For four days at the end of September, New York's New School for Social Research will host a chess tournament pitting human intelligence against artificial intelligence. Until recently, no computer has come close to beating a grand master, so staging a formal match seemed a waste of time. Then, a few months ago, a program dubbed Hitech became the first nonhuman to qualify for senior master ranking. Grand master Arnold Denker then agreed to defend human pride in September.
>
> Hitech still doesn't stand a chance of beating a grand master, admits the system's "father," Hans Berliner. While Hitech ranks among the top 150 U.S. players, it has lost eight straight games with senior masters rated among the country's best 25 players. So, Berliner just hopes for at least one draw.
>
> A computer scientist at Carnegie-Mellon University, Berliner has spent 18 years teaching Hitech to use so-called fuzzy logic—a technique that approximates human reasoning. But a grand master-level program remains years off. And should Hitech win through some fluke, Denker can cry foul. Hitech cheats: It needs two computers working in collusion.
>
> Source: *Business Week,* Oct. 3, 1988, p. 131.

work, where do they go to school, what activities do they participate in, where do they live? We would have to test all this knowledge with the rules at our disposal to see if any of it fit. For example, after testing dozens of different rules we might find that Agnes and Bernard have overlapping ancestors, and they live near each other. From this we might conclude that they are second cousins and neighbors.

This type of process is quite different from the procedural ones we are used to with computers—add this number to that and print the results. In the AI example, the computer must determine its own procedures. In doing so, it must make many tests and attempts, and go up many blind alleys, to find an answer. This requires a great deal more processing than following a set procedure. Until the last few years, memory was too limited, computers were not fast enough, nor were they cheap enough to make such processing practical. Now, in the early 1990s, prices have gone down, and speeds and capacities have gone up, so many companies are making use of AI techniques in their operations.

One use of AI is in **expert** or **knowledge-based systems** that actually make decisions rather than simply providing the information for human decision making. Only five years ago, just a handful of expert systems were in regular use. Now, there are over 3,000.

A Dialogue With an Expert System

An expert system reaches conclusions by applying rules to facts.

HOW IT REASONS
Dialogue With A Simple Expert System

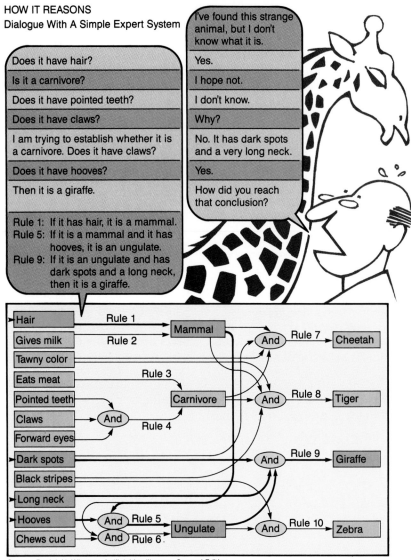

	I've found this strange animal, but I don't know what it is.
Does it have hair?	Yes.
Is it a carnivore?	I hope not.
Does it have pointed teeth?	I don't know.
Does it have claws?	Why?
I am trying to establish whether it is a carnivore. Does it have claws?	No. It has dark spots and a very long neck.
Does it have hooves?	Yes.
Then it is a giraffe.	How did you reach that conclusion?

Rule 1: If it has hair, it is a mammal.
Rule 5: If it is a mammal and it has hooves, it is an ungulate.
Rule 9: If it is an ungulate and has dark spots and a long neck, then it is a giraffe.

Source: Patrick H. Winston, *Artificial Intelligence, Second Edition*.

Applications for expert systems are cropping up in diverse fields. Ford Motor Company has "computerized" Gordy Kujawski, their auto-repair expert. Where auto dealers used to call Gordy with engine problems that stumped them, they now plug into a nationwide computer system that duplicates (or closely so) the reasoning processes Gordy uses to diagnose such problems. This frees Gordy's time for developing new diagnostic methods.

IBM uses a system called DEFT (Diagnostic Expert–Final Test) to perform the final test and diagnose problems on its disk drives. The Department of Defense has developed the ALBM (AirLand Battle Management) system to simulate almost every aspect of a battle and test various battle-management strategies.

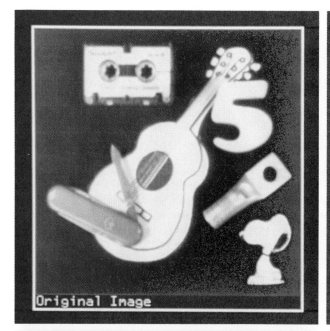 

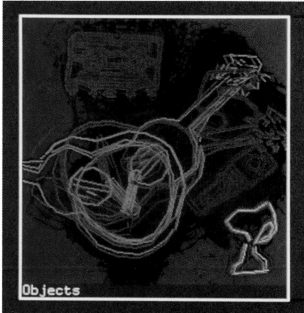 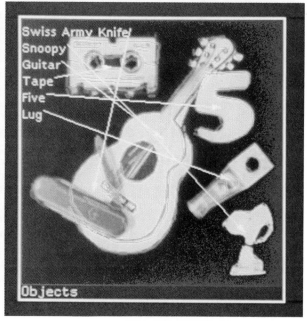

Another application of artificial intelligence is the simulation of human senses—especially sight, hearing, and touch. These, too, are applications of knowledge and rules, but the processes are even more complicated because the number of possible variations are so great. For example, if the computer "sees" a circular shape, is it a balloon or a manhole cover? If it is a sphere rather than a disk, it is more likely a balloon. However, if it has a pebbly surface, it is probably a basketball instead of a balloon. But if the pebbly surface is uneven, it is more likely to be a planet.

Object Recognition

(a) Image of various overlapping objects (b) Lines and their intersections are extracted from the image. (c-d) Connection Machine generates and verifies hypotheses for objects it detects, based on previously learned examples; and correctly identifies and displays the location of each.

Business Focus BOX 15-8

The Supercomputer Breaks Through: Europe's Parallel Performance

Europe has caught supercomputer fever. Commercial users in the U.K. as well as on the Continent are seriously evaluating high-performance systems—many for the first time. Native vendors are developing technologies that could challenge the dominance of U.S. and Japanese supercomputer superpowers. And the world's largest computer company is investing $40 million to seed European supercomputing initiatives at universities and research centers from Belgium to West Germany.

What's causing Europe's supercomputer temperature to rise so quickly is opportunity. An increasing number of European commercial users view supercomputing as a possible solution to their processing problems. In Europe, as in the U.S., there has been a steady—albeit slower—move of supercomputers into commercial engineering applications. Rolls Royce in the

U.K., automakers in West Germany, and now two banks—one in the U.K. and one in France—are in the process of evaluating supercomputers as high-volume transaction processing systems. Neither bank is prepared to talk about these projects at this stage.

Just who will supply those commercial solutions isn't clear, however. Foreign suppliers have built up a strong base of systems in Europe. Minneapolis-based Cray Research has populated the Old World with 30 supercomputers—some 15% of its worldwide installed base of 200 systems. A selection of high-end Control Data Corp. and Fujitsu systems, more than 40 IBM vector processing add-ons, and a host of minisupers from Convex, Alliant, Sequent, and Floating Point Systems also dot the European landscape. But there is rising competition from European-based companies.

In the time since U.K. chip maker Inmos launched its

innovative transputer system in 1986, European supercomputing has taken significant strides forward. The power of transputer technology—high-density VLSI processor chips whose design lends itself to parallel computing—has been harnessed by existing companies such as Beaverton, Ore.-based Floating Point Systems and emerging companies such as Sension and Meiko, both in the U.K. In fact, by the end of last year, when Intel was boasting about its shipments of 70 of its IPSC systems, Meiko had already shipped over 100 of its transputer-based Computing Surface products.

IBM also is doing some pushing. IBM Europe last fall launched a $40 million supercomputer initiative to establish five supercomputer centers—each equipped with 3090 600E systems and vector processing facilities—at European universities and research institutes, all free of charge. IBM also agreed to

Voice recognition is an important branch of artificial intelligence combining computer hearing, which consists of digitizing sound patterns and storing them, and natural-language processing. Again, this is an application of knowledge—stored sound patterns with which to compare the received ones—and rules—what the combinations of those patterns mean. Unfortunately, humans are both imprecise and flexible in their speech. If the computer cannot accommodate for variations in the speaker, speech dialect, and the context, it will have difficulty understanding. For example, "having a ball," meaning enjoying one's self, could just as easily be interpreted as possessing a round object.

donate 25 vector processing facilities to other European educational and research centers.

The motive behind IBM's largesse is to stimulate European development of supercomputing technology. "If Europe is to remain competitive," explains IBM Europe president C. Michael Armstrong, "we must ensure that we have the young scientists and engineers experienced in applying supercomputing to real problems."

Some of those young professionals are already involved in the European supercomputing business, especially in West Germany. Two companies there are now marketing homegrown supercomputer systems: Bonn-based Suprenum, a spin-off from GMD, the West German research institute, and Integrated Parallel Systems, Karlsruhe, a spin-off from Karlsruhe University.

Work on supercomputing products is also being done by researchers at the universities of Southampton and Edinburgh in the U.K. By the time these products and the results of the research become widely available, European users will be in a better position to judge their worth. The first major European conference on evaluating supercomputers is planned for London, June 1-3, cosponsored by Unicom Seminars of Uxbridge, England, and U.K.-based Reed International's *Computer Weekly*. Reed is also the parent company of Cahners Publishing Co., which owns DATAMATION.

Overall, the prospects for supercomputing in Europe are strong. As Eamonn Wilmott, San Diego publisher of the book *Supercomputing Review*, to be published in July, points out, "Europe's strength is definitely in parallel computing, especially on the software side. There are some very strong supercomputer software companies there."

Source: Paul Tate, *Datamation*, May 1, 1988, p. 53.

Voice recognition is currently being used in a number of applications, including IBM's Talkwriter and Kurzweil's VoiceWriter, which print out what you say to them.

The field of robotics, discussed earlier, depends on combinations of practically all of these AI techniques. The robot of tomorrow, and in limited cases, of today, can understand spoken commands, recognize objects by sight and/or touch, manipulate them, and decide what to do with them.

Computers may imitate some of the more mundane human thought patterns, but for the foreseeable future, the next few decades or centuries at least, they will still be no substitute for the human brain.

SUMMARY

Computers are no longer something special but just part of the normal job scene. They are used in almost all aspects of modern organizations.

Office automation is important because, while most other sectors of business have experienced large productivity gains, office tasks are by nature labor intensive. A number of computer applications have contributed to higher office productivity, however.

Word processing makes editing and output of documents much more efficient. Desktop publishing allows the office to produce high-quality documents that have that "published" look. Computers—through office networks, electronic mail, facsimile, and teleconferencing—have revolutionized office communications. Desktop organizers have made the many tasks that any individual in an office must perform more organized, neater, and more efficient.

In design and engineering, there is no substitute for human creativity, but computer-aided design and engineering have drastically reduced the amount of time it takes to create a design and produce it in a form for others to use.

Computer-aided manufacturing has come of age. In manufacturing management, materials-requirements planning systems monitor and direct the supply of raw materials. Manufacturing resource management includes MRP but also encompasses planning and evaluation of other manufacturing resources—inventories, machines, labor, and capital.

Computers are used extensively for manufacturing process controls. Numerical-control machine tools have been in existence for years, and now more flexible robots, some even with humanlike senses, are becoming commonplace. These types of controls allow for flexible manufacturing systems that can react to changes in product requirements with little human intervention or loss of production time.

Many firms are heading toward complete computer-integrated manufacturing where the computer assists in or controls all phases of product-oriented activities from design to distribution.

In the future, computers will be playing an even greater role in our business activities. Hardware advances will include even faster and more sophisticated processors, some utilizing parallel processing and superconductors. Storage devices, including erasable optical disks, will continue to pack more data into a smaller space. Input and output will depend less on the keyboard and printer and more on voice and flat-panel screens.

Advances in software will make the computer easier to use. Operating systems will become larger and perform services such as multitasking, communications, and implementing fault tolerance. Application software will continue to become more powerful and easier to use. Software development tools such as CASE and fourth-generation languages will allow programmers to communicate to the computer in more human terms. They will also accept instructions describing the desired result rather than the procedure required to obtain that result.

We will continue to advance in the field of artificial intelligence. Expert systems, now in their infancy, will become commonplace. Voice and object recognition will become accepted methods of inputting into the computer. Using AI techniques, robots will become more flexible and effective.

KEY WORDS

(in order of appearance in text)
Word processing
Desktop publishing
Page oriented
Document oriented
Electronic mail
Facsimile (Fax)
Teleconferencing
Desktop organizer
Clipboard
Cut
Paste
Computer-aided design (CAD)

Computer-aided engineering (CAE)
Computer-aided manufacturing
 (CAM)
CAD/CAM
Materials-requirements planning
 (MRP)
Manufacturing-resource planning
 (MRP II)
Robot
Flexible manufacturing system
 (FMS)
Computer-integrated manufacturing
 (CIM)

Parallel processing
Superconductor
Computer-aided software engi-
 neering (CASE)
Application generator
Procedural language
Fourth-generation language (4GL)
Natural language
Artificial intelligence (AI)
Expert system
Knowledge-based system
Voice recognition

REVIEW QUESTIONS

1. In which have we increased productivity most in the past 20 years, the factory or the office?
2. Are we shifting toward more factory jobs or more office jobs?
3. What are the major differences between word processing and desktop publishing?
4. What does it mean to import text?
5. Name the typical features of a sophisticated desktop publishing package.
6. What is the most important feature of a desktop organizer?
7. Name some of the other common features of desktop organizers.
8. Why is design becoming a more important part of the entire production process?
9. Name the features of a typical computer-aided design system.
10. How does computer-aided engineering differ from computer-aided design?
11. What is computer-aided manufacturing?
12. What is the difference between MRP and MRP II?
13. In what ways does a typical industrial robot resemble a human being?
14. What is the objective of a flexible manufacturing system?
15. What do we mean by computer-integrated manufacturing?
16. Describe parallel processing.
17. What new trends do we envision in input and output systems?
18. How will system software change in the future?
19. What changes in applications software should we see?
20. How do fourth-generation languages differ from the current procedural ones?
21. What is artificial intelligence?
22. How do the processes of expert systems differ from those of a traditional computer?
23. Why are expert systems only now becoming practical?
24. Why are voice and object recognition so difficult for the computer?

THINK ABOUT IT

1. Why is it easier to automate most factory processes than office processes?
2. List and explain the similarities between normal written mail (interoffice and post office) and electronic mail.
3. Compare and contrast the principles behind word processing and computer-aided design.
4. How do computer-aided design and computer-aided manufacturing interact?
5. How can the results of an MRP system be used in an MRP II system?
6. Given the limited sensory capabilities of a robot, describe a marble so that the robot could pick it out (and differentiate it from a grape, ball bearing, pearl, or anything else it might encounter).
7. How do robots help the worker? How do robots hurt them?
8. Describe the tests an expert system might use to determine a particular article of clothing.
9. Why does making things easier for humans demand more of the computer?

CHALLENGES

1. You are setting up your own office with a personal computer. Pick any personal computer (IBM or compatible, or Macintosh, for example), decide which office tools you would need, and pick the specific brands. Give reasons for your choices.
2. Since your office is for a company that custom designs deluxe doghouses, pick a CAD package for your PC. Give reasons for your choice.
3. Look at a local production facility. See how they use computer-process controls and suggest how they might use more.

Appendix

USER PRODUCTIVITY SOFTWARE

PREVIEW
At various points in the main text we have alluded to software that is typically available to users of personal computers. In this appendix we will look at the capabilities of the three most common types of user productivity software. After reading it you should understand:

■ The capabilities of typical word processing packages and when they should be used.

■ The capabilities of typical spreadsheet packages and when they should be used.

■ The types of graphics output capabilities of typical spreadsheet packages.

■ The capabilities of typical database management packages and when they should be used.

WORD PROCESSING

Word processing is the manipulation of text. It includes inputting, editing, and outputting text data—such as letters, memos, reports, and manuals—and has the dual objectives of clean output and operator efficiency. Word processing was the first popular productivity package for personal computers. Michael Schrayer's *Electric Pencil* package was developed in 1976, only a year after the introduction of the first commercially successful microcomputer, the Altair. Although *Electric Pencil* has dropped off the scene, today there are dozens of viable word-processing packages available for any of the popular personal computers.

Let us examine some of the capabilities of modern word-processing packages. The method of execution of these functions will vary from package to package, but the functions exist in almost all packages.

Text Entry

Straight entry of text is about the same on a word processor as on a typewriter. This is not the area of significant productivity gain. The major gains are a result of what you can do with the text once it has been entered.

Text Formatting

Lines may be single or double spaced; margins are set at specific points on the left and right; tabs are located at certain spots across the line; paragraphs may have hanging indents (lines after the first start at some place other than the margin); text may be left justified (lined up at the left margin), right justified, centered, or fully justified (spaced to line up at both margins); there may be two or more columns. All of these things define the format of the text. Word processors allow these format characteristics to be determined before the text is entered, and the software will enforce the formats—put text in two columns, for example. More importantly, most word processors will allow the user to change the format specifications for portions or all of the text, and the software will automatically change the text to conform to the new format.

One of the most straightforward of the formatting functions is **line wrapping.** As you enter text and your text goes beyond the right margin, the word-processing software will move the last word down to the next line along with the rest of what you type. This continues line after line until you

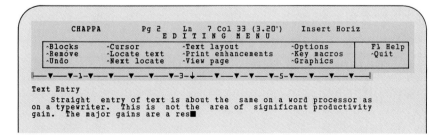

Text-Entry Screen

This screen shows text being entered onto a typical word-processing screen. A menu of commands appears at the top of the screen and the cursor is positioned at the end of the text where the character typed next will appear.

Line Wrapping

The *a* at the end of the top lines brings the text beyond the right margin. As you type, the word processing software moves the *ma* down to the next line as shown in the lower set of lines.

```
     One  of the most   straightforward of the  formatting functions is
line wrapping. As you enter text and the text goes beyond the right ma■
```

```
     One  of the most   straightforward of the  formatting functions is
line  wrapping. As you enter text and your text goes beyond the right
margin,  the word processing software will move the last word down to
the next line along with the rest of what you type.■
```

signal the word processor that the paragraph has ended by hitting the return or enter key.

Moving within the Document

A document created with a word processor may be hundreds of pages long. To work with the document, you must be able to access any part of it and the accessed area must appear on the screen. The screen becomes a "window" that may be "placed" over any part of the document. Combinations of keystrokes will allow you to move the screen forward or backward over the document, or to the beginning or end. Once your desired text is on the screen, you may use special directional keys (or perhaps a mouse) to move the **cursor,** a blinking line or block on the screen, to the desired character position. The next character you type will appear at the location of the cursor.

Editing

Before word processors, editing meant a lot of retyping or, at best, a lot of correction fluid and cutting and pasting. Word processors allow easy editing

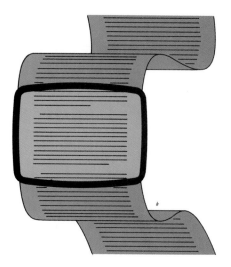

Word-processing Screen in Relation to Text

The screen can "see" only a small portion of the text in a document. To access other parts of the document, the screen is moved to a different location in the document.

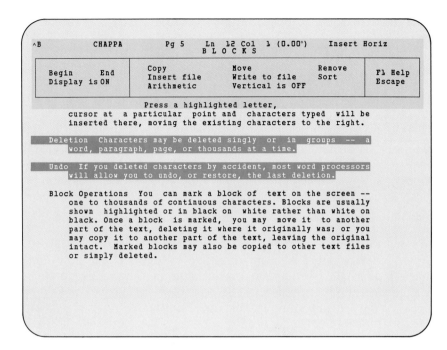

A Text Block

This shows a word-processing screen with a menu of options at the top and a block of text marked and ready to be moved, copied, deleted, or exported to another file.

of text by allowing you to manipulate the text in soft copy—on the computer screen—and having the computer produce the hard copy. Screen changes can be made at any time and new hard copy may be produced on demand. Adding a paragraph to a letter used to mean retyping it. Now the paragraph is added on the screen and the computer prints out the new letter.

Following are typical examples of the text-editing capabilities of word processors:

- *Overtyping.* You may change a character or a group of characters on the screen by moving the cursor to the character and typing over it. The new characters typed will replace the old. To change the word "typed" in the previous sentence to "input" we would move the cursor to the "t" and type "input."
- *Insertion.* Instead of typing over the text on the screen, you may change to the insertion mode. This allows you to set your cursor at a particular point so that characters typed will be inserted there, moving the existing characters to the right.
- *Deletion.* Characters may be deleted singly or in groups—a word, paragraph, page, or thousands at a time.
- *Undo.* If you deleted characters by accident, most word processors will allow you to **undo,** or restore, the last deletion.

Block Operations. You can mark a **block** of text on the screen—one to thousands of continuous characters. Blocks are usually shown highlighted or in black on white rather than white on black. Once a block is marked, you may **move** it to another part of the text, deleting it where it originally was; or you may **copy** it to another part of the text, leaving the original intact. Marked blocks may also be copied to other text files or simply deleted.

Importing and Exporting Text

Often, a document includes text that is already in electronic form. Since different systems use different methods of storing and organizing characters, they cannot be simply placed in the word processed document. The traditional way of handling the situation was to print this other text out and retype it into the word processor. Most word processors now are able to **import,** accept in different form, characters from a variety of sources. These sources include other word-processing packages, spreadsheets, database management systems, and even other computers through communications options. Now, instead of having to retype the material, you can have your word processor change its form and insert it directly into the text.

Many word processors are also able to **export** text in various forms—produce files with text in formats for other software. One popular export format is ASCII text—only the printable ASCII characters as they appear on the screen with no extra coding characters.

Search and Replace

If you are editing a document and want to look at the section about "VLSI chips," you can have the computer **search** for the key characters "VLSI chips." Most searches have a number of options, including searching for whole words only (so that if you search for "chip" the computer won't stop at "chips"), ignoring case (upper- and lowercase will be treated equivalently), and repeating the last search.

You can also search and **replace** sets of characters. If you wrote a scathing memo to Leonard Bellknap and discovered that it should have gone to Hatshepsit Freedle, you could direct the word-processing software to find "Leonard" and replace it with "Hatshepsit." All the search options will be available as well as some others. You could perform a **global replace,** directing the software to replace all occurrences of "Leonard," either stopping to confirm the replacement or replacing without confirmation.

Spelling Correction

Misspellings are hard to find and require a lot of human, therefore expensive, effort. Most word processors have a built-in **spelling dictionary** that will check the words in your document and even offer suggested corrections for those that they cannot identify. Although many word-processor spelling dictionaries are massive, some have over 80,000 words, you may use words that are not included. These words can be added to supplemental dictionaries. In fact, you can buy supplemental dictionaries for most word processors that contain medical, legal, or other special terms.

Spelling-correction programs are not infallible, they only check for the existence of a word, not its correct use in context. For example, if you spell "expert" as "export," the spelling correction software would never catch it.

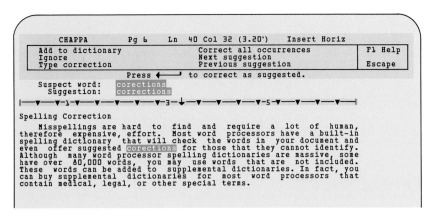

Spelling Correction

"Corections" is misspelled. The spelling checker has found it, highlighted it, has suggested another word, and is waiting for the user to respond.

In addition to spelling dictionaries, many word processors have a **thesaurus** available. Using the thesaurus, you can put your cursor on a word and the computer will suggest synonyms for it.

Headers and Footers

Many documents have the same thing at the top and/or bottom of every page—the name of the addressee and the page number, for example. If this is at the top, it is a **header;** at the bottom it is a **footer.** These usually may be multiple lines and may include options such as the page number (which changes with every page) or the current date.

Merging

Sending out form letters is a breeze when you can **merge** data from a file into the text. For example, if you were selling gold-plated key chains with the insignia of the customer's automobile on them, your data file might have the name, address, and make of car for each prospect, and the text file would be the letter with those spaces coded so that the word processor would fill in the proper data from the data file. Each letter would then be specific to each customer: "Mr. Feldermacher, think of the envy of your friends when you open the door to your Yugo with a solid gold, personalized key chain."

Output Options

You can customize your word-processing package to take advantage of the features of most of the popular printers on the market—from dot matrix to daisy wheel to laser printers. Most printers have a number of built-in **fonts** (type styles) and other features that the word processors can make use of with the right coding. For example, you might change from Times Roman to Courier type styles, or put some words in boldface or italics, or change from 10-pitch to 12-pitch or 12-point to 10-point character sizes.

Even if your printer does not have a separate boldface font, the word processor can simulate it by striking each character more than once (often called double-strike, instead of bold).

Graphics

Pictures, charts, graphs, and so forth, were usually made up by hand and pasted into documents. Many of these graphic images are produced by other software, such as graphics presentation, spreadsheet, integrated software, and art packages. Other images, such as photographs, can be scanned and stored in electronic form. Now, high-end word processors can accept those stored graphic images and include them in the printed, and often in the displayed, document.

SPREADSHEETS

An electronic **spreadsheet** is a grid of rows and columns that can be edited and manipulated by the computer. The electronic spreadsheet has a number of advantages over a manual one, that is, one done with pencil and paper. The first is the same advantage that a word processor offers—ease of editing. Changing one number does not necessitate cutting and pasting or retyping. The second is that only part of the spreadsheet need be entered as numeric values. Any calculated figures are entered as formulas, and the software calculates the numeric values. This relieves the user from having to make calculations, but more importantly, it means that if you change a number, the software will recalculate all the other values based on that number.

An electronic spreadsheet is laid out on the screen as it would appear in a manual version, that is, in rows and columns. Typically, the rows are labeled with numbers down the left side of the screen and the columns with letters across the top. The intersection of a row and a column defines a particular field on the spreadsheet called a **cell.**

There are as many cells as the product of the rows and columns, and most spreadsheets allow a large number of rows and columns. *Lotus 1-2-3,* for example, allows up to 8,192 rows and 256 columns for a total of 2,097,152 cells. If you were to fill up the entire spreadsheet and print it out, your paper would have to be over 19 feet wide and 120 feet long. Fortunately, you use only as much of the spreadsheet as you need. The portion of the spreadsheet bounded by the highest row and the highest column that you have actually used is the **active area.**

With so many cells available, the active area still could be much larger than the screen, so the spreadsheet screen works much like the word-processor screen. It provides a window that can be moved to the part of the spreadsheet on which you are working.

A Spreadsheet

In this spreadsheet example, only the sales by product and region were entered as numbers. The totals and percentages were all calculated by the spreadsheet software.

	A	B	C	D	E	F	G
1		Sales By Region and Category For the Year					
2							
3		Widgets	Parts	Access.	Service	Total	%
4	North	428615	27443	41750	21889	519697	18.45
5	South	309852	16102	24421	12200	362575	12.87
6	East	1014552	54004	71935	40625	1181116	41.92
7	West	622996	37927	61993	31150	754066	26.76
8							
9	Total	2376015	135476	200099	105864	2817454	
10	%	84.33	4.81	7.10	3.76		100.00

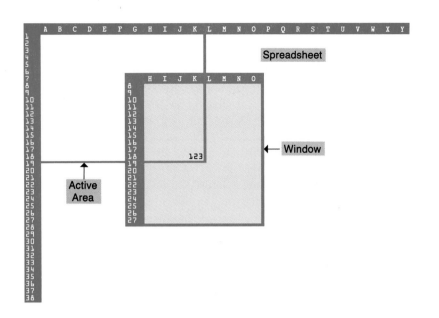

A Window and the Active Area

The screen acts as a window which you can move over any part of the spreadsheet. The active area is from the upper left corner to the highest row and column used.

Parts of the Spreadsheet Screen

A typical spreadsheet screen is divided into three areas. The first, often referred to as the **control panel,** contains information about the operations currently being performed on the spreadsheet. The next is the spreadsheet itself. The last is the **status area,** containing the current date and time, and information about the current condition of the spreadsheet.

Within the spreadsheet are the cells which we refer to by their **address**—the column letter and the row number. The cell at column E row

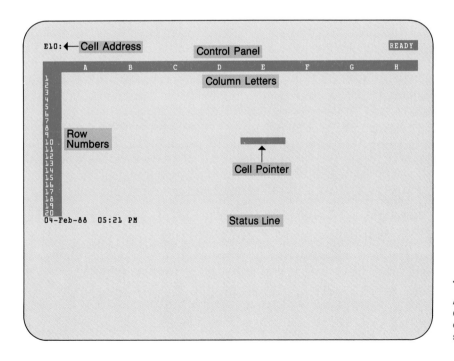

The Parts of a Spreadsheet Screen

A typical spreadsheet screen is divided into three areas: the control panel, the actual spreadsheet, and the status area.

10 is shown in figure and its address is E10. The column letter always comes first.

The position of the cell on which you are currently working is usually defined in two ways. First, its address appears in the control panel. Second, there is a **cell pointer** on the spreadsheet itself, typically indicated in inverse video (black on white rather than white on black). You can move the cell pointer around the spreadsheet as you would move the cursor around a word-processed document—using the cursor-control keys. You may also go directly to a particular cell by giving the spreadsheet a command and the address of the cell. If you move to a cell that is off the screen—out of the current viewing window—the spreadsheet software will position the window over that cell.

Contents of a Cell

A spreadsheet cell may contain one of three things: a label, a value, or a formula. A **label** is straight text, anything you want to type in. It could be a column or row label, the title of the report, "------" to indicate an underline after a column of figures, or a paragraph of comments at the end of the report. By using the correct codes, you may center the label in the column, or align it to the right or left. If the text is wider than the cell, it will overflow into the next cell if it is empty.

Values are numeric values—numbers. These may be the basis for calculations that the spreadsheet will make. If you change any of these values, the spreadsheet will recalculate any cells that are based on them. Values will never overflow into the next cell, even if it is empty. You must be sure your cell space is large enough to accommodate any values that might end up there. As you type in a value or a label, it will appear in the control panel. When you hit the enter or return key, it will be transferred to the cell.

A **formula** is just that—a mathematical expression made up of values, variables, and operators. The variables in this case are cell addresses. If the formula $(B4+A9) \div 100$ was in cell G6, the spreadsheet would take the value currently in B4, add the value in A9 to it, divide the result by 100, and display the result in cell G6. A formula never appears in a cell, only the calculated value. As you type in a formula, it will appear in the control panel. When you hit the enter key the value will appear in the cell.

As you move the cell pointer around on the spreadsheet, the content of the current cell appears in the control panel. For labels and values, the **content** of the cell is the same as the **displayed value** (that which appears on the screen in the cell). For formulas, the content is the formula and the displayed value is the result of the spreadsheet's calculations.

Functions

Functions can be used to perform more complicated operations in formulas than just adding, subtracting, multiplying, and dividing. Many of these operations could be performed using the arithmetic operators, but the function allows you to perform complicated operations with a single instruction. Following are some of the types of functions available with most spreadsheets:

- *Mathematical Functions.* These include trigonometric functions (sine, cosine, and so forth), turning a decimal number into an integer, use of logarithms, random numbers, rounded numbers, remainders of divisions, and others.
- *Logical Functions.* These test for certain kinds of conditions in a cell (greater than 1000, a set of characters rather than a number, and so forth) and become different values depending upon whether the condition exists or not. For example, if your company paid a $100 bonus if sales were over $10,000, a logical function in a sales-commission formula could test the cell containing the sales value. If the value exceeded $10,000, the function would be 100 rather than 0 and the bonus would be added.
- *String Functions.* Strings are sets of characters as opposed to numeric values. These functions take characters from specific positions in strings, find characters in strings, turn characters into upper- or lowercase, eliminate leading and trailing spaces from strings, and so forth.
- *Date and Time Functions.* These allow you to put the current date into a spreadsheet, as well as to perform mathematical operations on dates and times. For example, you can have the spreadsheet software find the exact number of days between two dates, or determine a date 180 days from now.
- *Financial Functions.* Since spreadsheets are often used for financial analyses, many common financial operations are included as functions. These usually include interest rate, present value, and payment formulas; rate of return calculations; and depreciation by various methods.
- *List Functions.* These calculate various figures on an entire range of figures, such as all the values between cell F5 and F14. They include the sum, average, maximum, minimum, and others.

Modes of Operation

When you are using a spreadsheet, you are always in one of four modes of operation: ready, enter, edit, or command. The **ready mode** allows you to move the cell pointer about the spreadsheet. To do anything else, you must be in one of the other modes.

The **enter mode** allows you to enter a new label, value, or formula into the current cell. The **edit mode** puts the current cell contents in the control panel where you can make changes to it. Here you may insert, delete, or overtype characters.

The **command mode** gives you choices from the hundred or so spreadsheet options—from saving the spreadsheet in secondary storage to copying entire sections to other parts of the spreadsheet.

Command Options

Most spreadsheets divide their command options into a hierarchy of **menus**—lists of choices in the control panel. When you initially make a

Spreadsheet Command Menu

When you invoke the command mode on a typical spreadsheet, you are given a menu of choices. This usually leads to submenus until you reach the actual command. Here, the main choice "worksheet" is highlighted and its submenu displayed below. If you move to another main choice, its submenu will be displayed. If you select a main choice, the submenu will become the top line and a further submenu or set of choices will be displayed below.

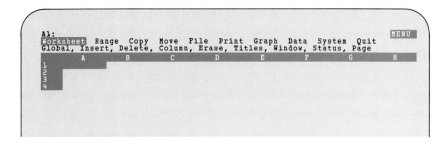

choice from the list, you are often given a **submenu**—a further list of choices—until the actual operation you wish to perform shows up.

Following are some of the more important options available with most spreadsheets:

- *Inserting and Deleting.* You may insert any number of continuous blank rows or columns with a single command. You may also delete or remove the contents of ranges of rows and columns.
- *Copying and Moving.* Ranges of rows and columns may be either copied or moved within the spreadsheet. Moving or copying formulas are given special treatment. Remember, formulas in a spreadsheet generally depend on the values of other cells. For example, the formula in D6 may be D5 × C6. When you move or copy a formula to another location, it should probably depend on cells relative to the new location. Spreadsheets take this into account. Unless you specifically code a cell address in a formula so that it will not change (you **fix** it), the spreadsheet will change the cell addresses to fit the new location of the formula. In our example, if the row 6 (containing D6) were copied to row 7, the formula in D7 would be D6 × D7.
- *Formatting.* You may make a column any number of characters wide, have it round to any number of decimal places, display with a percent or dollar sign, or right align, left align, or center a label.
- *Printing.* At any time, you may print your entire spreadsheet or a selected range from your spreadsheet. You may also print the cell contents. (Remember, this will show you the formulas rather

Menu Hierarchy

To insert rows in this spreadsheet, you would choose "Worksheet" from the main menu, "Insert" from the first submenu, "Row" from the second submenu, and then give the spreadsheet the range of rows you wished to insert.

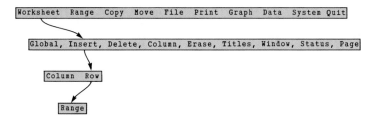

than the calculated values.) Most software allows you many other printing options such as printing a wide spreadsheet on two pages (which you can tape together to make one wide page).

■ *Saving and Retrieving.* Of course you may copy your spreadsheet into secondary storage and retrieve it later, but you may also save just part of it or save it in report format (usually referred to as **ASCII format** because just the ASCII codes for the output are saved, not the internal codes for formatting, cell formulas, and so forth). Saving it this way allows you to import it into other documents, such as one you might be using with your word processor. You may also retrieve parts of other spreadsheets or straight ASCII text and include them as part of a spreadsheet.

■ *Protecting Contents.* Spreadsheets are often used many times with different values. For example, you may make up financial statements using spreadsheet software. Each month the raw numbers change but the calculations and the format remain the same. The spreadsheet other than the raw numbers becomes a **template**—a pattern—for your financial statements. You may code all the cells other than the ones containing the raw numbers so that the cell pointer will not move there. This **protects** those cells so that they may not be inadvertently changed.

SPREADSHEET GRAPHICS

"A picture is worth lots of words—or a bunch of rows and columns on a spreadsheet."

Quantitative data are more effective and memorable if they can be shown visually, therefore spreadsheet software packages, or supplements that accompany them, will take your data and automatically produce graphs from them. All that is required of you is that you state a range of values to graph, and the spreadsheet will take care of the rest—scaling, axis scale figures, and drawing the lines. Almost any of the automatic defaults can be

Spreadsheet Data to Graph

We will use this spreadsheet of the sales of Wallbee Toys, a toy manufacturing company, as the basis for all the graphs in this section.

	Dolls	Electric	Rad/Cont	Fantasy	Games	All Toys
1st Qtr	447122	379260	179303	420575	203478	1629738
2nd Qtr	620846	563542	235463	637485	373262	2430598
3rd Qtr	836452	705743	406866	856450	506532	3312043
4th Qtr	735625	612036	326548	719033	376452	2769694
Year	2640045	2260581	1148180	2633543	1459724	10142073

WALLBEE TOYS
Sales by Quarter by Category

overridden, allowing you control of the type of graph, scales, titles, colors, patterns, and so forth. Let us look at the types of graphs you can produce.

Line Graphs

The **line graph** consists of a horizontal (X) and a vertical (Y) axis with the data shown as a line. It is useful for showing data trends, particularly over time. Examples might be sales over the last ten years, monthly net profit, or

A Single-Line Graph

Line graphs are useful for showing trends. For example, here we see sales rising toward the third quarter and then falling off.

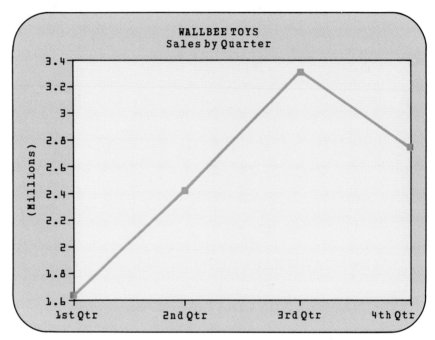

Multiple-Line Graph

Multiple-line graphs allow you to put different, but related, data on the same set of axes.

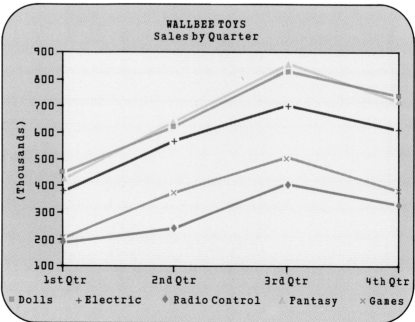

projected sales versus level of inventory. Most spreadsheets allow not only a single line graph but also multiple line graphs with many ranges of data shown on the same axes. The different lines are shown in different colors or patterns and the point on the lines with different symbols.

Bar Graphs

Instead of showing data as continuous lines, a **bar graph** shows the data

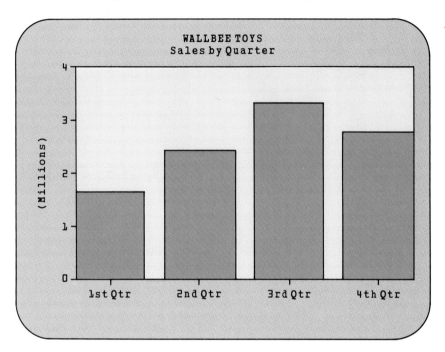

A Bar Graph

Instead of showing the trend of sales over time, this bar graph emphasizes the fact that peak sales are in the third quarter, presumably when retailers are building up inventories for holiday sales.

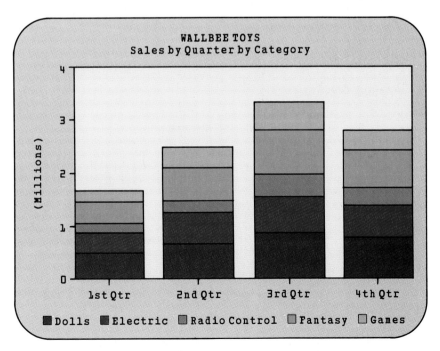

A Stacked Bar Graph

This stacked bar graph shows total sales in each quarter, but the sales are broken down by category within each bar.

A Grouped Bar Graph

The grouped bar graph shows sales in individual toy categories but does not show total sales in each quarter.

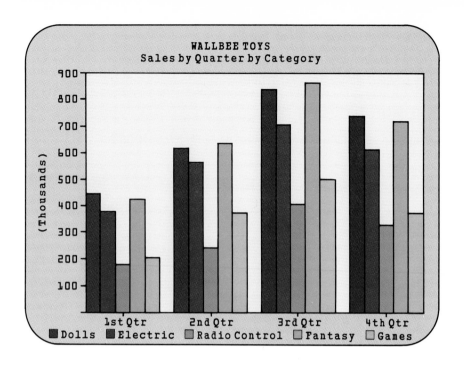

individually as bars extending out from either the X or Y axis. A bar graph is useful for comparing different pieces of data. Examples might be sales in different product lines, expenses by type, or profit by division. Related sets of data may be shown on bar graphs by using a **stacked bar graph,** which puts categories cumulatively on top of each other in the same bar, or a **grouped bar graph,** which puts categories next to each other.

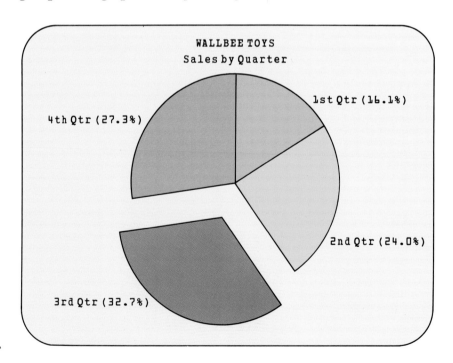

A Pie Graph

Wallbee's third-quarter sales are a major portion of the year's sales. This fact is easily seen in this pie graph and emphasized by exploding the third-quarter section.

Pie Graphs

A **pie graph** (or **circle graph**) is used to show the relationship between various pieces of related data. The data are almost always expressed in percentages. The graph is a circle divided into wedge-shaped sections. Often, one or more of these sections is **exploded**—pulled out slightly from the pie—to emphasize it. Examples of candidates for pie graphs are: expenses by category as a percent of total expenses, sales by region, and ingredients in a cake mix.

MICROCOMPUTER DATABASE MANAGEMENT

In Chapter 13 we discuss the conceptual framework of databases and database management systems. Most of the information there applies to large as well as small systems. Here we wish to examine the capabilities of database management systems from the user's standpoint. Users may have access to large-system DBMSs through query languages, but the majority of users will interface with a microcomputer DBMS, so we will concentrate on them.

The purpose of a database management system is to provide a flexible and efficient method of storing and retrieving data. Storing the data is important, but how you store the data will depend on how you want to retrieve it. The DBMS should make the organization and inputting of the data easy for the user, and it should provide for the retrieval of the data by many different criteria.

For example, you could store sales data very neatly by putting all your sales slips chronologically in a drawer. If you wanted to see sales that occurred on August 14, you would know exactly where to look. If you wanted total sales for the month of August, you and your calculator could start at the beginning of August and accumulate totals to the end of August. It would take time, but it would be a straightforward operation.

What if you wanted to know how many people made purchases of over $100 during the year? Or the names of the customers in a specific town who bought a certain type of product? Or you wanted to print a set of mailing labels for customers in a certain state who made large purchases within the last year? All the data would be there, but it would take a prohibitive amount of time picking through the sales slips one by one.

Once the raw data are stored as a database, the DBMS should be able to grant such requests without much trouble at all.

Setting Up a Database

As with almost any type of data-processing task, you must first consider the output—what kinds of information should the system supply? Once this question has been answered, you can work backward to determine the data required to provide the information.

In most microcomputer database systems your data will be stored in **files**—collections of related data. A phone book is a good example of a file. For a business, the data on all the company's sales or current inventories on hand might be stored in a file. These files will be made up of individual entities or transactions called **records.** In the phone book, each listing is a record. In the sales file, each sale would have a record.

Each record will have a number of details that make up the characteristics of that entity or transaction. These details will be put into the **fields** that make up the record. In the phone book each listing contains a name field, an address field, and a phone number field. Each sale record might have fields for the customer name, date, item purchased, quantity, and unit price.

The DBMS will have some capability to help you design your file. You will describe to the DBMS the make-up of a record by defining each field in the record. The following characteristics of each field must be decided upon:

- *Field Name.* In your retrieval of data you will want some easy way of describing the field where the data may be found. To each field, then, you give a **field name**—some title that indicates the kind of data in the field. The field name for the address in the phone book might well be "ADDRESS".
- *Field Type.* Are you going to put a name or a numeric value in the field? Internally, those data are handled differently. You may perform mathematical operations on a number but not on a name. A variety of **field types** are usually available to handle those differences. A **character field** can contain any characters—*A, B, C,* &, #, or a numeric character such as 6, or 2. Names, addresses, and phone numbers are stored in character fields. **Numeric fields** contain numbers on which you may perform arithmetic operations. Sales quantities and prices are examples. Often there are two types of numeric fields—integer (whole number) and real (numbers with decimal points).

  Date fields are allowable types in many DBMSs. By storing a date in such a field, you may use the date in calculations. For example, you can retrieve records between two dates or within 180 days of the current date. Some DBMSs have **memo fields** where you can enter any kind of data of any length. You may not do retrieval selection on these fields, however.
- *Field Width.* Each record must be consistent. It must contain the same number of fields in the same order with the various fields having the same number of characters in each record. For each field, then, you must state a **field width**—the number of characters each field will occupy. The field should be set to a sufficient width to accept almost any data you may wish to put in it. You cannot exceed the established width. Making a field too wide, however, wastes storage space. Any spaces not filled by you will be automatically filled with blanks by the software.

  Character field widths are set according to the number of characters. For numeric fields, the width usually is specified by a total number of characters, with some of those character positions reserved for decimal places. Dates are typically entered in mm/dd/yy form and so the field width is preset. Memos are the exception. Each memo can be any number of characters you type in.

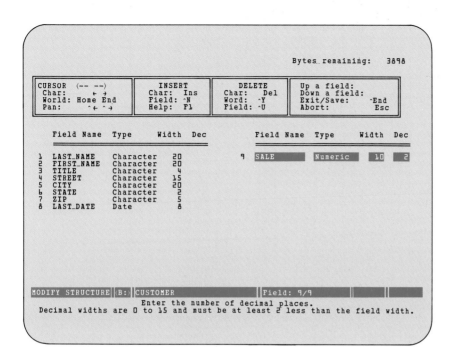

Setting Up a Database File

When creating a database file, you must define each field of a record. Here we are creating a file for a customer mailing list. TITLE is Mr., Miss, or whatever. LAST_ DATE is the date of the last sale to the customer. SALE is the total of all sales to that customer.

Once the fields are defined, you may still change them. If you do, however, the DBMS will have to reorganize all the data in the file, which could take some time if a lot of data has been entered.

Entering Data

Database management systems offer assisted data entry. You may design your own screen form for data entry or the DBMS will provide you with a few automatic choices. Whichever form you choose, the screen will show you the fields and limit you to entering the proper type of data within the allowed width. Using the same types of entry formats, you may either add data to the file or edit existing data.

Putting the Database in Order

Data are typically entered into the file in whatever order they are received. One of the major features of a DBMS is being able to put the data in whatever order you wish. There are two methods for organizing data. A **sort** of the file reorganizes the data file according to any **key field** you choose. For example you might sort the phone book by address or the sales file by item sold or date.

When a file is sorted, it is rewritten—the data are physically moved around on the disk. This can take a lot of time if the file is large. The sorting process also takes up storage space—at least twice as much as the size of the data file. At the completion of the sort, though, the file is its original size, and it can be easily viewed and accessed in the desired order.

You may also **index** a file. Indexing does not reorganize the file itself, it creates a second file, the index, which shows where each record is in the

Entering Data

The DBMS assists data entry by providing you with a screen with all the fields highlighted which you can fill in.

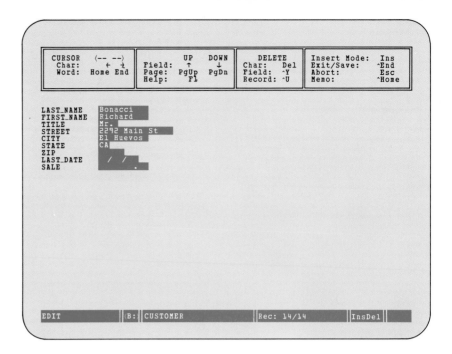

A Database File

After the database has some data in it, you may display it on the screen and/or at the printer. You may either use the DBMS's default format or design your own report format, as shown here.

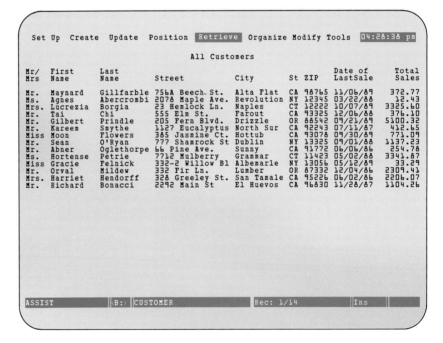

data file. We can illustrate the difference between sorting and indexing by thinking of an apartment house. The manager wants to be able to find each of the tenants easily according to their last name. One solution would be to have everyone move so their apartments would line up alphabetically. That is sorting. The other is to set up a directory with each tenant's last name and apartment number. The directory would have to be sorted, but that is easier than having everyone move. That is indexing.

```
Set Up  Create  Update  Position  Retrieve  Organize  Modify  Tools  02:11:06 pm
                          All Customers
Mr/   First      Last                                      Date of    Total
Mrs   Name       Name       Street        City    St ZIP   LastSale   Sales
Mrs.  Harriet    Hendorff   328 Greeley St. San Tamale CA 95226 06/02/86 2206.07
Mr.   Abner      Oglethorpe 66 Pine Ave.   Sunny      CA 91772 06/06/86  254.78
Mr.   Orval      Mildew     332 Fir Ln.    Lumber     OR 87332 12/04/86 2309.41
Mr.   Kareem     Smythe     1127 Eucalyptus North Sur CA 92243 07/11/87  412.65
Mr.   Richard    Bonacci    2292 Main St   El Huevos  CA 96830 11/28/87 1104.26
Ms.   Agnes      Abercrombi 2078 Maple Ave. Revolution NY 12345 03/22/88  12.43
Ms.   Hortense   Petrie     7712 Mulberry  Grammar    CT 11423 05/02/88 3341.87
Mr.   Sean       O'Ryan     777 Shamrock St Dublin    NY 13325 09/01/88 1137.23
Mr.   Tai        Chi        555 Elm St.    Farout     CA 93325 12/06/88  376.10
Miss  Gracie     Felnick    333-2 Willow Bl Albemarle NY 13056 05/12/89  33.29
Mr.   Gilbert    Prindle    205 Fern Blvd. Drizzle    OR 86542 09/21/89 5100.32
Miss  Moon       Flowers    385 Jasmine Ct. Hottub    CA 93078 09/30/89  771.09
Mrs.  Lucrezia   Borgia     23 Hemlock Ln. Naples     CT 12222 10/07/89 3325.60
Mr.   Maynard    Gillfarble 756A Beech St. Alta Flat  CA 98765 11/06/89  372.77



ASSIST        (B:) CUSTDATE          Rec: 1/14
```

Sorted Database
The database from the previous example was sorted by the date of last sale and a report displayed in the same format.

A sorted file allows faster access by the sort key because you do not have to refer to an index first. It also takes up less storage space because there is no separate index file. On the other hand, a file is indexed more quickly than it is sorted. In addition, a file may have many indices. Our sales file, for example, might be indexed by item sold, date, and customer.

Retrieving Data

The main objective of a DBMS is its ability to provide information from the database any way you want it. Admittedly, there will be a few limitations, but the better the database, the fewer the limitations. By sorting or indexing the database, you can put it in the proper order. By applying specific retrieval characteristics, you can get just the data you want. For example, let us say that you want an alphabetical report of customers from the sales file who purchased tractor treads. First you would index (or sort) the file alphabetically, then you would retrieve only those records in which the item sold was tractor treads.

You can retrieve specific things by setting up **filters**—retrieval characteristics in a language that the DBMS will understand. These filters consist of expressions using field names. For example,

```
STATE = "CA"
```

will look for only those records which have the characters "CA" in the STATE field. The filter expressions may be quite complicated, including many parts. For example,

```
STATE = "CA" AND SALE > 1000
```

will return only those records for California sales greater than $1,000.

Setting Up a Retrieval Filter

This screen is shown in the process of setting up a retrieval filter. The LAST_ NAME field can be compared to another set of characters by any of the criteria shown in the window on the right.

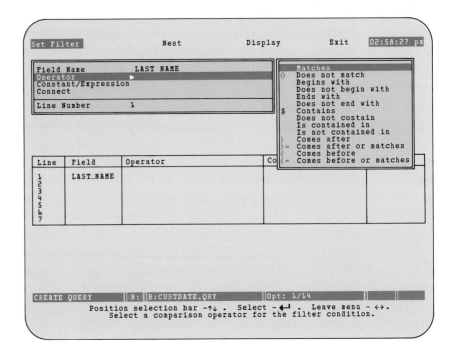

Things like $+$, $>$, and AND are **operators.** They tell the DBMS how to combine the field names and values together to execute a filter expression. Four categories of operators are available with most DBMSs:

- *Arithmetic Operators.* These perform some kind of arithmetic, such as adding, and subtracting. The typical **arithmetic operators** are:

  $+$ Add

  $-$ Subtract

  $*$ Multiply

  $/$ Divide

  $\wedge$ Exponentiate

  $(\ )$ For grouping operations together

- *Relational Operators.* Comparisons are specified by **relational operators** such as:

  $=$ Equal to

  $>$ Greater than

  $<$ Less than

  $>=$ Greater than or equal to

  $<=$ Less than or equal to

  $<>=$Not equal to

- *Logical Operators.* You can combine relationships together by using **logical operators** such as:

```
Filter: ZIP ( "20000"

Mr/   First     Last                                          Date of    Total
Mrs   Name      Name      Street       City       St ZIP      LastSale   Sales

Ms.   Agnes     Abercrombi 2078 Maple Ave. Revolution NY 12345 03/22/88   12.43
Mrs.  Lucrezia  Borgia    23 Hemlock Ln.  Naples    CT 12222 10/07/89  3325.60
Mr.   Sean      O'Ryan    777 Shamrock St Dublin    NY 13325 09/01/88  1137.23
Ms.   Hortense  Petrie    7712 Mulberry   Grammar   CT 11423 05/02/88  3341.87
Miss  Gracie    Felnick   333-2 Willow Bl Albemarle NY 13056 05/12/89    33.29

Filter: TITLE () "Mr."

Mr/   First     Last                                          Date of    Total
Mrs   Name      Name      Street       City       St ZIP      LastSale   Sales

Ms.   Agnes     Abercrombi 2078 Maple Ave. Revolution NY 12345 03/22/88   12.43
Mrs.  Lucrezia  Borgia    23 Hemlock Ln.  Naples    CT 12222 10/07/89  3325.60
Miss  Moon      Flowers   385 Jasmine Ct. Hottub    CA 93078 09/30/89   771.09
Ms.   Hortense  Petrie    7712 Mulberry   Grammar   CT 11423 05/02/88  3341.87
Miss  Gracie    Felnick   333-2 Willow Bl Albemarle NY 13056 05/12/89    33.29
Mrs.  Harriet   Hendorff  328 Greeley St. San Tamale CA 95226 06/02/86  2206.07

Filter: STATE = "CA" AND SALES ) 1000

Mr/   First     Last                                          Date of    Total
Mrs   Name      Name      Street       City       St ZIP      LastSale   Sales

Mrs.  Harriet   Hendorff  328 Greeley St. San Tamale CA 95226 06/02/86  2206.07
Mr.   Richard   Bonacci   2292 Main St    El Huevos CA 96830 11/28/87  1104.26
```

A Selective Retrieval

This is our database, retrieved using three different filters.

AND Conditions on both sides must exist for action to be taken

OR If conditions on either side exist, action will be taken

NOT Reverses the condition. If the condition does not exist, action will be taken.

■ *String Operators.* Strings are sets of characters. The **string operators** allow you to set up conditions based on characters that may be in a field. For example, you may want to pick out only those records with ZIP codes beginning with "940." See the figure for an example of the string operators that are provided by one popular database system.

Designing and Printing Reports

Most DBMSs are quite versatile in the types of reports you can produce. You can design report formats using any or all of the fields in a file, put them in any order you want, make them any width (be sure you do not lose data by making the field too narrow), add titles and column headings, and have the system show you totals and subtotals going both across the report and down. All the reports shown here used the same report format, even though the data shown varied. We could also have the same data output in many different forms. Most DBMSs, for example, have special report designs for printing data on address labels.

Programming Using Micro DBMSs

A large computer's database is available for access by high-level languages, such as COBOL and C. As the capacity of microcomputers continues to increase, this idea is filtering down to the microcomputer database management systems. All of them have their own limited programming languages that you can use to facilitate input, organization, and output of the data; but these languages are somewhat clumsy if you try to do anything but manipulate the data within its database.

More recent micro DBMSs, such as *Informix* and *Oracle* (which is a scaled-down version of their large-system DBMS), allow access by high-level languages. By using this feature, you can write a program in C, for example, and when you need to access something from a database, you can give instructions that will be passed to the database management system which will provide that access. This allows you the best of both worlds—the flexibility of high-level programming and the ease of data handling with the database management system.

SUMMARY

Word processing is the manipulation of text. Using a computer can enhance the productivity of the activity, principally by allowing you to manipulate the text after it has been entered. The word-processing software will help you format your text—keeping text within margins, wrapping words at the end of lines, making columns, and so forth. Formats may be changed, and the word processor will change the text to fit the new format.

Word processors can work with large documents. In order to give you visibility over the entire document, the screen acts as a working window which can be moved anywhere in the document. Once your window is in the correct place you can enter text or edit. Some editing features are overtyping; insertion; deletion; undoing deletions; and block moving, copying, and deleting.

If your text was originally entered using some other software, chances are you can import it into your word-processed document. You can also export text to other documents. In your document you can search for text or replace any or all occurrences of a set of characters with another set. Most word processors have spelling checkers that will find words that do not exist in their dictionaries, presumably misspellings. Many have thesauruses which will suggest synonyms for words.

Your document may contain headers and/or footers on each page. You may create form letters where data such as names and addresses are merged into the letter. Word processors will take advantage of the features of most popular printers—using the available type fonts, italics, bold, or whatever. Some word processors even allow you to merge graphics into your text.

Electronic spreadsheets facilitate working with data in rows and columns. Like word-processed documents, the active area of a spreadsheet can be quite large, so the screen acts as a window that you can move anywhere over the spreadsheet. The spreadsheet screen allows you to see not only the spreadsheet itself, but also, in the control panel and status area, information about the spreadsheet.

Spreadsheet cells may contain one of three things: a label (straight text), values (upon which you may perform mathematical operations), or formulas. Only the results of the formula are displayed in the spreadsheet; the actual formula may be seen in the control panel. Many functions

are available for use in formulas. Function categories are: mathematical, logical, string, date and time, financial, and list.

You may operate on the spreadsheet in a number of different modes: ready, enter, edit, or command. The command mode allows you many options such as inserting or deleting rows or columns, copying or moving ranges of cells, formatting columns, printing in various ways, saving and retrieving data, and protecting cells to make up templates.

Spreadsheets or companion packages will allow you to display your data graphically. Your typical choices are line and multiple-line graphs; simple, grouped, or stacked bar graphs; and simple and exploded pie graphs. The software will take care of scaling, labeling the axes, and choosing colors or patterns for the different elements of the graph.

Database management packages allow you to easily store and retrieve data. Your data is stored in files with records made up of fields which are consistent from record to record. When you set up a database file, you must define each field in terms of name, type (such as character, numeric, date, or memo), and width. The DBMS will provide you with an input screen depicting those characteristics so that you may enter data.

You may organize data by either sorting or indexing the database file. Sorting is more time consuming and the process requires more storage, but the final storage requirements are less and access according to the new order is quite efficient. Indexing does not rewrite the database but sets up a separate index file and requires that access first consult the index file to get to the data.

Data may be selectively retrieved by filtering the data according to many different criteria. Filters are expressions made up of values compared with field names. Expressions are put together using arithmetic, relational, logical, and string operators. Retrieved data may be displayed or printed in reports that you design.

Microcomputer database management systems have query languages and limited programming facilities. Some of the newer DBMS software packages allow you to write programs in common, high-level languages and access the DBMS from those programs.

KEY WORDS

(in order of appearance in text)

Word processing	Status area	Pie graph
Line wrapping	Address	Circle graph
Cursor	Cell pointer	Explode
Undo	Label	File
Block	Value	Record
Move	Formula	Field
Copy	Content	Field name
Import	Displayed value	Field type
Export	Function	Character field
Search	Ready mode	Numeric field
Replace	Enter mode	Date field
Global replace	Edit mode	Memo field
Spelling dictionary	Command mode	Field width
Thesaurus	Menu	Sort
Header	Submenu	Key field
Footer	Fix	Index
Merge	ASCII format	Filter
Font	Template	Operator
Spreadsheet	Protect	Arithmetic operator
Cell	Line graph	Relational operator
Active area	Bar graph	Logical operator
Control panel	Stacked bar graph	String operator
	Grouped bar graph	

REFERENCES

Literary Acknowledgments

BUSINESS WEEK For "Selling to the Hordes Who Are Working at Home." Reprinted from February 8, 1988, issue of *Business Week* by special permission, copyright © 1988 by McGraw-Hill, Inc. For "Unix: The Soul of a Lot of New Machines," by Richard Brandt and John W. Verity. Reprinted from March 14, 1988, issue of *Business Week* by special permission, copyright © 1988 by McGraw-Hill, Inc. For "Computer vs. Grand Master: Still No Contest." Reprinted from October 3, 1988, issue of *Business Week* by special permission, copyright © 1988 by McGraw-Hill, Inc. For "At Westinghouse, 'E-Mail' Makes the World Go 'Round," by Gregory L. Miles. Reprinted from October 10, 1988, issue of *Business Week* by special permission, copyright © 1988 by McGraw-Hill, Inc. For "Eureka! Now There's a Laptop for the Blind." Reprinted from February 8, 1988, issue of *Business Week* by special permission, copyright © 1988 by McGraw-Hill, Inc. For "Helping the Deaf Keep in Touch—From Anywhere." Reprinted from November 7, 1988, issue of *Business Week* by special permission, copyright © 1988 by McGraw-Hill, Inc. For "Put Enough PC's Together, and You Get a Supercomputer," by Port, Levine, Hammonds. Reprinted from September 26, 1988, issue of *Business Week* by special permission, copyright © 1988 by McGraw-Hill, Inc. For "If Computers Can Go Anywhere, Why Can't They Reach the Poor?" by Katherine M. Hafner. Reprinted from October 10, 1988, issue of *Business Week* by special permission, copyright © 1988 by McGraw-Hill, Inc. For "Will NEXT Usher in the Software of the Future?" by John W. Verity with Karen A. Frenkel. Reprinted from October 24, 1988, issue of *Business Week* by special permission, copyright © 1988 by McGraw-Hill, Inc. For "'Dumb' Terminals Are Getting a Lot Smarter." Reprinted from February 8, 1988, issue of *Business Week* by special permission, copyright © 1988 by McGraw-Hill, Inc.

COMPUTERWORLD For "Northrop Designs Own Systems to Answer Pressure to Integrate," by Glenn Rifkin, September 12, 1988. Copyright © 1988 by C. W. Publishing, Inc., Framingham, MA 01701. Reprinted from *Computerworld.* For "Friends and Foes Join to Build PCs," by Charles P. Lecht, February 22, 1988. Copyright © 1988 by C. W. Publishing, Inc., Framingham, MA 01701. For "Bad Language," by Dan Nolan, July 25, 1988. Copyright © 1988 by C. W. Publishing, Inc., Framingham, MA 01701. Reprinted from *Computerworld.* For "Programmers: *Not* a Breed Apart," by Brett Middleton, April 4, 1988. Copyright © 1988 by C. W. Publishing, Inc., Framingham MA 01701. Reprinted from *Computerworld.* For "Wingnet—It's Definitely for the Birds," by Tim Scannell, September 6, 1982. Copyright © 1982 by C. W. Publishing, Inc., Framingham, MA 01701. Reprinted from *Computerworld.* For "Linked PCs Deliver Newspaper," by Alan Ryan, April 18, 1988. Copyright © 1988 by C. W. Publishing, Inc., Framingham, MA 01701. Reprinted from *Computerworld.*

COMPUTERS IN BANKING For "Relational Data Base System Provides Speedy Information Services," by Scott Humphrey. Appeared in *Computers in Banking,* January, 1988. Copyright © 1988 by *Computers in Banking.*

DATA GENERAL For "Magnetic Resonance Imaging: A Dream Come True," by Fonar Corp. Appeared in *Technique,* vol. 3, no. 2. Copyright © 1988 by *Data General.*

DATAMATION For "Steady as She Goes," by Karen Gullo, January 15, 1987. For "Following Successful Project Management Steps," October 15, 1988. For "British Telecom Starts from Scratch," October 15, 1988. For "Europe's Parallel Performance," by Paul Tate, May 1, 1988. For "Learning Systems Integration the Hard Way," November 1, 1988. All appeared in *Datamation.* Copyright © 1987, 1988 by *Datamation.*

ASHLEY GRAYSON For "A Document-First Strategy May Cure Specification Indigestion," by John Barnes. Appeared in *Computerworld,* July 25, 1988. John Barnes is the Pacific Northwest area manager for ADA, a high-tech marketing firm based in San Pedro, CA.

INSIGHT For "Portable Computer Runs on Handwriting," by Susan Dillingham, August 22, 1988. Reprinted with permission from *Insight.* © 1988 *Insight.* All rights reserved.

MICROPRO INTERNATIONAL CORP. For "Word Processing Versus Desktop Publishing," by Ray Mussato, *Wordstar News,* Fall, 1988. Copyright © 1988 by Micropro International Corp.

MINI-MICRO SYSTEMS For "DOS-Easy: Putting on a Friendly Interface," by Terry Keene, August, 1988. Reprinted with the permission of Systems Integration Magazine, formerly Mini-Micro Systems, Cahners Publishing Co., Newton, MA.

ROBERT PERRY For "PCs Help Put Welch Competitors in a Jam," by Robert L. Perry. First appeared in *Business Solutions,* September, 1987. Reprinted by permission of the author.

RESELLER MANAGEMENT/COMPUTER DEALER For "Art-to-Part Gizmo Makes Plastic Models from CAD Data," by Ken Fermoyle, *Computer Dealer,* September, 1988. Reprinted by permission.

NEW SCIENTIST MAGAZINE For "Fast Moves in Computer Graphics," February 11, 1988. This first appeared in *New Scientist Magazine, London, the Weekly Review of Science and Technology.* Reprinted by permission.

PC COMPUTING For "Non-Computer Users Need Not Apply," by Kenan Woods; "How Scanners Scan"; "Security Blankets: Diskless PCs," by Deborah Asbrand; "Computer Angst," by Norman Boucher. Reprinted from *PC Computing* Nov., 1988; October 1988. Copyright © 1988 Ziff Communications Company. For "A Closer Look at the Superchip," by Winn L. Rosch; "New Coprocessors for a New Era," by Winn L. Rosch. Reprinted from *PC Magazine* Sept. 29, 1987. Copyright ©1987 Ziff Communications Company.

SENTRY PUBLISHING/SOFTWARE MAGAZINE For "Database Machine Watches the Options," by John Desmond, *Software Magazine,* April, 1988. Reprinted with the permission of *Software Magazine,* April 1988, Sentry Publishing, Inc., Westborough, MA 01581.

TIME MAGAZINE For "Quick, What Are the Prime Factors of . . ." October 24, 1988. Copyright 1988 *Time,* Inc. Reprinted by permission. For "Driving by the Glow of a Screen," by Philip Elmer-DeWitt, April 29, 1987. Copyright 1988 *Time,* Inc. Reprinted by permission. For "The Next Major Battleground," by Philip Elmer-DeWitt, April 25, 1988. Copyright 1988 *Time,* Inc. Reprinted by permission. For "Just Dig While You Work," March 28, 1988. Copyright 1988 *Time,* Inc. Reprinted by permission. For "From Mozart to Megabytes," by Philip Elmer-DeWitt, March 16, 1987. Copyright 1987 *Time,* Inc. Reprinted by permission.

Photo and Illustration Credits

2 & 3 © Erich Hartmann/Magnum Photos, Inc. **4** © 1989 Roger Ressmeyer-Starlight. **5** © Gerard Fritz, Journalism Services. **6** Courtesy of Apple Computer, Inc. **10** *(top left)* Courtesy Unisys Corporation/Unisys Archives; *(top right)* Courtesy of International Business Machines Corporation; *(bottom left)* Digital Equipment Corporation; *(bottom right)* COMPAQ. **12** *Datamation,* 6/15/87, p. 78. **13** *(top) Datamation* 6/15/88, p. 18; *(bottom)* © Jon Feingersh, 1986/Stock Boston. **14** Used with permission of Borland International, Inc. **17** Courtesy of Ford Motor Corporation. **18** *(top)* Courtesy of International Business Machines Corporation; *(bottom)* © Charles Feil, 1985/Stock Boston. **19** Commodore Business Machines, Inc. **21** *(top)* © Hank Morgan/Rainbow; *(bottom)* Courtesy of International Business Machines Corporation. **22** FONAR. **23** FONAR. **24** NASA. **26** ETAK.

30 © Hank Morgan/Rainbow. **31** *(top & middle)* Courtesy Intel Corporation; *(bottom)* Photo Courtesy of Quadram. **33** Copyright © 1987 by Blair Seitz. **34** Courtesy Intel Corporation. **35** AST. **36** *(left)* Courtesy of International Business Machines Corporation; *(right)* © Oscar Palmquist/Lightwave. **37** "Photo Courtesy of TeleVideo Systems, Inc. Sunnyvale, CA." **41** Courtesy of International Business Machines Corporation. **42** *(top)* Courtesy of International Business Machines Corporation; *(bottom)* by Amdahl. Used with permission of Amdahl Corporation. **43** © Steve Young/Lightwave.

54 Courtesy of International Business Machines Corporation. **56** Courtesy of International Business Machines Corporation. **57** Courtesy Oshman's Sporting Goods, Inc. **61** Courtesy Oshman's Sporting Goods, Inc. **74** Copyright © 1987, Ashton-Tate Corporation. All Rights Reserved. Reprinted by permission. RapidFile is a registered trademark of Ashton-Tate Corporation. **71** *(top)* © Holt Confer/ The Image Works; *(bottom)* Compaq. **72** © Dagmar Fabricius/Stock Boston.

78 & 79 Charles Lewis/PhotoEdit. **80** © Philippe Gontier/The Image Works. **92** © A. Mastrocola/Lightwave. **94** Motorola, Inc.

106 © Jon Feingersh 1988/Tom Stack & Assoc. **109** Courtesy of International Business Machines Corporation. **117** *(left)* Memorex Corporation; *(right)* © K. Murakami 1988/Tom Stack & Assoc. **119** Photos courtesy of Inmac Corporation, Santa Clara, CA. **120** *(left)* © Oscar Palmquist 1989/Lightwave; *(right)* Photo courtesy of Verbatim Corporation, an Eastman Kodak Company subsidiary. **121** Microsoft Corporation. **124** Maxtor Corporation.

131 © Joseph Nettis 1985/Stock Boston. **132** Lotus Development Corporation. **143** Courtesy of NCR Corporation. **145** Linus Technologies. **146** *(left)* Courtesy of NCR Corporation; *(right)* © 1989 A. Mastrocola/Lightwave. **147** Joystick Technologies, Inc. **148** *(bottom left)* C. W. Schwartz/Animals, Animals; *(top)* Great West Technology Limited; *(bottom right)* Courtesy of Summagraphics Corporation. **149** Hewlett-Packard Company. **150** *(top)* © Jim Olive; *(bottom)* Courtesy Houston Instrument Division, AMETEK, Inc.

155 Copyright © 1987 by Blair Seitz. **159** *(top left)* Photo Courtesy of Xerox Corporation; *(top right)* Photo courtesy of NEC Information Systems, Inc.; *(bottom)* Courtesy of International Business Machines Corporation. **160** © Oscar Palmquist 1989/Lightwave. **161** From 'Personal Computers' by Hoo-min D. Toong and Amar Gupta, copyright © December, 1982 by SCIENTIFIC AMERICAN, INC. All rights reserved. **164** Courtesy of International Business Machines Corporation. **167** *(left & right)* Photos courtesy of Toshiba America, Inc. Information Systems Division. **168** RE 5515 15" multiscan monitor from Relisys, Milpitas, CA. **170** © A. Mastrocola/Lightwave.

180 & 181 © 1988 M. Woodbury, Woodbury & Assoc./In Stock. **182** Hank Morgan/Rainbow. **187** *(left)* Photo courtesy of Hewlett Packard Company; *(right)* Courtesy of International Business Machines Corporation. **189** Quarterdeck Office Systems. **190** Used with permission by Borland International, Inc. **191** Courtesy of International

Business Machines Corporation. **200** Photograph courtesy of Tandem Computers Incorporated.

203 © bachmann/In Stock. **226** "From the *Wall Street Journal*—Permission: Cartoon Features Syndicate."

229 COMPAQ.

260 & 261 © Jim Olive. **262** Informatics General Corporation. **262** *(top)* © Christopher Morrow/Stock Boston. **262** *(bottom)* © Stacy Pick/Stock Boston.

289 Courtesy of AT&T Archives. **292** *(left)* Dan McCoy/Rainbow; *(right)* © Roger Ressmeyer-Starlight. All rights reserved. **293** Courtesy of AT&T Archives. **295** GTE.

317 Copyrighted by Amdahl. Used with permission by Amdahl Corporation. **318** *(top)* © 1986 Chris Beck/The Picture Cube; *(bottom)* © Brian Christopher 1989. **319** © Gary C. Bublitz **333** COMPAQ.

340 & 341 Courtesy of International Business Machines Corporation. **342** Photo Courtesy of Unisys Corporation. **343** © Oscar Palmquist 1989/Lightwave. **349** Lotus Development Corporation. **350** Microsoft Corporation. **357** Courtesy of Apple Computer, Inc.

366 Photo Courtesy of Toshiba America, Inc. Information Systems Division. **367** © Richard Pasley/Stock Boston. **375** Used with permission of Borland International, Inc. **376** © Paul Light/Lightwave. **377** © Jon Feingersh 1986/Stock Boston. **380** *(left & right)* 3D Systems, Inc. **381** *(top)* TM & © 1977 Lucasfilm Ltd. All Rights Reserved. Courtesy of Lucasfilm Ltd.; *(bottom)* Cincinnati Milacron. **383** Chrysler Corporation. **385** Texas Instruments. **388** Photo courtesy of NEC Systems, Inc. **391** Courtesy of Kurzweil Applied Intelligence, Waltham, MA. **394** P. H. Winston, *Artificial Intelligence,* © 1984, Addison-Wesley Publishing Company, Inc., Reading, MA. Adapted from pages 178–81. Reprinted with permission. **395** © Thinking Machines Corporation, 1988.

400 © Dick Luria/Photo Researchers, Inc.

Photo Essays *(Listed by photo number.)*

Making of an IC chip: *1* Motorola Semiconductor Products. *2* Motorola Semiconductor Products. *3* Motorola Semiconductor Products. *4* © Erich Hartmann/Magnum Photos, Inc. *5* Motorola Semiconductor Products. *6* Motorola Semiconductor Products. *7* Photo courtesy of Hewlett-Packard Company. *8* © 1989 Roger Ressmeyer-Starlight. All Rights Reserved. *9* Texas Instruments. *10* Motorola Semiconductor Products. *11* Motorola Semiconductor Products. *12* Photo courtesy of Hewlett-Packard Company.

13 Photo courtesy of Hewlett-Packard Company. *14* Motorola Semiconductor Products. *15* Photo courtesy of Hewlett-Packard Company. *16* Photo courtesy of Hewlett-Packard Company. *17* Photo courtesy of Hewlett-Packard Company.

Computer Hardware: *1* © 1989 Roger Ressmeyer-Starlight. All Rights Reserved. *2* Grumman Corporation. *3* © Mark Richards. *4, 4a, & 5* Joseph M. Waltz, M.D.,

Department of Neurological Surgery, St. Barnabas Hospital, New York. *6* Honeywell Inc. *7* National Medical Enterprises, Inc. *8* Bell & Howell. *9* NASA. *10* Photo courtesy of Wang Laboratories, Inc. Copyright © 1989. Freestyle™ is a trademark of Wang Laboratories, Inc. *11* Thinking Machines Corporation. © 1988. *12* Arnold Meisner/Defense Image. *13* Photo courtesy of Hewlett-Packard Company.

Computer Graphics: *1* © 1989 Roger Ressmeyer-Starlight. All Rights Reserved. *2* Robert Abel & Associates. *3* © Terry Wild Studio. *4* Robert Abel & Associates. *5* Gimeor, Inc. *6* Gimeor, Inc. *7* Genigraphics Creative Services, Liverpool, New York. *8* Genigraphics Network Services, Oakbrook, IL. *9* Genigraphics Creative Services, Liverpool, New York. *10* © 1989 Roger Ressmeyer-Starlight. *11* Robert Abel & Associates *12* Commodore Business Machines, Inc. *13* Commodore Business Machines, Inc. *14* Commodore Business Machines, Inc. *15* Courtesy of Lucasfilm Ltd. TM & © Lucasfilm Ltd. (LFL) 1983. All Rights Reserved. *16* NASA. *17* NASA. *18* NASA.

History of Computers: *1* The Bettman Archive, Inc. *2* Courtesy of International Business Machines Corporation. *3* Courtesy of International Business Machines Corporation. *4* Courtesy of International Business Machines Corporation. *5* The Bettmann Archive/BBC Hulton. *6* Courtesy of International Business Machines Corporation. *7* Courtesy of International Business Machines Corporation. *8* Courtesy of The Computer Museum, Boston, MA. *9* Courtesy of International Business Machines Corporation. *10* Courtesy of The Computer Museum, Boston, MA. *11* Courtesy of The Computer Museum, Boston, MA. *12* Courtesy of The Computer Museum, Boston, MA. *13* Courtesy of International Business Machines Corporation. *14* Courtesy of International Business Machines Corporation. *15* Courtesy Department of the U.S. Navy. *16* Courtesy of AT&T Archives. *17* Courtesy of International Business Machines Corporation. *18* Photo courtesy of Control Data Corporation. *19* Courtesy of The Computer Museum, Boston, MA. *20* Courtesy of The Computer Museum, Boston, MA.

Microcomputers: *1* Reprinted courtesy of Eastman Kodak Company. *2* Photo courtesy of NEC Information Systems, Inc. *3* Photo courtesy of NEC Information Systems, Inc. *4* Courtesy of Plus Development Corporation. *5* Courtesy of Seiko. *6* Courtesy of International Business Machines Corporation. *7* Wide World Photos, Inc. *8* Matsushita Electric Industrial Company, Ltd. *9* © D. Kirkland-SYGMA. *10* © Hank Morgan/Photo Researchers, Inc.

GLOSSARY/INDEX

A

Absolute positioning: Moving to a point on a display screen by pointing to that spot, either on the screen itself or a separate pad representing the screen. 147

Access arm: The arm which holds the read/write head in a disk drive. Similar to a tone arm on a phonograph. 116

Access rights: The types of access (select, update, insert, delete, or grant) a user may or may not be allowed to specific data. 327

Access time, 120, 337

Accumulator: A variable used in programming to keep a running total of values. 218

Accuracy
in communications, 291
key-and-verify process and, 138
See also Error checks

Acoustic coupler: A device used to connect a digital device to a telephone. The telephone handset fits into the coupler which sends and receives sound signals generated by a modem. 299

Active area: The actual rows and columns in use in a spreadsheet. Its boundaries are the highest row and highest column in use. 406, 407

Activision, 55

Ada: A high-level programming language which embraces structured methodology and is a candidate for becoming the required language for software sold to the United States government. 208, 247–48

ADABAS, 208, 324

Address: The reference (column letter and row number) to a cell in a spreadsheet. 407

ADS, 391

Advanced database query languages, 392

Advanced Micro Devices, 33, 38

AIX, 197

Albert, Fred "Al," 152–53

ALBM (AirLand Battle Management) system, 394

Alliant, 396

Allstate Insurance, 358

Alphanumeric: The combination of alphabetic and numeric symbols that we, as humans, use. 230

Altair, 401

Alternative development: The second step in the decision-making process. Identification of a number of possible ways to solve the problem. 352

Alternative selection: The third step in the decision-making process. Picking the best solution from the alternatives. 352

AmCom, 266–67

Amdahl, 89, 199

Amdek Corp., 312

American National Standards Institute (ANSI), 240, 248, 325

American Satellite Company, 309

American Standard Code for Information Interchange (ASCII): A coding scheme—specific patterns of bits which represent characters. 86

Ames Research Center, 43

Analog computer: A computer that works with data in continuous ranges rather than in discrete units. 81–82, 296–97

Anixter, Ben, 33

APL, 208

Apple Computer, Inc., 217, 357, 373, 388
education and, 384
HyperCard, 390–91
laptop, 73
Macintosh, 168, 187, 198, 236, 335, 336, 371, 389
microcomputers, 41
operating system, 198
SLA and, 380

AppleDos, 357

Application generator: Software which allows a programmer to give the computer task specifications and have the computer generate the actual software to perform the task. 391

Application program: A program that performs a specific task for certain users of the system. Examples are accounting, word processing, and sales order programs. 38–39

Apply By Computer (ABC) system, 9

Apollo Services, 249

Coding scheme: Agreed-upon patterns of bits used to represent various characters in the computer. 86

Comité Consultatif International Télégraphique et Téléphonique (CCITT): A world-respected, United Nations committee on communications standards. 307

Commodore, 37, 64, 93, 384

Command languages, 189

Command mode: The mode of spreadsheet operation that allows you to call up one of the many available operations, from saving the spreadsheet in secondary storage to copying sections to other areas. 409

Common carrier: A company whose business it is to provide communications channels and services to other companies. 309–11

Communications. *See* Data communications

Communications channel. *See* Channel

Communications processor: A secondary computer whose function it is to handle communications for the main computer. 301

Compact disc read-only memory (CD-ROM): A computer disk using the same discs and recording, reproducing, and playback processes as an audio compact disc. These have the data manufactured into them, like their audio counterparts. 121, 123

Compaq, 41, 73, 326, 357, 386

Compiler: A program that translates a high-level language into machine language. 234

Complex object: A data object consisting of more than one piece of data. 323

Compuserve, 314

Computer: A machine which, under control of a stored program, can manipulate data by itself. 10

construction, 31–33

diskless, 326–27

education and, 384

effect of, 22–26

future of, in business, 383–85

growth of, 9–10

history of, 7–8

home, 17, 37

networks, 303–9

number system, 82–85

portability, 389

problem-solving and, 40

resources, 138–39

sizes of, 40–46

underprivileged and, 384

user anxiety and, 368

uses of, 3–7, 10–12, 59–62, 390

versus humans, 13–14, 20–22

Computer-aided design (CAD): Using a computer rather than manual drafting-board methods to draw designs. 18, 170, 376–78, 380

devices, 377

software, 377–78

Computer-aided engineering (CAE): Adding to computer-aided design facilities for making engineering decisions, such as component layout or structural strength. 378

Computer-aided manufacturing (CAM): Using designs stored in the computer to control manufacturing processes. 18, 379

Computer-aided software engineering (CASE): A number of programming tools and techniques that allows the computer to help in the software-generating task. 391

Computer-integrated manufacturing (CIM): The catch-all term used for a system that aids, directs, and controls all phases of product-oriented activities. 382–83

Computerized Application Process (CAP), 9

Computerized axial tomography (CT), 18, 20–21

Computing Surface, 397

Concentrator: A computer-controlled device that divides a single physical communications channel into a number of logical ones. 300–301

Concurrent processing: Executing more than one program within the same period of time. 192

Configuration division: The section of a COBOL program that describes the specific hardware that is to be used with the program. 240–41

Connection Machine, 385

Connector: A flowcharting symbol (a small circle) used to represent a connection between lines, such as when two lines come together or where lines could not be drawn (as between two pages). 210

Consolidated Professional Systems, 327

Contention: A network protocol governed by rules similar to a polite conversation. Each node will listen before transmitting. If the line is free, then it will transmit. 306

Content: In a spreadsheet, the data stored for a cell address. It may be a label, value, or formula. 408

Control: The function of the central processing unit which allows it to direct, under program control, the rest of the computer system. 34

Control Data Corp., 396

Control panel: The area of a spreadsheet screen which contains information about the operation currently being performed. 407

Control structure: Any one of the three programming patterns used in structured programming. 212–16

Convergent, 32

Conversion: Part of the systems-implementation stage of the

Download: Transfer data from a larger computer, typically a mainframe or mini, to a smaller computer, typically a micro. 74, 357

Doyle, Jim, 248

Drive: The device that reads and writes storage media. The drive includes heads, mechanisms to move the medium, and circuitry to change the data from electronic bits to the kind required by the medium (magnetic regions, pits in optical media, and so forth) and vice versa. 108

DriverGuide, 24

Drum: On one type of line printer, the continuously moving cylinder that carries the character patterns to be printed. 162

Drum plotter: A type of plotter where horizontal motion is accomplished by a moving pen and vertical motion by rolling the paper back and forth over a drum. 168, 169

Duplex: In data communications, refers to two-way communications. 295

E

E. F. Huttonline, 314

EAPROM, 93

Earth-station-Ie, 327

ECLIPSE S/140, 20

ECRM, Inc., 312

Edge connector: A set of fingers etched onto the edge of a printed circuit board which acts as a plug allowing other plugs to be attached to the board or the board plugged into another board. 32

Edit mode: The mode of spreadsheet operation that allows you to change the contents of the current cell. 409

Edit report: A printed report typically produced in a batch input process. The report goes to the originator of the source documents who checks that the

data input into the system are correct. 133

Egoless programming: Viewing one's own software not as an extension of one's ego but simply as a product to be improved. 279

Electric Pencil, 401

Electro-luminescent display: One type of flat-panel display. 167

Electronic Associates, 38

Electronic Data Systems Corporation (EDS), 358

Electronic funds transfer (EFT): Transferring money from one account to another by data communications rather than paper. 312

Electronic Industries Association (EIA), 298, 347

Electronic mail: Sending, storing, receiving, and managing messages using computers and data communications. 16, 64, 312, 372–73

Electronic maps, 24

Electronic notepad, 145

ELSE: The key word in pseudocode that begins the false branch of a selection structure. 212

Encoding: Translating human characters into the bits which represent characters in a computer. This is typically done using a keyboard. 87–88

Encore, 387

END DO: The key words in pseudocode that end an iteration structure. 214

END IF: The key words in pseudocode that end a selection structure. 212

Engineering. *See* Computer-aided engineering (CAE)

ENIAC (Electronic Numerical Integrator And Computer), 7, 9, 230

Enter mode: The mode of spreadsheet operation that allows you to type a new label, value, or formula into a cell. 409

Environment division: The section of a COBOL program that

describes the specific hardware that is to be used with the program. 240–41

EPROM, 93

Epson America, 373

Error checks, 137, 234

Esprit Systems, 166, 326

Etak, 24

Ethernet, 309, 336

Eureka, 23

Even parity: A parity-checking scheme in which the added parity bit will make the number of one bits even. 112

Exception report: A report which shows only those things that are not within normal ranges. 344–45

Executable code: A program that is in machine language and can be run without further translation. 233

Execute: Perform an instruction or set of instructions. 12

Executive: Another term for the operating system. 184

Expansion slot: An extra socket on a motherboard which allows extra circuit boards to be added to the system. 33

Expert system: A computer system that simulates a human expert by using stored knowledge and rules for applying that knowledge to make decisions. 393–94

Explode: Emphasize data in a pie graph by moving one section out from the circle. 415

Export: Generate data from one software package in a format to be used or imported into data from another software package. 404

Extended binary coded decimal interchange code (EBCDIC): A coding scheme—specific patterns of bits which represent characters. 86–87

External data: Data from sources outside the company. 347

F

Facsimile (fax): A process which

OLTP (*continued*)
occur from many different sources. 75, 346

One Source, 123

OOPSLA conference, 217

Open systems interconnection (OSI): An OSI model for defining communication systems standards. 307–8

Operand: The value, register, or memory location that will be affected by a computer operation. 232

Operating environment: An enhanced operating system, usually set up to make operations easier for the user. 189

Operating management: The people responsible for carrying out the tactics of middle management and directing the people producing the output. 355–56

Operating system: A resident system program placed between the user and the actual hardware which translates user or program instructions into the detailed ones required by the central processing unit. This provides services, such as secondary-storage access and input and output, to application programs. 39, 184–85
multiuser, 190–99
single-user, 186–90

Operator: (1) The person who runs the computer system itself. Operators turn the computer on; queue programs to run; attend to the printers, storage devices, and other hardware; and monitor the operation of the system. 67 (2) In a programming or database language, the symbol or code that tells the computer what operation is to be performed. Examples are: ADD, +, and so forth. 232, 420–21

Operator's manual: The procedures that the operators in the computer information systems department will follow to run the system. 282

Optical character recognition (OCR): Reading human characters into the computer using optical (light-sensing) means. 142–43, 144

Optical disc: A disk (often spelled disc, especially for the CD-ROM variety) that uses a laser to read and write data. 121
erasable, 121–22, 368–88
versus magnetic disks, 122–24

ORACLE, 325, 331, 422

Oracle Systems Corporation, 75

Ortiz, Gary, 152

OS/2, 187, 188–89, 197, 325

OS/2 Presentation Manager, 371, 391

Output: Deliver information from whatever computer process is being performed. 65–66
criteria, 156
displays, 166–67
graphics, 167–70
machine-readable, 170–71
options, 405
types of, 156–58
voice, 170

P

Package: The case surrounding a component or integrated circuit which provides protection and a means of electrical connection. 31

Packet: The fixed-size block of data defined by the communications protocol. In a packet network, data will be sent a packet at a time. 307

Packet-switching network: A communications network in which the data are broken into packets, each packet is routed to its destination in the most efficient way, and the packets are reassembled on the other end. 311

Pad: Lengthen data to a specific number of characters by adding blanks. 69

Page oriented: Directed toward producing high quality, one page at a time. 371–72

Page previews, 370

Page printer: A printer which forms an electrostatic page image, raster fashion, on a moving belt or drum, then transfers the image to paper. 164–66

PageMaker, 369

Paging: A technique used in a virtual-memory operating system where fixed-length sets (pages) of data or programs are moved between main memory and secondary storage. 193

Paragraph: A number of sentences, or instructions, in COBOL dealing with the same function. 240

Parallel conversion: Running the old and new systems side by side for a time to compare data and have a system to fall back on if there are problems with the new one. 283

Parallel processing: Executing a process on more than one processor simultaneously. 200, 385–86, 387

Parallel recording: Storing data "crosswise," with the bits of a byte next to each other so that they can be read or written simultaneously with a multipart head. ANSI standard, nine-track tapes are parallel. 111

Parity: An error-checking scheme where an extra bit is added to a byte before recording or transmitting to make the total number of one bits even (or odd). After reading or receiving, the nine bits are counted to see whether the number of one bits is still even (or odd). 111–12

Parity bit: The extra bit added in a parity-checking scheme. 111–12

Partition: A separation of main memory to provide discrete areas for the programs and data of concurrently running programs. 192

Pascal, Blaise, 243

Pascal: A high-level programming language, one of the first to

meant to be accessed, the tape stopped, the data processed, the tape started, more data accessed, and so forth. 113

Statement: An instruction in a program. 212

Status area: the area of the spreadsheet screen containing information about the current condition of the spreadsheet. 407

Stepstone Corp., 199

StereoLithography, 380

StereoLithography Apparatus (SLA), 380

Stone, Antonia B., 384

Storage: Devices that retain data and/or programs. 35, 107–9
See also Secondary storage

Storage program concept: The capacity for a computer to store, or remember, a set of instructions and execute it on command. 12

Stratus Computer, Inc., 387

Streaming tape: A tape with little or no interblock gaps that is meant to be accessed continuously without starting and stopping. 114, 115

Stream file: A file not ordered in repetitive fashion—by records and fields. Text is stored in a stream file. 70

String operator: A symbol or code that tells the computer to perform some operation on a set of characters (rather than a numeric value). 421

Strings, 409

Structured decision: A decision in which the process follows specific rules, procedures, or guidelines. 352–53

Structured design: Designing an information system using top-down, structured methodology. 265

Structured programming: A method of designing programs using combinations of three simple programming patterns (structures). 212–18
applications, 218–20

rules, 217–18
in software development, 391

Structured Query Language (SQL): A standard language for retrieving data from a database management system. 208, 325, 335, 391, 392

Structured walkthrough: Explaining in detail the software specifications of the system to other people involved to elicit their comments, criticisms, and assistance. It is a way of testing the software before it is written. 279

Stylus: A penlike device used to specify a location on a graphics pad or digitizer. 151

Subdirectories, 189

Submenu: A menu of subordinate choices that is invoked from another menu. 410

Substrate: The material, usually plastic or aluminum, under the coating on a storage medium. The substrate exists to give the medium shape and strength. 107

Summary report: A report which shows only summaries of groups of transactions, not individual transactions. 344, 345

Sun, 33

SuperCalc, 357

Supercomputer: A high-capacity, high-speed, very large computer. They are typically used for scientific applications. 43, 46, 396–97

Superconductor: A material that allows electrical currents to pass with virtually no resistance and generating almost no heat. 386

SuperKey, 189

Supervisor: Another term for the operating system. 184

Suprenum, 397

Swap: To exchange one page of data for another in a virtual memory system. 193

Switched lines: Communications lines which reach their desti-

nations through central switching facilities. 309–10

Symmetry, 387

Synchronous communication: Communication in which the sender and receiver are first matched in speed and frame, and then a block of data is transmitted. 297–99

System V, 199

System adjustments: During the systems maintenance stage of the systems development cycle, maintenance programmers change the software to reflect changes in the organizational environment. 285

System flowchart: Part of the systems design stage of the systems development cycle, a diagram of all the parts of the system and how they interact. 274, 277

System program: A program which helps all the users of the computer by delivering system resources to the users. Its typical function is to translate the relatively simple instructions of the user into the detailed ones required by the central processing unit. 39

System requirements: Part of the systems analysis stage of the systems development cycle. A complete description of the proposed system as it will appear to the user. 271–72

System software: A collection of programs that manage and deliver system resources to the user or application program. 183
components, 184–86
fault-tolerant, 200–201
multiprocessing, 200
multiuser, 190–99
single-user, 186–90
trends in, 389
types of, 184–86

Systems analysis: The first stage in the systems development cycle, starting with determining the user's needs and ending